Negotiating Essentials
Theory, Skills, and Practices

Michael R. Carrell

Dean of the College of Business and Founding Director of the Alternative Dispute Resolution Center
Northern Kentucky University

Christina Heavrin, J.D.

Special Counsel to the Mayor
Louisville/Jefferson County Metro Government
Louisville, Kentucky

PEARSON
Prentice
Hall

Upper Saddle River, NJ 07458

Library of Congress Cataloging-in-Publication Data

Carrell, Michael R.
 Negotiating essentials : theory, skills, and practices / Michael R. Carrell, Christina
Heavrin.
   p. cm.
 Includes bibliographical references and index.
 ISBN 0-13-186866-7 (pbk. : alk. paper)
 1. Negotiation. I. Heavrin, Christina. II. Title.
 BF637.N4C363 2008
 302.3—dc22

                              2006035864

Senior Acquisitions Editor: Michael
  Ablassmeir
VP/Editorial Director: Jeff Shelstad
Product Development Manager:
  Ashley Santora
Assistant Editor: Denise Vaughn
Assistant Editor, Media: Ashley Lulling
Marketing Manager: Anne Howard
Marketing Assistant: Susan Osterlitz
Associate Director, Production Editorial:
  Judy Leale
Managing Editor: Renata Butera
Production Editor: Kelly Warsak
Permissions Coordinator: Charles Morris

Associate Director, Manufacturing:
  Vinnie Scelta
Manufacturing Buyer: Michelle Klein
Design/Composition Manager: Christy
  Mahon
Cover Design: Jayne Conte
Cover Photo: Getty Images, Inc.
Composition: Laserwords
Full-Service Project Management:
  Thistle Hill Publishing Services, LLC
Printer/Binder: Courier-Stoughton
Cover Printer: Courier-Stoughton
Typeface: (10/12 Palatino)

Credits and acknowledgments borrowed from other sources and reproduced, with
permission, in this textbook appear on appropriate page within text.

Pearson Education LTD.
Pearson Education Singapore, Pte. Ltd
Pearson Education, Canada, Ltd
Pearson Education–Japan

Pearson Education Australia PTY, Limited
Pearson Education North Asia Ltd
Pearson Educación de Mexico, S.A. de C.V.
Pearson Education Malaysia, Pte. Ltd.

10 9 8 7 6 5 4 3 2 1
ISBN-13: 978-0-13-186866-3
ISBN-10: 0-13-186866-7

DEDICATION

We dedicate this work to thousands of former students who have inspired us to write yet another book because negotiating can be fun!

In addition, we dedicate it to our colleagues on both sides of the negotiation table, from whom we have learned through practice much of the material presented in this book.

Finally, we dedicate it to our families who have given us time on weekends, holidays, and evenings to write books:

Colleen Sue, my wife and life partner
Shari Diane, my firstborn and model parent
Amber Maureen, my Hanover College and sorority student
Lexi Savannah, my Notre Dame junior and Camp Ernst staffer
Annabelle Michael, my Governor's Cup medal winner and straight-A student
Autumn Rain Carrell, Boompa's little angel

MRC

Mike, Jasper, and *Kevin Ward,* all master negotiators in their own right and the men in my life, and Amanda, my new daughter-in-law, who is helping me even the odds

CH

BRIEF CONTENTS

CONTENTS

PREFACE

Welcome to *Negotiating Essentials!* This is an exciting new book that presents, in a unique student-centered focus, time-tested negotiation concepts, skills, and practices developed by nationally recognized authors, experienced professionals, and the most recent findings of distinguished academic researchers. This book was written in response to faculty who requested a comprehensive negotiation textbook that can be utilized in a wide variety of college courses—negotiation, conflict resolution, labor relations, and managerial decision making—either as a textbook or as a supplement. In society today, almost everyone has the opportunity to be a successful negotiator—managers, business professionals, engineers, lawyers, teachers, public sector administrators, health care professionals, consumers, parents, and neighbors. That is the reason negotiation courses are found in colleges of business, law, education, engineering, psychology, and public administration. This book is designed for those programs.

Negotiation situations occur in a person's professional and personal life. In fact, most people are faced with hundreds if not thousands of opportunities to negotiate issues of importance to them during their lifetime. Unfortunately, many people choose not to negotiate but instead accept what is offered to them—the terms of a job offer, the listed sale price, a standard rate, or perhaps a work estimate. Why? Either they simply do not recognize that bargaining is possible in the situation before them, or they feel uncomfortable negotiating. They may believe they lack the skills to negotiate successfully. Or they simply detest the negotiating process and will avoid it at any cost—but they often pay a higher cost for their lack of negotiating skills.

Based on our own combined 60-plus years of negotiating experience, as well as the hundreds of years of combined experience of the highly successful professionals who made contributions to this book, we are convinced that almost everyone can become an effective negotiator. A considerable amount of scholarly research and classroom teaching shows that one can become a successful negotiator by mastering the concepts, skills, and practices presented in this text and applied to real-world cases. Our former students have told us that not only have they learned and applied these skills themselves, but that negotiating can be fun!

From the beginning, our major goal was to write a book that could be utilized in a variety of courses. To enhance its readability and versatility, we intentionally chose not to use a "textbook" writing style, but rather a conversational voice. To further enhance that style and to reinforce learned skills, we have incorporated several elements that provide insights into negotiating in everyday situations. These elements include *Zits* and other cartoons, which provide a humorous but realistic viewpoint, as well as many practical "Tactics for Success" and "Traps to Avoid." In addition, we have included boxed features and discussions of actual negotiations to illustrate major concepts throughout the book. Even the end-of-chapter summaries and exercises, as well as the real-world cases provided by experienced negotiators—all of which enable readers to apply the key skills of the chapters to their own professional and personal lives—are presented in a visually interesting and lively voice.

The theme of this book is that negotiating skills can be learned: Successful negotiation requires only that one employs a defined set of concepts, skills, and practices that have been identified by negotiation professionals and academic researchers. Therefore, we do not believe in the old saying, "Good negotiators are born"—it is simply not a valid statement. No "negotiator gene" has been identified by science. Good negotiators are those individuals who have mastered and who routinely apply this set of concepts, skills, and practices to appropriate situations.

The book includes several features that together provide the reader with an integration of those negotiation skills, concepts, and practices:

- Each chapter opens with the description of a set of *Negotiation Skills* that will be presented three times in each chapter: defined at the beginning; explained and applied within the chapter; and then, at the end of each chapter, applied to the Learning Exercise or other negotiation situations.
- The *Chapter Cases* at the beginning of each chapter present real-world negotiation situations that then are applied to the chapter content.
- Practical, time-tested, easy-to-learn, and easy-to-apply *Tactics for Success* and *Traps to Avoid* are presented in boxes throughout the book. These features not only provide many critical "tools" to apply during a negotiation, but the tactics and traps help students recognize tools that are used by others.
- At the end of each chapter, a *Summing Up* section uses a question-and-answer format to allow the reader to review the chapter's contents by applying each of the skills presented to a negotiation situation. This immediate application of skills and interactive style reinforces understanding and retention of the chapter's content.
- Each chapter concludes with a *Learning Exercise.* The purpose of this exercise is to let the student apply the negotiation skills presented in the chapter to an actual negotiation situation.

The book contains 10 chapters, which have been carefully organized to introduce novice negotiators to concepts, skills, and practices of negotiation and then build their knowledge of the subject in a logical, easy-to-learn progression. Chapter 1, "An Introduction to Negotiation," explains the five essential elements in any negotiation—multiple parties/interests, interdependency, a common goal, flexibility, and the ability to make a decision. The chapter discusses negotiation techniques, personal negotiating styles, understanding motivation, and the importance of setting collaborative goals. Chapter 2, "The Negotiation Process: Four Stages," describes the most common series of steps utilized by experienced negotiators, from setting ground rules and making initial offers to reaching a final settlement. Chapter 3, "Distributive Bargaining," and Chapter 4, "Integrative Bargaining," address the two most common negotiation models: distributive bargaining (sometimes called win-lose or zero-sum negotiation) and integrative bargaining (sometimes called win-win or mutual-gains negotiation). Chapter 5, "Gaining Leverage Through Power and Persuasion," and Chapter 6, "Strategy," describe various techniques that the novice negotiator should learn to identify and consider employing during negotiation sessions. Chapter 7, "Impasse and Alternative Dispute Resolution," presents several methods by which negotiators may move stalled negotiations forward to achieve a favorable settlement. Chapter 8, "Ethics, Fairness, and Trust in Negotiation," focuses on two personal factors that are critical to the successful negotiator—ethical behavior and developing trust. Chapter 9, "The Influence of Culture and Gender on Negotiations," discusses how demographic factors can impact the negotiation process and how to create a strategy that considers their effect on the process. The perspectives in this chapter are becoming more and more critical as the world shrinks through increased communications and international transactions. Finally Chapter 10, "Closing the Deal," teaches a negotiator to claim value right up to the end of a negotiation and suggests a template on how to successfully close a deal.

ACKNOWLEDGMENTS

We gratefully thank the individuals who contributed case material or other content to this book based on their own professional negotiation experiences: Rick Thiemann, President and CEO, Hunkar Laboratories, Cincinnati, Ohio; Kevin Cranley, President, Willis Music Company, Florence, Kentucky; Timothy Rawe, President and CEO, Fifth Third Bank, Florence, Kentucky; Richard Buddeke, President, Barge Exchange, Louisville, Kentucky; Randy Coe, Executive Director, Kosair Charities, Lousiville, Kentucky; Chris Comte, Artist, Burlington, Kentucky; Steve Harper, President, Harper Oil Products, Florence, Kentucky; Vivian Llambi, President, Vivian Llambi & Associates Inc., Cincinnati, Ohio; Mike Vogt, Vice President of Human Resources, Mazak Corporation, Florence, Kentucky; James Monton, Director, Research and Development, Procter & Gamble, Cincinnati, Ohio; Bill Schuler, President and CEO, Castellini Company, Wilder, Kentucky; Kenzie Baker, Vice President, IBEW Local 1347, Cincinnati, Ohio; Jerry E. Abramson, Mayor, Louisville/Jefferson County Metro Government, Louisville, Kentucky; William E. Summers IV, Deputy Mayor, Louisville/Jefferson County Metro Government, Louisville, Kentucky; Donald Cox, Partner, Lynch, Cox, Gilman & Mahan, Louisville, Kentucky; Donna Heitzman, Portfolio Manager, Prisma Capital Partners LP, Jersey City, New Jersey; Jacqueline Strange, Vice President Director of Employment Practices, Brown-Foreman Corporation, Louisville, Kentucky; Kay Wolf, Partner, Ford & Harrison LLP, Orlando, Florida; Larry Hayes, Deputy Mayor and Finance and Administration Cabinet Secretary, Louisville/Jefferson County Metro Government, Louisville, Kentucky; Kathleen McDonald, President, IDS Group Inc., St. Petersburg, Florida; and William D. Norris, Business Representative, Teamsters Local Union No. 783, Louisville, Kentucky.

We also thank the following individuals who reviewed drafts of our text and provided valuable comments and suggestions: Janet K. (Jess) Alberts, Arizona State University; Mark A. Arvisais, George Washington University; Michael P. Bochenek, Elmhurst College; Moshe Cohen, Boston University; Edward Kass, Saint Joseph's University; Laura Kray, University of California–Berkeley; Olenka Krupa, Golden Gate University; Donavan Ropp, California State University–Bakersfield; Greg Saltzman, Albion College; and Manuel J. Tejeda, Barry University.

Finally, we wish to gratefully thank Michael Ablassmeir of Prentice Hall, who encouraged us to write this book, as well as several others including Mary Baker, Denise Vaughn, Ashley Santora, Judy Leale, and Kelly Warsak, who assisted in the development of this and other Prentice Hall books.

ABOUT THE AUTHORS

MICHAEL R. CARRELL

Dr. Carrell is the Founding Director of the Alternative Dispute Resolution (ADR) Center and Dean of the College of Business at Northern Kentucky University. The ADR Center provides negotiation, mediation, and arbitration services in the greater Cincinnati region. Dr. Carrell received his doctorate from the University of Kentucky, and MBA and B.A. in Economics from the University of Louisville. His professional career has included positions as a personnel director and labor negotiator in Louisville, Kentucky. These positions enabled him to build a sizable management consulting practice while teaching at the University of Louisville. In addition to collective bargaining agreements, he has negotiated numerous employment, business, and personal service contracts. Dr. Carrell was elected to the City of Louisville Board of Aldermen for five terms, and served as President of the Board and Mayor Pro-tem for three terms.

Prior to his tenure at Northern Kentucky University, Dr. Carrell held academic positions at California State University–Bakersfield, the University of Nebraska–Omaha, Marshall University, Morehead State University, and the University of Louisville. He has authored more than 50 scholarly works in some of the leading management and human resource journals including *The Academy of Management Journal, The Academy of Management Review, Organizational Behavior and Human Performance, Personnel Journal, The Personnel Administrator, HR Magazine, Labor Law Journal, Business Forum, Personnel, The Journal of Accountancy, Training,* and *Public Personnel Management.* Books published by Dr. Carrell are in the fields of negotiations, collective bargaining and labor relations, organizational behavior, and human resource management. During his academic career he has received awards for both outstanding research and teaching.

CHRISTINA HEAVRIN

Ms. Heavrin has practiced municipal and labor law in both the public and private sectors since 1976. She received her undergraduate degree from Spalding University and her J.D. from the Louis D. Brandeis School of Law at the University of Louisville. She served in the Peace Corps in the West African countries of Liberia and The Gambia.

As an attorney for local government, she served as the City of Louisville's Director of Law and oversaw the activities of 17 attorneys and 11 law firms. In addition to numerous litigation settlements and contracts, she negotiated agreements on behalf of the government, primarily in intergovernmental relations and economic development activities. These agreements resulted in the development of an award-winning public park along the city's waterfront, a successful industrial park, the construction of a Minor League Baseball stadium in downtown Louisville, and tax-sharing between governmental jurisdictions. Recently voters approved the merger of the City of Louisville and Jefferson County governments, and Ms. Heavrin is currently serving as Special Counsel to the first Mayor of Louisville/Jefferson County Metro Government. Her duties include negotiating labor agreements between Louisville Metro Government and the nearly 5,000 employees represented by seven unions in approximately 36 bargaining units.

Ms. Heavrin is a member of the Kentucky Bar Association and the Louisville Bar Association and was named a Woman of Achievement in 1990 by the Business and Professional Women, River City, and was named a Distinguished Alumni in 1993 by the Louis D. Brandeis School of Law at the University of Louisville.

Chapter 1

An Introduction to Negotiation

*H*istory marks the dawn of civilization at the point when humans discovered that farming and domesticating animals offered a better way to sustain life than hunting and gathering. Permanent communities were formed to plant and reap crops and domesticate animals. Individuals, who might have previously observed each other only at a safe distance or as enemies on a battlefield, began to rely upon one another for survival. That survival not only involved joining together for mutual protection from outsiders, but also required internal agreement on the distribution of work and the allocation of resources. Some agreements would have flowed naturally: Men, because of their strength and endurance, would hunt and protect; and women, who would bear and raise children, would also plant and nurture the farms. Other agreements would have come by necessity: Those men and women who were most successful in fulfilling their roles would naturally wield the most influence and would therefore decide how work and resources were to be distributed.

Later the reliance on mores and myths, as well as the establishment of rules and laws, all contributed to the evolution of a society that united individuals for a common goal and made them dependent upon each other for success. And while such dependency did not eliminate disagreements, self-preservation did require these individuals to find ways to resolve internal conflict without weakening their ability to withstand external threats. In other words, they had to find ways to resolve conflict that did not involve destroying each other.

Millennia later, not much has changed. Conflicts continue to arise on both a grand and smaller scale. Most parties find ways to resolve such conflicts through an agreement of some sort. Many people today reach agreement through negotiation. However, many others avoid negotiating situations and some even fear them! Why? They may lack the simple skills, techniques, and experience to prepare and succeed at negotiations. The focus of this book is on understanding how negotiation works and what skills, knowledge, and abilities are necessary to succeed. If you avoid or fear negotiating situations, realize you are not alone and that negotiation skills can be learned.

Negotiation Skills

In this chapter we present five negotiation skills that can be learned and developed by the novice negotiator, and applied to the end-of-chapter Learning Exercise, "House For Rent."

Skill 1.1   *Recognize the* **five essential elements** *in a negotiation.*

Skill 1.2   *Be able to model* **bargaining behaviors** *used by skilled negotiators.*

Skill 1.3   *Learn to recognize* **bargaining styles** *and how such styles impact bargaining behaviors and strategies in a negotiation.*

Skill 1.4   *Learn how to set* **collaborative goals** *to successfully resolve a conflict.*

Skill 1.5   *Recognize and avoid* **cognitive biases** *that hinder successful negotiation.*

CHAPTER CASE: ZONING CHANGE

Robert, who had just recently passed the Bar exam, has been approached by a condominium developer, Sophia, who is seeking a change in zoning on a piece of property adjacent to a neighborhood of single-family homes. She would like to hire Robert because her current lawyer is charging her $300 per hour and she believes that a beginning lawyer would charge less. She is also of the opinion that the legal work involved in the zoning change is minimal, so the fact that Robert has very little experience in this area does not concern her. Robert is eager to have Sophia as a client because this type of work—zoning representation—can be a very good specialty for a lawyer. He is a little concerned about never handling a zoning case before, but he knows that a great deal of the work will involve negotiating and he has had a lot of experience negotiating.

At their initial meeting, Sophia was impressed by Robert's preparation. He knew a great deal about her company and specifically about the neighborhood where the condominium was to be built. When she brought up his fees, Robert, who knew what her last lawyer's firm usually charged per hour, suggested that his fee be a structured fee that reflected the kind of tasks involved. He was willing to discount his hourly rate of $150 by $75 for time spent on legal research because, as he admitted to Sophia, he would be doing some on-the-job learning that would benefit him as much as it benefited her. He would discount his hourly rate of $150 by $50 for time spent at meetings of the Zoning Commission and its subcommittees when he attended those meetings to gather information—but Robert felt his full hourly rate was appropriate for any appearances before the Zoning Commission and its subcommittees on Sophia's behalf and for any legal documents he would prepare. Sophia, who had been through the zoning process many times before, countered Robert's proposal by agreeing to the fees he suggested for research and drafting legal documents but wanted to specify that the time spent at meetings when Robert was waiting to appear before the Zoning Commission or subcommittees also be discounted. Such meetings could go on all day, and paying Robert the same to sit there as she paid him for "doing something" was a problem for her. Robert's initial reaction to her counter was annoyance because Sophia seemed to be saying that his time was not valuable. He decided, however, that he would give Sophia these rates in order to get her business, so the deal was made.

The zoning approval process involves three basic steps: staff approval, neighborhood notification, and Zoning Commission approval. Robert and Sophia's first meeting with the Zoning Commission staff went well. They made a very thorough presentation and worked through the issues raised by the staff. Sophia agreed to add a tree line along one side of the development to shield it from the neighborhood and to limit the number of condos to 65 rather than the 70 she had originally proposed. Even though her plans for parking met the zoning standards, the staff wanted the number of parking spaces increased. Sophia would not agree to do that, however, because she would have to eliminate another five condos. Because 65 was her break-even number, she told the staff that the development could not be built with more parking spaces than the rules required. The staff dropped this request and completed its review, making a recommendation for approval to the Zoning Commission. Robert was feeling very good about the process so far, when the notice of the zoning change was published in the local paper as required by the Zoning Commission.

The adjacent neighborhoods of single-family homes, whose residents first learned of the development from the newspaper, started flooding the Zoning Commission with phone calls and e-mails. The staff directed all of these comments to Robert, and his phone began to ring off the hook. Many of the neighbors were misinformed about the project, not familiar with the zoning process, and misunderstood their legal rights as to how the property was to be developed. Robert and Sophia attended a meeting to discuss the condominium plans with the neighbors. The meeting did not go well. The residents were not interested in hearing what Robert and Sophia had to say. They were there to express their objections to the project in no uncertain terms. Their list of objections included the possibility of increased traffic through their neighborhood, a negative impact on their property values, a fear of subsidized condo owners (i.e., those who qualified for government assistance), and noise. After about an hour of listening to angry complaints and being interrupted when they tried to address the concerns, Robert and Sophia simply left the meeting.

After conferring with the Zoning Commission's staff, Robert suggested to Sophia that a three-party meeting be arranged at which Sophia, the zoning staff, and representatives of the affected neighborhoods would sit down and try to resolve some of the neighbors' complaints. Robert was afraid that if Sophia did not address their concerns, the neighbors would convince the Zoning Commission to turn down her zoning change. The parties agreed to the meeting to resolve the conflict.

Negotiation is a way to resolve issues without resorting to actions that hurt or destroy relationships. Not every interaction between two parties is a negotiation.

However, every negotiation requires an interaction between at least two parties who have a relationship. The parties must be motivated to negotiate. That is, each party must need or at least perceive that he or she wants or needs something that the other party has or can control. Furthermore, both parties must be able to propose options, make decisions, and deliver on their agreement.

There are three basic types of negotiations: deal-making negotiation, decision-making negotiation, and dispute-resolution negotiation. When people think of "negotiating" they are usually thinking of a type of **deal-making negotiation**, such as the purchase or sale of a home or a car, collective bargaining between a company and its employees, or entering into a contract for construction or legal services, as Robert and Sophia did in the Chapter Case. It is generally an exchange of something of value between the two parties. **Decision-making negotiation** is when the object of the negotiation is to arrive at a mutually beneficial decision. It occurs in numerous settings such as the exchange between Robert and the Zoning Commission staff, or within a workplace between co-workers who must jointly decide upon a course of action. **Dispute-resolution negotiation** occurs when an issue has reached an impasse and the parties are attempting to resolve the dispute. In the Chapter Case, there is the possibility that if Sophia is granted her zoning change but cannot satisfy the concerns of the neighbors, the issue might land in litigation. Settlement negotiations in litigation are a common type of dispute resolution.

For purposes of this text, rather than focus on the difference between these types of negotiations, we will focus on the five elements common to them all: (1) at least more than one party or interest, (2) interdependency, (3) common goals, (4) flexibility, and (5) decision-making ability or authority.

THE FIVE ELEMENTS OF NEGOTIATION

Not all conflict situations can be resolved through negotiations. As noted in the preceding paragraph, the elements that must be present for negotiations include multiple parties or interests, interdependency, a common goal, flexibility, and the ability to make a decision. In the Chapter Case, there are multiple parties and interests involved in the proposed zoning change: Robert, Sophia, the zoning staff, the neighbors, and the Zoning Commission. They are certainly interdependent because without approval of the Zoning Commission, Sophia could not proceed with her project and Robert would not have a client or an opportunity to learn how to handle a zoning case. The neighbors need the Zoning Commission to stop Sophia's development or at least to make changes in it that they can live with. Sophia needs the assistance of the Zoning Commission staff to help her satisfy the neighbors' concerns, or else she will risk not getting the zoning change. The parties have a common goal in having the zoning request decided—although at this point their individual goals on how the request is decided may be in conflict. The parties probably have sufficient flexibility in how they address the competing interests, although Sophia's decision to go forward may be limited by the feasibilities of developing a profitable project. Finally, it remains to be seen if the parties can make the decisions necessary to move the decision forward. Representatives of the neighborhood, for example, may not be in a position to speak for all of the neighbors, and the zoning staff's role is limited to making a recommendation to the Zoning Commission, which has the final say. Let's explore these elements to a negotiation in more detail.

The Parties and Their Interests

The parties to a negotiation can be friends trying to agree on what movie to see, co-workers trying to come up with a solution to a work-flow problem, a business owner and her vendors, world leaders trying to avoid war, or a developer and disgruntled neighbors as in the Chapter Case. Conflicts occur when the parties believe that their goals and/or needs cannot be satisfied at the same time. This perception can come from the parties' beliefs about their own goals and needs, beliefs about the other parties' goals and needs, a belief that they lack viable solutions. Conflict resolution experts Robin L. Pinkley and Gregory B. Northcraft explain that disputants have a certain orientation by which they view a conflict situation. That orientation, or frame, leads them to focus on some characteristics of the conflict and ignore others. These *conflict frames* are relationship/task, emotional/intellectual, and cooperate/win.

- The **relationship/task frame** refers to the extent that the parties focus on either their ongoing relationship or the subject matter of the dispute. A person with a relationship orientation will focus on interpersonal concerns, and a person with a task orientation will focus on the material aspects of the dispute (such as money or property).
- The **emotional/intellectual frame** reflects the degree of attention that the parties pay to the emotional components of the dispute. An emotionally oriented person will be concerned with the emotions displayed in the dispute, whereas an intellectually oriented person will be concerned with the behaviors that the parties exhibit.
- The final orientation, the **cooperate/win frame,** reflects the attitude of the parties about responsibility for the dispute. A person with a cooperative orientation will see both parties as sharing some responsibility and focus on increasing the benefit to both parties to reach agreement. The person with a win orientation blames the other party for the dispute and seeks to win, maximizing personal gain at the expense of the opponent.[1]

The Negotiators Negotiations can take place between two individuals who are representing their own interests, such as an individual and her lawyer who are negotiating a representation deal. Or it can be between a group of people engaged in a decision-making process, such as the developer and the staff of the Zoning Commission in the Chapter Case. Or it can be between two parties representing interests other than their own, as is typically found in a business transaction between a company and its suppliers. *Independent agents*, such as a lawyer or broker, are *outside parties* that are often hired because they have the expertise that their client believes is needed to negotiate with the other party. Outside parties are also hired when the client is worried about preserving the relationship with the other party, while still wanting a good deal. An agent can put distance between the client and the other party, thus enabling the agent to be more aggressive than the client would be while pursuing a better deal. *Non-independent agents* are *inside parties*, individuals who are identified with and who act on behalf of the principal party. A Human Resources director will often negotiate union contracts on behalf of the employer. The ability of an inside agent to put distance between the boss and the other party is more limited.

The challenge in being an agent of a principal party who is not in the negotiations is to make sure the principal party is aware of how the negotiations are progressing. **Bargaining** is a process that includes gathering general information, learning the priorities of the other side in the specific negotiation, and assessing the strengths and weaknesses of their positions. If the principal is not a direct part of that process, the agent must discuss the information gathered at the negotiating table and get direction from the principal about how to proceed.[2]

Traits of Skilled Negotiators   Negotiators can aid or impede the progress of a negotiation. In a study of "successful" negotiators, researchers were able to identify behaviors that can make the difference between the success or failure of a negotiation.[3] The negotiators were observed bargaining and were identified as "successful" in the following circumstances:

- If they were rated effective by both sides
- If they had a track record of significant successes, where the parties agreed
- If they had a low incidence of failures where the parties could not reach agreement

Prior to the actual negotiations, skilled negotiators spent about the same time planning as average negotiators, but, the skilled negotiators also did the following:

- Considered a wider range of outcomes or options
- Averaged twice as many discrete ideas
- Gave three times the attention to areas in which the parties might agree
- Referred to long-term considerations twice as often
- Developed a range of possible settlement points rather than a single goal

During negotiations, techniques used by skilled and average negotiators also differed. Average negotiators planned to cover issues sequentially in a predetermined order, whereas skilled negotiators allowed issues to be separated, dealing with them independently in order to promote both flexibility and an atmosphere of agreement.[4] Skilled negotiators used neutral phrases such as "another offer," rather than the more irritating phrase "generous offer," and skilled negotiators did not immediately offer a counterproposal as often as average negotiators, because an immediate counterproposal indicates that the party didn't take the proposal seriously. The skilled negotiators focused on one or two very specific reasons why their proposals or positions were good. By focusing on the key or best reason for their argument, these skilled negotiators did a much better job of communicating the needs of their side. The average negotiators, on the other hand, generally gave the opposing side at least three or more reasons why their position was superior in each area of disagreement. Such overkill can leave their bargaining partner without a clear idea of their needs.

After the negotiations, differences also surfaced between the skilled and the average negotiators. Two-thirds of the skilled negotiators reviewed the process afterward to see what they could learn, whereas fewer than half of the average negotiators bothered to do so.

Thus, in general, skilled negotiators differed from average or less successful negotiators in nine behavioral areas, summarized in Table 1.1.

Developing Negotiating Skills   Throughout this text, you will find skills that you can learn and practice to become a better negotiator. The following points give you an idea of what to focus on as you begin to build these skills.[5]

Negotiations are rarely pure win-lose or win-win propositions. The typical win-lose negotiation involves a strictly distributive result—for instance, in buying a house, more money paid to the owner represents less money for the purchaser. A win-win negotiation is when both parties' interests have been integrated into the result—as when an elderly homeowner is relieved of the obligation of keeping his house up to code and the purchasers could afford the house because they can do home improvements themselves. However, in reality most negotiations are mixed-motive situations where one party benefits more than the other, although both have some of their interests satisfied. A skilled negotiator remains flexible in order to respond to the changing dynamics of a negotiation.

Negotiations take place under conditions of ambiguity and uncertainty. Negotiators are constantly faced with the choices of accepting what's been offered, breaking off the negotiations, or continuing to negotiate in hopes of forging a better agreement. This decision must be made when the parties cannot be sure that they have all the information or that they have explored all of the possible areas of agreement. Both sides have likely attempted to shape the other side's perceptions by framing the issues,

Table 1.1   Contrasts Between Skilled and Average Negotiators

SKILLED NEGOTIATORS	AVERAGE NEGOTIATORS
Considered a wide range of outcomes or options	Considered a narrow range of outcomes or options
Gave three times the attention to common ground areas	Considered one-third as many common ground areas
Anticipated twice as many long-term areas	Anticipated half as many long-term areas
Developed upper and lower limits for possible settlement points	Planned goals around fixed settlement points
Were flexible on the order of issues to discuss	Addressed issues in an inflexible, predetermined order
Used neutral phrases when proposing offers	Used judgmental phrases when proposing offers
Took time to consider proposals before countering	Offered counterproposals immediately
Gave only one or two key reasons why their position was better, quality over quantity	Gave numerous reasons why their position was better
Reviewed the negotiations afterwards for improvement	Did not review negotiations afterwards

selectively providing information, invoking principles of fairness, and perhaps making threats or promises. A skilled negotiator learns to navigate through the ambiguities and uncertainties by preparing for the negotiation as thoroughly as possible and by being vigilant during negotiations in paying attention to the other side's real interests.

Most negotiations involve existing or potential sources of conflict that impede reaching agreement. A negotiator is often called upon to diagnose such sources of conflict and to play a mediator's role in managing the conflict between the sides or within one's own side. By doing this, a skilled negotiator establishes and sustains a productive working relationship with a bargaining partner.

Negotiations are chaotic and seldom pass sequentially through distinct phases such as pre-negotiation, deal structuring, detailed bargaining, and agreement. Skilled negotiators are imaginative and creative in order to cope with the chaos. They have a firm grasp of their goals but are flexible on how to get there.

Negotiations involving multiple parties and complex issues challenge a negotiator. A skilled negotiator knows when and how to create coalitions in multiparty negotiations, and how to structure the negotiation so that the right parties are at the table and the right interests are being addressed.

Most negotiations are linked to other negotiations. Negotiations are seldom self-contained or stand-alone processes. Even a simple negotiation like the purchase of an automobile can involve more than just the purchaser and seller, because there are competitors who might affect the dynamics of that exchange. Certainly, the parties to a negotiation may have a long history with each other or with the same third party or other types of linkages that can influence the negotiations. Skilled negotiators seek to advance their interests by creating or neutralizing those linkages depending upon the desired result.

Negotiating progress comes in stops and starts. Movement toward or away from agreement occurs in surges rather than an even flow. The parties make choices when they lack more attractive alternatives but know that doing nothing is not an option. Skilled negotiators employ techniques to build such momentum toward agreement— including establishing ground rules that prevent backsliding, making unilateral concessions to pressure concessions from the other side, and setting deadlines.

Most complex negotiations take place between agents of groups and not the groups themselves. Often the skilled negotiator is called upon to work within his or her own group to shape their negotiating goals and expectations. Good negotiators play a leadership role in managing the multiple, interacting levels of negotiations within the group itself and between the group and the other side.

Complex negotiations often involve a team approach. A skilled negotiator knows when and how to use a team approach to negotiations For example, complex negotiations requiring a diverse set of knowledge, expertise, and abilities and with the potential for integrative solutions are ideal for teams. Negotiations involving diverse constituencies and interests, such as labor negotiations, lend themselves to a team approach. The skilled negotiator shows trust and respect for team members and takes the time to organize and coordinate the team effort.[6]

Negotiating skills can be learned. Although certain people may have more inherent ability, everyone can learn to be a better negotiator. Research suggests that the difference between a novice and an expert negotiator includes the ability to see familiar patterns, such as coalition alignments, in negotiations; to filter out irrelevant clutter in order to grasp threats and opportunities in a timely manner; and to develop action and contingency plans on the spot that anticipate reactions, and to refine or discard those plans as necessary.

Bargaining Styles   People have different bargaining styles—relatively stable, personality-driven clusters of behaviors and reactions that arise in negotiating encounters.[7] A popular way of describing bargaining styles is the **dual concern model** described by noted educators Dean G. Pruitt, Jeffrey Z. Rubin, and Sung Hee Kim.[8] The dual concern model, pictured in Figure 1.1, explains how one's behavior while bargaining or during a conflict is based on two concerns: the desire to satisfy oneself and the desire to satisfy the other party.[9] The bargaining styles associated with the dual concern model stem from two personality dimensions: *assertiveness* and *cooperation*. Assertiveness measures the attempt to satisfy oneself, and cooperation assesses the attempt to satisfy the other party. These two dimensions yield five negotiation styles commonly designated as follows:

- Avoiding
- Accommodating
- Collaborating
- Competing
- Compromising

Avoidance and accommodation are used to deescalate a negotiating conflict. Competition, compromise, and collaboration are used to engage in the negotiating conflict and, if possible, resolve it. Avoidance, accommodation, and compromise are essentially unilateral behaviors, whereas competition and collaboration require active participant by both parties.

Negotiators with a strong predisposition to *avoiding* are adept at deferring confrontational aspects of negotiation. As a positive trait, avoidance can be displayed as tact and diplomacy. As a negative trait, however, it can lead to stalemate. By avoiding conflict, a negotiator may eliminate the communication necessary for the parties to indicate what is truly critical to reaching agreement.

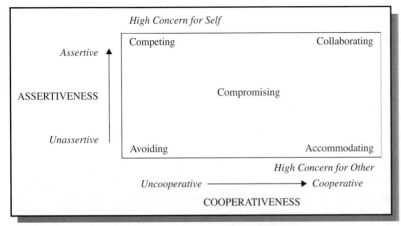

Figure 1.1
Dual Concern Model of Bargaining Style

Source: Adapted from Dean Pruitt, "Strategic Choice in Negotiation," in *Negotiation Theory and Practice,* eds. J. William Breslin and Jeffrey Z. Rubin (Cambridge, MA: Harvard Law School Program on Negotiation, 1991), 27–46.

A negotiator with a strong predisposition to *accommodating* derives satisfaction from solving someone's problem. This negotiator is a good team-builder and is sensitive to others' emotional states and body language. The accommodating style is useful in joint decision making negotiations, sales-based deal making, and conflicts when emotions are running high. The tendency to emphasize the relationship over the content of a negotiation, however, may cause an accommodating negotiator to make unwise concessions.

Competitively inclined negotiators see negotiations as an opportunity to win what they view as a game or a sport. These negotiators, with a predisposition to *competing,* thrive on winner-take-all situations. Self-interest—that is, achieving one's goals at the other's expense—is the primary motivation. They have excellent instincts for pressure tactics such as creating leverage through the use of deadlines and threats or taking advantage of positioning techniques such as initial offers and ultimatums.

Collaboration as a negotiating trait is the cornerstone of integrative bargaining. Negotiators with a strong disposition to *collaborating* enjoy negotiations because they enjoy participating in the joint solution to a problem, recognizing the interdependence of the parties and the need to satisfy the interests of both. As a positive trait, collaborative negotiators bring both parties to the same side of the table so they can confront the problem on the other side. They instinctively probe beneath the surface of conflicts to discover the real interests of the parties.

Finally, a negotiator with a predisposition to *compromising* is eager to conclude the negotiation based on fair standards or established formula. As a positive trait, compromising negotiators are at their best when time is short and the stakes are small.[10]

What determines one's bargaining style: Is it personality driven, or does it come from the bargaining situation itself? And can we relate a negotiator's bargaining *style* to bargaining *behavior*—or do behaviors come also from the bargaining situation itself?

In a recent study conducted with 138 undergraduate students using a negotiation simulation, researcher Zhenzhong Ma sought to determine whether personality factors could predict an individual's bargaining style and whether one's bargaining style adequately predicts bargaining behaviors. Using the **Five Factor Model (FFM)** (also called the "Big Five" personality dimensions, which are detailed in Table 1.2), Ma determined that people high in *neuroticism,* who you might think would find conflict threatening, did not display a preference for any of the negotiating styles. Likewise, *openness* and *conscientiousness* were found not to relate to any specific behavior preference in a conflict situation. The personality dimensions that did relate were *agreeableness*, which was positively related to compromising and negatively related to competing, and *extroversion,* which positively related to competing or collaborating, negatively related to avoiding, and not particularly related in either way to compromise or accommodation. His study did find that conflict styles can predict actual bargaining behaviors: Assertive styles, such as competing and collaborating, led to more competitive behaviors; a collaborating style also showed a positive relationship to compromising behavior; avoiding was negatively related to the assertive styles; and, surprisingly, accommodating and compromising styles didn't predict compromise behavior.[11]

Table 1.2   The "Big Five" Personality Dimensions

DIMENSION	ASSOCIATIONS	OPPOSING
Neuroticism	Anxious, depressed, worried, insecure	Emotionally healthy, calm, free from persistent negative feelings
Extroversion	Sociable, assertive, talkative, active	Introverted, quiet, low-key, deliberate
Openness	Imaginative, curious, original, open-minded	Conventional, narrow-minded, straightforward, conservative
Agreeableness	Courteous, flexible, trusting, cooperative, tolerant	Suspicious, unfriendly, uncooperative, critical, disciplined
Conscientiousness	Careful, responsible, organized, persistent	Unreliable, lacking ambition, easily distracted

Authors Grant T. Savage, John D. Blair, and Ritch L. Sorenson suggest that the classic negotiating styles, with some modifications, can be used as negotiating strategies. For instance, *actively avoiding negotiations,* when employed as a strategy as opposed to a style, can be used when a party is simply not interested in negotiating.[12] Perhaps the matter at issue is not important enough or worth enough to engage in negotiations. However, if the opponent is interested in negotiating, then *passive avoidance,* letting someone else take over the negotiations, for example, makes sense.

Accommodation as a strategy is known as *open subordination,* where a negotiator chooses a yield-win strategy to dampen hostilities, increase support, and foster more interdependent relationships. To protect oneself from a less than optimal situation at the negotiating table because the other party is not as interested in the relationship, one can adopt a *focused subordination* strategy, which limits the areas in which the negotiator is interested in reaching an accommodation.

As a strategy, *firm competing* can be used when the substantive interests are important but the relationship is not. Under some circumstances, such as when the parties have unequal bargaining power, the directness of firm competing should be modified to soft competition. The relationship may not be of much importance, but it is still wise to consider it on occasions.

Trusting collaboration, as a strategy, can be used when both the relationship and the substantive outcomes are important to the negotiator. If the other party does not reciprocate, then the negotiator can use a modified collaborative strategy known as *principled collaboration* by which the parties agree to conduct negotiations based on a set of mutually agreed-upon principles.

Behaviors during a negotiation can change. Anyone might employ any of the techniques in a negotiation situation depending upon the circumstances. A negotiation may begin in one behavioral style and move through others. Situational variables that influence the type of behavior exhibited include the following:

- Subject matter of the negotiation (resources, power, dependency of the parties)
- Previous success in using a particular style
- Relationship of the parties (family, supervisors, peers, or subordinates)[13]

The behavior by one party is obviously influenced by the response received. It is the interaction of the parties that determines the negotiating dynamics.[14] If avoidance is matched by accommodation, then the negotiation is probably over. But if avoidance is met by competition, the negotiation can escalate in a negative way. And if avoidance is met with a collaborative style, the negotiation may result in agreement. Table 1.3 summarizes the bargaining styles discussed here.

The Role of Emotions in Negotiation   Negotiation or conflict resolution is a process where the outcome is ultimately a choice made by the parties from among available alternatives. Deciding which alternative is one's preference involves not only an evaluation of facts but also an investment of some emotion. Emotions (anger, happiness, fear) and moods (grumpy, depressed, apprehensive) collectively influence a party's judgment and decision tendencies. Many decisions have pros and cons on both sides with no rational way to distinguish among the options. As you will see in the experiments described next, emotion may be a critical component of the decision-making process by giving the individual a basis for making a choice.

Table 1.3   Attributes of Bargaining Styles

Conflict Style	Strong Predisposition	As a Positive Attribute	As a Negative Attribute	Weak Predisposition	As a Strategy
Avoiding	Defers confrontational negotiation	Displays tact and diplomacy	Causes stalemates	Prefers hard-nosed bargaining	Used when not interested in negotiating
Accommodating	Derives satisfaction from solving problems	Is good team-builder	May make unwise concessions	Has little patience for other party's needs	Used when hostilities need to be lessened
Competing	Views negotiation as a game or sport to win	Has excellent instincts for claiming value	Focuses on issues that are easy to define as win-loss	Believes in treating people fairly and avoiding needless conflict	Used when substantive interests are important, but not the relationship
Collaborating	Enjoys participating in joint problem solving	Instinctively tries to discover and satisfy the real interests of the parties	May transform a simple problem into a complex one	No patience for the give-and-take that comes with collaborative thinking	Used when relationship and the substantive outcomes are important
Compromising	Is eager to conclude negotiation on fair standards	Is best when stakes are small and time is short	Can rush the process and agree to unnecessary concessions	Refuses to compromise on principle	Used when stakes are small, time is short, or in a weak bargaining position

Neuroscientists have studied the effect of emotion on decision making. Patients with damage to the frontal cortex of their brain experience greatly diminished emotional responses, although their intellectual function and memory are unaffected. In one experiment, when given a choice of two possible dates for an appointment, one patient spent 30 minutes trying to choose, using a sophisticated cost–benefit analysis that far exceeded the demand of the task. In another experiment simulating gambling, the parties were asked to choose a card from one of four decks. Every time a party chose a card from A or B deck, he won $100; when he chose a card from C or D deck, he won $50. After a while the parties were told that they had to begin returning some of the winnings. The rate of unpredictable losses per 10 cards from stacks A and B averaged $1,250, whereas the average unpredictable losses per 10 cards from stacks C and D averaged $250. So choosing cards from C and D decks resulted in the most gain. The normal subjects learned to pick from C and D, and experienced signs of tension as they selected a card. The impaired subjects, on the other hand, continued to select from the A and B decks and showed no signs of tension.[15]

Author Daniel Goleman, in his book *Working with Emotional Intelligence*,[16] promotes the idea that for individuals to negotiate effectively, they need to identify and use their emotional intelligence. **Emotional intelligence** is a term encompassing the following five characteristics and abilities as they relate to a bargaining situation: (1) *self-awareness*—the ability to be aware of which emotions, moods, and impulses one is experiencing and why, as well as being aware of the effect one's emotions are having on others involved in the negotiation; (2) *self-regulation*—the ability to keep one's emotions and impulses in check, to remain calm in potentially volatile negotiations, and to maintain composure regardless of one's emotions; (3) *self-motivation*—the ability to remain focused on one's goals in the negotiation despite setbacks, to operate from a hope of success rather than a fear of failure, and to accept change as necessary to attain goals; (4) *empathy*—the ability to understand the feelings being transmitted at the negotiations through verbal and nonverbal messages, to provide emotional support when needed, and to understand the link between others' emotions and their behavior; and (5) *managing relationships*—the ability to deal with problems without demeaning the opponents, not to let others' negative feelings prevent collaboration, and to handle conflict with tact and diplomacy.[17]

In the Chapter Case, Robert and Sophia could have drawn on their emotional power and intelligence during the meeting with the neighbors, to defuse their anger and facilitate a healthy dialogue.

Interdependency

If there is no **interdependency** between the parties, there can be no reason to negotiate and no motivation to reach agreement. If one party is totally dependent upon the other, the dependent party has nothing to offer and the other party can simply dictate the terms of the relationship. Likewise, if both parties are totally independent, there may be no need to negotiate because either party can survive without the other. Interdependency means that for some reason each of the two parties depends upon the other—at least as it concerns the object of the negotiation—and therefore the parties are motivated to enter into a negotiation and to reach agreement.

The degrees of interdependency can vary based on the depth and duration of the relationship. In a *one-shot negotiation,* such as a negotiation for the purchase of a car or a home, the transaction is generally between strangers in which one party supplies the other party with the car or house in exchange for money. The interdependency between the parties in this instance is shallow and of short duration. *Repeat transactions* between parties, as might occur between a manufacturer and its suppliers, can create a deeper relationship in which the parties have more interdependency than in a one-shot negotiation. The relationship can be of long duration because they have the possibility of more transactions in the future. But the parties, while interdependent in these transactions, are still *free agents*—that is, if either party becomes dissatisfied with the other, both could walk away.

Some negotiations occur between parties in a long-term relationship in which one side controls more of the resources, such as an employer and her employees. In a situation like this, the relationship from the employees' standpoint is deep, as they have the greater dependency because the employer controls the resources needed to pay them. In terms of duration, it is a long-term relationship as long as the employees perform so that the employer can stay in business. The employer, in turn, is dependent upon the performance of the employees—but because employees can be replaced, the employer's dependency is less.

A negotiation between parties in a long-term relationship of equal standing, such as a business partnership, typifies a very deep interdependency. The parties have a common identity, goals, risks, and rewards—so if either party became dissatisfied with the other, walking away would be difficult. The tactics in Box 1.1 can help you identify the interdependency in a negotiation.

BOX 1.1   Tactics for Success

Find Common Interests by Asking the Right Questions

Interdependency means that the parties to a negotiation have some reason to reach agreement. If a negotiator can identify the common interests, then he or she may be able to offer solutions that address those interests. One way to find common interests is to ask the right questions. Following are some examples:

Open-ended questions seek information: What were you hoping to settle today? How can we move this issue forward?

Leading questions point in a particular direction: Don't you think that our last proposal gave both of us some benefit? Don't you think that it is important that we resolve at least this issue today?

Clarifying questions focus the discussion: Do you find the discipline troubling mainly because of this past year's experiences? You want me to agree that the new bonus system will not begin until the new fiscal year?

Gauging questions aid in finding the other's point of view: Is it important to you if we finish up today, or can we have another day to consider the offer? How do you feel about our latest proposal?

Decision questions seek to reach agreement: If I could guarantee an abbreviated hearing process, would you be willing to limit appeals to dismissals? If all of the salespeople could report to the office on a regular schedule, could we begin using flextime?

Common Goals

There are two types of goals within every conflict: content goals and relationship goals. A **content goal** is the substance of the issue, such as getting a development plan approved, landing a client, or satisfying neighbors. The **relationship goal** defines how the parties intend to relate to each other—for instance, whether the parties are important to each other, whether they are willing to share decision-making authority, whether they intend to dictate to one another. The parties may not be aware that there are two goals within a negotiation. They might resolve the content goal without ever addressing the relationship goal. If this happens, the conflict continues after the negotiation is complete, albeit in subtler ways. In the Chapter Case, Robert and Sophia wanted to cooperate with the Zoning Commission staff in order to establish a good working relationship for this project and for projects in the future.

The parties may have a **prospective goal**—that is, the goal they identify at the start of a negotiation. In the Chapter Case, for instance, Robert and Sophia's prospective goal for the three-way meeting with the Zoning Commission and the neighborhood was to eliminate the neighborhood's opposition. Goals may change or emerge as the negotiation progresses. **Transactional goals** are those that either arise or become apparent during the negotiations, not before or after. Adaptability is crucial to successfully resolving transactional goals; the parties must be able to change their expected result during the negotiation. For example, in the Chapter Case, Sophia initially did not have any reason to agree to the Zoning Commission staff's suggestion on increasing parking spaces. However, after the neighbors began to protest her development, she decided it would be beneficial to have the enthusiastic support of the staff, so she agreed to the parking change.

Retrospective goals are those that emerge after a negotiation has concluded. People continue to make sense of a negotiation after it is over—either as a way to justify their decisions or as a learning process on how to resolve similar issues in the future. If, for example, employees whose encounter with their employer did not result in a raise but did give them a sense of how the employer values or does not value their work, the goal of clarifying the relationship may become, in retrospect, the point of the negotiation.

In integrative negotiations, the parties set **collaborative goals**—that is, they attempt to identify and satisfy mutual goals. A negotiation that takes the interests of both sides into account results in a fair and durable agreement. It has both solved the content dispute and enhanced the relationship of the parties.[18]

Flexibility

In a study to determine how people who have not negotiated regularly view the negotiation process, 25 undergraduates were asked to generate a sequence of 20 actions that occur when two people negotiate. The results showed that when the term *negotiate* is used, most individuals characterized the interaction as "competitive" and involving "incompatible interests."[19] In such a negotiation, a distributive model* would dictate that the negotiator should approach the bargaining table expecting a lot, giving up a little, and willing to walk.[20]

Although that might work well in simple negotiations, such bargaining is less productive in negotiations involving multiple hard-to-quantify issues where no obvious common ground exists. In those kinds of negotiations, integrative and interest-based bargaining models are more productive. Participants in a negotiation need to be flexible about the processes they are willing to use. If they approach a negotiation with a closed mind as to how the negotiation is to be conducted, it is unlikely they will reach agreement.

Why do we continue to think of negotiation as a win-lose proposition? For one thing, society encourages us to engage in hard bargaining. Certainly in U.S. culture we learn to win at games, beat opponents, and get the best grades, car, or deal, regardless of anyone else's needs. Such an attitude is difficult to unlearn because hard bargaining may have worked in the past, so changing to something that is seen as weaker or emotional is not very appealing. Negotiators often feel they have taken the moral high ground in a negotiation and that any change would compromise their principles. But being flexible does not require compromising principles or acquiescing for the sake of an agreement. Being flexible means protecting and fulfilling your own interests, while finding creative ways to minimally satisfy the interests of others as well.[21]

Participants must be flexible to respond to power plays in a negotiation. Negotiators often make tactical moves—such as belittling a proposal, making threats, or appealing for sympathy—in an attempt to shift power in the bargaining situation. A negotiator must be able to respond to such tactics in a strategic way. For instance, strategies for responding to power moves made by the other side include taking a break, asking a question, correcting a misstatement, or ignoring the attempt and continuing to negotiate.[22] A power shift can quickly occur in a negotiation situation. Just the addition of new facts can quickly alter the balance of power between parties—even between a father and son as illustrated in the accompanying cartoon, or in an actual negotiation as described in Box 1.2.

Zits

Source: Zits is syndicated by King Features Syndicate Inc. Used by permission.

---

* In later chapters we will examine in detail the negotiation models commonly called *distributive bargaining* (Chapter 3), *integrative bargaining* (Chapter 4), *interest-based bargaining* (Chapter 4), and *alternative dispute resolution* or *ADR* (Chapter 7).

Decision-Making Ability

When conflict is at the core of negotiations it manifests itself in three areas: relationship conflict, resource conflict, and process conflict. *Relationship conflict* comes from interpersonal incompatibilities, friction or tension between parties, their lack of familiarity, or their lack of trust. *Resource conflict* is a disagreement or difference of opinion over the object of the conflict, or incompatible goals or disagreement over the allocation of resources between the parties. And *process conflict* can arise when the parties use different strategies for resolving conflicts—competing versus collaborating, for example.[23]

Underlying all those manifestations of conflict is the fact that negotiation is an activity that involves at least two people making decisions that require judgments and choices. *Judgment* involves recognizing and evaluating the content of the options presented. *Choice* involves actually selecting an option. Negotiators or the parties to a conflict often differ in how they think or process information and in their beliefs and value systems, so when called upon to make judgments, conflict can escalate. The parties may differ on how they react emotionally to a conflict or by what motivates them. Both of those factors can influence their choices, making agreement more difficult.

People develop *schema* as a way of organizing current knowledge and as a way to process future information. A **schema** is a framework or structure for one's beliefs about a particular issue. Through the use of schemas, people can quickly organize most everyday situations and act effectively without effort. For example, most people have a stairway schema, and can apply it to climb staircases they've never seen before. Because one's schema, or *frame of reference,* is determined by personal experience and expertise, the parties to a conflict may not be experiencing the particular situation in the same way. In Box 1.3 you can see how a schema might affect a bargaining situation.

It is essential to the negotiating process that both parties are in a position to *make a decision* and are *willing to commit* to the agreement reached. Keep in mind that in many situations the parties doing the bargaining may be representing other parties. For instance, two or three union negotiators may represent 1,000 workers in an assembly plant, while the management representatives across the table from them represent its owners. A car salesman may have to check with the manager before reducing the price of a car, while a buyer may have to check with a spouse before committing to buying it. In those circumstances, even though both sides have to "go back" to their respective principals for "ratification," the negotiators must be empowered to reach agreement or the negotiations are a waste of time.

Max H. Bazerman and Margaret A. Neale applied behavioral decision theory to negotiation and moved researchers away from simply focusing on the bargaining process of moves, countermoves, goals, and expectations to understanding the cognitive process of judgment and choice involved in negotiation.[24] Howard Raiffa refined this research by noting that the study of negotiation must include not just the study of what negotiators *should* do—the rational or normative perspective—but also what negotiators *are likely* to do—the behavioral or descriptive perspective.[25] Decision making in negotiations thus involves cognition, personal biases, and motivation.

Cognition and Heuristics **Cognition** refers to the process of assimilating information to make rational choices. Negotiation is an activity that requires participants to make judgments and choices. Theoretically, negotiators gather the optimal amount of information needed for decision making, make accurate assessments of that information, compare the expected value of an agreement to the expected value of nonagreement, and choose the alternative that maximizes their interests. This *rational choice theory* is the basis for the most frequently used bargaining processes. However, when judging the contents of options, two people can look at the same information and draw totally opposite conclusions, because each is seeing it from his or her own vantage point.

Parties in a negotiation are faced with a constant stream of choices and many choices involve uncertainty. They may also be called upon to process information quickly, which they may do intuitively rather than rationally. To aid the cognitive process as they try to assimilate information, individuals often react to such uncertainty and make intuitive decisions by relying upon a small number of general-purpose **heuristics**, or rules of thumb, to simplify decision making. Heuristics are helpful, but they can also misdirect a negotiator when used inappropriately.

Biases   Certain heuristics employed in negotiations can create knowledge-based or cognitive biases, which cause negotiators to make faulty or irrational decisions. One example of such a bias is an **availability bias** that occurs when the negotiator estimates the probability of an outcome based on how easy that particular outcome is to imagine—that is, how readily it comes to mind. For example, it is normal for vividly described, emotionally charged possibilities to be perceived as being more likely than those that are harder to picture or are difficult to understand.[26] People who are afraid of dying in an airplane crash have no problem riding to the airport in a car, even though more people die from car crashes than airplane crashes. But because airplane crashes involve multiple deaths and are widely reported in the media, and deaths from car accidents, unless drinking is involved, receive less attention, the possibility of being in an airplane crash is more "available." In the Chapter

Case, the neighborhood may have reacted negatively to Sopia's development because the picture of unsightly multi-family dwellings was more *available* than a picture of a tastefully developed condomimium.

Another example of a congitive bias is a **representativeness bias**, or *stereotyping*. This occurs when one uses superficial qualities rather than essential characteristics in deciding that two things are similar when they are actually unique. In the Chapter Case, it would seem that the neighbors assumed that Sophia was an irresponsible developer who had no concern for the impact of her development on the neighborhood, simply because some developers had no such concern.

An *egocentric* or **self-serving bias** occurs when people believe an uncertain option will more likely be beneficial to them than is objectively true, because their perceptions and expectations are biased in a self-serving manner. Research by Max A. Bazerman and Margaret Neale has demonstrated that individuals in final offer arbitration, for example, consistently overestimate the likelihood of their success. They believe that the arbitrator will rule in their favor because they perceive their final offer to be the most fair.[27] A related perception, **self-enhancement bias**, occurs when one party to a conflict views his or her behavior as more constructive and less distructive than that of the opponent—again, seeing oneself in the best light.[28]

One cognitive bias that is often the cause of an unresolvable conflict is an **impact bias**, which occurs when a person—who may accurately predict that he or she will feel positively or negatively about a certain outcome—**overestimates** the intensity and duration of those feelings. Lawyers often have this problem with clients in litigation when settlement discussions begin. By the time most lawsuits reach the settlement stage, the parties have been engaged in an adverserial process for some time. During that time, one of the parties may have anticipated vindication that his cause was just, which is more important to him than money to compensate for the injury he believes he suffered. So, when the financial offer during settlement negotiations is the amount expected, but the accountability falls far short of what he had imagined, he doesn't want to settle. He believes that he will feel much better if the jury finds the other party "guilty" rather than just settling the case. In fact, the satisfaction he derives from such a finding is short-lived. For example, in the Chapter Case, the neighbors anticipated that the building of condos would be so detrimental that they reacted emotionally to its development. However, if the condominiums were developed as Sophia contended, they would probably become such an integral part of the neighborhood that any lingering concerns would be minor.

These biases—availability, representativeness, self-serving, self-enhancement, and impact—lead to an unrealistic assessment of the value of various options to the parties in a negotiation. Such assessments either cause the parties to greatly overestimate what can be achieved at the bargaining table or cause them to fear agreement, thinking that they may have been taken advantage of by the other party.

Motivation Experienced negotiators know that the key to reaching agreement is to ascertain the other party's motivations. What is influencing the decisions that the other party makes? Of course the obvious and certainly most common motivation is to claim more value from the negotiation than the opponent claims. Beyond that, however, motivation affects both information processing and the strategies one employs in a negotiation.[29]

Social motivation refers to the negotiator's preference for particular outcome distributions between the parties—either *selfish* (trying to maximize one's gains with no regard for the other party) or *prosocial* (trying to maximize both parties' gains). Research indicates that a negotiator's inclination toward selfish versus prosocial preferences will influence what information he or she recalls.[30] In a typical distributive bargaining situation in which both parties are attempting to claim as much value for themselves as possible, a negotiator could easily "forget" conciliatory statements made by the other party earlier in the negotiations.

Epistemic motivation refers to the effort a negotiator uses to process information relevant to the negotiation. An epistemic motivation attempts to get at the truth and avoid error through the process of knowing and, more precisely, of being aware—knowing, thinking, learning, and judging. The extremes are between a negotiator who jumps to a conclusion, relying to a large extent on heuristics, and a negotiator who tries so hard to develop a complete understanding about the issue that he or she is never able to reach a conclusion. And while a negotiator's personality may lend itself to one extreme or the other, in negotiations it is often the situation itself that causes an individual to be either highly motivated to gather extensive information or motivated to move on with limited information. Generally, when one is accountable to other parties for the outcomes in the negotiation, or when one has less power at the negotiating table, or when the task at hand is complex, the motivation to process more information will be high. Fatigue and deadlines tend to undermine the need for more information.

Impression motivation is defined as the desire to make a good impression and to get along. It may stem from the negotiator's need for confidence and self-esteem. Or, as in the Chapter Case, the negotiator's need to land a client caused Robert to suppress any annoyance he had toward Sophia's fee arrangement. But such motivation can be difficult when the negotiator wants to be seen as a hard bargainer. An impression motivation may be a function of a negotiator's cultural background, such as someone with collectivist values, or may stem from a negotiator's accountability to a constituency.

MULTIPARTY NEGOTIATIONS

Generally the discussion and the examples given for negotiating techniques involve two-party negotiations. But as in the Chapter Case, many negotiations involve multiple parties and multiple interests. Multiparty negotiation occurs when three or more parties, each representing their own interests, try to resolve a conflict or agree upon a course of action. Multiparty negotiations can present significantly different and difficult challenges in finding common goals, balancing the interdependency, being flexible, and identifying the true decision makers. For example, although most collective bargaining negotiations involve numerous individuals on both sides of the table, they actually involve only two interests: management and labor. However, collective bargaining in the public sector can be a multiparty negotiation if a legislative body such as a city council inserts itself between a mayor (management) and the public employees (union). In that instance, the legislators' goal may be to win political points with the union rather than helping the goal of the mayor to finalize a contract fair to both the taxpayers and the employees. Certainly interdependency suffers if the union can abandon the negotiations with the mayor and go to the legislators for an agreement.

The war in Iraq provides an example of multiparty negotiations, as represented by the U.S.-established Iraqi Governing Council (IGC). The IGC was specifically designed to bring together the diverse ethnic and religious groups of that post-Saddam country, to make decisions for reordering Iraq's political life and government. The 25 members represented a varying number of individuals from five key groups: Shiite and Sunni Muslims, Kurds, Turkmen, and Christians. In order to reach agreement the groups had to form coalitions that shared at least one interest. Such coalitions can cause otherwise minor players to have a greater influence on the outcome of the negotiations than their numbers might warrant. In this case, the Shiite members, who represented approximately 60% of the nation's population originally, refused to sign the interim constitution because they thought it gave too much power to the Kurds. Eventually, through negotiation, the Shiite representatives were brought back to the table and the document was signed.

Some specific issues to consider in multiparty negotiations include dealing with coalitions, formulating trade-offs, voting and majority rule, reaching consensus decisions, and coping with complicated communication patterns.[31]

Coalitions

In a multiparty negotiation often two or more of the parties will form a coalition in order to have more influence on the outcome. But because these parties are coming together only to wield greater influence and most likely agree only on narrow goals, they will find it difficult to sustain common positions and may lack the flexibility necessary to respond to events as the negotiations continue. For example, the Iraqi Governing Council, which had originally excluded the Shiite members and was formed primarily to reach agreement on an interim constitution, would be a very fragile coalition that one might expect to dissolve quite easily.

Trade-Offs

In a multiparty negotiation, each party has the ability to negotiate with one or more of the other parties and can engage in a trade-off that may have considerable influence on the eventual agreement. To garner support for its most important objective, for example, one party might be willing to give up on an issue important to the other parties and throw its support behind one of the major players, giving that player the ability to "win." In the Chapter Case, Sophia might decide to go back to the Zoning Commission staff and agree to their parking lot request if she thinks that doing so will gain for her the staff's assistance in overcoming the neighbors' objections.

Majority Rule

Majority rule arrived at by voting in a multiparty negotiation fails to recognize the strength or interest of individual positions. One person who has very little invested in a particular issue has the same vote as one who considers the issue paramount.

One neighbor in the Chapter Case may be very interested in the outcome of the zoning negotiation, but Sophia has invested time and money and may not accept that the weight of one neighbor's vote should equal hers.

Finding Consensus

Another approach to reaching agreement in multiparty negotiations is to try and find a consensus. A consensus agreement does not imply that all of the parties are in complete agreement on all of the issues, but rather that they have agreed that the total agreement is acceptable, even if some of its parts are less than desirable. Returning to our earlier example, the Shiite representatives came back to the negotiating table and agreed to the Iraqi Governing Council's interim constitution even though they originally thought the provisions concerning the Kurds were unacceptable. Finding consensus is time-consuming and difficult among multiple parties, but often it is the only way to reach a lasting agreement.

Communication

In multiparty negotiations the process of sending and receiving messages, understanding and interpreting those messages, and coping with perceptions can become more complex simply because of the number of people involved. Active listening techniques can help, but the party trying to use such techniques has to be careful not to be perceived as taking over the negotiations. When clarifying a statement made by one party, for example, the party repeating it should make sure that all of the parties agree with the restatement.

MYTHS AND FACTS

To understand how negotiation works and what skills, knowledge, and abilities are necessary to succeed, it is also necessary for you to dispel common myths about negotiations. Which of the following statements do you think are true and which are myth?

> Good negotiators are born.
> Experience is a great teacher.
> Good negotiators take risks
> Good negotiators rely on intuition.
> Good negotiators make concessions.
> Good negotiators never lie.
> Good negotiators look for common interests.
> Everyone is a negotiator.

According to Leigh Thompson, in her book *The Mind and Heart of the Negotiator,* the first four statements are all myths.[32] Good negotiators are not born, but rather learn negotiation skills and, with practice, perfect them. Many people believe negotiators are born and not made because of their own experience in such common negotiations as buying a car or a house. In that isolated event, a person may or may not be very successful because of things totally outside of his or her control. The next time, or on a different day, the negotiations may have had a completely different result. Effective negotiation requires practice and feedback. One is not born knowing how to assess a negotiation situation, how to recognize conflict resolution techniques, or how to diffuse a difficult situation. Furthermore, experience in negotiations is not necessarily a great teacher. Experience alone will not develop negotiating skills, because in the absence of feedback one cannot improve. Just because the end result of a negotiation is a "win" does not necessarily mean that the negotiator was skilled. In fact, such experiences may encourage a negotiator to take risks—but good negotiators don't take uncalculated risks. They are trained to evaluate risk so they can know when and how to proceed successfully. Nor do they act on intuition. Rather, good negotiators rely upon deliberate thought and preparation.

The last four statements in the list are all true. A good negotiator can and most probably must concede something during a negotiation. After all, a key to successful negotiation is compromise! Good negotiators do not enter discussions with the idea that they must get a certain number of things—but instead, enter with a range of things in mind and remain willing to consider alternatives. They are flexible! It is also true that good negotiators never lie. One of the most difficult skills to master in a negotiation is being candid and yet not revealing important information. A negotiator may not want to reveal all the details of her position early in a negotiation, but she must be careful not to misrepresent that position to such an extent that the opposite party believes she has lied. Successful negotiations depend upon trust, which can be established only if the parties interact truthfully. Good negotiators look for common ground and realize the value of starting discussions on a positive note by identifying common interests and agreeing to some issues quickly. If both sides realize that they do, in fact, have common interests and thus both can gain from a settlement, they are more likely to adopt a positive, compromising strategy. Also, early agreement on some issues often helps to resolve differences on other issues later in the process. Finally, the simple truth is that everyone who is able to communicate is a negotiator. Why? Because everyone is faced with negotiation situations every day—some realize their potential to negotiate a better deal, while others simply accept what is offered to them. Everyone can learn to be a competent negotiator by learning three things: (1) *when* a situation is appropriate for negotiation, (2) *who* to negotiate with, and (3) *how* to prepare and use common negotiation strategies and tactics.

SUMMING UP

You may have many opportunities each day to use negotiations to make a deal, make a decision, or resolve a problem. Select one of the parties in the Chapter Case and answer the following questions from that party's perspective.

1. Identify your interests in the zoning dispute.

Then name the other parties and describe what you think their interests are.

_____

_____

2. Describe five techniques a skilled negotiator might use to assist you in getting what you want from the zoning dispute.

   a. _____

   b. _____

   c. _____

   d. _____

   e. _____

3. Determine how you can complement or counter each of the following bargaining styles to keep a negotiation moving in your direction.

Competing: _____

Collaborating: _____

Compromising: _____

Avoiding: _____

Accommodating: _____

4. Explain how each of the following attributes can help you in a negotiation.

Self-awareness: _____

Self-regulation: _____

Self-motivation: _____

Empathy: _____

Managing relationships: _____

5. Describe the degree of interdependency you have with each of the other parties in this dispute and explain why.

_____

_____

6. What relationship goals could you employ to move this zoning dispute to resolution in your favor?

_____

_____

7. Identify issues in this zoning dispute that you could be flexible on if given the opportunity.

_____

_____

Identify issues that you cannot be flexible on and explain why.

_____

_____

8. Explain how an availability bias may keep the parties from reaching agreement.

_____

_____

9. Describe possible alliances that the parties to this zoning dispute might form.

_____

_____

10. Describe four myths about negotiators, and four truths.

Myth: _____

Myth: _____

Myth: _____

Myth: _____

Truth: _____

Truth: _____

Truth: _____

Truth: _____

LEARNING EXERCISE: HOUSE FOR RENT

You have been relocated by your employer to a new city for an assignment that will probably last for two years. You do not want to sell your home—a four-bedroom, two-bath Tudor—so you decide to rent it. A friend of yours in real estate has a potential lessee for you to meet. He is a 30-something single doctor beginning a two-year residency in the local hospital. You have some concerns about a single guy living in your house and taking care of it the way you would, but you agree to meet with him and possibly negotiate a lease. Answer the following questions.

Skill 1.1: Who are the interested parties in this negotiation and what are their prospective goals? How would you compare the parties' dependencies and motivations? What are four options you are willing to propose in this negotiation so that all parties' goals are met?

Skill 1.2: Which bargaining behaviors of a skilled negotiator would be most advantageous to you in this negotiation?

Skill 1.3: Why is collaboration the only bargaining style applicable to this negotiation?

Skill 1.4: What are the collaborative goals in this negotiation?

Skill 1.5: Have you gone into this negotiation with a cognitive bias? If so, explain.

ENDNOTES

1. Robin L. Pinkley and Gregory B. Northcraft, "Conflict Frames of Reference: Implication for Dispute Processes and Outcomes," *Academy of Management Journal* 37 (February 1994): 193–205.
2. *Harvard Business Essentials: Negotiation* (Boston: Harvard Business School Press, 2003), 122–128.
3. Richard Graham, "Developing Effective Negotiation Skills," available at Web site of Huthwaite International http://www.huthwaite.co.uk/pdf/whitepapers/NEGS-developing_effective_negotiation_skills.pdf (accessed September 9, 2006).
4. Phillip R. Harris and Robert T. Moran, *Managing Cultural Differences* (Houston: Gulf Publishing, 1991): 64–67.
5. Michael Watkins, "Negotiating in a Complex World," *Negotiation Journal* 15 (July 1999): 245–271.
6. Elizabeth A. Mannix, "Strength in Numbers: Negotiating As a Team," *Negotiation* 8 (May 2005): 1–4.
7. G. Richard Shell, "Bargaining Styles and Negotiation: The Thomas-Kilmann Conflict Mode Instrument in Negotiation Training," *Negotiation Journal* 17 (April 2001): 155–174.
8. Dean G. Pruitt and Jeffrey Z. Rubin, *Social Conflict: Escalation, Stalemate, and Settlement* (New York: Random House, 1986); Dean G. Pruitt and Sung Hee Kim, *Social Conflict: Escalation, Stalemate, and Settlement, 3rd Ed.* (New York: McGraw-Hill, 2004), 40–47.
9. Keith G. Allred, "Distinguishing Best and Strategic Practices: A Framework for Managing the Dilemma Between Creating and Claiming Value," *Negotiation Journal* 16 (October 2000): 387–397.
10. Shell, "Bargaining Styles and Negotiation."
11. Zhenzhong Ma, "Exploring the Relationships Between the Big Five Personality Factors, Conflict Styles, and Bargaining Behaviors," June 1, 2005, paper presented at the IACM 18th Annual Conference, Seville, Spain, available at the Web site of the Social Science Research Network, http://ssrn.com/abstract=735063 (accessed August 26, 2006).
12. Grant T. Savage, John D. Blair, and Ritch L. Sorenson, "Consider Both Relationships and Substance When Negotiating Strategically," *Academy of Management Executive* 3 (February 1989): 37–48.
13. Joyce Hocker and William Wilmont, *Interpersonal Conflict*, 3rd ed. (Dubuque, IA: Brown, 1991), 128–129.
14. Karen A. Jehn and Elizabeth A. Mannix, "The Dynamic Nature of Conflict: A Longitudinal Study of Intragroup Conflict and Group Performance," *Academy of Management Journal* 44 (April 2001): 238–251.
15. Margaret A. Neale, "Emotional Strategy," *Negotiation* 8 (February 2005): 9–11.
16. Daniel Goleman, *Working with Emotional Intelligence* (New York: Bantam Books, 2000), 180–181.
17. M. Afzalur Rahim and Clement Psenicka, "A Model of Emotional Intelligence and Conflict Management Strategies: A Study in Seven Countries," *International Journal of Organizational Analysis* 10 (2002): 302–326.
18. Sybil Evans, "Negotiation Can Be Positive," *HR Magazine* (May 1992): 49–51.
19. Kathleen M. O'Connor and Ann A. Adams, "What Novices Think About Negotiation: A Content Analysis of Scripts," *Negotiation Journal* 15 (April 1999): 135–146.
20. Daniel L. Shapiro, "Supplemental Joint Brainstorming: Navigating Past the Perils of Traditional Bargaining," *Negotiation Journal* 16 (October 2000): 409–419.
21. Joshua Weiss, "Why Has Negotiation Gotten a Bad Name?" available at Mediate.com, www.mediate.com/articles/weissj.cfm (accessed December 8, 2003).
22. Deborah M. Kolb, "Staying in the Game," *Negotiation* 6 (December 2003): 1–4.
23. Karen A. Jehn and Elizabeth A. Mannix, "The Dynamic Nature of Conflict: A Longitudinal Study of Intragroup Conflict and Group Performance," *Academy of Management Journal* 44 (2001): 238–251.
24. Max H. Bazerman and Margaret A. Neale, "Heuristics in Negotiation: Limitations to Effective Dispute Resolution," in *Negotiating in Organizations*, eds. M. H. Bazerman and R. J. Lewicki (Beverly Hills: Sage, 1983), 51–67.

25. Howard Raiffa, *The Art and Science of Negotiation* (Cambridge, MA: Harvard University Press, 1982), 20–32.

26. Leigh Thompson, Margaret Neale, and Marwan Sinaceur, "The Evolution of Cognition and Biases in Negotiation," in *The Handbook of Negotiation and Culture*, eds. Michele J. Gelfand and Jeanne M. Brett (Stanford, CA: Stanford Business Books, 2004), 7–44.

27. Margaret A. Neale and Max H. Bazerman, "The Effects of Framing and Negotiator Overconfidence on Bargaining Behaviors and Outcomes," *Academy of Management Journal* 28 (1985): 34–49. See also Max H. Bazerman, "When Self-Interest Is Sabotage," *Negotiation* 6 (2003): 7–9.

28. Thompson, Neale, and Sinaceur, "The Evolution of Cognition and Biases in Negotiation," 24.

29. Carsten K. W. DeDreu, "Motivation in Negotiation: A Social Psychological Analysis," in *The Handbook of Negotiation and Culture*, eds. Michele J. Gelfand and Jeanne M. Brett (Stanford, CA: Stanford Business Books, 2004), 114–135.

30. Ibid., 117.

31. Jeffrey T. Polzer, Elizabeth A. Mannix, and Margaret A. Neale, "Interest Alignment and Coalitions in Multiparty Negotiation," *Academy of Management Journal* 41 (1998): 42–54.

32. Leigh Thompson, *The Mind and Heart of the Negotiator*, 2nd ed. (Upper Saddle River, NJ: Prentice Hall, 2001), 6–8.

Chapter 2

The Negotiation Process:
Four Stages

*I*n a negotiation process the goal of both parties is to reach a settlement. If it is not the goal of both parties, then it is very likely that no settlement will be reached. The two parties have interdependent goals—that is, they both expect to gain more by reaching a settlement than if no deal is reached. Thus a negotiator must understand that a deal must meet his or her own interests *and* the interests of the other party. Why? In their classic book, *Getting to Yes*, Roger Fisher and Bill Ury noted that both parties have an alternative to a negotiated settlement: no settlement.[1] They can always choose an alternative ending: no agreement.

Thus, it is absolutely critical to realize that any settlement must include gains by both parties, or one party will likely walk out. Too often negotiators become solely preoccupied with their own interests and forget that to reach a settlement both parties must achieve something. Noted mediator Ted Kheel summarized this critical point: **"Negotiations are about changing the status quo. Unless both parties can receive something more that what the status quo provides, there is nothing for them to negotiate."**[2]

In this chapter we describe the general stages of the negotiation or bargaining process. For our purposes the two words *negotiation* and *bargaining* will be used interchangeably—however some people may consider the term **negotiation** as a more formal process meaning "to settle a business transaction, treaty, etc.," and **bargaining** more commonly used in the exchange of commercial goods "to reach an agreement with regard to worth."[3] The term *collective bargaining* generally refers to yet another arena: the process that an employer and labor union utilize to negotiate and administer terms of employment. The goal of this chapter is to provide an overview of the total negotiation process, to enable readers to more easily understand the various components discussed in later chapters.

In this chapter we present five negotiation skills that can be learned and developed by the novice negotiator, and applied to the end-of-chapter Learning Exercise, "Heirs to an Estate."

Skill 2.1   *Recognize that before entering a negotiation, **preparation** is critical to success and usually includes identifying all tangible and intangible issues that will be of interest to either party, and then prioritizing those issues, making sure to include some throwaway issues. Always decide a BATNA before starting to negotiate.*

Skill 2.2   *Begin negotiation by adopting **ground rules** that address the questions Who, What, Where, When, and How. Also consider the setting because the place and environmental factors can impact the outcome.*

Skill 2.3   *Learn the importance of the **initial offer** in negotiations.*

Skill 2.4   *Anticipate some **posturing** by the other participants in the negotiations, who might select one of several common techniques.*

Skill 2.5   *Decide if you are primarily negotiating a **single-issue or multiple-issue negotiation** and choose an appropriate strategy. Also decide at what point you would walk away from negotiation, thus causing an impasse, and how it might be resolved.*

CHAPTER CASE: THE BUDGET PRESENTATION

Francis was excited beyond anything he had ever experienced when he was appointed department head at the age of 28. He had landed his dream job only three years earlier and then worked long hours to prove himself worthy—loving every day of it. Then his supervisor retired and Francis was promoted to his first administrative position. Yesterday he was informed by the company's CEO, Gail Watson, that he needed to prepare a budget in five days and present it to the budget committee in a meeting, with all other department heads present. Suddenly he felt inadequate and nervous. He had absolutely no budget experience and was totally unaware of the process. His supervisor had several years of experience and never mentioned the annual budget process. Francis then asked the head of another department to describe the process. The head told him, "It's a vicious, competitive process—we all know that we are fighting for a share of a fixed pool of funds. After the meeting you sit down with the CEO and try to get the most you can for your department, keeping in mind the presentations of the rest of us."

Francis is now asking himself, "How do I prepare for this? What are the department's most important needs? How can I negotiate with the CEO? What do I tell my staff?"

A negotiation process does not always follow the exact same steps or stages. Most experienced negotiators recognize four basic stages or general phases of the process. The four phases, as shown in Figure 2.1, include (1) *preparation*—gathering relevant information, deciding the issues of interest to one or both sides, setting priorities, and developing supportive arguments; (2) *the opening session*—establishing ground rules, determining a framework or plan of action, and exchanging initial proposals; (3) *bargaining*—engaging in the give-and-take of negotiations, including discussion of issues and exchange of counterproposals; and (4) *settlement*—reaching a final agreement or "closing the deal." These phases may even be expanded to seven or more stages in complicated, lengthy negotiations. Keep in mind, however, that negotiation is both an art and a science—thus it is not an *exact* science with exact processes (specified by law, scientific experimentation, and so forth).

Academic researchers and real-world negotiators generally agree that the process has changed over the years. The hard-bargaining process generally used in the 1950s utilized a win-lose strategy that included setting aggressive targets, making only few and small concessions, using threats and bluffs, holding firm commitments to initial positions—and often resulting in no negotiated agreement. In the 1980s the Fisher and Ury book *Getting to Yes* described the win-win negotiation process, a strategy that was then growing in popularity, based on the realization that an agreement can most likely be reached if both sides gain something more than they would have achieved if no settlement was reached. Also in the 1980s, the impact of game theory and a focus on the people involved in the process received attention following publication of Howard Raiffa's *The Art and Science of Negotiation*. In the 1990s, interest-based bargaining (IBB) began gaining momentum as negotiators in different settings developed an approach that focused on a new problem-solving process utilizing brainstorming techniques. Today all of these views of the negotiation process have merged to produce a new understanding of the negotiation process.[4]

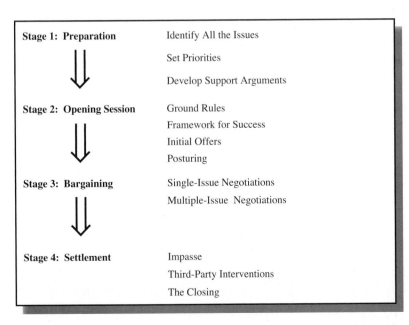

Figure 2.1
The Basic Stages of Negotiation

STAGE 1: PREPARATION

The first stage of the negotiation process is *preparation*, which begins with the identification of key goals—that is, what exactly do you want or expect to gain from the process? The importance of clearly defining the expected goals cannot be overemphasized. Before entering into any negotiation, *always* clearly decide upon your **BATNA—Best Alternative To a Negotiated Agreement**—or "walk-away" value. Absent a clear BATNA, you start off in a weak position because you lack a distinct reference point and thus may accept a poor offer—one with a value *less* than if you achieved no agreement at all. Examples of exercising one's BATNA include a buyer walking away from a salesperson, a labor union declaring a strike, a manager deciding to search for a new vendor, a lawyer going to court, an investor seeking other uses for her funds, or an employer declaring a lockout of employees.

Besides determining the BATNA, the preparation stage also includes identifying all the issues in the negotiation, setting priorities, and developing support arguments for the adopted position.

Identify All the Issues

Too often the "heat of the battle" causes novice negotiators to lose sight of what they are trying to achieve, which is especially likely if they were not clear on their goals at the start. They should constantly compare proposals to their goals to ensure they don't get sidetracked. Experienced negotiator Charles Craver suggests that this critical step begin with the identification of *all* of the issues that may be of interest to either party. A negotiator might identify these issues by answering two simple questions: Which outcomes do you expect to achieve from the negotiation? And, which outcomes might the other party want? When writing the initial list of issues, consider the following:[5]

• The *greater* the number the better—you are more likely to achieve a satisfactory settlement because nothing will be overlooked or forgotten.

• *Intangible issues* should be listed as well as tangibles like price and quantity. The intangibles might include things such as timing of payment (for example, half the settlement price to be paid on the first working day, the other half when all work is completed to the owner's satisfaction), color (to be approved by the owner before painting a room), or delivery arrangements and cost of delivery materials (to be borne by the contractor).

• Add *throwaways* (extras), or issues that have little or no value to you but that may have value to the other party (and thus can be traded for an issue of value to you!). Because parties are rarely able to negotiate everything they want without giving up something, having a few throwaways can help achieve the issues that are most valued or desired. For a throwaway issue to be used effectively, however, negotiator "Smith" must convince negotiator "Jones" that Smith actually values it. Even after a settlement is reached, the throwaway nature of the issue should not be disclosed, or else Smith risks retaliation in future negotiations and will probably lose the ability to effectively use throwaway issues in the future. For example, when negotiating a new job, Eileen asked for a housing allowance because many employers in her new high-cost city provided such an allowance. The employer responded that the human resource policy did not allow for such an allowance, but offered her a modest salary increase to compensate. Eileen had planned on living with her cousin—and thus the housing allowance was actually a throwaway issue—but suggesting it gained her an increase in pay.

Set Priorities

After listing all possible issues, it is often helpful to set priorities. This can be achieved by one of several methods, or a combination thereof: (1) ranking all the issues from the highest priority to the lowest priority; (2) assigning percentage weights (relative importance) to the items—the total must be 100% and throwaway items can be given a zero weight; or (3) dividing the items into four broad categories, as follows:[6]

Level I: *Essential items*—Issues that *must* be gained for a settlement, or else you will accept your BATNA, and not accept the agreement

Level II: *Important items*—Items that you would like to gain but are willing to trade to achieve essential or other important items

Level III: *Desirable items*—Issues that have secondary value and could be exchanged for essential or important issues

Level IV: *Throwaway items*—Items that you are perfectly willing to concede, that may have value only to the other party

As a general strategy, one is always willing to trade a lower-level issue to gain a higher-level issue, and may exchange issues on the same level—but will never give up a higher-level issue, such as Level I, for a lower-level issue, such as a Level II. Figure 2.2 provides an example of ranking, assigning weights, and categorizing negotiable items.

Develop Support Arguments

Once all the issues have been identified, prioritized, and framed, a convincing argument to support each needs to be developed. Why *each* issue? No negotiator is likely to give in on an issue simply because it is desired by the other side! However, facts, logic, and a persuasive argument certainly can enable you to prevail on an issue. In addition, when armed with strong arguments, you are more confident and may cause less prepared negotiators to question their own positions on issues. Business negotiations often utilize arguments based on published trade information, government data, expert witnesses, the results of similar recent deals, and so forth. In personal negotiations, supporting arguments based on facts can be extremely valuable and can "level the playing field" between the novice buyer and the experienced salesperson. The new car buyer, for example, who enters the dealer showroom armed with the exact dealer cost from the Consumer Reports New Car Price Service (available by calling 800-933-5555, for a modest fee) and relevant information from other published services—such as the fact the model desired has a high average inventory period (120 days) and often can be bought online for just $200 over true dealer cost (not including dealer holdbacks)—certainly has a persuasive argument to support an exact, well-researched offer![7] (However, using facts and logic doesn't always work when negotiating with teenagers, as illustrated in the accompanying cartoon.)

Zits

Source: Zits is syndicated by King Features Syndicate, Inc. Used by permission.

Figure 2.2 Setting Priorities: Which Items Are Negotiable?

Barry and Myrtle Woods have a limited budget ($30,000) for upgrades and extras for the new house they are constructing. They have different interests and have agreed to negotiate how they spend the $30,000. Each independently lists all the items they desire, as well as a few throwaways that they can trade. Then they assign weights to help them consider the importance of each item before negotiations begin. Here is a chart showing the items that Barry and Myrtle identified as open to negotiation, along with the weights they assigned to each item.

Barry's List	Weight	Myrtle's List	Weight
Essential			
A. brick & stone exterior	20	A. granite countertops	25
B. 4-car garage	20	B. carpet upgrades	15
C. front porch	15	C. custom cabinetry in kitchen	15
Important			
D. brick walkway & porch	10	D. lighting upgrades	10
E. fireplace master bedroom	10	E. leaded glass front doors	10
F. 9-ft. basement ceilings	10	F. crown molding first floor	10
Desirable			
G. finished garage	5	G. plantation shutters	5
H. custom cabinetry in office	5	H. built-in vanity in master suite	5
I. security system	5	I. dutch oven	5
Throwaways			
J. exterior spotlights	0	J. berber carpeting	0
K. separate electric panel for garage	0	K. dining room tray ceiling	0
L. argon gas-filled windows	0	L. wooden shutters (inside)	0
		M. mother-in-law wing	0
	100%		100%

Recent research by Deborah Kolb and Judith Williams on the negotiation experiences of more than 300 executives suggests that developing persuasive support arguments is a necessary but not sufficient condition for adequate preparation. Sometimes negotiations may break down or stall due to a **shadow negotiation**—the game, sometimes played by negotiators, which does not center on the facts or information of the issues but instead focuses on how the negotiators will deal with each other. For example, if there is an unequal balance of power between the two sides—possibly due to their different status levels within an organization, or their age, experience, race, or gender—a negotiator may lack the clout needed to bring the other side to the table or to engage in serious negotiations, and therefore phone calls are unanswered, meetings are postponed, and so forth. The shadow negotiation has thus diminished the legitimacy of one party. Then the person of higher status or greater power sees no "compelling need" to negotiate, and prefers the status quo in favor of a negotiated settlement, sometimes even when a negotiated settlement would benefit that party, because the person wants to maintain the perceived higher status or power base.[8]

In the Chapter Case, Francis realized that all of the preparation issues (discussed in this chapter) were important to him, especially because this was his first budget preparation and subsequent negotiation with the CEO. He began his preparation by talking with his predecessor and the other department heads—some of whom were open and helpful, others not because they viewed him as competing for the same budget resources. From these discussions, as well as input from his staff, Francis identified three key tangible priorities—(1) a new staff position, (2) travel expenses, and (3) new laptops—as well as two intangibles—(1) longer reporting periods and (2) fewer approvals required for budget transfers. In addition he added six throwaway items with a total value more than double the value of the essential items. Why? He found out that in the past, the CEO often uses the strategy of giving all department heads an equal proportion of their total requests. Thus with the throwaways added, the essential priorities are a small percentage of the total package, and he has a better chance of receiving more of his essential requirements.

The key person, Francis determined, is not the CEO but her budget analyst Mary Ryan, who attends all the meetings. Ms. Ryan reacts strongly to how issues are framed, preferring to hear how items will help the unit contribute to the bottom line, and not why a unit feels it "deserves" something for "equity." This information enabled Francis to prepare his presentation and defend each issue.

STAGE 2: OPENING SESSION

The second stage of negotiations is the process of bringing together the two parties for the general purpose of presenting a list of specific issues. This stage often begins quickly, with both parties ready to begin discussing issues based on past similar negotiations. However, in some cases one or both sides may be reluctant to begin negotiations—possibly due to a shadow negotiation, a fear of failure, or simply inexperience. Regardless of whether the parties are eager to start or reluctant to begin, they should take the time to establish ground rules. Ground rules can clarify the process to all parties involved. They can alleviate concerns about how to proceed by determining a plan of action—clarifying what actions or behaviors will be allowed and what will not be tolerated—and can set a framework for success by specifying exactly how the parties will "settle this."

Ground Rules

In general, a few basic ground rules can reduce anxieties and help get the process started—and completed. Some negotiators, especially inexperienced ones, may want to "skip talking about rules and get on with it," and they may negotiate successfully. But consider the fact that highly experienced negotiators almost always begin by agreeing on the ground rules. Obviously, however, in some situations there will be no ground rules—especially if the negotiations were unanticipated, if it is a one-shot negotiation situation, or if the parties are not sure they can or want to negotiate.

What are ground rules? They can be as simple as a parent who tells two fighting children, "These are the rules: Only one of you speaks at a time, and not until I say so …" In general, the "5 Ws" of negotiation ground rules often address the following:

- **Who** speaks for each party—is authorized to make offers, and accept or reject offers made by the other party?
- **What** form of agreement is acceptable?
- **Where** will the negotiators meet, and what will be the seating arrangement?
- **When** will meetings begin, and how long will sessions last?
- **How will** formal proposals be made and issues be presented?

In some negotiation situations the answers to these questions will be obvious, and ground rules unnecessary. However, quite often how one or two of them are answered can be critical—for example:

- *Who is authorized to make a deal?* In one situation a neighbor thought he had an agreement to buy a piece of property, only to discover that the person he negotiated with was only one of three owners. The other two owners did not accept the deal and, armed with knowledge of what the neighbor had offered to pay, negotiated a higher price.

- *Where will negotiations occur?* Often boardrooms, dining rooms, conference rooms, or similar neutral locations are used for formal negotiations so neither side has an advantage. In one unusual labor–management negotiation situation, the union challenged management to negotiate nonstop, 24 hours a day, until a settlement was reached. Management agreed, but only if the location was moved to the boardroom of its headquarters. The union negotiators agreed, but after 72 straight hours began to tire faster than the management negotiators—who were sneaking naps in an adjourning room!

- *When will negotiations start, and for how long will they last?* Usually two- to four-hour blocks of time, three to five days per week, with hours convenient to both sides, are agreed to until a settlement is reached.

- *How will formal offers be made?* Novice negotiators as well as experienced ones can benefit from specifying exactly how proposals will be made. A proven method is to exchange lists of issues at the first session with the ground rule that no additional issues can be added. This causes both sides to carefully consider exactly what tangible and intangible issues are important, and enables them to reach "closure" once those issues have been resolved. Otherwise, one party may try to "nickel and dime" the other side—meaning when all issues have been settled and both sides are anxious to sign papers and leave, one side says something like "there is one more thing we need …" Many car buyers have experienced this tactic when closing a deal with the dealership finance manager, who adds several hundred dollars for undercoating, an extended warranty, or "dealer prep" to the just-negotiated price.

• *What form of agreement is acceptable?* It is recommended that the parties agree at the start of the bargaining process, as a ground rule, exactly how the agreement will be finalized. One of three methods is generally utilized in negotiations. The first two are informal. A *handshake* between friends may suffice. The second method, *written settlement terms* signed and dated by all parties, often takes less than five minutes but serves several important purposes. Most important is that written words don't change, although memories of an oral agreement almost always change. Furthermore, the clarity of a written agreement is always superior to spoken words. Moreover, the signatures attached to the agreement can have a powerful impact. Parents, for example, have discovered that the act of writing down and signing agreements with their children—covering chores, allowance, and so forth—can be a valuable lesson. Too often children have short memories, which can be quickly refreshed by showing them a piece of paper with their signature! And a written agreement is most helpful in cases where it is necessary to seek enforcement by a third party—for example, when a cousin buys an old car and promises to pay for it next month, but then can't be found! The third method of finalizing an agreement, used in most business deals of substantial value, is a formal *legal contract*—for which both parties may have to pay a fee, but due to the nature of the agreement is worth the cost.

Framework for Success

Successful negotiators formulate a general negotiation framework or plan that guides their actions from the initial offers through final agreement. Unfortunately a common error made by novice negotiators is the failure to clearly define success and develop an overall strategy that enables them to achieve that success. Danny Ertel, a former senior researcher at the Harvard Negotiation Project, offers an analytical framework for defining success in negotiations. Once success is defined, choosing a framework that can guide the negotiator to settlement is possible. Ertel's framework for success contains the following points:[9]

1. *Better than BATNA.* As pointed out at the start of this chapter, any agreement must contain (for both parties) a deal that is better than their BATNA. Thus each side must first determine its own BATNA (see Box 2.1), and then formulate a strategy in which both sides achieve gains greater than their BATNAs. This requires each negotiator to estimate the other side's BATNA.

BOX 2.1   Tactics for Success

How to Determine Your BATNA

A negotiator who starts without a clear BATNA is in a very weak position. Deciding your BATNA, however, is not always easy. If a monetary value can be determined—even for nonquantitative items, then a general BATNA can be estimated and used as a basis to compare with any negotiated proposed agreement. However a BATNA is not only a monetary consideration, it may include alternative courses of action, or simply choosing no agreement as an acceptable alternative.

If you need help identifying your BATNA, answer the following questions:

1. If the other party withdrew from negotiation today, what would be your alternatives?
   a. Not pursue any further negotiations
   b. Bring another party to the table, possibly a mediator
   c. Consider the timing and begin a new attempt to negotiate at a future, more advantageous, date

2. What are the variables that can estimate a general value of your BATNA?

   Price: $ _____
   Timing: $ _____
   Options: $ _____
   Warranty: $ _____
   Color/condition: $ _____
   Other: $ _____
   Total BATNA $ _____

3. How important is your long-term relationship with the seller/buyer, vendor/supplier, or partner? Is this relationship so critical that it overrides any dollar value assigned to your BATNA? If not, can you assign a dollar value to the relationship?

4. Can you improve your BATNA by searching for new alternatives to no agreement?

Source: Adapted from *Harvard Business Essentials: Negotiation* (Boston, MA: Harvard Business School Press, 2003), 15–18, 146.

2. *Satisfy interests, not positions.* It is critical that *interests* be separated from *positions.* For instance, two brothers settling their father's estate fought over an apartment building. Unable to reach an agreement, it was sold to the dismay of both—each had taken the position that he solely should inherit it. Shortly after the sale, a third brother realized the interests of the two were very compatible—one wanted the building as an investment, the other only wanted to manage it in retirement. A negotiated settlement easily could have met both interests, but unfortunately each assumed the *position* that he alone had to own it to achieve his goal and did not realize that they had compatible *interests.*

3. *Do not leave value on the table.* Howard Raiffa, author of the classic book *The Art and Science of Negotiation,* notes that the longer and more complex the deal, the greater the probability that some value can be left on the table—gains that both sides could have received.[10]

4. *Saving face is important for both parties.* Neither party should feel "taken" after a settlement is reached and both parties should be able to explain the outcome to other interested parties without "losing face" because it appears they got the short end of the deal.

5. *Insist on a clear and operational settlement.* Exactly what actions are expected of each party in the settlement should be clearly communicated and achievable—and a written document always provides clearer interpretation and therefore is preferable to a handshake or verbal agreement.
6. *Strive for an efficient process.* Don't waste time talking in generalizations, changing strategies, reneging on offers, and so forth. Make specific offers on issues, and once an issue is resolved don't bring it up again.
7. *Consider the long-term relationship.* Good business negotiators always consider the deal to be but one step in a long-term relationship with a customer, supplier, or partner. An agreement that causes one side to feel forced to accept a bad deal—and thus seek revenge in the next negotiation—can destroy the relationship and cost many times what is gained in the short run.

Thus, in summary, a good general strategy or framework is one that develops offers enabling both sides to realize gains better than their BATNA, to save face, to leave nothing of value on the table, and to leave them with the desire to engage in future negotiations. In the Chapter Case, Francis wisely realized that the long-term relationship with his CEO and budget analyst was the most important factor to consider in forming his budget negotiation strategy. At the same time, the multiparty negotiation process required him to bargain effectively to secure needed resources for his department. Thus he chose to frame each issue according to how it would enable his unit to meet its annual sales and operational targets. His BATNA was to accept no gain for his department, if necessary, but to ask for consideration in the midyear budget adjustment. For him to save face as the new department head, he needed to achieve at least his top priority—and he would present that concern as a last alternative strategy.

Initial Offers

The opening bargaining session often involves the parties getting together in a pre-negotiation meeting. They informally discuss their interests, how negotiations will commence, possible ground rules, and the form of the settlement. How open and honest they are in this process depends largely on their history together and their experiences in other negotiations, which have formed their bargaining styles.

Howard Raiffa encourages negotiators to adopt a style of **FOTE**—Full, Open, Truthful Exchange (also known today as FOTN—Full, Open-Throttle Negotiations). If both parties have successfully utilized FOTE in the past, they are likely to try using it in present negotiations, especially if the other party was involved in the past. How often do negotiations use FOTE in real life? Seldom, admits Raiffa—mostly only wives and husbands, long-time business associates, and students choose the FOTE style. A third-party mediator can help both sides use FOTE if they are willing to adopt it, but usually the initial sessions involve **POTE**—Partial, Open, Truthful Exchange.[11] In the initial session both sides will determine whether POTE or FOTE will be used, but will generally assume a POTE position—which includes the use of tactics such as posturing, bluffing, and the concealment of real interests. Thus we find the negotiation rituals of give-and-take, making and receiving offers and counteroffers—also generally called the "negotiation dance."

Posturing

Because the parties are not being completely open with each other, the opening session generally involves a certain level of **posturing**—the dramatic presentation by one side of its view of the issues, facts, and feelings about the other side. This posturing can become heated and involve emotional outbursts, name-calling, finger-pointing, and other nonproductive behaviors. How long it lasts and how emotionally charged the parties become depends largely on their prior relationship, the perceived balance of power, and the issues at hand. Several factors can increase posturing, such as strain due to past heated negotiations, the existence of divisive issues at hand, or even a perceived exact balance of power. The more these issues are present at some level, the more posturing can be expected to sway the other negotiators—or at least convince them of the firmness of one's position.

However, if past negotiations have generally been harmonious, if the issues at hand can be easily negotiated, and if the power largely rests with one side, then a minimum of posturing can be expected. Why? In these situations, the parties have a long-term positive relationship, and they often realize the issues can be rather easily negotiated to the benefit of both sides—and especially if one side clearly enjoys the balance of power, the process can be more harmonious. It is always important for negotiators to anticipate a certain degree of posturing and accept it is an important element in negotiations.

Posturing can play a positive role in negotiations. How? It allows parties to "blow off steam" and it provides a level of face-saving to parties who must present a strong position to others outside of the negotiations who also have a vested interest—union members, businesses partners, spouses, neighbors, friends, and so forth.[12] Posturing can even be entirely for the benefit of these outside, but very interested, parties. In one case, for example, a labor negotiator called his counterpart on the management side and suggested that he prepare his team for some possible "theatrics" the next day—because some new members of his team wanted to express themselves. Due to their past relationship, the management negotiator did not ask any questions, but warned his teammates. The next day his members were subjected to a barrage of name-calling and foul language—and a walkout by the other side. However, the following day negotiations picked up where they were before the walkout—the posturing and blowing-off steam was over.

As the two sides make their initial offers and engage in posturing, there are several common negotiation elements and techniques that should be anticipated by the participants, as follows:

• *Conflicting viewpoints*. One element of negotiations is conflict, which can cause tempers to rise as parties become emotionally involved. However, both sides need to remember that despite conflicting viewpoints, their goals are interdependent. Neither side can achieve success without the other.[13] Thus, as in the example just cited, both sides should "keep their cool" and expect to resume collegial negotiations after a session of theatrical posturing.

• *Concealment of objectives*. During POTE negotiations, parties often conceal their real goals and objectives to enhance the probability for the best possible settlement. Every negotiator must decide how open and honest to be in communicating needs and preferences—it is a key strategy decision. Negotiators who are completely open and honest may end up settling for less than if they conceal goals and fight harder for a better settlement. However, if negotiators are completely deceptive about goals, the talks may never move in the direction of the desired settlement because the other side is unable to develop proposals that benefit both sides, since the deceptive party's real objectives are unknown. This dilemma of trust poses a key problem for negotiators: Initial discussions may reveal little of the parties' true interests, with disclosure of their objectives offered only in an effort to move discussions forward. As both sides begin to trust each other, however, this process becomes easier.[14]

• *Caucusing*. After a proposal or counterproposal is received, a team usually asks for a **caucus**, or private meeting with its own members. In the caucus they can openly discuss the merits of the proposal and their willingness to accept it, or formulate a counterproposal—without having to worry about posturing. A major part of negotiation strategy is not to reveal at the table how the party feels about a proposal received from the other side. Even when receiving a very desirable proposal, negotiators will call for a caucus without showing their joy—and then the team returns and accepts the proposal, again without showing emotion. Why? An expression of happiness over a proposal may lead the other side to believe that it does not need to concede any further on issues, or that it has conceded too much. Caucusing is also used for resolving disagreement among members of the same team or for gathering additional information about unanticipated or costly proposals.[15] It is always best for negotiators on the same team to not disagree among themselves in front of the other side—and thus possibly weaken their position.

• *Flexibility*. Posturing should not insist on an attitude of inflexibility. The successful negotiation process often requires the exchange of many proposals and counterproposals. Every proposal received should be studied and responded to with acceptance or a counteroffer—but seldom with outright rejection. Immediate rejection of a proposal implies inflexibility and a response of "we will accept only our position." This attitude often angers the other side and may in fact be considered bad faith bargaining. Also, most proposals must be carefully evaluated before their merits can be accurately estimated. If even a small portion is acceptable, then it should be included in the counterproposal to help move both sides toward a settlement.[16]

• *Compromise*. The single most important key to successful negotiations is compromise—by both parties. Posturing aside, if either side really believes it will achieve its position on every issue, then probably no settlement will be reached. Instead, both parties must realize that their goals may be in direct conflict; if one side gains on an issue, the other side loses. If one side loses on too many issues, most likely it will not sign the agreement—or if forced to sign, then it will certainly be looking to even the score during the next round of negotiations.

• *Saving face*. It is important to recognize the need for both parties to save face. Patrick J. Cleary, former chairman of the National Mediation Board, described how the face-saving process at the end of labor–management negotiations typically works: When a tentative agreement is reached, the union negotiator claims victory while management remains silent. Why? Because the union must still win ratification by the membership. If management boasted about the gains it made at the table (and both sides always make some gains), then the union negotiators might lose face, and the members might reject the deal, sending their negotiators back to the table for more management concessions. Most important, notes Cleary, is reaching a final agreement. Getting a final deal—the ultimate goal—is also the most effective way of saving face.[17]

STAGE 3: BARGAINING

After the opening session, the serious bargaining begins. It may be helpful for the novice negotiator to recognize that almost all negotiation situations can be generally categorized by two critical variables: (1) the *number of parties* involved in the negotiation and (2) the *number of issues.* As Table 2.1 illustrates, an analysis of these potential variables can describe four common negotiation situations.

The first involves two parties and only one issue, usually price. In this situation—*two parties, single issue*—the negotiators engage in a zero-sum distributive bargaining process. In most real-life business and personal circumstances, however, there is more than one issue of importance to both parties that must be negotiated. These situations can be described as having *two parties, multiple issues.* Although price is often the primary issue, other issues—such as payment terms, options, delivery cost, add-ons, and so forth—are usually important as well. With multiple issues, the negotiators often find that they have similar interests on some issues, and can trade off other issues to achieve a settlement that contains gains for both parties, sometimes referred to as an *efficient* settlement.

Sometimes a situation can involve *three or more parties, single issue*—such as a public auction where multiple buyers bid on an item offered by a seller. While conventional wisdom might suggest that a seller would always prefer an auction with a large number of potential buyers, in practice auctions can be riskier than negotiations, and empirical research indicates other limitations.[18]

Finally, a fourth potential situation involves *three or more parties, multiple issues*—which produces highly complex negotiations with multiple possible outcomes. These situations are usually resolved either by reaching a full consensus by all parties on all issues, which is extremely difficult, or by each party strictly utilizing its BATNA on each issue. The classic example is several adult children seeking to divide many items included in the estate of their parents. One method to resolve the negotiation would be for all to agree to a proposed split of the items. Alternatively, the items could be

Table 2.1
Possible Negotiation
Situations

NUMBER OF ISSUES	NUMBER OF PARTIES INVOLVED	
	Two	Three or More
One	Zero-sum outcome	Auction process
Multiple	Efficient outcomes	Consensus by all parties on all issues, or only some issues resolved by some parties following their BATNAs

sold to the family members one at a time—thus each could exercise his or her BATNA price on each item—with the total proceeds divided equally among the children. On a global scale, United Nations debates on how to restrict the proliferation of nuclear arms often involve many countries and multiple issues including oil, foreign intervention, human rights, or trade restrictions, with no consensus possible as nations choose to remain with their BATNA, which is often self-determination.

Single-Issue Negotiations

The two-party, single-issue negotiation situation is the most common model and involves only one issue to be negotiated—usually price. Both sides begin by making an initial offer while concealing their **resistance points**—defined as the seller's minimum price (or BATNA), and the buyer's maximum price (or BATNA). Once the opening offers are made, the bargaining process called *bracketing* occurs. **Bracketing** is a common negotiating process of moving toward a middle point between the opening offers (or brackets). The two parties will most likely reach a settlement by using either distributive bargaining or integrative bargaining. These two bargaining strategies are described briefly in the next section and are discussed at length in Chapters 3 and 4.

Multiple-Issue Negotiations

In **distributive** (win-lose) bargaining both sides view their own goals as being in direct conflict with those of the other side—with any one of the multiple issues, whatever one side gains, the other side loses. The negotiators view each issue as a "fixed pie"—thus the larger one piece is, the smaller the other. Each side wants to maximize its share of the resources, or pie. It is critical that all negotiators be prepared to use distributive bargaining, because many negotiators use this method and if one side uses it exclusively, then the other is usually forced to adopt it as well. The distributive approach is often chosen by negotiators who wish to triumph over the other party or maximize their outcome at all costs.

Some of the common tactics used by distributive or win-lose negotiators include the following:

1. *Making extreme or even ridiculous opening offers*. This tactic is designed to cause the other side to question its own opening positions.
2. *Claiming limited authority*. The negotiators at the table claim that they do not have the authority to make concessions.
3. *Making emotional outbursts*. They shout, curse, call the other side names, and often walk out in a huff—all part of their posturing strategy.
4. *Offering few concessions*. They view concessions as a sign of weakness, and thus offer few themselves and seldom offer a concession in return for concessions made by the other side.
5. *Resisting deadlines*. They move very slowly and use time as their ally, preferring a delayed settlement if it gains something, however small, for their side.[19]

A negotiator also needs to be aware of specific tactics that can be used as "traps" (see Box 2.2), and must be prepared to respond to them appropriately.

BOX 2.2 Traps to Avoid

Four Common Negotiating Tactics

Experienced negotiators and even some novices are very likely to try some of the following tactics—but a skilled negotiator should always be aware of these traps and know how to avoid them with the proper response.

1. Lowball (or Highball) Offer

When price is the main issue to be negotiated, and the buyer is not worried about maintaining a positive long-term relationship, then he or she may consider making a "lowball" offer—one that is significantly lower than the seller expects. Likewise, a seller may consider asking a "highball" price that is far higher than the buyer would expect. Why? For two reasons.

First, it just might work given the right circumstances; if a seller or prospective buyer is "desperate," then that party may agree to a deal that is less than optimal. For example, a corporate executive moving to a new city looked at about 20 pieces of property one weekend with his real estate agent. One was a large condo within a block of his new office, with a great view of a river. Asking price was $300,000. Unfortunately, however, the previous tenants were the teenage sons of a wealthy businessman who had moved out six months before his sons—who then completely trashed the condo. The prospective buyer's agent called him late one night to let him know the condo owner's agent had confided in her that the owner wanted to sell it quickly. "I would need to spend $100,000 just to have it gutted and refurbished," the executive replied to her suggestion that he make an offer. "Fine, then offer them half," she said. Thinking he had no chance of getting it at that price, but knowing it would be a steal if he did, the executive offered $150,000. The owner, 6,000 miles away and wanting to unload the condo, accepted the lowball offer. It worked because this situation, like others in which a lowball offer might be successful, involved unusual circumstances that caused the market price to be less relevant. A $300,000 listing price might have been appropriate for another similar condo in the same building, *if* it had not been trashed, and *if* it had not been owned by a highly motivated seller 6,000 miles away.

Even if it is rejected, which it usually is, the second reason that a buyer might make a lowball offer is to significantly lower the seller's aspirations or seriously question the validity of the price.* In the example just cited, if the condo owner had rejected the $150,000 offer, he may in fact have accepted a second offer of $190,000 ($110,000 below the listing price) because now he questions his original listing price—and $190,000 doesn't sound so bad if the only other offer you've received is $150,000! Therefore, if you are the buyer and your strategy is to use lowball offers until you find a great deal, and you are patient and understand that it may never work, your losses may only be time and effort. However, if you are the seller, be aware of the lowball tactic, which might trap you into lowering your price unreasonably or questioning the validity of your position. Recognize the lowball offer for what it is—a negotiating tactic—and don't let it unduly influence your position or BATNA.

2. Good Guy/Bad Guy Routine

This "good guy/bad guy" tactic is similar to the good cop/bad cop routine portrayed on many police dramas in which a person is questioned by two detectives—one who acts tough, uses foul language, threatens the person, and then leaves the room, while the other expresses sympathy and offers assistance if the person cooperates before the "bad" cop returns. In negotiation situations, the classic case is a husband and wife looking to buy a house. The husband could, for example, tell the owner all the things he loves about the house, but also confide that his wife has a few reservations and is not certain that they can't find one more to her liking—if they don't buy *this* house quickly and at a good price. Whether or not that is in reality the case, the owner is likely at least to partially believe it, and therefore may accept the buyers' offer or make a counteroffer.

3. The Whole Pie Versus Single Slices

When a negotiation situation involves several issues to be decided—even if one issue such as price is the most important—negotiators sometimes suggest settling the issues one at a time, agreeing to them and then signing off on each as it is decided. The alternative to discussing and agreeing to single issues is the tactic of looking at the "whole pie." This means each proposal will include a position on all the issues on the table, and none will be agreed to unless all are agreed to at the same time.

The "single-slice" strategy allows each individual issue to be discussed on its own merits and keeps the discussions focused on only one issue at a time. (This process can also package two or more issues together to provide for trade-offs, as we will discuss in Chapter 4.) Although it may appear to be reasonable, the tactic can trap inexperienced negotiators into exceeding their total BATNA, as they resolve individual minor issues one by one before tackling the main issue.

If they know the other party well and can easily evaluate the whole proposal as well as the individual issues successfully, experienced negotiators may choose a whole-pie strategy. More often, however, negotiators prefer to discuss and reach conclusion on individual issues, especially if each requires attention or the whole involves many complex elements. The complexity of dealing with several issues at the same time may lead a novice negotiator to agree to discuss the issues separately, but the single-slice trap should be avoided.

4. The Nibble

Novice negotiators are often excited when they are on the brink of concluding a negotiation, especially if it is their first one. However, they should be aware of

As opposed to the distributive or win-lose strategy, in an **integrative** or win-win approach to multiple-issue negotiations the parties do not assume they want to triumph over the other side at all costs, but instead seek a reasonable settlement of the issues. They recognize the cardinal rule of negotiations we discussed earlier—that both sides must see the deal as better than their BATNA, or no deal can be reached. Thus both parties also realize three important facts: (1) that they may have *common positions* on some issues (not all issues are win-lose), (2) that they will probably need to use *trade-offs* and make concessions on some issues to achieve their goals, and (3) that they want *to maintain a positive long-term relationship* with the other party, and thus will compromise on some issues.

The integrative (win-win) process generally begins with the parties developing a common list of all issues of possible interest to either side. They do not assume they have opposing goals on all issues. Instead, together they review the issues and classify them as either *compatible* or *exchange*. Compatible issues are those for which they have identical or very similar goals and thus agreement can be reached quickly and the issue settled. Exchange issues are those of generally equal value that can be traded one for the other, allowing one party to achieve its goal on one issue and the other party to achieve its goal on another issue.

Finally, the remaining issues, often few in number, but important—such as price or salary—must be settled in a distributive manner similar to the win-lose process. However, in strict win-lose bargaining it is likely that all the issues were settled by the adversarial distributive process, whereas in integrative (win-win) negotiations many of the issues can usually be settled by implementing the compatible or exchange concepts—far more friendly processes that are also likely to achieve an agreement of greater total gain for both sides, because fewer issues are left on the table.[20] Table 2.2 illustrates how the win-win process might be utilized in negotiating a new job.

Table 2.2

How the Win-Win Process Might Be Utilized in Negotiating a New Job

The human resource (HR) manager of a regional firm offered a job to Alexis Lewis. Alexis asked for 24 hours to "think it over" and during that time spoke with two friends at the firm who helped her identify eight issues she might negotiate before accepting the job. The next day the HR manager and Alexis discussed the issues and, using the win-win approach, found two issues with "compatible goals" and four issues with which they could "trade" (two pairs of approximately equal value), leaving two issues for "distributive" bargaining. The results can be summarized as follows:

	ISSUE	AGREEMENT	WIN-WIN METHOD	WHY?
1.	Office	Suite E (window)	Compatible goals	Important to Alexis—who wanted a window. The HR manager had four open offices available.
2.	Primary sales region	Columbus, Ohio	Compatible goals	Alexis preferred it to seven other regions. The HR manager had planned on Lexington, Kentucky, for Alexis—but when asked, the Columbus agent volunteered to switch to Lexington.
3.	Technology budget	$0	Traded for the signing bonus	The cost was about the same as the signing bonus—cash that Alexis really needed. Thus Alexis gave up $3,000 that others receive for new technology.
4.	Signing bonus	$2,500	Traded for the technology budget	Since he saved $3,000 in his technology budget, the HR manager was willing to give Alexis a $2,500 signing bonus.
5.	Moving expense	$0	Traded for clothing allowance	Alexis had nothing to move—but rather than give up the standard moving expense asked if the same dollars could be used for a clothing allowance—as a recent MBA, she desperately needed professional outfits.
6.	Clothing allowance	$2,000	Traded for moving expense	The HR manager was sympathetic to Alexis's desire to buy new professional clothes and thus was willing to give her the standard moving expense.
7.	Travel days per month	16	Distributive negotiation	Alexis wanted to keep her travel days to 14, but 16 was the average for the staff.
8.	Salary	$45,000 plus bonus	Distributive negotiation	The HR manager's opening offer was $40,000, Alexis responded that she was currently making $43,000 (no bonus) and had hoped to get $50,000.

STAGE 4: SETTLEMENT

Although negotiators in some cultures do not actually enter into bargaining with the hope of reaching a settlement—the negotiations may be simply a means of information sharing, or perhaps an exploratory process—most U.S. negotiators begin the bargaining process expecting to reach an agreement. It is important, however, to keep in mind that while you may genuinely desire to reach a settlement, you should never knowingly agree to a bad deal. If the best deal you can negotiate is a bad deal for you—just walk away. So why do people, in rare cases, agree to a bad deal? Probably for one of two reasons—either they have become emotionally involved to the point that they "gotta have" that house, sports car, or new contract no matter what the cost; or else, due to fatigue, outside pressure, or inexperience, they simply want to end the process.[21] This emotion is sometimes called "the over factor" because a negotiator simply wants the process "over with". It can, however, become a significant source of motivation to a fatigued, emotionally drained negotiator and therefore should not be underestimated.

On the road to settlement, sometimes negotiations stall and reaching an agreement seems improbable. Sometimes a third party is called upon to facilitate negotiations and improve chances for a satisfactory settlement. And of course, sometimes the parties reach an agreement that provides optimal benefits to all involved.

Impasse

Negotiators fail to reach an agreement when one party simply walks away from the deal and the process ends, or when both sides still desire a settlement but realize they have reached a stalemate, often called an **impasse.** An impasse occurs when both sides believe no gains can be achieved through the negotiation process they have been utilizing—and thus further bargaining sessions would be a waste of time—but both sides do still prefer a settlement to walking away.

Why do such breakdowns occur? Victor Gotbaum, based on his 35 years of negotiating experience, believes breakdowns are due to one of the following three causes: (1) noncommunication of interests; (2) excessive emotional involvement; or (3) failure of one party to understand the interests of the other party—and thus failure to offer a settlement that is a mutual-gain proposition, that exceeds their BATNA, and that avoids one party walking out.[22] Remember the first point we made in this chapter? The last cause cited by Victor Gotbaum should remind you of it. To reach a settlement, *both* parties must gain more from a settlement than if no deal is reached. Always begin a negotiation with your BATNA determined—and thus with a clear walk-away price. If negotiations fail to reach the walk-away price, be prepared to end negotiations. Box 2.3 more fully explains how important this concept is in negotiation strategy.

Third-Party Intervention

When an impasse occurs, the parties do have alternative methods of continuing to seek an agreement. The methods generally involve a third-party facilitator who can bring an objective viewpoint to the discussions. The facilitator is often a person (or persons) known and trusted by both parties—family member, attorney, judge, college professor, or someone selected from known organizations such as the American Arbitration Association (AAA) or Federal Mediation and Conciliation Service (FMCS). The distinct goal of the third party is to get an agreement. Once selected, the third party meets with the negotiating parties to outline a process to be followed, then establishes trust and may control the process by meeting with the parties separately,

BOX 2.3 Tactics for Success

What Is Your Walk-Away Price?

In any negotiation you must start by determining your "walk-away" price—the top price you are willing to pay when the final price is discussed. The walk-away price should not include the full potential value of the synergies of the deal. Why? The synergies are possible additional positive outcomes that *may* happen—but they are not part of the deal and thus should not influence your negotiation or walk-away price. In addition, for a walk-away price to be real—and it is a critical part of any negotiation—you must be ready to walk away.

For example, when Carlos Gutierrez, CEO of Kellogg Company, the cereal giant, was negotiating the purchase of Keebler, the cookie company, he was most eager to close the deal. Keebler had a direct-to-buyer delivery system that enabled it to carry products to stores in its own trucks, bypassing the retailers' warehouses altogether, which Gutierrez viewed as an enormous synergistic benefit of acquiring Keebler. However, his staff had calculated that at maximum Keebler was worth $42 a share—less than Keebler negotiators would accept. As in similar situations, the staff who established the walk-away price consisted of a decision-making group of highly trusted senior managers given veto power over the final number. They were not concerned with synergies, but with the goal of establishing a balanced, objective estimation of the facts.

In the final bargaining session Gutierrez told Keebler's management that $42 was his walk-away price—and left to watch a Mets baseball game and forget the deal. Two days later, after Gutierrez had made it clear that he had made his final offer, Keebler accepted the $42 BATNA offer.

The next time you begin a negotiation, ask yourself—or better yet, ask other trusted individuals: What is your walk-away price? *Write it down and stick to it.*

Source: Adapted from Geoffrey Cullinan, Jean-Marc Le Roux, and Rolf-Magnus Weddigen, "When to Walk Away from a Deal," *Harvard Business Review* (April 2004): 96–104. Used by permission.

making suggestions, and seeking a settlement. The third party is careful not to take sides, express support for suggested options, or question the interests of the parties. Third-party interventions generally take one of three common forms, as follows:[23]

1. *Settlement facilitation*. The third-party facilitator has only one goal—to reach an agreement between the parties. Thus the facilitator may put pressure on the parties to agree—often to avoid further steps such as legal action. These facilitators generally separate the parties, discourage communications between them, and meet with the parties individually to offer suggested solutions in an effort to reach a deal. These facilitators often refer to themselves as mediators, but use different processes from most mediators, primarily creating their own settlement terms and convincing the parties to accept the deal.

2. *Mediation*. The third-party mediator assists the parties in crafting a settlement agreement that the parties voluntarily accept. The mediator strives to remain nonjudgmental and has no authority to force an agreement. Mediators strive to maintain open communications with both sides and assist them in developing mutually agreeable solutions.

3. *Arbitration.* The third-party arbitrator is empowered by the parties to make a written decision on all unresolved issues. The parties agree in advance to accept the arbitrator's decision as "final and binding." Arbitrators may choose a compromise position on unresolved issues, or may choose one of the final offers made by the parties. The binding power given to the arbitrator assures the parties that a settlement will be reached. However, by agreeing in advance to abide by the arbitrator's decision, the parties lose their ability to reject the final proposal (made by the arbitrator), or to choose to continue negotiating.

The Closing

At some point the parties have completed the bargaining stage and thus reach the closing stage, which is discussed in detail in Chapter 10. The feeling of relief and sense of closure tells the negotiators that a deal is near. All issues have been addressed and settled. With a written, signed, and dated document in hand, the parties involved can feel confident their negotiating produced an agreement that achieves gains for both sides. In addition, they have a document that can be referred to at a later date if needed.

SUMMING UP

Think about the next negotiation situation in your personal life or at work. You can prepare yourself for the four basic negotiation stages by answering the following questions.

1. Describe the situation. What are the central issues to be negotiated?

   _____

   _____

2. Can you create a list of issues that includes essential, important, desirable, and throwaway items? (See Figure 2.2.)

   Essential: _____

   Important: _____

   Desirable: _____

   Throwaway: _____

3. Who are the other people involved?

   _____

   What are their primary goals?

   _____

   _____

4. How can you best present each issue?

_____

_____

5. What is your BATNA or walk-away price or value?

Your BATNA: _____

Can you estimate your opponents' BATNA and thus identify the settlement range?

Opponents' BATNA: _____

Settlement range: _____

6. What ground rules will you propose in the opening session (such as Who, What, Where, When, How)?

_____

_____

_____

7. What is your general strategy or framework for bargaining as you begin discussions? Does it provide gains for both sides beyond their BATNAs?

_____

_____

_____

8. Do you prefer to make the opening offer? What will it be?

_____

_____

9. Will your style be FOTE (Full, Open, Truthful Exchange) or will you conceal at least some of your goals (POTE: Partial, Open, Truthful Exchange)?

_____

10. Is your preferred bargaining method distributive or integrative? Why? If the other side uses a different method, how will you respond?

Preferred method: _____

If other side chooses a different method: _____

11. If an impasse occurs, will you utilize a third-party intervention? Which method? Who?

_____

12. Exactly how do you plan on closing the deal?

_____

_____

LEARNING EXERCISE: HEIRS TO AN ESTATE

Recently you and your brother and sister inherited the estate of an aunt who lived in Chicago. All three of you loved your aunt, but even though you all lived in the same city, you had not kept in contact in recent years due to career and family obligations. Your aunt's last will and testament requires that the three of you divide her assets any way that you can agree upon within 30 days of her death. However, if you fail to provide her attorney with a written agreement within the 30 days, all of her assets will be given to charity. The estate consists of the following: (1) about $320,000 in cash and Certificates of Deposit; (2) a 2004 Lincoln Town Car; (3) two houses, valued at $360,000 and $525,000; (4) all of the furnishings of both houses; (5) an art collection valued at $250,000; (6) season tickets to the Chicago Cubs (behind the home dugout); and (7) a large box containing family photos and slides. The three of you are meeting in six days to negotiate a settlement. In preparation, ask yourself the following skills questions:

Skill 2.1: Recognize that before next week's meeting, preparation is critical to success, and usually includes identifying all tangible and intangible issues that will be of interest to either party, and then prioritizing those issues, making sure to include some throwaway issues. What preparations do you need to make before the meeting?

Skill 2.2: Should you propose that the three of you begin negotiation by adopting ground rules that address the "5 W" questions; Who, What, Where, When, and How? Also, carefully consider the "who"—will spouses and children be included, and the "where" or the setting—where should you meet?

Skill 2.3: The initial offer in negotiation could affect the tone and outcome. What will be your initial offer?

Skill 2.4: Anticipate some posturing by your brother and sister. While the three of you get along fairly well, this estate represents a great deal of money for each family. What posturing might you encounter?

Skill 2.5: Decide whether you are primarily negotiating a single-issue or a multiple-issue situation, and choose an appropriate strategy. Should you consider a third-party intervention?

ENDNOTES

1. Roger Fisher and William Ury, *Getting to Yes* (Boston: Houghton-Mifflin, 1981).
2. Theodore W. Kheel, *The Keys to Conflict Resolution* (New York: Four Walls Eight Windows, 1999).
3. *Webster's New World Dictionary*, 4th ed. (Cleveland: Wiley, 2002).
4. James K. Sebenius, "Six Habits of Merely Effective Negotiations," *Harvard Business Review* (April 2001): . 7–8.
5. Charles Craver, *The Intelligent Negotiator* (Roseville, CA: Prima, 2002), 23–27.
6. Ibid., 25.
7. Ibid., 27–32, 236–242.
8. Deborah M. Kolb and Judith Williams, "Breakthrough Bargaining," *Harvard Business Review* (February 2001): 89–97.
9. Danny Ertel, "How to Build An Effective Negotiation Strategy," 1997, available on the Web site of Vantage Partners, www.vantagepartners.com (accessed January 9, 2004).
10. Howard Raiffa, *The Art and Science of Negotiation* (Cambridge, MA: Harvard University Press, 1982).
11. Howard Raiffa, *Lectures on Negotiation Analysis* (Cambridge, MA: PON Books, 1997), 11–14.
12. Michael R. Carrell and Christina Heavrin, *Labor Relations and Collective Bargaining*, 7th ed. (Upper Saddle River, NJ: Pearson/Prentice Hall, 2004), 217–219.
13. Roy J. Lewicki and Joseph A. Litterer, *Negotiation* (Homewood, IL: Drivin, 1985), 7–9.
14. Ibid.
15. Carrell and Heavrin, *Labor Relations and Collective Bargaining*, 218.
16. Ibid.
17. Patrick J. Cleary, *The Negotiation Handbook* (Armonk, NY: Sharpe, 2001), 20–21.
18. Guhan Subramanian and R. Zeckhauser, "For Sale, But How? Auctions Versus Negotiations," *Negotiation* 7 (October 2004): 7–9.
19. Herb Cohen, *You Can Negotiate Anything* (New York: Bantam Books, 1980), 120–123.
20. Carrell and Heavrin, *The Everyday Negotiator*, 94–98.
21. Craver, *The Intelligent Negotiator*, 135–136.
22. Victor Gotbaum, *Negotiation in the Real World* (New York: Simon & Schuster, 1999), 158–163.
23. Kathy Domenici and Stephen W. Littlejohn, *Mediation: Empowerment in Conflict Management*, 2nd ed. (Prospect Heights, IL: Waveland Press, 2001), 19–25.

Chapter 3

Distributive Bargaining

*T*he negotiation model known today as *distributive bargaining* was first identified by R. E. Walton and R. B. McKersie in their seminal work on negotiation theory, *A Behavioral Theory of Labour Negotiations.*[1] In their work they defined the differences between distributive bargaining and integrative bargaining in the field of labor–management relations. (Integrative bargaining will be discussed in Chapter 4.) Today both terms are commonly used in all discussions of negotiation theories and processes. **Distributive bargaining** is a negotiation method in which two parties strive to divide a fixed pool of resources, often money, each party trying to maximize its share of the distribution. Distributive bargaining is a *fixed-sum* game, and the limited resource is often termed a *fixed pie.* It is also called a *zero-sum* process because one party loses whatever amount is gained by the other. For example, if a seller is paid $1,000 (and thus realizes a $1,000 gain), then a buyer has paid the same amount (and realizes a $1,000 loss)—and the sum of the two is zero. Distributive bargaining is described as *win-lose bargaining* because whatever one side gains comes at the expense of the other party—what is "won" by one is "lost" by the other. It is also sometimes referred to as *hard bargaining* because it is usually a highly competitive process designed to reach a formal written agreement, such as a purchase contract. Probably the most easily identified example of distributive bargaining would be the sale or purchase of a big-ticket item such as a house or a car.[2]

The general nature of distributive bargaining is highly competitive and the objective of the parties involved is to maximize their share of the fixed resource. As a result, both parties may use a variety of tactics including making threats, concealing their true objectives, misrepresenting information—or even lying and utilizing leverage or power if they perceive it is balanced in their favor. A common example in labor relations would be a union threatening to strike when it perceives that management cannot afford the loss of production.

Why is it necessary for all negotiators to be prepared to use and/or respond to distributive bargaining tactics? The basic reason is that, for many novice as well as some experienced negotiators, distributive bargaining is the heart of negotiation. For them, the word *negotiation* brings to mind the classic car-buying situation: a single-deal negotiation in which only one issue (price) is key, and both sides view the transaction as a zero-sum game. Thus, many negotiators will view any situation as distributive and therefore will use distributive strategies and tactics, even though it may not best serve their long-term interests.

In general, the distributive bargaining model is identified by three components: (1) the parties involved view each other as *adversaries;* (2) the objective of both parties is to *maximize their self-interest* or their "share of the pie"; and (3) they are *only concerned about the current negotiation,* interacting with each other as though they have no past relationship and expect no future relationship—and thus are willing to use tactics they might not use if they had a continuing relationship.[3] It is important to recognize, however, that sometimes the parties do have a past and a future relationship—as in labor–management contract negotiations—but they use the distributive model in spite of this fact and bargain strictly as adversaries, trying to get a maximum "share of the pie," seemingly unmindful that in later months or years they may suffer from the retaliatory tactics of the other party, who has been waiting to "even the score."

Negotiation Skills

In this chapter we present five negotiation skills that can be learned and developed by the novice negotiator, and applied to the end-of-chapter Learning Exercise, "Buying a House."

Skill 3.1 *Recognize a* **distributive bargaining** *situation by the three key components and therefore prepare to utilize appropriate strategies and tactics to reach a desired settlement.*

Skill 3.2 *Begin by determining a* **reservation price** *to prevent "the heat of the moment" from causing you to agree to an unacceptable offer.*

Skill 3.3 *Learn how to use* **bracketing** *of the other party's offer to achieve your desired outcome in a distributive negotiation.*

Skill 3.4 *Recognize and use common social* **norms** *and accepted practices to evaluate offers, make counteroffers, and reach a settlement point.*

Skill 3.5 *Learn the important role of* **framing** *offers to influence how others perceive and respond to offers.*

CHAPTER CASE: BUYING A WORK OF ART

Chris Comte is an artist with studios in Morro Bay, California, and Cincinnati, Ohio. She has built a following of admirers in southern California and in Ohio and is considered to be very talented by those who collect her paintings. Many of her works have appeared in magazines such as *Southern Living* and *San Luis Obispo Magazine* and have been purchased and displayed in many prominent locations including art galleries, courthouses, and private collections. However, like most struggling artists, she always needs to sell her works for a fair price to pay the bills. One of her favorite (and she believes one of her best) paintings is of two young women dressed in their finest Sunday white outfits, sitting in a rowboat on a sunny, lazy August afternoon, with a beautiful wildflower garden behind them. The painting is simply titled *Sunday*. A retired couple from Texas is vacationing in the area for a few days and by chance stop in the studio. While browsing they pause to admire *Sunday*. The next day they decide to return to the studio and possibly buy the painting. The listed price is $12,500. The buyers believe they cannot afford to pay the asking price, and have decided to offer $7,500, knowing that artists often negotiate the price of their works. It is a classic distributive bargaining situation. The only real issue is price. Both parties would like to make a deal, but both also know they can walk away from the deal.

CLASSIC DISTRIBUTIVE BARGAINING SITUATION

The classic distributive bargaining situation is one that everyone has experienced. The issue is the sale of a piece of furniture, an automobile, or perhaps, as in the Chapter Case, a work of art. The buyer and seller do not know each other, and do not expect to have any meaningful future relationship. The only issue to be negotiated is price. The goal of the buyer is to minimize the price, and the goal of the seller is to maximize the price. Both view the situation as win-lose bargaining. It is important to consider that in most such distributive bargaining situations, there actually is no "fair" or "best" price. What is a house worth? It's worth whatever price the two parties will agree upon.

Howard Raiffa, in his classic book *The Art and Science of Negotiation*, provides an analytical model of this classic distributive bargaining situation. Raiffa explains that when the two parties enter discussion, each has some idea of what they consider to be their **reservation price**—the absolute minimum price that the seller will accept or the absolute maximum price that the buyer is willing to pay. Let's call the seller's reservation price s and the buyer's reservation price b. What happens if negotiators do not decide their reservation price before the negotiation begins? They will be at a real disadvantage because they may easily agree to what they will later admit to being too much or too little because they were "caught up in the heat of the negotiation." Unfortunately this is not a rare situation.

The reservation prices can also be thought of as the BATNA of each party, as we discussed in Chapter 2. For sellers, the BATNA or s is the price at which they will simply continue to seek another buyer, and for buyers the BATNA or b is the price at which they will look for another car to buy. If b is larger than s—that is, if the buyer's maximum price is greater than the seller's minimum price—then there exists a **zone of possible agreement (ZOPA)**, also called the *bargaining range, negotiating latitude,* or *settlement range* because any offer outside of the range will be quickly rejected by one of the parties. The ZOPA exists because the buyer is willing to meet or exceed the seller's minimum price.

However, the mere existence of a positive ZOPA does not guarantee that an agreement will be reached. After all, negotiators do not usually share with each other their reservation prices and thus may not realize that a range of possible settlement prices exists, and in fact they may not reach agreement if they are poor negotiators. Also consider what happens if s is greater than b. Then the seller's minimum acceptable price is higher than the buyer's maximum price, and thus no ZOPA exists, and no agreement can be reached.[4] The distributive bargaining situation can be represented as illustrated in Figure 3.1.

In Figure 3.1, the seller, of course, wants X to be the highest possible price, or as close as possible to b, and the buyer wants X to be the lowest possible price, or as close as possible to s. However, during negotiations both parties are only aware of two values: their own reservation price and the proposed value of X. So how do they negotiate a final price? Typically, in a distributive bargaining situation, they enter into the **negotiation dance** with one party making an opening offer, the other party responding with a counteroffer, and then possible multiple counteroffers, until an agreement price, X, is reached—which will be somewhere between the two reservation prices, within the zone of possible agreement.

An interesting finding by negotiation researchers is that all things being equal, such as the negotiation abilities of the two parties, each point in the ZOPA has an equal probability of becoming X, the final agreement price.[5] In the real world, of course, all things are seldom equal. One or more of several factors may enable one party to negotiate a final price, X, that is more favorable to them and thus closer to their reservation price.

One critical piece of information that can provide a distinct advantage is the *reservation price of the other side*, or how eager the other party is to reach an agreement. For example, a husband and wife are negotiating to buy a pleasure boat they found on the Internet. The seller listed the price as $35,000 in the ad—but, unknown to the buyers, has decided he will take $28,000 (reservation price). Upon inspecting the boat in person, the wife offers $25,000. The seller declines and the husband and wife begin haggling over the good and bad points of the boat. They discuss, in front of the seller, other boats they found online, and how far they would need to travel to inspect them. The husband keeps saying, "This is the nicest one we've seen." The seller

Figure 3.1 Classic Distributive Bargaining Model

0	s		X		b		$ Dollars

s = Seller's reservation price
b = Buyer's reservation price
X = Negotiated price or final agreement

senses they are eager to make a deal, so he responds with: "I'm willing to come down to $33,000 if we can close the deal today." The buyers counter with an offer of $32,000, which is accepted. The seller in fact is just as motivated as the buyers, if not more motivated, but their discussion gave him the sense they were very eager to buy—information that allowed him to lower his price by only $2,000 and gain a settlement price of $4,000 more than his reservation price.

Another important factor is the *opening offer,* which can often be critical in the negotiations that follow. In the example just cited, the seller's opening offer was $7,000 above his reservation price and gave him room to negotiate downward, thus appearing to compromise. In his second offer he reduced his opening offer by $2,000 instead of raising their opening offer by $2,000, which would have been an equal movement. However by saying "I'm willing to come down" he based his counteroffer on his opening offer—a tactic that was critical to reaching a higher final price.

A third important factor is the *skill of the negotiator.* Negotiators who prepare in advance and successfully utilize commonly practiced negotiation tactics will reach agreements that are more favorable to them. The tactic that the seller used in our example was a simple but important one: He listened and learned about the circumstances of the other party. Experienced negotiators realize that careful listening to the other party during negotiations may enable them to determine the true interests of the other party, and thus give them valuable information. Negotiation scholar Kathleen L. McGinn compares this important negotiation skill to that of improvisational jazz musicians who practice with other musicians for hours every day, listening carefully to notes, scales, chords, and progressions. After much practice they can begin to improvise to create exhilarating new music. Skilled negotiators, like jazz musicians, are to a degree improvisational because they "play it by ear" and skillfully listen to the interests, needs, and concerns expressed by the other party and then, based on that information, make adaptations in the negotiations to their advantage. McGinn believes that negotiators can develop their improvisation skills by seeking out, recognizing, and then utilizing three types of information during a negotiation:[6]

1. *Relational information:* Facts, beliefs, and feelings about the relationships between the parties. For example, when asked "How can I trust that this is your best price?" a manager responded by showing the buyer his company price list. This information helped build a relationship as well as gain the sale.
2. *Substantive information:* Facts, pertinent data, and questions about the other party's offer, utilizing reason and logic. For example, the seller of a house asked the buyers why their latest offer was an odd number ($183,256), when their previous offers were nice round numbers ($170,000 and $180,000). The buyers responded by showing the seller a form with their bank's approved loan limit, saying "We really want this house, but this is the maximum amount the bank will loan us under their first-time-owner plan—if you can't accept it, we have to keep looking." The owner accepted the offer because she was convinced the form was legitimate and appreciated their sharing the information.
3. *Procedural information:* Open discussion of the negotiation process that helps understand and manage the process. For example, at the start of the annual round of labor contract negotiations between the city and nine unions, one

union president informed the city's new chief negotiator, "Don't bother setting information sessions with us—no matter what we tell our members, we are not in a hurry, and in fact will not engage in serious negotiations until the city has settled with all the other unions." Then, true to his word, the union negotiator accepted the city's opening offer that day but refused suggestions that they meet again—for 11 months, until the city had settled with all the other unions. Once they did meet again, they settled on a new contract in less than 30 days. By first explaining the process his union would follow, the president provided valuable procedural information that gave the city negotiator a realistic expectation of the process and helped maintain a positive relationship.

OPENING OFFERS

At this point we will expand upon the discussion of the two party, single-issue distributive bargaining situation presented in Chapter 2. The single-issue negotiation situation is the most common, and the one issue to be negotiated is usually price. As we discussed earlier in this chapter, both parties begin by determining their reservation prices. The next critical step is for one side or both sides to make an initial opening offer. Keep in mind that they are concealing their resistance points—defined as the seller's minimum price (or BATNA) and the buyer's maximum price (or BATNA). Experienced negotiators appreciate the critical importance of the opening offers. They realize that novice negotiators, such as the ones in the accompanying cartoon, may simply accept an opening offer and not really negotiate. Once opening offers are made the bargaining begins. Opening offers can easily determine the nature of the bargaining and greatly affect the settlement value.

Anchoring

Opening offers can easily determine the nature of the bargaining and greatly affect the settlement value by effectively setting the outer limits of the bargaining. No

Zits
Inexperienced negotiators may simply accept an opening offer, or make a counteroffer that is very close—thus in reality "accepting" the opening offer of the other party.

Source: Zits is syndicated by King Features Syndicate, Inc. Used by permission.

buyer will pay more than the asking price, and no seller will accept less than the buyer's lowest offer. Therefore, many experienced negotiators often prefer to make the opening offer and thus **anchor** the discussion at their chosen point. Still other negotiators prefer to have the other party make the first opening offer. Once they have the other side's opening offer they can adjust their own opening offer to keep their desired outcome in the middle of the two opening offers. Negotiation researchers have shown that people irrationally fixate on the first number put on the table in a negotiation—the offer becomes an anchor for the following negotiations, regardless of how arbitrary it may be. In fact, research shows that even when people know that the anchor has little or no relevance, it still influences their decision making. This curious phenomenon is illustrated in Figure 3.2.

Experienced negotiators therefore know that the first offer on the table, especially in situations of great uncertainty, can substantially influence the other party's perception of the ZOPA, and thus the outcome of the negotiation. Remember that in fact there are two ZOPAs—each side estimates the ZOPA based on its own reservation point and the reservation point it guesses has been set by the other party. If an opening offer causes the other party to change its perceived ZOPA, then the negotiator has anchored the bargaining in a most effective manner.

Negotiators often make opening offers with one of three types of anchors:[7]

1. *Facts:* "My agent told me no house in this neighborhood with this square footage has sold for more than $350,000."
2. *Extreme offer:* "I believe highly experienced CPAs like myself can command a $95,000 salary in this region."
3. *Precedent:* "My last supervisor always gave me the highest possible rating, in all 12 categories."

The first offer clearly anchors the negotiation discussions. Who, then, should make the first offer? By what mechanism does an anchor affect even experienced negotiators who believe they are immune to such influence? According to anchoring research

Figure 3.2 The Power of Random Numbers

In an experiment on the effects of anchoring, Daniel Kahneman and Amos Tversky spun a wheel marked with random integers ranging from 0 to 100. Participants were then asked whether they thought that the percentage of UN member countries from Africa was greater than or less than the number just spun on the wheel. Participants were then asked for their best estimate of the proportion of UN member countries that were from Africa.

For one group of the subjects, the wheel stopped at 10. The vast number of these subjects said that the proportion of the UN member countries that were from Africa was more than 10%; on average, they guessed that the actual percentage was 25%.

For another group of the subjects, the wheel stopped at 65. Almost all of these participants said that the proportion of the UN member countries that were from Africa was less than 65%. In contrast to the first group, this group's average guess was that 45% of UN member countries were from Africa.

The only difference between the two experimental conditions was the number on the wheel, yet the groups' best estimates differed by 20 percentage points! The purely random number the subjects were given by the wheel dramatically—and irrationally—anchored their assessments.

Source: Adapted from Daniel Kahneman and Amos Tversky, "The Power of Random Numbers," *Negotiation* Vol. 7, No. 9 (2004): 10.

by Adam D. Galinsky of Northwestern University, the answers can be found in the fact that all items on the table have both positive and negative qualities, and a high anchor may direct the negotiators' attention to the positive qualities. In addition, those making the first offer are more likely to have confidence in their position. By contrast, the lack of an aggressive first offer to anchor the discussions leaves you with only two unappealing options—make small concessions to the other party's opening offer, or stand by your positions and appear to be uncompromising.[8] And a word of caution: If the other party begins with an extreme opening offer, it may be a trap (see Box 3.1).

Bracketing

Once the opening offers are made the real haggling process, often called *bracketing*, occurs. **Bracketing** is the logical bargaining process of moving toward a middle point between the opening offers, or brackets.[9] Consider, for example, the negotiation described in the Chapter Case, "Buying a Work of Art," as illustrated in Figure 3.3. The seller listed the price at $12,500 and the buyers approached the seller with an opening offer of $7,500. The two sides then began bargaining in the bracket range between the opening offers ($7,500–$12,500). In general, negotiators should "bracket" their initial offer, or initial counter, about the same distance away from

---

BOX 3.1 Traps to Avoid

How to Respond to an Extreme Opening Offer

How should you respond to an extreme opening offer—which might set an anchor in favor of the other party? Keep in mind that an unrealistic opening offer is often simply a tactic employed by the other side, not an insult. The other party simply is trying to lower your expectation, and in the process establish its extreme offer as an anchor point. Negotiators are especially likely to use this tactic if they believe you may end up agreeing to split the difference between your reasonable offer and their extreme offer. Thus you should first recognize their extreme offer for what is it—and quickly dismiss it with a response such as "Outrageous!" or "Ridiculous—$11,000 is not in the ballpark!" The goal is to get them to abandon the possibility that their offer will be considered at all in the ensuing negotiations. Then quickly follow up with your own opening offer based on facts or a defensible position. For example: "The Blue Book on this vehicle is $18,500, and that is for a car in average condition. This one has low mileage and is in excellent condition, so I believe $20,500 is a fair price. Now what is your offer?" With this response, you accomplished two important objectives—first, you dismissed their extreme offer, effectively removing it as a potential anchor, and then you focused the discussion on your price by basing your offer on facts.

Source: Roger Fisher, William Ury, and Bruce Patton, *Getting to Yes,* 2nd ed. (New York: Penguin Books, 1991), 138–140.

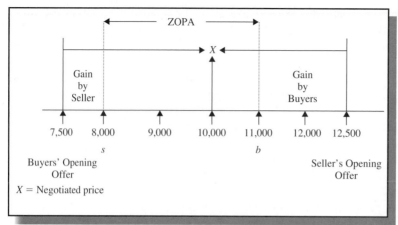

Figure 3.3 Two Party, Single-Issue Negotiation (applied to the Chapter Case, "Buying a Work of Art")

their desired price (in the opposite direction, of course) as the offer made by the other party.

Bracketing can be used in small deals and large deals. For example, Roger Dawson suggests that if a car dealer is asking $15,000 and you want to pay $13,000, make an opening offer of $11,000. Dawson also cites an example of how bracketing was used in a large deal—the 1982 international loan between the governments of Mexico and the United States. The two sides first agreed that Mexico would pay off its $82 billion loan with oil. Then Federal Reserve Chairman Paul Volcker and Treasury Secretary Donald Regan asked Mexico to pay a $100 million negotiating fee—which is a politically acceptable way of paying accrued interest. Mexico's President José López Portillo balked at the idea and said he would not pay any negotiating fee—zero dollars. Thus he bracketed the deal with his "zero dollars" counter, and the two sides agreed to a fee of $50 million.[10]

Thus if the other side makes the first offer, a good response strategy is to bracket the negotiation, and possibly end up splitting the difference, as is often the case, and therefore getting your desired objective. That is why some negotiators, when they believe the other party is inexperienced, want the other party to make the first offer—so they can bracket the negotiation. Real estate agents, when counseling clients, commonly apply bracketing. For example, a house is listed for $370,000 and potential buyers ask their agent, "What offer should we make?" They already told the agent they don't want to go over $350,000 on any house. Thus the agent responds, "Offer them $330,000, and let's hope they counter with $360,000. and then you can counter with $350,000."

In the Chapter Case, if the buyers' goal is to purchase the painting for no more than $9,000, then instead of an initial offer of $7,500 they should make a more extreme opening offer of $5,500—creating a midpoint of $9,000. Both sides have already decided their reservation price or BATNA; the seller will not accept less than $8,000, a minimum profit on the item (s), and the buyers decided that $11,000 is their absolute limit (b) to spend on any item. Obviously, in most negotiations, both sides do not reveal their reservation prices. The distance between the two therefore becomes the ZOPA because any agreed-to final price will be between these two points, which are the limits each party has determined.

The final negotiated settlement price (X) usually will be a point approximately in the middle of the two opening offers (if each side accepts the other's opening offer as reasonable), because although the opening offers are known, the reservation prices have not been revealed. In the Chapter Case example, for instance, the midpoint is $10,000. If the final price is larger than the midpoint, say $11,000, then the seller perceives a "negotiated gain" of $3,500 and the buyers perceive a "negotiated gain" of only $1,500. (The seller would have haggled for $3,500 more than the buyers' opening offer of $7,500, but the buyers would have realized only a $1,500 drop from the seller's opening offer of $12,500.) Neither wants to realize a smaller negotiated gain than the other side, and thus both sides often move to a price near the midpoint.

Inexperienced negotiators may be hesitant to set the opening offer higher or lower just to create a desirable midpoint, for fear of offending the other party. A critical novice mistake! The best strategy is to allow for adequate negotiating room between the two initial positions by proposing an opening offer that both anchors your position and provides an acceptable midpoint. However, prepare a logical argument to give your offer credibility, or else it may be ignored by the other side and thus does not function as an anchor. A strong defense of the initial offer can achieve two objectives: (1) it convinces the other party that the offer has merit, and (2) it begins to call into question the credibility of the other party's opening offer. In fact the other party may begin to question its own position and thus be more willing to move toward your opening offer.[11]

If you must give the first opening offer, or choose to do so for strategic reasons, then you should choose *the most extreme offer that you can logically defend* and carefully gauge the reaction. If the other side quickly makes is own opening offer—either very close to yours or extremely far from yours—be ready to walk away and reassess the situation. If their opening offer is very close to yours, then ask yourself if you set your offer too conservatively. If their offer is extremely far from yours, then it may be difficult to reach an acceptable midpoint. Either case may cause you to walk away or break off negotiations. Perhaps the worst scenario of an opening offer is when the other side quickly accepts your offer. This situation is called the **winner's curse**—you achieve your offer, but you are "cursed" with worry over why they quickly accepted your opening offer without even proposing a counteroffer!

THE ROLE OF NORMS

Once each party has determined its reservation price and the two parties have exchanged initial offers, now they must arrive at a price somewhere in the range between the two initial offers. This situation represents the basic distributive bargaining question—how to distribute the possible gain available to both parties. How do the negotiators proceed? What motivates them to make a particular counteroffer, or accept or reject a counteroffer made by the other party? Negotiations seldom take place in a vacuum. Instead they are often guided by social norms and accepted practices that are based on the context of the situation. The two negotiators in this situation might proceed according to one or more common norms, which research and theory indicate, will most likely guide their behavior.

Table 3.1 How Norms Can Be Used to Support an Offer, or Evaluate a Counteroffer

Norm	How Negotiator Utilizes the Norm
1. Relational	Desires to maintain a positive long-term relationship
2. Fairness	
A. Equality	Evenly splits the difference between offers (50-50)
B. Equity	Splits the difference between offers based on proportional inputs of the parties
C. Need	Splits the difference between offers based on proportional perceived needs of the parties
D. Status quo	Leaves the current situation unchanged
3. Reciprocity	Responds to a counteroffer or action with one of equal value
4. Good faith bargaining	Will (1) honor and not retract an offer, (2) meet and discuss issues, (3) make sincere proposals, and (4) provide honest information and share sources of information

In general, there are four major types of norms that might influence a negotiator's behavior: (1) *relational norms,* (2) *fairness norms,* (3) *reciprocity norms,* and (4) *good faith bargaining.* Table 3.1 provides a summary of each norm and the basis upon which a negotiator will use it to develop or react to a proposal.

Relational Norm

In a negotiation situation the parties may be involved in a strictly win-lose relationship, as described earlier in this chapter. They are concerned only with maximizing their outcomes. However, in many real-world situations the parties often have a communal relationship—they are family, friends, neighbors, or may have a continuing business or organizational connection. Organizational cultures, like national cultures, can produce shared ideas and practices—causing negotiators to seek the maintenance of long-term positive relationships even as they seek to maximize their outcomes when negotiating. This desire is referred to as a **relational norm** and can easily cause tension between the desire to maximize outcomes and the desire to maintain a positive relationship.

Research on relational motives and norms indicates that, when present in a negotiation situation, such norms can cause negotiators to overlook maximum outcomes in favor of suboptimal or less efficient trades that are viewed as providing a more satisfying relationship. Perhaps the most extreme application of relational norms occur in romantic relationships among "negotiators" whose concern for the relationship far exceeds the desire to achieve maximum exchange outcomes. O. Henry's classic 1905 story "The Gift of the Magi" describes the extreme romantic relational situation in which a young couple each sacrifice their most prized possession, only to receive in return something that has no practical value.[12] O. Henry, however, might argue that the couple made the wisest possible *relational* exchange (see Figure 3.4).

Why are relational norms important? Too often people, especially novice negotiators, view a negotiation situation in a purely exchange mode or one-time interaction,

Figure 3.4 Lesson from "The Gift of the Magi"

In a story by O. Henry, one Christmas Eve a young couple who are very much in love, but also very poor, each seek to buy a present for the other. They have no money, but each has a prized possession: Jim, the husband, has a gold watch handed down from his grandfather, and Della, the wife, has beautiful, long flowing hair. Jim decides to sell his watch to buy Della a set of tortoise-shell combs for her hair, which she had long desired. On the same day, Della has her hair cut and sells it to buy Jim a chain for his watch.

That evening the two lovers exchange gifts and realize the irony of their actions. The two had sacrificed for each other their greatest treasure. O. Henry ends the story by advising readers: "But in a last word to the wise of these days let it be said that of all who give gifts these two were of the wisest." Why were they "the wisest"? Some might call the couple's exchange foolish since both gave up their most prized possession for no good reason. But in terms of their *relationship,* their exchange was, as O. Henry noted, "the wisest" because each had made the ultimate sacrifice for the other, and thus their relationship became far stronger than if they had exchanged ordinary gifts.

Source: Adapted from O. Henry, "The Gift of the Magi," 1905.

without regard for the future relationship between the parties. Therefore their objective is to win at all costs, to maximize the gain in a purely distributive bargaining context. This one-time "car-buying" situation may indeed be valid in many negotiation situations, but in many other situations it is not a valid assessment because the parties have a future relationship, at least to some extent. Organizational examples of relational norms include the common ones between managers, suppliers, co-workers, and vendors. Two major organizational developments in the past 20 years have contributed to the increased importance of relationships in negotiations: First, "flatter organizations"—those with fewer levels between president and the entry level—have become more common. Within flatter organizations, employees are given greater decision-making autonomy, and thus are increasingly empowered to negotiate with others within the organization. Second, organizations have become more inclined to develop partnerships with suppliers and other outside organizations, and therefore are more inclined to maintain long-term relationships. Due to these developments both within and between organizations, relational norms are more important today than in the past, primarily for three reasons:[13]

1. Future negotiations with the same party are often anticipated, and therefore negotiators will seek to avoid harming the future relationship between the parties (see Box 3.2). Thus the relational norm effectively moderates the exchange relationship.
2. People from other organizations expect negotiated "favors" to be repaid at a later date.
3. Trust is critical to a long-term relationship, so agreements must include less nitpicking, fewer what-ifs or contingency clauses. A higher level of trust is expected.

Fairness Norm

According to Richard Shell, professor of legal studies and management and academic director of the Wharton Executive Negotiation Workshop, the negotiation process involves one of human nature's most basic psychological drives: the need to

BOX 3.2 Traps to Avoid

How to Avoid Harming Future Relationships

How can you avoid harming a future relationship with the other party by appearing to be greedy in a current deal? Alternatively, can you give up too much in the current negotiation for the sake of preserving a positive long-term relationship? Negotiating expert Danny Ertel provides three useful tips for negotiating exchange issues for maximum gain while also not harming future relationships.

The first tip is to clearly separate the issues of "the deal" from the issues of "the relationship." A strong relationship is built largely on trust, and thus the parties when negotiating will share information freely—and therefore can mutually identify issues that might harm the relationship. However sometimes negotiators pay *too much* attention to the relationship, and therefore give away too much in the deal. On the other hand, if they push for the best possible deal they may jeopardize their side's ability to do business with the other party in the future. Ertel recommends that at the start of a negotiation the parties categorize the issues, for example:

Deal Issues

1. Price and volume discounts
2. Service and maintenance agreements
3. Equipment replacement due to obsolesce
4. Termination clause
5. Delivery specifics

Relationship Issues

1. Specific mutual long-term goals
2. Individual personal interests (CEO, officers, and so forth)
3. Specific areas for future collaboration
4. Mutual desire to maintain trust and respect, open communication

A second useful tip for maintaining a positive relationship during negotiations is to continually ask for feedback from the other party: "Is everything happening as you expected?" or "Did this agreement include all the points of interest to your company?"

The third suggestion is to negotiate using FOTE (see Chapter 2)—full, open, truthful exchange of issues, information, and positions. Total communication can improve the level of trust and therefore help build a positive relationship.

Source: Adapted from Danny Ertel, "Turning Negotiation into a Corporate Capability," *Harvard Business Review* 77 (May–June 1999). Used by permission.

---

maintain an appearance of consistency and fairness in both words and deeds. Psychologists call this need to appear reasonable "the consistency principle." Negotiations of all types provide situations in which people seek consistency due to the high level of uncertainty. The use of a norm to provide consistency in a bargaining situation can give a negotiator what Shell calls "normative leverage." Negotiators who correctly anticipate the other party's norm and therefore frame their proposal within that context can gain an advantage.[14]

Negotiation researchers have concluded that the **fairness norm** may be the most commonly employed norm. It includes four major variations: (1) the **equality norm,** which negotiators often call the "50-50" or "split-the-difference" (which certainly sounds fair since both sides gain an equal amount, but is really fair only if the initial offers were equally fair to both parties, which is highly unlikely); (2) the **equity norm,** or a split based on the proportional input of the parties; (3) the **need norm,** which can be a powerful social norm; and (4) the **norm of maintaining the status quo,** which keeps all significant issues in their current state. Figure 3.5 provides an example of how the fairness norm works.

To illustrate the first three of these fairness norms, consider three adult children who must decide how to divide the estate of their parents. Only three items of value remain. The most valuable of these is a new Mercedes-Benz; the other two items are a set of dining room furniture and a kitchen table and chairs. One child proposes they sell the items and split the proceeds 33-33-33, thus utilizing the *equality norm.* A second child notes that she provided the majority of the care for the parents over the last several months, and thus she believes she has earned the Mercedes. She is utilizing the *equity norm.* The third child explains how her car has more than 200,000 miles and is constantly in the shop, and therefore she could really use a new car. Therefore she is utilizing the *need norm.*

A fourth fairness norm employed by some negotiators and arbitrators is *maintaining the status quo.*[15] Many labor contracts, for example, leave most current provisions unchanged, although a few key ones are negotiated. It's not always assumed that the status quo is fair, but if things were accepted and used once, then they may work again. And sometimes it's easier not to change something than to try to reach an agreement on a new proposal.

In the employer–employee relationship, what is commonly termed the *equity principle* is actually just the fairness norm—in this case, the equity norm variation—at work. The equity norm is based on the work of J. Stacey Adams,[16] who found that employees compare the ratio of their own organizational outcomes/inputs to the perceived ratios of other employees' outcomes/inputs—where *outcomes* include pay, recognition, bonuses, and so forth, and *inputs* include factors such as work effort, hours, and ideas. If employees perceive the ratios to be roughly equal, then they experience job satisfaction. However, if they perceive the ratios to be unequal, then they feel unfairly treated by the employer and will usually attempt to balance the ratios by seeking an increase in the outcomes received or, more likely, reducing their inputs or work effort, or even looking for another job. Thus the employee equity norm is quite similar to the fairness norm in a negotiation situation, except that the other party is the employer. Both are generally based on one of the cornerstones of Western culture—fair treatment. Religious, political, and labor organizations have often worked hard to achieve equity or fairness in our society. Issues such as gay marriage or discrimination based on race, religion, or age are often framed in terms of fairness or equity.

It is important to note that the common use of fairness norms in negotiations should not be confused with what is the "right," "best," or "fairest" solution. A fairness

Figure 3.5 Fairness Norm Example

Individuals in our society, when faced with a distributive decision as discussed in this chapter, often apply the "fairness norm." This can be demonstrated easily with a group of individuals of almost any age from 8 to 80. The following exercise usually utilizes a group of 24 or more. It often leads to a lively conversation of the participants' definition of fairness and the norms they apply in bargaining.

Exercise 1

Begin by choosing something of minimum value that can be easily divided into two parts, such as Snickers candy bars. Divide the participants into two groups (group A and group B) of equal size, and if possible locate the groups in separate rooms. In each room ask everyone to select a partner. Distribute a Snickers bar and a knife to one volunteer from each pair and provide this instruction: "Divide the Snickers into *two parts of any size*. Keep one part for yourself and give the other to your partner, but don't eat them until I tell you." Then inspect each pair of divided bars and determine how many are approximately of equal size, and how many were divided into one part larger than the other.

Then in the second room, with group B, repeat the exercise, but this time give the volunteers this instruction: "*Fairly* divide the Snickers into two parts. Keep one for yourself and give the other to your partner, but don't eat them until I tell you." Again, inspect each pair of divided bars and determine how many are of approximately equal size.

Now bring the groups together and explain what just took place in each room. Did most of the volunteers in group A divide the Snickers bars into two parts of approximately equal size, even though your instruction was to divide them into two parts of any size? Did most of the volunteers in group B follow your instruction to "fairly" divide the Snickers bars into two parts of approximately equal size as well? If the volunteers in group A (the control group) are like most people, they choose to split the Snickers into two approximately equal parts, just like the volunteers in group B who were instructed to "fairly" divide the bars. Why? Ask the volunteers to explain their action. The explanation offered by most people is that even though the volunteers in group A were told "any size," they chose to divide the bars into approximately equal size because *they wanted to be fair!* This is a demonstration of how the fairness norm affects behavior when individuals are in a distributive situation.

Exercise 2

A possible discussion point of the first exercise is the value of the good to be distributed. Some may posit that the value of a Snickers is too small to cause participants to slight their partners by dividing the bar unequally. To further explore the fairness norm, raise the value. The volunteers would be asked to distribute something of more value, such as a hypothetical $10,000 bonus from their employer, given to a group of employees who worked without an accident for the prior year. Volunteers would divide the bonus into portions of "any size," keeping one portion for themselves and distributing the other portions to the other group members. Volunteers in the control group would be asked to divide the bonus "fairly." Then of course the critical question for the group to discuss is: "Does raising the value change the outcome? Why or why not?"

As a variation, to possibly change the outcome, ask each volunteer to divide the $10,000 bonus among a group of three employees, one of whom only worked half the year while the others worked the entire year. In this scenario volunteers usually apply the fairness norm of equity, and the employee who worked only half the year will usually receive half as much as the other two employees.

norm or any other norm is simply an external standard that people employ to guide them in negotiations. However it may provide a very convincing argument in support of a proposal. Using norms or standards does not provide negotiators with a means of reaching the "fairest" outcome. Why? Reasonable people can use different norms and facts to reach different solutions. However utilizing norms or standards can assist negotiators in their efforts to reach an agreement in at least three ways: (1) Making decisions based on a norm such as fairness is easier than making decisions on offers that are randomly tossed out. (2) An offer based on a norm is more persuasive than an arbitrary number, and thus more likely to receive serious consideration. (3) It is easier to agree to the other party's offer if it is based on a norm, because you are agreeing to a principle, not a pressure tactic.[17] For example, would you find it easier to agree to "That is my final offer—it's what I want, and I don't have to explain it!" or "I can't lower the price any more—it's already $2,000 less than what we sold the last one for, and I matched your concession, which I think is only fair, so do we have a deal?"

Reciprocity Norm

The **reciprocity norm**, or the human tendency to respond to the actions of others with equal or similar actions, is a third major type of norm. Someone who believes that "an eye for an eye" is the most reasonable response to another party is applying the reciprocity norm. For example, a seller who drops her price by $2,000 may expect the buyer to counter with a $2,000 higher offer. At the negotiation table, a single act of hostility—or one of respect and cooperation—can be responded to with like action, and start an ongoing cycle that can last for years, even after the individuals who initiated it are long gone. Such cycles, which often grow from a perception of hostility or unfairness, can become vicious. Alternatively, they can be positive or virtuous if the negotiation process itself is perceived to be fair and the outcomes are perceived to be fair. Such cycles are often perpetuated by other human behaviors, including (1) *naïve realism*—when people assume their view of the world, and only their view, reflects reality, (2) *confirmatory bias*—when people tend to seek only information that confirms their original position or belief, and (3) *accuser bias*—when we tend to hold someone who has harmed us once excessively responsible for other actions. These human tendencies cause the cycles of vicious or virtuous behavior to be perpetuated, and the reciprocity norm to be practiced.[18]

Good Faith Bargaining

Good faith bargaining is a fourth major type of norm, and in a negotiation situation generally means that people expect certain behaviors from the other negotiators, including the following:

1. They will honor what they propose in bargaining; they do not retract an offer once made and accepted, and if necessary they sign written agreements.
2. They are willing to meet together, at reasonable times and places, to discuss issues.
3. They are willing to make proposals on each of the issues at hand.
4. They will engage in a process of give-and-take or compromise.
5. They provide only honest information, and if necessary will share their sources of information.

It is important to realize that in most negotiation situations, however, there are no legal or prescribed rules for good faith bargaining, and unfortunately reasonable people can disagree as to exactly what behaviors define "good faith." Thus, one party may feel that the other has violated the rules of good faith bargaining, and discussions can be prematurely terminated. Why? It is often said that a negotiator's greatest asset is integrity. Few negotiators will continue to meet with someone they no longer trust to be negotiating in good faith, since they cannot expect to reach an agreement, or if one is reached, they fear it will not be implemented as negotiated.

Workplace collective bargaining in the United States is a specialized negotiation situation that involves representatives from labor and management—an example of the good faith bargaining norm in action. The National Labor Relations Act of 1935 and its amendments require the representatives to meet at reasonable times and confer in good faith on issues such as wages, benefits, hours, and working conditions. This requirement includes active participation with an intention to reach an agreement and to sign binding agreements on mutually acceptable terms. It does not however, require either party to make a concession or agree to a proposal.

COUNTEROFFERS

Returning to the Chapter Case, the buyers and the seller of the work of art (refer again to Figure 3.3) will draw upon one or more of the negotiation norms just discussed as a basis for making counteroffers to the other party and for evaluating the counteroffers received. In addition, during this give-and-take process they may choose to utilize one or more of the common negotiation tactics described in Chapter 2. As you recall, these tactics include (1) making extreme or even ridiculous opening offers—designed to cause the other side to question its own opening positions; (2) claiming limited authority to make concessions; (3) using emotional outbursts such as shouting, cursing, name-calling, and even walking out in a huff as part of a posturing strategy; (4) offering few concessions, they view concessions as a sign of weakness, and thus offer few themselves, and seldom offer a concession not even in return when concessions are made by the other side; (5) resisting deadlines and using time as their ally, preferring a delayed settlement if it gains something, however small, for their side; and (6) waiting to counter after receiving an offer (see Box 3.3).[19]

In time, the buyers and the seller in our Chapter Case (refer again to Figure 3.3) agreed upon a negotiated price, X, that fell within the ZOPA of $8,000–$11,000 and thus met the reservation price of both parties. Exactly which price a party accepts often depends on how the offer is framed when it is presented.

Framing Positions

After identifying the issues to be negotiated, the next step in the preparation process is to carefully "frame" each issue (or group of issues)—that is, decide exactly how the issue will be presented to the other side in a context that is convincing. Framing is recognized as a key variable in the negotiation process because how an offer is framed has a significant impact on how it will be viewed by the other party. In general, the **framing** of a position refers to the wording and context of the offer. The art

BOX 3.3   Tactics for Success

Wait to Counter

After receiving the opening offer from the other party—or in fact any offer—a good tactic is to wait before responding. Why? A response delivered too quickly may cause the other party to think you did not seriously consider the merits of their offer, and may even appear that you are belittling them. Waiting a respectful amount of time to respond, even if you never had any intention of accepting their offer, will make your opponent feel better about the process. After waiting a respectful period of time, you can reject the offer, or even better, respond with, "We have considered your offer and would like to propose that you consider this counteroffer …" This tactic of waiting to respond to an offer shows a level of respect for the other party—and can help both parties reach an agreement.

Source: Adapted from Michael R. Carrell and Christina Heavrin, *The Everyday Negotiator* (Amherst, MA: HRD Press, 2004), 99–102.

---

of framing positions, offers, and counters is considered one of the key negotiation skills that must be learned by the novice negotiator.

Why is framing so important? Noted mediator Theodore Kheel explains that while the facts and numbers in a proposal are important, people often attach significant meaning to words, which therefore affects their view of the proposal. Kheel cites an interesting example in U.S. history. One Gallop survey taken the day after President Bill Clinton confessed his affair with Monica Lewinsky used traditional wording: "Now I'd like to get your opinion about some people in the news. As I read the name, please say if you have a favorable or unfavorable opinion of this person …" The result was 55% favorable, 42% unfavorable. Yet another Gallop survey on the same day used different wording: "Now thinking about Bill Clinton as a person, do you have a favorable or unfavorable opinion of him?" The result was 40% favorable, 48% unfavorable. Two polls taken on the same day by the same professional polling organization, with different wording, which therefore framed the question differently, produced significantly different results.[20]

One example of framing that received national attention occurred in the O. J. Simpson murder trial. The prosecution chose to frame the trial as *"O. J. Simpson the wife-beater v. The female victim,"* while the defense chose to frame the trial as *"O. J. the ethnic minority victim v. The racist police force"*—the frame accepted by the jury that acquitted him.[21]

People often view the same issue quite differently, especially when they sit across from each other in negotiations. They naturally bring different perspectives, expectations, biases, and experiences to the table. How should an issue be framed? First, consider each issue simply as a point of disagreement between the parties. Issues may focus on *procedures*—exact payment method, the timing of delivery, and so forth—or on *content*—price, contract length, quantity. In general you can frame an issue in a *slanted* manner that puts your position in the best possible light ("A fair price is $20,000 because that is the book value"), or in a *nonjudgmental* manner that states the issue as a question and invites the parties to search for a solution ("How can we objectively estimate a fair price?"). This latter method of framing is less antagonistic and moves discussions toward a process of creative problem solving if both parties are open to using it.[22] Herb Cohen suggests that issues should be presented in terms of three critical elements:[23]

1. *Information:* What do you know about the priorities, limits, and strategy of the other side?
2. *Time:* Is either side operating under a deadline? Is there pressure from an outside party to settle quickly?
3. *Power:* Who has the ability to exercise control over the situation? Power can originate from different sources: (a) competition—if three parties make offers on the same house, who has the power? the seller, of course; (b) expertise—a third party supports your position and thus gives it validity; (c) persuasive capacity—experienced negotiators clearly present the issues, provide strong evidence to support their positions, and offer proposals that meet the needs of both sides.

The framing of an issue can greatly affect the outcome of the bargaining. Even a one-word change can significantly alter how both sides view the issues. For example, in negotiations to merge two organizations, the managers were reviewing the personnel files of each key person. In each case only one person would be retained. In the case of one high-ranking position, a manager stated, "Now in thinking about Taylor, he is too valuable not to keep him, and in the HR director's job." The second manager who wanted his own person, Lane, in that position needed to quickly reframe the issue of Taylor and repeated the statement with a one-word insertion: "In thinking about Taylor, he *thinks* he is too valuable not to keep him, and in the HR director's job!" The issue of Taylor's worth in the new organization was totally changed from fact to only his lofty opinion of himself, and Lane ended up in the position.

Negotiation scholar David Venter suggests four types of frames to consider in a negotiation situation: reframing the issue, focus framing, contrast framing, and negative framing (see Table 3.2).

Reframing Offers   To be perfectly clear, the value of two offers can be identical, but the manner in which they are framed or worded can substantially affect how they are received and thus possibly accepted. For example, in a research study people were asked to choose between two plans of action, when three plants were scheduled to be closed and 6,000 employees laid off:

Plan A: This plan will save one of the three plants and 2,000 jobs.
Plan B: This plan has a one-third probability of saving all three plants and all 6,000 jobs but has a two-thirds probability of saving no plants and no jobs.

Then participants were asked to choose between plan B (same wording) and plan C:

Plan C: This plan will result in the loss of two of the three plants and 4,000 jobs.

The two pairs of choices contained the exact same values or facts—plans A and C both will save only one plant of the three plants, and 2,000 of 6,000 jobs. Yet 80% of

Table 3.2 Four Types of Frames

TYPE OF FRAME	PURPOSE	BUYER'S INITIAL POSITION: "THE PRICE OF $12,000 IS TOO HIGH …"
1. Reframing	1. Change buyer's context from a purchase decision to an investment decision.	*Seller:* "This work is a solid investment—the only other Ireland piece by this artist just sold at auction for $20,000!"
2. Focus framing	2. Change buyer's context from a simple purchase decision by focusing on the uniqueness of the painting.	*Seller:* "This is the only painting of a lake the artist has done, and he'll probably never get back to Ireland to paint another."
3 Contrast framing	3. Change buyer's context from a single price of $12,000 to much smaller, affordable monthly installments.	*Seller:* "If you pay for it over 24 months, the cost per month is less than the price of four tickets to a first-run play, but you will enjoy the painting for many years."
4. Negative framing	4. Because humans are loss averse, frame buyer's decision in terms of avoiding a loss.	*Seller:* "You can wait to decide—but another couple looked at it earlier today and said they would be back."

Source: Adapted from David Venter, "Framing—An Important Negotiation Tool," *The Negotiator Magazine*, October 2004, www.negotiatormagazine.com/article224_1.html (accessed March 2006).

the people in the study choose plan A in the first set of options, but then 80% chose plan B in the second set. The only difference was the positive framing of plan A compared to the negative framing of plan C.[24]

In his book *Getting Past No*, William Ury suggests that negotiators should, in practice, never reject an opponent's offer, but instead *reframe* it or literally "change the frame around the picture" so it satisfies the interests of both parties. Ury further suggests that reframing is the most valuable tactic in negotiations—and the single most valuable tool in reframing is the question asked, which should focus interests on each side. Ury suggests that the most useful reframing questions include the following:[25]

- *Ask why:* Instead of treating the other party's offer as an adversarial position, use it as an opportunity to better understand their interest or to test the firmness of the position. For example, "Why did you choose that exact number?" or "Why are you so determined to settle on that number—where did it come from?" A powerful "why" question can invoke the fairness norm: "Why is that a fair price?" Even if the other party refuses to directly defend the fairness of their number, the very fact that it cannot be easily defended inserts doubt in their mind about their own position, and thus makes it easier to achieve a concession.

- *Ask why not:* If the other party will not reveal the source of their position, asking "why not" can help uncover their real interests. For example: "Why not simply divide the difference equally?" or "Why not change our assumptions and see what figure the actuary gives us?" The answer to your question may reveal important information about the true interests of the other party.

- *Ask what if:* Instead of disagreeing with the offer of the other party, acknowledge it and respond with an option. For example: "I understand you believe you must have a 12% increase. What if we agreed to that figure—but to help pay for it, health care co-pays were changed?"
- *Ask for advice:* If asked in a constructive manner, the other party may develop an option that represents positive movement toward a settlement. For example: "How would you suggest I present that offer to my manager when company policy restricts us from providing service beyond one year?" or "I can agree to your price, if you can find a way to cover my delivery charges." Opponents often appreciate the opportunity to help develop mutually agreeable options, and once involved, may even develop a sense of ownership in the options suggested, and thus help one of them become a settlement point.

Reframing Personal Attacks   Making personal attacks has, unfortunately, become a common tactic in negotiations. The other party may simply get caught up in the "heat of battle," or may actually plan on using personal attacks as a means of getting the other party emotionally involved and thus possibly less focused on their objectives. Personal attacks may be direct, such as: "I can't stand dealing with low-life people like you!" or "You are simply too stupid to realize that I'm going to win." Or, they may be indirect, attacking your skill as a negotiator: "Are you sure you can afford this vacation home?" or "I don't think you can analyze this proposal in time for us to reach a deal—you'd better get help."

How should you respond to personal attacks? First and foremost, prepare yourself for the possibility. If you have never been exposed to such a tactic, but expect it might occur in your next encounter, then as part of your preparation think about how you will respond—and most important, don't let a personal attack get you emotionally involved. If your emotions take over your strategy, then you have given the other party a major advantage.

For example, a few years ago a real estate developer bought two-thirds of a valuable piece of lakefront property, expecting to buy the other third that was for sale and was the key to the total development project. The developer had already made one critical mistake by purchasing the first two-thirds of the property with no guarantee that he could buy the other third; he failed to realize the significant leverage he had given the other party who owned the last one-third of the property. Then in the first face-to-face meeting to discuss the remaining third of the property, he became enraged when the owners indicated they would prefer to sell their third of the land to someone else, even if at the same price. The developer took this negotiation tactic—introducing the existence of another buyer who is not at the table—as a personal attack and repeatedly asked, "Why isn't my money just as good as theirs?" and "Why do they only need to match my offer, but I must beat their offer?" In what is an all too common response when someone becomes emotionally involved, the developer angrily left the meeting, hired an attorney, and spent the next several months in court. In the end, he paid the same amount that the owners of the last one-third of the property had asked in the beginning, which was approximately just a little more than what he paid per for acre for the first two-thirds of the property. But his emotions led him to waste thousands of dollars on legal expenses and court fees.

What are successful responses to personal attacks on your character or abilities? First, as was just discussed, prepare yourself for the possibility. If you have never experienced such an encounter, then consider role-playing with someone who is experienced. Get used to the name-calling and keeping your mind focused on the issues at hand. Practice resisting the temptation to defend yourself—or worse, to respond with similar personal attacks. Both of these responses are perfectly natural, and tempting, but almost never productive. Instead they usually raise the emotional level of the other party to even higher levels, and decrease the likelihood of reaching an agreement. Instead, consider the advice of Roger Fisher and William Ury in their landmark book *Getting to Yes*. First, *recognize a personal attack for what it is,* and respond by sitting back and letting the other party blow off steam. Keep in mind, it's only a tactic to gain advantage over you, so don't let it reach your emotions. It might be helpful to respond with: "I think we all need a break, and in fact let's take a 15-minute break." Second, *reframe their attack on you as an attack on the problem or issues at hand.* In the real estate example just described, the buyer—instead of reacting emotionally and hiring an attorney—could have responded with: "When you indicate that you would just as soon sell your property to someone else, even at the same price, what I hear is there may be other interested buyers, and since this is a valuable piece of property, that is certainly a possibility. But I'm prepared to make you a fair offer today. What do suggest is a reasonable price?" That response would have reframed the personal attack back to the issue of settling on a price for the property. And it would have advanced negotiations without insulting the seller or falling for their tactic of introducing another possible buyer. Third, consider *responding with silence or a question.* Silence is a powerful tool in many negotiation situations (see Box 3.4). Silence after receiving a personal attack may cause the other party to become uncomfortable, and feel they have caused a stalemate. Thus, they may feel compelled to break the silence by making a positive statement and getting things back on track: "Well, that is not really a fair thing to say, let's get back to work." A carefully worded statement might achieve the same response. In the previous real

---

BOX 3.4   Tactics for Success

"Silence Is Golden"

When negotiations reach a critical point—such as when one party makes a verbal attack, refuses to make any concessions, or threatens to walk out—one tactic that might turn the tide is silence. A negotiator who says nothing in response to a verbal attack, unreasonable demand, or threat does, in fact, send a clear signal to the other party. Often, after a few minutes of silence, the negotiator who caused the breakdown will feel uncomfortable and make a conciliatory statement or concession in order to get the other party to continue to negotiate. If not, the silent party has not lost anything, and most likely will have communicated his or her displeasure with the actions of the other side. Experienced negotiators have learned that "silence is golden" when applied in appropriate situations.

Source: Michael R. Carrell and Christina Heavrin, *The Everyday Negotiator* (Amherst, MA: HRD Press, 2004), 118–121.

estate example, the buyer might have responded with: "Would you prefer to end this discussion and bring the other party to the table to negotiate a deal?" The question would have reframed the discussion to focus on the issue at hand.[26]

FINAL NEGOTIATED PRICE

At some point in the negotiation process, the parties involved believe they are close to a settlement. Before making a declaration such as "Well, I guess we're done" or "I think we have a deal," an experienced negotiator will consider a few critical points.

First, although price was the major issue being negotiated, ask if it is really the *only* issue. For example, a homeowner and home repair contractor agree on a price for siding installation, and they sign a standard form stating the price and a brief description of the work to be done. However, after the work is finished, the homeowner refuses to pay the contractor, perhaps because he is unhappy with the work, or it was completed later than they expected, or perhaps just because the homeowner thinks he can get away with not paying. If other issues had been negotiated as well—such as exactly how it will be determined when the work is finished (does the contractor or homeowner alone decide?), what interest the contractor is entitled to collect if payment is late, and who pays legal fees if the case goes to court—then both parties would be better served. A contract that specifies these issues in addition to the price can be critical to preventing common disputes, which arise in about 12% of all home repair contracts, according to the National Association of Remodeling Industry.[27]

In most simple distributive bargaining situations, shaking hands and exchanging a product for cash is all there is to it. However, if an immediate exchange of cash for goods is not possible, the bargainers should consider the classic economic principle of "the time value of money." This basic concept has caused many deals to sour after an agreement is reached. Thus a second point to consider is the need for a contingency contract. A **contingency contract** is an agreement that specifies how a future event will change specific issues contained in the contract. If such a future issue cannot be foreseen, a contingency contract can allow the parties to reach agreement on all other issues, and then provide for exactly how the terms will be finalized once the future event is known.

Contingency contracts are commonplace in business, but they can also be useful in personal negotiations among family, friends, or neighbors. For example, three adult children over a period of several months distributed all of the property, household, and personal items in the estate of their late parents. As their parents wished, the process had gone smoothly and without any serious disagreements. Only the disposition of their parents' home of 40 years remained to be negotiated. The parents' Will specified that all estate items were to be divided equally, thus the logical solution was to sell the home and divide the proceeds into equal thirds. One of the three, however, asked her siblings if she could buy their two-thirds interests in the house so she could live in it. Because the other two had no similar desire and liked the idea of a family member keeping the house, they responded positively to the proposal. Exactly how should they negotiate a "fair" sale price might be considered a common distributive bargaining situation, except the parties were not adversaries and had a continuing relationship (relational norm). They agreed to hire a trusted real estate agent to inspect the house and suggest a market price. Then they signed a written contract, which of course contained the market price. All three believed they had negotiated in a fair and responsible manner for all concerned. However, at the request of the one who was buying the house, the other two agreed to wait until she sold her existing home before closing the deal on their parents' home. They thought this a reasonable request, since she could not easily afford two house payments. Unfortunately none of the three foresaw what then happened. The daughter listed her home well above its market value and it took 18 months to sell. During the first few months, she moved into their parents' home. The contract had not included any specified maximum period of time to closing, or who would pay the utilities and taxes until the closing, or if any "rent" should be paid by the daughter during what became 18 long months of escalating tension among the three siblings. By the time the daughter did sell her house, these issues caused bitter feelings among the three. The two other children believed they had lost at least $12,000 each due to the length of the process. If, in addition to price, a contingency contract had been negotiated, the three siblings might easily have avoided a great deal of anguish. For example, the contract on the house could have included a standard clause requiring closing at the agreed-to price within 90 days, and a contingency clause could specify that if the daughter did not sell her house within 90 days she would owe a specified amount of rent, plus utilities and taxes to be paid at the closing. The clause might also specify a maximum period of two years for the closing, after which the house would be put on the market.

Contingency contracts can be valuable in many negotiation situations if any future event will likely alter the outcome of the negotiated deal. In a noted *Harvard Business Review* article, researchers Max H. Bazerman and James J. Gillespie cite several possible benefits of using a contingency contract, as follows:[28]

- The parties can counter negotiation biases by including future scenarios predicted by each party (such as mortgage rates in 12 months), and then letting future events decide which was correct.
- An impasse can be avoided by allowing the outcome of a future event to determine a critical portion of the agreement. For example, Bazerman and Gillespie recall when negotiations between a television production company and an independent station broke down over different expectations of the ratings of the show in question, with each ratings point worth about $1 million. A contingency contract could have specified that a $1 million license fee per ratings point, as determined by the Nielsen ratings on a specified future date, would be paid per the terms of the contract.
- It can motivate parties to perform at higher levels. For example, in the estate house dispute just discussed, a contingency contract may have motivated the daughter to sell her own house at a lower price or spend more time and effort fixing it up before she put it on the market—to avoid paying rent and other expenses after the 90-day period.

- The potential risk involved can be shared by the parties, rather than specifying an outcome at the present, when uncertainty about future events may make them uneasy about their level of risk. Retailers, for example, often share the potential risk of unsold products through contingency contracts with vendors by agreeing to rebates on unsold inventory.

Bazerman and Gillespie also point out that contingency contracts may not be right in every situation due to their potential limitations. First, they require a continuing relationship between the parties, which might not always be possible. Second, they may not be easily enforceable, and court costs can be prohibitive. And third, they require *transparency*—the future event must be easily and objectively measured and not subject to manipulation by either party.[29]

Let us now return to the Chapter Case. The bargaining situation is illustrated in Figure 3.6, including a summary of the negotiations. The seller listed her initial price or opening offer at $12,500 and the buyers made an opening offer of $7,500. The parties then decided, but kept confidential, their bottom line or reservation price. The seller decided she could accept no less than $8,000 and still realize a reasonable profit. The buyers decided their absolute limit was $11,000. Thus the range of possible settlement amounts, or zone of possible agreement (ZOPA), became $8,000–$11,000—although neither side could know the range since neither knew the other party's reservation price.

So how might this classic distributive bargaining situation have been settled? Because the buyer made the first verbal offer of $7,500, it is likely that the seller would make the first counteroffer. She would likely utilize the good faith bargaining norm and decide to show her willingness for give-and-take by making a counteroffer

Figure 3.6
Negotiation Settlement (applied to the Chapter Case, "Buying a Work of Art"

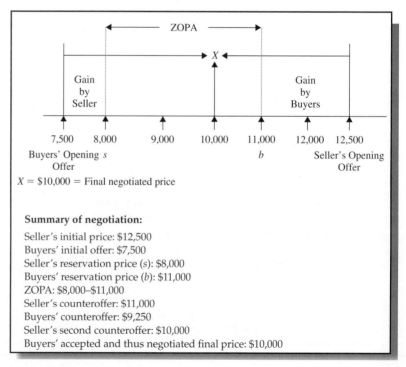

X = $10,000 = Final negotiated price

Summary of negotiation:
Seller's initial price: $12,500
Buyers' initial offer: $7,500
Seller's reservation price (s): $8,000
Buyers' reservation price (b): $11,000
ZOPA: $8,000–$11,000
Seller's counteroffer: $11,000
Buyers' counteroffer: $9,250
Seller's second counteroffer: $10,000
Buyers' accepted and thus negotiated final price: $10,000

of $11,000, and frame her offer with, "I'm very pleased that you are sincerely interested in *Sunday.* I know you have looked at it before. But this work is similar in size, detail, and content to three others that I sold in this price range over the last year, all with about the same number of hours invested. Also, I consider it to be one of my best paintings. For you I'm willing to come down $1,500, to $11,000." By citing the number of hours she has invested in the painting, the seller brought the need norm (see p. 67) into the negotiation. The buyers realize that $11,000 is their reservation price, and if they are particularly anxious to close the deal, or perhaps if they are inexperienced negotiators, they might agree to $11,000. But they likely would rely on the equality fairness norm and offer to split the difference of $3,500 ($11,000–$7,500) and thus offer $9,250. They would decide to make this offer because it is an equal sacrifice by both parties, and because it's not a round number and is based on a defensible position, which makes them more comfortable in offering it to the seller. Since the new counteroffer of $9,250 is higher than her reservation price, the seller might accept it if she was significantly motivated to sell. Or, she might decide that since the buyers have only made one counteroffer, they have not made their "highest and final offer," and thus she offers to make a second, but smaller, concession of $1,000, again noting that the work is similar to others that sold at higher prices. At this point the buyers might agree to her second counter of $10,000, and thus close the deal. Both parties will likely believe they have negotiated a "good deal." The seller gained $2,500 over the buyers' opening offer, and realized $2,000 more than her reservation price. The buyers also perceived they gained, because the final price was $2,500 less than the listed price, and they paid $1,000 below their reservation price.

SUMMING UP

Think about the next negotiation situation in your personal life or at work. Can it be categorized as a distributive bargaining situation?

If two parties are primarily negotiating a single issue such as price, and if each intends to maximize their outcome and the likelihood of a continuing future relationship is small, then consider it a distributive situation and prepare yourself by answering the following questions.

1. Describe the situation. What is the primary issue to be negotiated?

   _____

2. What do you expect will be the opening offer by the other party (listed price, last year's price, and so forth)?

   _____

3. How can you best anchor your opening offer in the mind of the other party? (With facts, an extreme offer, past precedent, or something else?) What will be your opening offer?

   Anchor: _____

   Offer: _____

   _____

4. What is your resistance point?

_____

5. What is your best guess of the resistance point of the other party?

_____

6. Given the answers to questions 4 and 5, what is the estimated ZOPA?

_____

7. Which of the norms presented in this chapter (Fairness: equality, equity, need; Reciprocity; Good faith; Maintaining the status quo) are you most likely to use in deciding and stating your offer(s)?

_____

8. Can you anticipate how you might reframe the position of the other party?

Ask why: _____

Ask why not: _____

Ask what if: _____

Ask for advice: _____

9. How can you best defend against an excessive anchor set by the opening offer of the other party?

_____

10. Do you have a possible future relationship with the other party? If so, how should you protect it while negotiating this exchange?

_____

_____

LEARNING EXERCISE: BUYING A HOUSE

The purpose of this exercise is to apply the five negotiation skills presented in this chapter to an actual negotiation situation. You wish to buy a home in a particular neighborhood because you like it and it is in the best school district. Your family needs at least four bedrooms, $2\frac{1}{2}$ baths, and a two-car garage. At this time you have twice viewed one house that meets all of your needs and is located at 5656 Valley Oak Court. Your agent has provided you with the information on this house as well as five other houses in the neighborhood (A through E in the table below) that meet your criteria and have sold in the past year. The house on Valley Oak Court is listed for $329,000. Review the following information and answer these skills questions:

Skill 3.1: Is this a *distributive bargaining* situation? Why or why not?
Skill 3.2: How will you determine your *reservation price?*
Skill 3.3: What initial offer should you make to use *bracketing* and achieve your target price of $310,000?

Skill 3.4: Which *norm(s)* can you utilize in presenting your initial offer?

Skill 3.5: How can you *frame* an initial offer that incorporates the norm(s) you are applying?

House	Price (000)	Square Feet	Rooms	Bed Rooms	Finished Basement	Baths	Garages	Time on Market	Miscellaneous
5656 Valley Oak	???	3,600	10	4	No	2.5	2	6 mo.	Large wooded lot, pantry, all brick
A.	$359	3,900	12	4	Yes	3.5	3	2 mo.	River view, central vac, large pantry
B.	$349	4,100	12	4	Yes	2.5	2	3 mo.	Large wooded lot, cul-de-sac, crown molding
C.	$319	3,600	13	5	Yes	4	2	6 mo.	Large deck w/arbor, Corian counters, alarm
D.	$275	3,400	9	4	No	2.5	2	8 mo.	Wooded lot, pantry, fans
E.	$246	3,100	8	4	No	2.5	2	8 mo.	Private yard, brick, custom shelves

ENDNOTES

1. R. E. Walton and R. B. McKersie, *A Behavioral Theory of Labour Negotiations* (New York: McGraw-Hill, 1965).
2. W. David Rees and Christine Porter, "Negotiation: Mystic Art or Identifiable Process? Part 2," *Industrial and Commercial Training* 29 (1997): 153–157.
3. Susan Cross and Robert Rosenthal, "Three Models of Conflict Resolution: Effects on Intergroup Expectancies and Attitudes," *Journal of Social Issues* 55 (Fall 1999): 561–580.
4. Howard Raiffa, *The Art and Science of Negotiation* (Cambridge, MA: Harvard University Press, 1982), 44–65.
5. Ibid.
6. Kathleen L. McGinn, "Planning to Play It by Ear," *Negotiation* 1 (November 2003): 4–6.
7. David A. Lax and James K. Sebenius, "Anchoring Expectations," *Negotiation* 7 (September 2004): 9–11.
8. Adam D. Galinsky, "Should You Make the First Offer?" *Negotiation* 7 (July 2004): 1–4.
9. Charles Craver, *The Intelligent Negotiator* (Roseville, CA: Prima, 2002), 41.
10. Roger Dawson, *Secrets of Power Negotiating*, 2nd ed. (Franklin Lakes, NJ: Career Press, 2001), 18–19.
11. Craver, *The Intelligent Negotiator*, 41–42.
12. Jared R. Curhan, Margaret A. Neale, Lee Ross, and Jesse Rosencranz-Englemann, "The O. Henry Effect: The Impact of Relational Norms on Negotiation Outcomes," *Proceedings,* Annual Meeting of the Academy of Management, Denver, Colorado, 2002, available at the Web site of the Social Science Research Network, http://ssrn.com/abstract=321448.
13. *Harvard Business Essentials: Negotiation* (Boston: Harvard Business School Press, 2003), 110–114.
14. G. Richard Shell, *Bargaining for Advantage* (New York: Penguin Books, 1999), 39–51.
15. "Being Fair and Getting What You Want," *Negotiation* 7 (February 2004): 12.
16. J. Stacey Adams, "Toward an Understanding of Inequity," *Journal of Abnormal Psychology* 67 (1963): 422–436.
17. Roger Fisher, William Ury, and Bruce Patton, *Getting to Yes,* 2nd ed. (New York: Penguin Books, 1991), 153–157.
18. Keith Allred, "The High Cost of Low Trust," *Negotiation* 7 (June 2004): 1–4.
19. *Harvard Business Essentials: Negotiation,* 2–6.

20. Theodore H. Kheel, *The Keys to Conflict Resolution* (New York: Four Walls Eight Windows, 1999), 3–4.

21. David Venter, "Framing—An Important Negotiation Tool," *The Negotiator Magazine*, October 2004, www.negotiatormagazine.com/article224_1.html (accessed March 2006).

22. Kathy Domenici and Stephen W. Littlejohn, *Mediation: Empowerment in Conflict Management*, 2nd ed. (Prospect Heights, IL: Waveland Press, 2001), 84–88.

23. Herb Cohen, *You Can Negotiate Anything* (New York: Bantam Books, 1980), 51–113.

24. Max H. Bazerman, "Picking the Right Frame: Make Your Offer Seem Better," *Negotiation* 7 (October 2004): 9–11.

25. William Ury, *Getting Past No* (New York: Bantam Books, 1991), 59–71.

26. Fisher, Ury, and Patton, *Getting to Yes*, 111–113.

27. Erika D. Smith, Knight Ridder News Service, "Specific Contracts Can Save the Day," *Cincinnati Enquirer*, January 29, 2005, D6.

28. Max H. Bazerman and James J. Gillespie, "Betting on the Future: The Virtues of Contingent Contracts," *Harvard Business Review* 77 (September–October 1999): 155–160.

29. Ibid.

Chapter 4

Integrative Bargaining

*T*he *integrative bargaining* technique, like the distributive technique, was largely developed within the field of collective bargaining and labor negotiations in the 1970s. Since then it has evolved into a very popular method of negotiations. Integrative bargaining is a cooperative approach to negotiation or conflict resolution. It is often referred to as a *win-win* or *mutual-gains* approach. Unfortunately the term *win-win* today is so popular that has become a cliché and is used to refer to any collaborative process. The integrative approach, like distributive bargaining, involves making concessions to reach an agreement—but in addition, it involves searching for mutually profitable options and logical trade-offs. It is also called an *expanded-pie* approach (in comparison to the distributive *fixed-pie* approach) because negotiators search for better proposals than the obvious ones that meet only their own interests. Integrative techniques include a clear understanding of the issues, open sharing of information, and the joint exploration of solutions that benefit both parties.[1] In an integrative bargaining process the parties generally cooperate to achieve maximum total benefit of the final agreement while also competing to divide the value of the package.

The essence of the integrative process is sometimes attributed to the work of Mary Parker Follet in the 1920s, who described the classic story of two sisters who each coveted the same orange. They decided to share it and used the distributive tactic of splitting it in half. After each sister took half of the orange home, one sister who wanted only the juice, squeezed out the juice, drank it, and threw out the peel. The other sister, who wanted only the peel for a cake she was baking, threw out the pulp and added her half of the peel to her cake batter. Neither sister considered expressing her true interest in the orange, but rather chose to negotiate for as much of the total orange as possible. Both sisters would have realized a greater settlement if only they had chosen to be open and truthful about their interests.

Integrative bargaining, then, can be broadly defined as a negotiating process in which the parties involved strive to integrate their interests as effectively as possible in the final agreement. Integrative negotiators generally strive to achieve two goals: (1) to create as much value as possible for both sides, and (2) to claim as much value as possible for their own interests. The integrative technique does not require negotiators to give in to demands made by the other party or to sacrifice any of their own objectives. It does require the parties to seek out creative options and not simply to focus on trading concessions. Integrative bargaining generally requires the existence of several issues to be negotiated—which enables the negotiators to find common ground on some issues, trade-off positions on some issues, and distributive bargaining on some issues. To create value and discover mutual benefits, or common ground, on some issues requires the parties to share information and present more options than is typical of distributive bargaining, in which the parties seldom share their true interests and seldom seek new options, but instead focus on exchanging concessions and reaching agreement on one issue.[2]

Negotiation Skills

In this chapter we present six negotiation skills that can be learned and developed by the novice negotiator, and applied to the end-of-chapter Learning Exercise, "Negotiating a New Job."

Skill 4.1   *Learn the key elements of the **integrative bargaining** process—including sharing interests, creating and claiming value, mutual-gain objectives, and valuing a long-term relationship with the other party.*

Skill 4.2   *Learn how to apply the five steps of the **categorization method** to an integrative bargaining situation.*

Skill 4.3   *Recognize that an important first step is to identify all issues and **focus on the interests of the parties involved** in the negotiation process.*

Skill 4.4   *Learn to develop different types of questions that can be used to advance negotiations, and to practice **active listening**.*

Skill 4.5   *Utilize the tactic of **packaging** when negotiations involve many issues that must be resolved.*

Skill 4.6   *Consider applying concepts of **interest-based bargaining (IBB)** to a negotiation situation, including brainstorming to create new options and joint problem solving.*

CHAPTER CASE: LABOR CONTRACT NEGOTIATIONS

The Ohio Metals Company and Local 56 of the Primary and Sheet Metal Workers of America, AFL-CIO, developed a positive labor–management climate over their 50-year relationship. As their current three-year contract is about to end, they begin negotiations for a new agreement. In general the company, the union, and the workers have experienced prosperity in recent years and certainly expect to continue their positive relationship. In their first meeting they openly share several important sources of information. Management provides the company's financial data for each of the past three years as well as sales projections for the current year. The union negotiators provide copies of contracts negotiated within the past year within the industry and for similar regional employers within other industries. The union shares the results of a recent survey of its members that indicates the issues that are important to them and their rank priority. Management lays on the table a copy of the ground rules that they adopted three years ago, and both sides quickly agree to adopt them for the current negotiations. One ground rule provides that both sides will bring a list of all economic and noneconomic issues they want to negotiate to the next meeting.

INTEGRATIVE VERSUS DISTRIBUTIVE BARGAINING

The integrative bargaining process is different from the distributive process in many aspects, although both are broad, not exact, concepts—and therefore in practice a negotiator might utilize aspects of both in a given negotiation situation. However, it is helpful to recognize that the two methods begin with distinctly different strategies. In distributive (or win-lose) bargaining both sides view their own goals as being in direct conflict with those of the other side (see Box 4.1). The negotiators approach each issue as a "fixed pie"—the larger one piece is, the smaller the other. Each side wants to maximize its share of the resources, or pie.

Generally all negotiators must be prepared to use distributive bargaining, because many negotiators use the method—and if one side uses it exclusively, then the other is usually forced to adopt it as well. Negotiators who wish to triumph over the other party, or maximize their outcome at all costs, often choose the distributive or win-lose approach. In integrative bargaining, on the other hand, both parties begin with a spirit of collaboration and seek to identify mutual-gain options (to "expand the pie") as well as gain their share of the resources (or claim their share of the pie).

To help recognize the differences, consider the factors and common strategies of the two methods, as presented in Table 4.1.

The Integrative Negotiation Process

Complex negotiations such as collective bargaining between management and union representatives, supplier–buyer contracts, agreements between employers and health care providers—as well as some personal negotiations such as building a new house, dividing an estate among heirs, or reaching a divorce settlement—often involve multiple issues. Novice negotiators sometimes utilize the single-issue distributive process described in Chapter 3 for each of the 10, 20, or more issues—settling each separately, one at a time. By comparison, an alternative method would be to consider all the issues simultaneously, and reach agreement on all issues at the same

BOX 4.1 Traps to Avoid

Using Win-Lose or Win-Win Metaphors

Should negotiators think in terms of "win-lose" or "win-win" bargaining? Are these metaphors appropriate in the context of negotiations? Leonard Greenhalgh, in a classic *Negotiation Journal* article, made an argument that scholars and practitioners should not think about negotiations or conflict resolution in such terms. These metaphors, he noted, are primarily rooted in the military and sports of Western cultures where they may be appropriate. They are not, however, appropriate in describing negotiations.

Greenhalgh listed five disadvantages to using the win-lose metaphor in describing negotiations:

1. The win-lose metaphor carries a zero-sum quality, which is not a useful context for a negotiation settlement that contains a *mutual gain* for both parties—or else why would they agree on the deal? Furthermore, "win-lose" implies that one party has gained something at the expense of the other party, which is not always the case. In addition, the win-win metaphor is not useful because it cannot be used without also using the win-lose metaphor.
2. Sports metaphors emphasize rules rather than relationships. Thus, negotiators may believe that any tactic may be tolerated as long as a rule or law is not violated, even though the long-term relationship between the parties may be damaged.
3. Ethical considerations tend to be subordinated when sports metaphors are applied, and therefore the level of trust between the parties may be severely damaged.
4. Sports metaphors induce participants to focus on the immediate conflict rather than the long-term perspective. Sports contests are isolated events and the score is set at zero at the start of each contest, whereas most negotiations involve parties that have a continuing relationship, and thus the concepts of "winning" and "losing" are less useful.
5. The win-lose metaphor induces negotiators to strive to fractionate the other party and throw its group into disarray. This practice may, however, make it more difficult to negotiate an agreement because, once divided, the other party will have more difficulty evaluating alternatives and agreeing to a settlement.

Try to avoid the trap of thinking in terms of a sports metaphor such as *win-lose* or *win-win*, which can lead you to visualize a bargaining situation in counterproductive ways. Instead, terms such as *mutual gain* or *problem-solving* or *cooperative agreement* might lead to a positive visualization of the bargaining situation.

Source: From Leonard Greenhalgh, "The Case Against Winning in Negotiations," *Negotiation Journal* 3 (April 1987): 167–173.

Table 4.1   Common Differences Between Distributive and Integrative Bargaining Techniques

Factor	Distributive Bargaining	Integrative Bargaining
1. Number of issues	One (or with several issues, one at a time)	Several
2. Technique	"Win-lose"	"Win-win"
3. General strategy	Maximize share of a "fixed pie"	"Expand the pie" by creating value and claiming a share
4. Relationship of the parties	One time only	Continuing, long-term
5. Interests	Keep interests hidden	Share interests with other party
6. Possible options	One expressed position (for each issue)	Many options—create new options for maximum mutual gain
7. Information	Keep information hidden	Share information with other party— explain the "why" of an interest

time—but that can easily become unwieldy. Thus, most experienced negotiators try to divide the issues into general groups—such as "highly important," "somewhat important," and those "of little value." Usually negotiators prefer to start negotiations by quickly resolving a few of the issues of little value, which creates a positive atmosphere and a sense of progress.[3]

Experienced negotiators of multiple-issue situations will usually utilize one of three proven negotiation strategies: (1) *distributive bargaining* (discussed in Chapter 3); (2) *integrative bargaining,* possibly using a categorization method as discussed later in this chapter; or (3) *interest-based bargaining (IBB),* also discussed in detail later in this chapter. Of these three strategies, the integrative process is more commonly utilized because it can generate deals that are more beneficial to both parties, and also because the parties today do usually have some continuing relationship and therefore are not solely interested in maximizing their gain in the current negotiation.

Thompson's Pyramid Model

Integrative negotiation, according to negotiation researcher Leigh Thompson of Northwestern University, can be described as both a *process* and an *outcome* of negotiation.[4] The parties involved seek to integrate their interests and therefore produce negotiated outcomes that exceed those normally achieved through distributive bargaining. Thompson further suggests a pyramid model of integrative agreements, as illustrated in Figure 4.1. In the model, Level 1 agreements are those in which both parties achieve an outcome that is better than their reservation point, and thus is within the ZOPA, as discussed in Chapter 2. Level 2 agreements produce an outcome that is even better for both parties than Level 1 agreements, possibly by introducing a new issue for which both parties have a similar objective. Finally, Level 3 agreements are those for which it is impossible to improve the outcome from the perspective of both parties, one in which any change that would benefit one party would

Figure 4.1 A Pyramid Model of Integrative Agreements

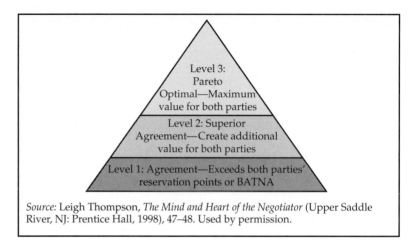

Level 3:
Pareto
Optimal—Maximum
value for both parties

Level 2: Superior
Agreement—Create additional
value for both parties

Level 1: Agreement—Exceeds both parties'
reservation points or BATNA

Source: Leigh Thompson, *The Mind and Heart of the Negotiator* (Upper Saddle River, NJ: Prentice Hall, 1998), 47–48. Used by permission.

harm the other party. Parties ideally seek to reach Level 3 agreements, and therefore "leave nothing on the table." Integrative negotiators do not stop at Level 1; they seek to gain the benefits of higher, mutually beneficial levels 2 and 3.

In reality it is more likely that negotiators can achieve Level 1 agreements in which both parties exceed their reservation points and BATNAs or, through the development of new options, that they can negotiate Level 2 agreements that create additional value for both parties above the minimums achieved in Level 1. Level 3 agreements can be described as pareto optimal[*] because they represent improvements above Level 2 for both parties and achieve an agreement that cannot be improved for one party without harming the other party.[5]

Thus the outcome of any level of an integrative negotiation is superior to that of a distributive negotiation. In this chapter we will describe two integrative processes. The first is the categorization method of integrative bargaining, and the second method is commonly called interest-based bargaining (IBB).

THE CATEGORIZATION METHOD

How does the integrative process work? First we will discuss the five steps of the **categorization method** of integrative bargaining (see Figure 4.2). For the sake of learning the integrative technique, we present this process as a linear process—one in which the first step must be followed by the second step, and the second by the third, and so forth. However, in reality, negotiators experienced in integrative bargaining may not utilize a linear model, but instead may choose to follow a process that best meets their interests in a given situation.

Unlike the distributive process, the parties generally do *not* begin by tossing out a number—their opening offer on an issue. The **first step** is for the parties to begin by exchanging information and seeking to identify all of the issues to be negotiated, listing them, and explaining their position on the issues. The negotiators seek to learn about

---

[*]*Pareto optimal* is a term used in economics, game theory, and the social sciences to describe a situation in which there is no other outcome in which every individual is at least as well off. The outcome cannot be improved upon without hurting at least one participant.

Figure 4.2 The Five Steps of the Categorization Method of Integrative Bargaining

Step 1:	Exchange information and identify all of the issues to be negotiated. Each side explains its interests and concerns on the issues.
Step 2:	Develop a common list of all issues that were discussed by either side during the first step, and seek to classify each issue as (1) *compatible*—similar interests; (2) *exchange*—approximately equal value, which may be traded; or (3) *distributive*—not compatible, cannot be traded, and therefore whose value must be distributed.
Step 3:	Reach final agreement on each of the compatible issues and remove them from further negotiation.
Step 4:	Trade or exchange issues of approximately equal value—in some cases including several issues in a single exchange.
Step 5:	Resolve any remaining issues—often accomplished through distributive bargaining on each separate issue.

the other party's concerns and interests, which helps them identify potential areas of common ground. Generally they do not make a proposal at this step, as it would be premature and could shorten the discovery phase of the process. The key here is to learn about the other party's issues and determine their interests and objectives. Rather than respond to any issue, a negotiator should focus on listening and interpreting what is presented. Key techniques in this first step include the following:[6]

- Use *active listening* (see Box 4.2). Active listening is perhaps the single most useful integrative bargaining skill because it indicates that you are genuinely interested in understanding what the other person is thinking, feeling, and needing. Listen closely to the other party's explanation without interrupting, disputing a fact or belief, or objecting to a statement—even if it may be critical of your position on an issue.
- Ask *open-ended questions* about the level of need, interest, or concern of the other party on each issue discussed. Ask *why* an issue is important, to help better understand the position presented. Ask "why not" to consider another approach to resolving an issue.
- Express empathy for the other party's feelings, using *reflective statements* such as "I can see why it is important that you have delivery by that date," while being careful to not agree with their position.
- Probe for the other side's willingness to *trade-off* an issue for another issue—a key to integrative bargaining. Ask questions such as: "Would you be willing to give up X if we were able to guarantee Y?"
- Assert your own needs. Explain your interests and positions.
- Refrain from making personal attacks or criticizing the other party's positions. Use humor when possible.

The **second step** in the categorization method generally begins with the parties developing a common list of all issues of possible interest that were discussed by either side in the first step. The participants do not assume that they have opposing goals on all issues. Instead, together they review the issues and classify them as one of three types: (1) **compatible issues**—those with identical or very similar goals, and thus where agreement can be reached quickly and the issue settled; (2) **exchange issues**—those of generally equal value that can be traded one for the other, and thus with one party achieving its goal on one issue and the other party achieving its goal on another issue; or (3) the remaining **distributive issues**, often few in number, but important—such as

BOX 4.2 Tactics for Success

Practice Active Listening

A critical negotiation skill that can be utilized in many situations—such as conducting job interviews, resolving grievances, and performing annual job evaluations—is called *active listening*, and involves far more than just keeping silent while the other party is talking. It is focusing on what the other person is saying from that person's point of view, understanding both the content and emotion. Active listening is a skill that must be developed for successful integrative negotiations because it enables you to recognize issues that can be successfully resolved. It also signals to the other side that you care about their concerns and are open to new options. Active listening requires you to confirm that you understood what the other party said before you respond, often by restating or paraphrasing the message. This *verification process* is what distinguishes active listening and makes it an effective skill. The active listener does not pass judgment—neither critical nor favorable—on what the other person is saying. Why? Because the primary goal of active listening is *comprehension*, not agreement or disagreement.

You can practice active listening by following these tips:

Tip # 1: Maintain eye contact with the other person.

Tip # 2: Think only about what the person is saying. Resist the urge to begin formulating your reply or your position on the issue.

Tip # 3: Take notes that summarize their thoughts and can be used later as you reflect on their concerns. This attention to detail also shows your sincere interest in what they are saying.

Tip # 4: Pay close attention to their body language, including any significant aspects in your notes.

Tip # 5: Ask reflective questions to let the person know you are listening and that you understand their position. Repeat in your own words what you've heard to ensure that you have understood it and to let the other party know you understood it correctly. Ask probing questions about any aspect that is not entirely clear to you.

Source: Adapted from *Harvard Business Essentials: Negotiation* (Boston: Harvard Business School Press, 2003), 59. Used by permission.

price or salary—which can be settled using the distributive process discussed in Chapter 3. However, if the distributive (win-lose) process had been utilized to settle all issues, it is likely that the process would have been far more adversarial, compared to integrative negotiations in which many of the issues can usually be settled by the compatible or exchange methods—which are far more friendly processes that are also likely to achieve an agreement of greater total gain for both sides. Why? Because less value is "left on the table"—a common goal of integrative negotiators.[7]

The **third step** involves reaching final agreement on the compatible issues, and therefore removing them from further negotiation. This step often passes quickly, since the parties are essentially in agreement as to substance and usually only need to record the specifics of the issues. However, this step can be critical in establishing a positive climate for the entire negotiation process. By first identifying at least some issues and reaching mutual agreement the parties involved begin the process with a sense of openness, collaborative, and accomplishment.

The **fourth step** involves the trade-off of issues—the heart of the integrative process. Both parties review the list of issues identified in the first step and categorized in the second step, noting the compatible issues that were removed in the third step—which leaves the remaining unresolved issues to be resolved through the exchange of one issue for another. In an open brainstorming process, either party can suggest exchanges of issues of approximately equal value. In the process, one party receives its position on an issue, then in return gives the other party its position on another issue. In some cases, two or more issues might be exchanged for a single issue if the approximate values are equal. If all remaining issues can be exchanged, the negotiation process is over, but in most situations one or more unresolved issues are left on the table.

The **fifth step,** then, is the resolution of the last issue or issues, which often is accomplished through distributive bargaining. However, because the prior steps resolved most of the issues, neither party is likely to walk away from the table over the last issue. Why? First, they have reached agreement on several important issues—a settlement that will be lost if they walk away. Second, the integrative process has established a positive bargaining climate that is more conducive to resolving the last issue. And third, both parties have invested time and effort into the negotiation and therefore are more motivated to reach a final settlement.

Returning to the Chapter Case, "Labor Contract Negotiations," let's apply the five steps of integrative bargaining just presented. In their second meeting, the union and management negotiators "lay on the table" or openly discuss each issue they would like to negotiate, and explain their interests or position on each. Management explains that it is seeking a five-year contract that would enable it to enter into longer-term contracts with buyers, which they have requested more often over the past several months. Management would also prefer a drug-testing program in cases involving accidents or injuries to protect the interests of employees, the owners, and customers. In exchange for any wage increase, management also wants workers in the bargaining unit to pay a greater portion of their health insurance, the cost of which has risen sharply since the last contract negotiation. Finally, management presents a proposal that would allow it to subcontract work to outside firms under certain conditions. Next the union negotiators present several economic items that they believe are needed to increase the total value of the contract until it is closer to other contracts in the region. Those items include a wage increase of 5%, the initiation of a profit-sharing plan to include 12% of net profits annually, an increase in the pension benefit formula, three days of paid funeral leave annually, a monthly clothing allowance, and an increase in the current shift differential provision. In addition, the union leaders present three noneconomic job security issues of importance to their members: a no-layoff provision, voluntary overtime assignment based on seniority, and a no-lockout provision.

In their next meeting (the third step) the negotiators review the common list of items developed in the previous meeting and agree that they have compatible interests on three of the 13 issues. Both sides desire the security of a long-term contract, and thus agree to a five-year term for the new contract. Both also agree that a new drug-testing policy is needed, and that testing should be conducted only in cases involving accidents or injuries. Finally, both agree that disruptions over contract disputes—which can be settled through the grievance arbitration process provided in the contract—are harmful to all parties involved, and thus should be prevented through a no-strike/no-lockout provision (see Table 4.2). With 10 issues left on the table, the two sides begin looking for items they can exchange (the fourth step).

In general, the exchange process involves one side receiving its desired position on one issue by giving the other party its position on another issue. In the first exchange, both sides agree to the union's proposal on job security—a no-layoff clause—in exchange for management's proposal on subcontracting, which allows up to 20% of the bargaining unit jobs to be subcontracted to outside firms for economic reasons. Next, they exchange two economic issues of approximately equal value—first, the union's pension increase proposal of 2% for future retirees in exchange for management's shift differential proposal (no change); and second, the union's new clothing allowance proposal ($50 per month) in exchange for management's funeral leave proposal, which combines funeral leave with personal leave and reduces the total number of days per year by two. Then, after several proposals are exchanged on the remaining issues, management's profit-sharing proposal, which changes the current program to 10% of net profits, is exchanged for the union's proposal that overtime be voluntary and assigned based on seniority. After these four trades of issues, only two issues remain on the table—wages and health care.

The negotiators on both sides at this point are feeling a sense of accomplishment because 11 of the 13 issues have been resolved. However, they also recognize that the two remaining issues are critical ones that both sides at the start had listed as top priorities, and which are high-value items, zero-sum economic issues. Thus they begin a distributive bargaining process on each item independently. Eventually, by making counterproposals with concessions, a settlement point is reached on both issues, and with all 13 resolved, an agreement was signed. The issues involved, positions of both sides, and bargaining categories (compatible, exchange, distributive) utilized in the bargaining are summarized in Table 4.2.

Keys to Successful Integrative Bargaining

Willing Participation of Both Parties   Negotiation practitioners and researchers have discovered several keys to the successful utilization of integrative bargaining. Perhaps the most helpful would be an initial agreement by all of the people involved that an integrative process will be employed. This agreement means that all parties will participate in *Full, Open-Throttle Negotiations* (FOTN) (see Chapter 2), and therefore will openly discuss as well as list all issues of concern to either party and be willing to explore new options. If one party is not willing to participate in an integrative process, or if one party says it is willing but then resorts to concealing its interests or rejecting options without careful consideration, then the integrative process may not be employed as easily as if both parties utilized it. Thus, the first key to integrative bargaining is the willing participation of both parties to openly seek mutual gains.

One party can use integrative bargaining to move the negotiations toward an agreement even if the other party chooses not to use the technique. Some experienced negotiators, however, believe that if one party does not fully participate in an integrative process, then the other party may at some point recognize it, choose to use only distributive bargaining techniques itself, and thus make it difficult for the first party to successfully use integrative bargaining. The negotiation process may then resort to one of strictly distributive bargaining, with both sides concealing their interests and striving to maximize their gain on each issue.

Table 4.2 Labor Contract Negotiations Through Integrative Bargaining

The following table summarizes the 13 bargaining issues described in the Chapter Case, "Labor Contract Negotiations." The chapter text describes the negotiation process in detail.

Issue Number	Description of Issue	Management's Initial Position	Union's Initial Position	Integrative Bargaining Category
1.	Length of contract	5 years	4 years	Compatible
2.	Pension increase	None	2%	Exchange
3.	Wage increase	1%	5%	Distributive
4.	Profit-sharing	10% of net	12% of net	Exchange
5.	Drug-testing program	Only in cases of accidents/injuries	Only in cases of accidents/injuries	Compatible
6.	Health care insurance	Employees pay 20%	Continue current program co-pay	Distributive
7.	Paid funeral leave and personal leave	4 days	6 days	Exchange
8.	No strike/no lockout provision	Continue current provision	Continue current provision	Compatible
9.	Shift differential	10% (no change)	15%	Exchange
10.	Subcontracting	20%	15%	Exchange
11.	Job security	No provision	No-layoff provision	Exchange
12.	Clothing allowance	$25/month	$50/month	Exchange
13.	Overtime	Management right to assign	Voluntary, based on seniority	Exchange

Source: Michael R. Carrell and Christina Heavrin, *The Everyday Negotiator: 50 Practical Tactics for Life and Work* (Amherst, MA: HRD Press, 2004), 94–98.

Recognition of the Relationship   Integrative bargaining can be more easily utilized if the parties involved value a long-term positive relationship. Negotiations between parties who place value on their relationship will be substantially different from negotiations between parties that do not value their relationship. Therefore, a second key to integrative bargaining is for the parties to openly recognize they have a valuable relationship that they seek to maintain after the negotiation process has ended. Thus, unlike purely distributive bargaining situations, the negotiators acknowledge that their continued relationship is of equal or even greater importance than one-time distributive gains. If this is not the case, then the negotiations will likely resort to a distributive process.[8]

Collaborative Atmosphere   A third key to integrative bargaining is to start with a collaborative atmosphere, which, according to negotiation consultants Peter Stark and Jane Flaherty, requires several things of each party. First, begin by looking for all factors of importance that can be negotiated, and therefore avoid the common pitfall of "fighter pilot lock-on" over just one issue, such as price. For example, if you contact a vendor about buying a large quantity of new computers, don't jump to lock on the price per unit. Instead, ask exactly what variables can be negotiated, such as delivery cost and date, financing, extended warranty, 24-hour on-site service, loaded software, training, or quantity discounts. All of these issues can be important factors in the overall price or deal, and should be considered, as well as the price.

Second, consider the needs and concerns of the other party and don't assume they are identical to your needs and concerns. In the computer example just cited, you might jump to assume that the vendor is only concerned about price and service. However, in one such situation, the vendor was a new company that needed to achieve a critical level of volume in less than 30 days, and wanted to add people to its training classes to give them critical mass—and therefore was willing to sell the computers at almost no profit, as long as they could also sell the training service package.

A third way to foster collaborative atmosphere is not to assume you know the "real" needs of the other party. In many negotiations, each party has both explicit needs, such as the product or service, but also has implicit needs, which might include the long-term relationship, loyalty, trust, and so forth. Negotiators often verbalize their *explicit* needs, but only through careful questioning and listening can you learn their *implicit* needs. In the computer example, only through the use of probing questions and attentive listening could the buyer discover the vendor's implicit need to sell the training service package.[9]

Thus, effective questioning and listening to responses is a critical negotiation skill. Yet research on the interaction in negotiation sessions has indicated that negotiators typically spend more time arguing for their positions and defending their stance on issues than they do asking questions. With the effective use of questions, negotiators can gain important insights into the implicit needs and concerns of the other party, and therefore respond with proposals that are more likely to reach a settlement. Furthermore, the effective use of questions can break a pattern of arguing for and against positions and move negotiations into conversations that uncover the true interests of the parties, and therefore potential positive outcomes. Why do even experienced negotiators spend more time defending their positions and not enough time asking questions? When asked that question, they admit that "asking questions leaves them feeling vulnerable and open to exploitation."[10] How can negotiators ask questions that advance the negotiation process? Linda L. Putnam, the former director of the Program on Conflict and Dispute Resolution at Texas A & M University, provides a variety of "Tactics for Success" in Box 4.3. Of course, some negotiators use questions to make the *other* party feel vulnerable! How should you respond to a loaded question? See Box 4.4.

Packaging the Issues   A fourth key to integrative bargaining is the ability to package issues for trades. **Packaging** generally refers to the process of combining two or more issues into one proposal that provides something of value to each party. When several issues are identified in the first steps of integrative bargaining, the process may appear to be unwieldy. Certainly if 40 or 50 issues are on the table, which is not uncommon in complex negotiations, the task at hand can be overwhelming. In addition to the trade-off exchanges of step 4 in the integrative process (see Figure 4.2), in which only two issues at a time are traded by the parties, packaging of several items at once can provide two distinct advantages. First, by including several issues in a single packaged proposal, the entire negotiation process can move forward faster, as more issues are "removed from the table" when the package is

BOX 4.3 Tactics for Success

Questions to Advance Negotiations

A carefully worded question can help you discover the other party's real interests—which in turn can help you reach a settlement quicker. Here are some questions designed to advance the negotiation process.

Type of Question	Purpose	Examples (Negotiation between a Training Director and a Potential Provider)
1. Open-ended	To generate useful information on interests, define issues, provide rationale for positions	"What type of clientele would this advanced course attract?"
2. Open-ended with explanation	So that question will seem less confrontational or intrusive than simply asking the open-ended question	"The basic course targets entry-level IT employees." "What type of clientele would this advanced course attract?"
3. Moving from debate to dialogue	To shift negotiations from debate over an issue to a discussion of the underlying issues or needs	"What profit margin do you need for the advanced course to be successful?"
4. Broad-based, clarification	To identify underlying differences on an issue	"You're clearly concerned about taking on additional risks, so what exactly do you see as the risk to you in offering the advanced course?"
5. Circular	To expand discussion beyond the immediate situation to a larger context; to clarify positions	"How do you conduct a marketing campaign?" "What is the difference between marketing a basic and an advanced course?" "So how does marketing both courses together affect the campaign of each course?"
6. Leading	To state a position, causing the other party to confirm your position	"Can you see that my firm is taking all the risks in this proposal?"
7. Loaded (avoid using, or responding to if asked)	To trigger an emotional or defensive response	"Are you saying these unfair payment terms are the only ones you will accept?"
8. Uncovering underlying concerns	To shift discussion from one of competition to mutual recognition of concerns	"What type of payment arrangement would reward you for the risk and provide your firm an adequate profit?"
9. Seeking creative solutions	To generate proposals that meet the needs of both parties on an issue (compatible outcomes)	"Why is it essential to offer the classes on different days?"

Source: Linda Putnam, "Are You Asking the Right Questions?" *Negotiation* 3 (March 2005): 7–9. Used by permission.

agreed to by both parties. Second, the ability of the negotiators to create combinations of approximately equal value to the parties is significantly increased by the ability to include more than two issues in the package. If, for example, one issue is worth $100,000 to one party and no single issue is worth more than $40,000 to the other party, trading any two issues would not be practical. However, if a package of four issues whose total value was approximately $100,000 could be created, and therefore traded for the single issue worth $100,000, both parties might be agreeable to the deal and five issues would be resolved.

In complex negotiations that involve both economic factors (issues that can be given an approximate monetary value such as price, delivery cost, or service fees) and noneconomic factors (issues such as product quality, safety, time, color, or job seniority), it is often practical first to trade-off or package the noneconomic factors and then the economic factors. While some might argue that integrative bargaining would not contain any throwaway items due to its full, open discussion of issues, packages in fact do also include some throwaways, as we discussed in Chapter 2. Note that in the accompanying cartoon, Blondie successfully includes nine throwaways to achieve her top goal.

Limitations of the Categorization Method

Negotiation researcher Leigh Thompson points out that there are often problems with the win-win or categorization method of integrative bargaining. Negotiators may believe they have utilized a win-win process because they showed genuine interest in the other party and negotiated an agreement in which both sides achieved

Blondie

Blondie includes nine "throwaways" to get Dagwood to agree on the only one she really wants!

Source: Blondie is syndicated by Reed Brennan Media Associates. Used by permission.

some true gains. However, a close analysis of the settlement determines that the deal in fact "left money on the table" or failed to maximize the total gains possible. Why? The parties mistakenly assumed that if they tried to fairly and evenly split the differences on each issue, then they would automatically achieve a win-win settlement. In reality, however, parties often mistake *good intentions* for a *good negotiation process.* The inability of the parties to look for and recognize the compatible and exchange issues and thus realize maximum gain for both sides is a common mistake made by novice negotiators—possibly 50% of all negotiators![11]

A second limitation of traditional integrative bargaining involves the perception of the balance of power between the two parties. If the balance of power is perceived by the parties to lean heavily to one side, then the integrative process may easily slide into a distributive process on each issue. Why? The party with the power advantage, if it so chooses, can ignore the possible mutual gains that might be obtained through integrative negotiations and instead leverage its power to gain its most desired position on each issue. That tactic would sacrifice the long-term relationship between the parties—which as we stated at the start of this chapter is a significant issue to negotiators who choose to utilize integrative negotiation strategy, even when they realize the power balance is in their favor. The term *power* is often misused in the context of negotiations. In any negotiation, each side evaluates the relative power of the parties involved and then evaluates its willingness and ability to use power. There is no question that both sides have some type of power—a union can call a strike, management can lock out the union, a buyer can walk away, and a vendor can provide poor service. However, the real question is: Considering the long-term relationship between the parties, when is it appropriate to use that power? In the United States, for example, fewer days are lost to strikes or lockouts than in any other industrial country—indicating that at least in labor relations, the decision to utilize power is probably more rare than some would guess.[12]

A potential third limitation to traditional integrative bargaining involves the common cognitive bias called *overconfidence.* At the core of integrative bargaining is the process of trade-offs, which enable each party to gain its desired interest on one issue while giving another issue to the other party. Negotiators, like most people in

Figure 4.3   Are You Overconfident? Take the Harper's Magazine Index Quiz

Without receiving any outside assistance, write down your best estimate of the 10 items below and put a lower and upper bound around your estimate so that you are 98% confident your range surrounds the actual quantity.

1. As of 2003, the amount, in dollars, of annual governmental worldwide fishing subsidies
2. As of 2001, the number of U.S. children under age 18 who become regular cigarette smokers each day
3. The 2002 GDP of Liberia
4. Rank of Belgium's water quality among 122 countries, as assessed by the United Nations
5. According to the World Health Organization, the estimated cost of vaccinating the 745,000 children worldwide who died from measles in 2001
6. The average salary of a U.S. state legislator in 2002
7. The average amount spent lobbying a U.S. state legislator in 2002
8. The total amount of money the U.S. Defense Department has lost track of as of 2000, according to a report by its inspector general
9. The amount of money owed the U.S. government by securities-law violators between 1995 and 2001
10. The rank of Hungary among nations whose residents are most likely to be obese

Now go to endnote 13 to determine how many of your 10 ranges included the actual quantity. If your ranges included 9 or 10 of the actual quantities, you were "appropriately confident," according to Bazerman. If your 10 ranges included 3 to 7 of the actual quantities, despite your 98% confidence interval, you were *overconfident*—which is how most people score on this quiz. If your 10 ranges included 0 to 2 of the actual quantities, well …

How can you avoid being overconfident in your next negotiation? Research is the key. Anticipate the key issues and seek data that will help you accurately estimate the other party's position on each issue. If that is not possible, seek assistance from a third party who might better know the other party or how the other party has settled similar past negotiations.

Source: Max H. Bazerman, "Great Expectations: Overconfidence Can Make the Best Negotiators Overestimate Their Chances of Success—And Underestimate the Value of Wise Tradeoffs," *Negotiation* 7 (January 2004): 9–11. Used by permission.

society, believe they know what the other party will accept on a given issue. Then, due to this overconfidence in their knowledge of the other party, they fail to listen carefully and learn the other side's underlying interests, and therefore fail to adjust their belief of what is acceptable.

Are you an overconfident person? To help you answer that question, take the quiz in Figure 4.3 by noted negotiation researcher Max Bazerman.[13]

INTEREST-BASED BARGAINING (IBB)

The practice of **interest-based bargaining (IBB)** has emerged in recent years as one of the most visible innovations in negotiations. It has also become the subject of considerable debate and discussion among labor relations practitioners and scholars. Some claim that IBB represents a critical improvement that will revolutionize the bargaining process. Yet others see IBB as just a new label for what Walton and McKersie called "integrative bargaining" in their 1965 book, *A Behavioral Theory of Labor Negotiations*,[14] or as simply an implementation of what Fisher, Ury, and Patton introduced as "principled negotiations" in their landmark 1991 book, *Getting to Yes*.[15]

The concept did not catch on then, and in fact was met with considerable skepticism by labor relations professionals until recent years. Today IBB is a fully developed approach to bargaining, including a set of principles, going beyond the concepts of these early works. According to a recent national survey of 1,557 negotiators, approximately 80% of management negotiators and 60% of union negotiators who have employed IBB prefer it to traditional bargaining methods.[16]

Principles of IBB

Interest-based bargaining has a different philosophy from that of distributive or traditional integrative methods of negotiation. At the core, it requires negotiators to think of themselves as joint problem solvers who seek solutions to mutual problems or issues of interest. The Federal Mediation and Conciliation Service (FMCS) is often credited as having developed the basic principles and steps of IBB. A 2000 report by the FMCS noted that IBB was the training method most requested by new negotiators. The principles and steps of IBB are as follows:[17]

1. *Sharing of information:* Both sides fully share all relevant information including economic forecasts, financial data, industry reports, costs, and so forth.
2. *Willingness to forgo power or leverage:* The parties strive to find mutually agreeable solutions to issues of concern and commit to not using their perceived power or leverage to sway the other party. Objective standards instead of power are used to evaluate options.
3. *Brainstorming to create options:* When issues are presented, rather than state their position or demand, as is common in traditional bargaining methods, the parties engage in brainstorming sessions to identify new options to resolve the issues. These options are mutually agreeable to both parties.
4. *Focusing on issues, not personalities:* By discussing the interests that underlie the issues, IBB negotiators can treat others with dignity and courtesy because they are not focused on discrediting the position of the other party. IBB advocates claim that in traditional negotiations, because the bargainers must defend their own "arbitrary" positions—saying things like "I must have this price" or "This is my position, take or leave it"—and because they must also attack the arbitrary positions of the other party, they often must resort to yelling and threatening as a means of making their points.
5. *Leaving past issues behind:* Discussions are focused on current issues and how to resolve them. The parties agree to not bring up past disagreements or try to settle old scores.
6. *Expressing interests, not positions:* Once options are identified through brainstorming, the parties—unlike the process in traditional negotiations—do not each take a position and defend it, and then try to exchange concessions until a middle ground is found. Instead they ask probing questions, use objective analysis, and seek to develop options that meet the mutual goals of both parties.
7. *Both parties committing to IBB:* An essential factor of most IBB negotiations is that both parties agree at the start to receive IBB training (if they have not in the past) and to accept and utilize the IBB process.

The FMCS does not believe that IBB can become a universal bargaining method that replaces distributive, integrative, or other traditional methods. In fact, it notes that unless the parties have had a positive past relationship and have received joint IBB training, it is not likely to succeed in a given negotiation situation. The growth of IBB as a bargaining method, according to the FMCS, is likely due to the realization by both labor and management leaders that they have a fundamental mutual interest in the long-term success of the organization.[18]

Advantages and Disadvantages of IBB

What are the possible advantages and disadvantages of IBB compared to traditional negotiation methods? According to Ira B. Lobel, a 30-year veteran mediator with the FMCS, advantages may include the following:

- IBB negotiators, by focusing on interests and not stating positions, will have improved communications and thus are more likely to fully understand the underlying interests of the other party, and do most of their work in joint open sessions.
- The joint development of options through brainstorming is more likely to uncover additional ideas and thus superior solutions to problems.
- Traditional methods, which focus on defending stated positions, are more likely to break down because the parties become too invested in their positions instead of trying to uncover new options.
- The focus on interests in IBB is more likely to cause the parties to explain the critical "why" behind an interest or proposal.

Disadvantages include these:

- The IBB method may waste a great deal of time as negotiators discuss interests and possible options when a mutual solution could be quickly reached.
- IBB negotiators may have difficulty transferring a proposed option into a practical, concrete solution.
- The standards suggested by IBB negotiators are often not precise, and are subjective, thus not easily agreed to by both parties.[19]

IBB at Work

Does Lobel consider IBB to be a "new and improved" method of negotiation? No. Instead he views it as a new "label" on what he considers to be the concepts and practices used by competent negotiators for many years. For example, good negotiators, have always explored the underlying interests of the positions of others. In addition, good negotiators avoid becoming entrenched in positions and are always open to new options that have mutual gains. Good negotiators also seldom use power indiscriminately and do not let personalities affect negotiations. Thus, whereas IBB and traditional methods can be thought of as different approaches, they also have a great deal of overlap in practice. If, however, interest-based bargaining provides negotiators with the concepts and practices utilized by good negotiators, then it serves a purpose. The ultimate outcome of a bargaining process, notes Lobel, depends on the skills and flexibility of the negotiators.[20]

One interesting case involving interest-based bargaining occurred in Alameda, California. In 1995 the city of Alameda and the members of its fire department entered into "meet and confer" negotiations for a new wage and benefit agreement. After three years of unsuccessful negotiations, an impasse was declared. The process then went to arbitration, and the relationship between the parties, according to city manager James Flint, became adversarial and highly emotional. In 1997 management and labor leaders identified IBB as a possible vehicle to resolve their differences, and the city agreed to fund joint IBB training for the members of the negotiating teams. After the training was completed the negotiators began the IBB process of brainstorming and searching for mutually agreeable solutions. They reached a solution within 12 months and agreed to set aside the arbitrator's decision in favor of their own new solution. In the three years under the solution, which became a wage and benefit *memorandum of understanding* (MOU) several remarkable achievements were realized: In 2001 a new five-year extension of the MOU was signed; the use of IBB was institutionalized as a business practice to resolve workplace differences; not a single grievance was filed during the first three years of the MOU, a first in the history of the city; more than $1 million in overtime costs was saved under the MOU; and the union actively participated in the selection of the new fire chief. According to Flint, however, the most remarkable achievement was replacing the previous hostile workplace environment with one that utilizes joint problem solving to address new problems—and the practice spread to other city departments in Alameda.[21]

Another interesting use of IBB occurred in Irvine, California. In only two days the city and three employee groups revamped the city's retirement plan. Judy Vonada, assistant city manager, credited IBB with giving the parties involved "So much good will, that it was almost like a scene from *The Twilight Zone*." And, Vonada noted, "We couldn't have done it if we were negotiating the old way. But we built relationships that allowed us to do this."[22]

How widespread is the practice of interest-based bargaining? Joel Cutcher-Gershenfeld and Thomas Kochan reported the first comprehensive study of IBB in labor relations in 2004. The study was commissioned by the Federal Mediation and Conciliation Service and included responses of 1,557 union and management negotiators. The survey results are presented in Table 4.3 and include some interesting findings. For example, joint training in IBB principles and practices occured in about one-third of the cases where IBB was utilized, and further analysis indicates that the training was essential to the use of IBB in negotiations. Second, during bargaining there was substantial use of brainstorming, sharing of information, and consensus decision making—all essential elements of the IBB process. Third, at the conclusion of bargaining a substantial percentage of both union (67.5%) and management (42.0%) negotiators reported that they continued to use IBB in future negotiations. However, a substantial percentage of each group (58% union, 57.2% management) also reported that at the end of negotiations, usually when only the most difficult issues such as wages, health care, and job security remain, they shifted back to traditional bargaining methods and even received some backlash or criticism of the IBB process (19.8% union, 17.0% management).

The study also reviewed the agreements that were negotiated and found that IBB had positively affected the outcomes of issues including pay, profit sharing,

Table 4.3 Union and Management Negotiators' Reports on IBB Activities

REPORTED EVENTS	MANAGEMENT (%)	UNION (%)
Pre-Bargaining Activities		
Joint pre-training in IBB	33.0%	40.4%
Joint task forces	26.5%	17.5%
Prior notice of IBB use to union members	22.2%	7.3%
Prior notice to management constituents	0.0%	22.0%
Activities During Bargaining		
Joint task forces (heavy use)	20.2%	17.6%
Brainstorming and problem solving	44.0%	34.5%
Use of a facilitator	6.1%	5.5%
Union sharing of data	61.1%	27.9%
Management sharing of economic performance data	61.4%	66.6%
Activities at Conclusion of Bargaining		
Further brainstorming at conclusion	66.0%	55.0%
Shift to traditional bargaining at conclusion	57.2%	58.0%
Backlash/criticism of the IBB process	17.0%	19.8%
Use of IBB in further contract negotiations	42.0%	67.5%

Source: Joel Cutcher-Gershenfeld and Thomas Kochan, "Taking Stock: Collective Bargaining at the Turn of the Century," *Industrial and Labor Relations Review* 58 (October 2004): 14. Used by permission.

increased worker input into decisions, team-based systems of work, and joint problem-solving committees. Other interesting results of the study included the fact that female union negotiators were more likely to bargain for new language that provided for worker input, and initial contracts were more likely to include such provisions. The authors concluded that IBB does encourage a problem-solving process in negotiations, and determined that atmosphere is more likely to provide a "supportive umbrella" for innovative provisions in agreements.[23]

SUMMING UP

Consider a bargaining situation that you are likely to encounter, which involves two parties and multiple issues to be negotiated. If the parties may be willing to share information, to explore options that create additional value for mutual gains, and are likely to have a long-term relationship, then consider it an integrative bargaining situation and prepare yourself by answering the following questions.

1. Describe the situation. Can you list the primary issues that are likely to be negotiated?

_____

_____

_____

_____

_____

_____

_____

_____

_____

_____

2. Can you easily categorize each issue as potentially either: (1) compatible, (2) exchange, (3) distributive?

Compatible issues:

_____

_____

_____

Exchange issues:

_____

_____

_____

Distributive issues:

_____

_____

_____

3. What is your best description of a proposal for each compatible issue that is likely to be acceptable to both parties?

_____

_____

_____

4. What trade-offs of the exchanges issues can you suggest that will provide approximately equal values for both parties?

_____

_____

_____

5. How will you suggest that you and the other party negotiate the remaining, more difficult issues (by using distributive, integrative, IBB, or another technique)? What metaphor might best describe the technique you are proposing?

_____

_____

_____

6. How can you create a collaborative atmosphere to start the bargaining over the remaining issues?

_____

_____

_____

7. Can you list three techniques of "active listening" that you can use to focus your attention while the other party explains its interests?

a. _____

b. _____

c. _____

8. What will be your prepared response to any loaded questions you might receive?

_____

_____

9. Can you list three questions you are prepared to use to advance the negotiation on the remaining issues if the talks should stall?

a. _____

b. _____

c. _____

10. What relevant information are you prepared to share with the other party?

_____

_____

_____

LEARNING EXERCISE: NEGOTIATING A NEW JOB

The purpose of this exercise is to apply the negotiation skills presented in this chapter to an actual negotiation situation. You recently received a telephone call from the vice president of sales for a large national office machine supplier. She invited you to an interview—and she made it clear that she wants to hire you and will try to negotiate a contract with you during the interview. You responded that you are quite content in your sales position with a regional competitor of her firm. She also made it clear, however, that this could be a very lucrative move for you, and thus you agreed to the interview. You then suggested that both of you consider carefully all of the issues that might be included in a negotiated contract. To better prepare yourself, you contacted a good friend who is currently a sales agent for her firm and asked him what issues he would suggest that you put on the table, because they might be important to you and she had the authority to negotiate, at least to a limited degree, on those issues.

After your conversation with your friend, and after giving the matter some thought, you developed a list of eight issues that you would like to discuss: (1) annual salary, (2) primary sales territory (your friend indicated that due to expansion five territories are available), (3) expense account, (4) office location within the building, (5) signing bonus, (6) number of travel days per month, (7) automotive usage plan, and (8) starting date. In final preparation for today's interview you decided to list several possible outcomes for each of the eight issues, and as a means of "creating value" for each you assign a "point value" to each outcome so you can compare them. The accompanying table includes the eight issues and your estimated value of the possible outcomes for each. In the right column are the vice president's point values as well—although you, of course, don't know them. Review the issues and your values for each possible outcome, and answer the following skills questions.

Skill 4.1: Why is this an *integrative bargaining situation?*

Skill 4.2: How could you utilize the *categorization method* in the interview? Which issues are likely to be compatible issues? Traded issues? Distributed issues?

Skill 4.3: How would you implement the first step of the categorization method—*identifying all the issues and focusing on the interests of both of you?*

Skill 4.4: How can you prepare yourself to use *active listening* in the interview?

Skill 4.5: Which initial *package* of issues would you propose?

Skill 4.6: Which *IBB tactic* might you utilize during the interview? Why?

If integrative bargaining is utilized by both sides, and given the values of the options in the table, what is the best possible total point outcome (combined for both parties)?

Issue	Possible Outcome	Your Point Value	The VP's Point Value
1. Annual salary	$45,000 + commission	10	30
	$50,000	15	25
	$50,000 + commission	20	20
	$55,000	25	15
	$55,000 + commission	30	10
2. Primary territory	St. Louis	10	5
	Indianapolis	8	4
	Evansville	6	3
	Louisville	4	2
	Springfield	2	1
3. Expense account	$20,000	2	10
	$25,000	4	8
	$30,000	6	6
	$35,000	8	4
	Unlimited	10	2
4. Office location	Suite A, no window	0	0
	Suite A, window	2	0
	Suite C, no window	0	0
	Suite C, window	2	0
	Suite E, window	4	0
5. Signing bonus	$1,000	1	15
	$2,000	2	10
	$5,000	5	4
	10% first year's net sales	10	2
	20% first year's net sales	20	0
6. Number of travel days per month	Less than 5	5	2
	5–10	4	4
	10–15	3	6
	15–20	2	8
	Unlimited	1	10
7. Automotive usage plan	Use own car, 50¢/mile	5	15
	Company luxury car plus gas expenses	3	5
	Company economy car plus gas expenses	1	10
8. Starting date	Next Monday	0	20
	Two weeks	2	10
	One month	4	0
	Two months (after your notice plus one month vacation)	10	–10
	Three months	12	–20

ENDNOTES

1. Susan Cross and Robert Rosenthal, "Three Models of Conflict Resolution: Effects on Intergroup Expectancies and Attitudes," *Journal of Social Issues* 55 (Fall 1999): 564–566.

2. *Harvard Business Essentials: Negotiation* (Boston: Harvard Business School Press, 2003), 2–11.

3. Charles Craver, *The Intelligent Negotiator* (New York: Roseville, CA: Prima, 2002), 85–87.

4. Leigh Thompson, *The Mind and Heart of the Negotiator* (Upper Saddle River, NJ: Prentice Hall, 1998), 47–48.

5. Ibid.

6. *Harvard Business Essentials: Negotiation,* 57–60.

7. Michael R. Carrell and Christina Heavrin, *Labor Relations and Collective Bargaining,* 7th ed. (Upper Saddle River, NJ: Pearson/Prentice Hall, 2004), 264–265.

8. *Harvard Business Essentials: Negotiation,* 2–11.

9. Peter B. Stark and Jane Flaherty, *The Only Negotiating Guide You'll Ever Need* (New York: Broadway Books, 2003), 13–16.

10. Linda Putnam, "Are You Asking the Right Questions?" *Negotiation* 3 (March 2005): 7–9.

11. Thompson, *The Mind and Heart of the Negotiator,* 48–49.

12. Ira B. Lobel, "Is Interest-Based Bargaining Really New?" *Dispute Resolution Journal* 55 (February 2000): 8–17.

13. Max H. Bazerman, "Great Expectations: Overconfidence Can Make the Best Negotiators Overestimate Their Chances of Success—And Underestimate the Value of Wise Tradeoffs," *Negotiation* 7 (January 2004): 9–11.

QUIZ ANSWERS: 1. $15 billion; 2. 3,000; 3. $560 million; 4. 122; 5. $558,750; 6. $30,300; 7. $130,000; 8. $1.1 trillion; 9. $3.1 billion; 10. 3

14. Richard Walton and Robert McKersie, *A Behavioral Theory of Labor Negotiations,* (Ithaca, NY: ILR Press, 1965).

15. Roger Fisher, William Ury, and Bruce Patton, *Getting to Yes,* 2nd ed. (New York: Penguin Books, 1991).

16. Joel Cutcher-Gershenfeld, Thomas Kochan, and John Calhoun Wells, "In Whose Interest? A First Look at National Survey Data on Interest-Based Bargaining in Labor Relations," *Industrial Relations* 40 (January 2001): 1–21.

17. Federal Mediation and Conciliation Service, *Interest-Based Bargaining: A Different Way to Negotiate* (Washington, DC: Federal Mediation and Conciliation Service, 1999).

18. Ibid.

19. Lobel, "Is Interest-Based Bargaining Really New?"

20. Ibid.

21. James Flint, "Mending Labor–Management Relationships," *Public Management* 84 (August 2002): 18–21.

22. Jeff Siegel, "Mutual Satisfaction: Interest-Based Negotiating Means Getting What You Want by Knowing What They Want," *Southwest Airlines Spirit* (September 2004): 54–58.

23. Joel Cutcher-Gershenfeld and Thomas Kochan, "Taking Stock: Collective Bargaining at the Turn of the Century," *Industrial and Labor Relations Review* 58 (October 2004): 3–26.

Chapter 5

Gaining Leverage Through Power and Persuasion

L everage in negotiation is like a seesaw. If the two people on the seesaw are of the same weight and are in the same relative position on both ends of the seesaw, then it is perfectly balanced. For one person or the other to take control, that person must add or redistribute weight so that he or she pushes to the ground and leaves the other person up in the air and out of control. The person up in the air can change the dynamics of the game by repositioning his or her weight, or perhaps finding a friend to join in. The two parties can continue to change or readjust their respective sides of the seesaw until they are back in perfect balance or until one person quits the game and goes home. In a negotiation, both parties come to the bargaining table with some bargaining power. Their attitude toward the negotiation depends, among other things, on the perceived balance of the bargaining power of the parties.

As you've learned in earlier chapters, there are a number of bargaining approaches. Distributive bargaining is a competitive approach in which two parties divide a fixed pool of resources, each trying to maximize its share of the distribution. Unequal bargaining power might lead to distributive bargaining, because the party with the most power may have little incentive to give up its advantage. Integrative bargaining, on the other hand, is a cooperative, win-win, mutual-gains bargaining method in which the parties focus on interests, not positions, and attempt to satisfy both parties. Interest-based bargaining (IBB) is also a cooperative approach that requires negotiators to think of themselves as joint problem solvers seeking solutions to mutual problems. IBB uses brainstorming, sharing of information, and consensus decision making. When the parties have more balanced bargaining power or a strong desire to maintain a positive long-term relationship, the situation would lend itself to the win-win scenario of cooperative processes such as integrative or interest-based bargaining. However, regardless of which approach is taken, any negotiation involves the leveraging of power. A negotiator must know how to leverage power and must be able to recognize and counter the leveraging of power by others. In this chapter, then, we will discuss how to leverage power in a negotiation by using your BATNA, traditional power bases, and persuasion.

Your BATNA, or best alternative to a negotiated agreement, is the most important source of bargaining power. Certainly a *great* BATNA gives you automatic control over the negotiation. For example, homeowners who are in a position to downsize and whose mortgage has been paid off may want to take advantage of a seller's market by putting their house up for sale at a very inflated, but possible, price. If the house sells for that amount, they are happy to move, but if the price is not met, they are just as happy to stay put. A potential buyer has very little leverage in this case. But you can also leverage a *less than great* BATNA by controlling the perceptions that others have of your BATNA, by challenging the opponent's perspective of your BATNA, or by repositioning the parties to change both BATNAs. A negotiator may also be able to control the power dynamics of a particular negotiation by using traditional power bases—such as by controlling resources, time, or information. And finally, techniques for persuading people to your point of view can be learned and used to your advantage.

Negotiation Skills

In this chapter we present five negotiation skills that can be learned and developed by the novice negotiator, and applied to the end-of-chapter Learning Exercise, "Unhappy Co-Owners."

Skill 5.1   *Learn to use your **BATNA** to reach agreement.*

Skill 5.2   *Recognize the **sources of power** in a negotiation, both yours and your opponent's.*

Skill 5.3   *Learn to marshal **persuasive arguments** to support the position you have framed in the negotiation.*

Skill 5.4   *Learn to use both verbal and **nonverbal communication** to persuade.*

Skill 5.5   *Learn when and how to use **threats** to get concessions.*

CHAPTER CASE: DEATH IN A POLICE EXCESSIVE FORCE INCIDENT

Wilma Mathis filed a wrongful death lawsuit after her husband James, an 18-year-old African American male, was shot and killed in an undercover drug bust by Officer Jones, a white police officer. Allegedly Mr. Mathis had approached Officer Jones as a drug dealer, but then tried to rob her of her cash. Officer Jones identified herself, and then she and Mr. Mathis struggled over her gun. It went off, but no one was injured. Mr. Mathis began to run, not heeding Officer Jones's order to stop. As he got a few feet away, he began to turn—and Officer Jones, who believed Mr. Mathis was pulling a gun, fired and shot him three times. Later, the coroner would determine that Mr. Mathis did not have a gun in his belt and that Mr. Mathis had been shot in the back.

This incident was the latest of a number of incidents involving African American men allegedly engaged in some criminal enterprise, killed by white police officers in this southern city of a half million people. Many people in the African American community were incensed over this incident and believed the case warranted an indictment. The grand jury, however, failed to indict the police officer, believing she had been in fear of her life. Officer Jones was later dismissed from the force for failing to follow a number of departmental policies in the undercover assignment.

Mr. Mathis's widow never accepted the premise for the shooting—that her husband was involved in drugs or robbery. After the criminal investigation cleared Officer Jones, Wilma Mathis sued Officer Jones for negligently causing the death of her husband. It was Mrs. Mathis's hope that she would be able to clear her husband's name if all the facts of the case were made public. Soon after the lawsuit was filed, Officer Jones made an offer to settle the lawsuit for $350,000. Officer Jones hoped to avoid a trial. Because of the publicity over the shooting, Officer Jones was not able to get another job as a law enforcement officer and she and her family suffered from the notoriety brought on by the negative publicity. Wilma Mathis refused the initial offer but asked Officer Jones to negotiate a settlement, which she agreed to do.

A month before the negotiation, another police officer was involved in a shooting. However, this time a 22-year-old police officer, while investigating a stolen car report, was killed in the line of duty, having been shot by a 17-year-old white male with a prison record and history of mental problems. The outpouring of shock and sorrow, as well as support for the police officer's wife of one year, united the community in a very visible way. The officer's funeral was telecast live on local TV stations and fellow officers, firefighters, and other emergency personnel from the city and many surrounding areas lined the funeral's 16-mile route to the cemetery.

Officer Jones and Wilma Mathis held their negotiation session as planned. Mrs. Mathis, who had already turned down $350,000, began the negotiations by reducing her original demand of $3 million to $2 million. But by now, Officer Jones was beginning to reconsider her desire to settle the case by paying Mrs. Mathis a large settlement. Realizing that the awful death of the 22-year-old police officer had changed the public's perception of what police officers face daily in their effort to "protect and serve," Officer Jones now believed a jury trial could exonerate her and perhaps enable her to resume her career as a police officer. Officer Jones withdrew her original offer and offered Mrs. Mathis a token $50,000. The negotiation ended abruptly.

LEVERAGING POWER FROM YOUR BATNA

In negotiations, **power** is the ability to induce the other party to settle for less than it wanted. **Leverage** refers to the use of that power to achieve your aims. Power in this context is *relational*, not personal. That is, power does not reside in the person but in the relationship of the parties to the situation being negotiated. For example, in the Chapter Case, if Wilma Mathis were to cross paths with Officer Jones in a routine traffic stop, no one would expect Mrs. Mathis's bargaining power in relation to Officer Jones's bargaining power to result in no traffic ticket being issued. However, in the context of the Chapter Case, Wilma Mathis does have the ability to affect Officer Jones's decisions regarding the excess force claim.

The most essential source of bargaining power in any negotiation is the ability to walk away. Remember that negotiation is a voluntary interaction between parties who are interdependent. Interdependency puts the parties into a bargaining relationship, gives them an incentive to work together to coordinate their wants or goals, and makes it advantageous for them to forge an agreement. But the voluntary aspect of negotiations gives parties the freedom to walk away and not to enter into an agreement if the advantage fails to overcome the disadvantage of settling. One of the first things you should do prior to a negotiation is determine your BATNA. As discussed in Chapter 2, each party's BATNA can determine who has more bargaining power in a negotiation.

For example, in a 2002 negotiation of a collective bargaining agreement between the United Parcel Service (UPS) and the Teamsters, the Teamsters signaled that their best alternative to an unfavorable labor agreement was a strike by appointing Ken Hall as the lead negotiator. In 1997, Hall had helped lead the Teamsters to victory against UPS following a successful 16-day strike. The 1997 strike lasted three weeks and caused UPS to lose $750 million in revenue, and many longtime customers switched to its competitors FedEx and DHL. As the renegotiation time neared, UPS experienced a decline in business as customers, fearing another strike, began using other delivery services. UPS could not afford another strike and needed a settlement quickly—giving the Teamsters significant leverage. The Teamsters were seeking major improvements, such as a 25% increase in wages for drivers and 50% for part-time workers, no reduction in health care or retirement benefits, converting 10,000 part-time jobs to full-time jobs, and a six-year agreement to provide job security. Thus, in a weak economic climate and while many employers were cutting health care and pension benefits in new contracts, the Teamsters were able to gain a historic contract because of their bargaining power.[1]

Believing You Have a Strong BATNA

Your BATNA does not have to be objectively "better" than the other party's to give you negotiating power. A BATNA, like beauty, is often in the eye of the beholder.

When you *believe* the possible negotiated outcomes of a particular transaction are inferior to your alternatives, you may reasonably decide to quit the negotiation. This can cause the other party to question its own commitment to the negotiation and the range or advisability of its own BATNA. Even if you overestimate the attractiveness of your alternatives, such belief adds to your power. Like a self-fulfilling prophesy, if you believe you have power within the negotiation because of available alternatives, then what you see and hear in the negotiation tends to confirm that belief.[2] If you are convinced that your BATNA is better than your opponent's, and that conviction is conveyed to your opponent, then you have increased your leverage in the negotiation.

Convincing Others of the Strength of Your BATNA

Likewise, if you know your BATNA is inferior to your opponent's BATNA, you may still convince your opponent that you have a better alternative than reaching an agreement. Three techniques to do this are (1) making sure your opponent doesn't know your BATNA, (2) increasing your value by leveraging the weakness of your opponent's BATNA, and (3) teaming up with other parties to increase your strength.[3]

In the Chapter Case, for example, if the police officer convinced the widow by her very low offer at the negotiation that she believes her best alternative to a negotiated agreement is to go to trial—regardless of whether she really believes it or not—her negotiating position is strengthened, even if going to trial is, objectively, a bad idea. In addition, when the death of the young police officer shifted sympathy away from the widow's claim for damages, the officer could have pointed out to the widow that a public trial to clear her husband's name could backfire if there was evidence that he was involved in drugs. Shifting back to the widow in this example, when she found her position weakening she could seek out some of the other people in the community who had made previous claims of excessive force and join with them to try and gain concessions from the police department on officer performance.

Changes in BATNA During Negotiations

Many negotiation theories assume that the parties' alternatives to negotiation are fixed before bargaining starts. But researchers David Lax and James Sebenius suggest that alternatives can change during the course of negotiations.[4] New information, new developments in the overall situation, renewed attempts to cultivate alternatives, and the culmination of ongoing processes can all change alternatives and thus change the range of possible acceptable settlements.

As demonstrated in the Chapter Case, initially the widow believed her best alternative was to file suit against the officer and let a jury decide the question. The officer initially preferred not to go to trial, not wanting to place her future in a jury's hands. However, by the time of the negotiation session, the situation was different and the police officer's BATNA changed, forcing the widow to prove her case at trial. The officer believed that a jury would understand that she was in fear for her life, even though the young man did not have a gun, because she *believed* he had a gun. Furthermore, she believed that even if the case was lost at trial, the likelihood that the widow would receive as much money as she was demanding was slim. So for the officer, either a win or a loss at trial was an acceptable alternative to a negotiated settlement. The widow's BATNA in light of the officer's non-offer was also to go to trial. For her, however, losing the trial was not an acceptable alternative. A win would not only serve to punish the officer for her actions and exonerate her husband's name, but it would also provide money as compensation for her loss. If she lost at trial, she would be left with nothing. The power in this negotiation *shifted* from the widow to the police officer, because the officer believed public support had changed and thus she had a better BATNA. Had the widow understood that, she might have reconsidered her demand.

Lax and Sebenius suggest that to increase their bargaining power, negotiators need to invest some of their effort, time, or money while negotiating toward improving their alternatives to a settlement, or by generating new alternatives constantly throughout the negotiation. For example, the widow in the Chapter Case might try to find out if the undercover drug program of her city's police department was either designed or managed according to best practice standards of police departments across the country.

As noted earlier, negotiators should be aware that people tend to overestimate the attractiveness of their alternatives and the likelihood of their success at the bargaining table. You can counteract this tendency by sharing your own best alternative or by offering the perspective of an uninterested third party. For example, either of the parties in the Chapter Case could ask an attorney, who did not represent either party, to give them an assessment of each party's case. Such an assessment could moderate one or both of their BATNAs.

The more intense a party's preference is for *one* alternative, the less power it has in negotiations because the range of possible negotiated outcomes is set by the available alternatives. Thus, negotiations may become blocked when one or both parties have inconsistent and overly optimistic assessments of their alternatives. In such cases the biased perceptions must be moderated in order to make the dispute ripe for negotiation. Lax and Sebenius suggest shifting bargaining power and jump-starting the negotiations by *altering the other party's perception* of your alternatives. For example, if you have to move from a rental property by a certain date and decide that the house you are making an offer to purchase is the *only* house you are willing to buy, then you have shifted a great deal of power to the seller—but your bargaining power increases if you can find one or more *other* houses that appeal to you. As another example, making irrevocable commitments in some instances can increase your bargaining power if it restricts the bargaining range in your favor.[5] If, for example, you hire a mover for a certain date and notify the seller that you are moving on that date—if not into the seller's house then into one of the other houses you have identified—then the seller may be pressured to accept your price.

LEVERAGING THE SOURCES OF POWER

Power can be acquired and used in a negotiation in the same way it is acquired and exercised in organizations. In studies of organizations, a number of power bases have been identified. The work most commonly referred to was done in 1956 by John R. P. French and Bertran Raven, who described the generalized power sources shown in

Table 5.1 Sources of Power

POWER TYPE	POWER SOURCE	EXAMPLE
Reward power	Controlling resources that could reward.	Only dealer in region to sell popular sports car. Company employee with authority to use the company's Major League Baseball tickets.
Coercive power	Controlling resources that could punish.	Managers assigning undesirable tasks at work
Legitimate power	Authority vested in you by your position or through an ally.	Manager's role in approving employee's raise. Being the "boss" able to make final decisions.
Expert power	Controlling necessary knowledge or information.	Releasing information when it is strategic to do so. Being a recognized "expert" on a subject.
Reference power	Being attractive to others so they seek you out	Engendering cooperation by appealing to shared values and the duty to contribute to their achievement. Building consensus by understanding people.

Source: Adapted from Rosabeth Moss Kanter, *Men and Women of the Corporation* (New York: BasicBooks, 1993), 174.

Table 5.1. These same sources of power can often be found in a negotiation—namely reward power, coercive power, legitimate power, expert power, and reference power.

Reward Power and Coercive Power: Controlling Resources

Control of the object of the negotiation is, of course, the most common source of power in a negotiation and the easiest to understand. You can use your control over the object as a reward for a favorable outcome in the negotiation or to force the other party to make concessions in your favor. For example, if you are a car dealer and you control a very popular sports car model, then you have considerable negotiating power when a consumer who wants that model comes to your dealership. If you are the *only* dealer in the region with the franchise to sell that sports car, you have even more negotiating power. When professional ball players are allowed *free agency* (that is, players may bargain for employment with any team), the star players have control over a resource that gives them considerable **reward power** (power to bestow favors or rewards) or **coercive power** (power to impose one's will on the other party) over the team owners: Star performances bring in the fans, and fans are the team owners' source of income. So the star players can always cut a better deal with another team. As a result, free agency leads to higher player salaries for many players.

Legitimate Power: Position or Authority

A person may have **legitimate power** in a number of ways as a result of the position he or she holds. For instance, in most situations the negotiator has the authority to bargain and reach agreement, even if he or she is merely an agent for someone else. But, sometimes the "boss" or employer is the actual negotiator, and his or her presence conveys additional power because it reinforces the boss's ability to reward or punish through the granting or withholding of resources in the negotiation.

It is very common in business negotiations not to have the actual decision makers present during bargaining. The negotiating teams simply represent the decision makers and do in fact have certain authority delegated to them—but when the time comes for reaching an agreement, the discussion moves from the bargaining table to a back office or hallway where the real decision makers meet informally and hammer out the settlement. It is not necessary that the decision makers have a title or position. If they are the ones who can make the deal happen, then they have legitimate power by virtue of their position in the organization. How often have you witnessed a salesperson "take the offer to the manager" in another room? When the salesperson comes back, he or she has the "deal" that the manager authorized.

Negotiators can also obtain a form of legitimate power by creating alliances with those who control resources. So even though they do not control an asset directly, they can influence the situation through control of the ally. For example, an outside negotiator representing a public employer at the bargaining table with an employee union generally has no real authority over the resources that the public employer can commit to the labor agreement. However, if the negotiator is able to influence the allocation that the employer is going to include in the city's annual budget, then the negotiator has control of the resources at stake in the negotiation through influence over the budget process.

Expert Power: Controlling Information

In a negotiation, a person can have considerable power through the control of information. The negotiator can use this **expert power** by choosing to communicate or not to communicate that information or by deciding when and in what form to present the information to the other party. For example, in a lawsuit filed by an inventor against multiple parties who had infringed on his invention—a riding lawnmower with plowing attachments—the plaintiff reached a confidential agreement with one of the defendants in which the defendant admitted to infringing on the patent with one of the other defendants. That defendant, who did not know of the settlement, agreed to meet with the plaintiff to discuss settlement, although he had no real intention to settle. The defendant spent an hour at the beginning of the negotiation denying any wrongdoing on his part *and* on the part of the co-defendant. The plaintiff was able to surprise the defendant with the executed settlement and admission of his co-defendant, thereby weakening the defendant's position.

A negotiator might control information also because of his or her *expertise,* a special skill or knowledge that the other parties do not share. Because of that skill or knowledge, the parties give greater weight to the information that person presents. For example, an architect who is a member of a citizens' group trying to negotiate with a national company on its plans for a new shopping center in their neighborhood may command considerable influence with both sides of the negotiation on design issues, even though he is not the architect who will actually design the center.

Reference Power: Personal Attributes

Charisma, which has been defined as a special magnetic charm or appeal, is one source of *influence power* or **reference power**. In a negotiation, charisma is less a function of personality than it is a technique of shaping what others want. It comes from engendering cooperation based on shared values and the justness or rightness of contributing to the achievement of those shared values.[6]

A skilled negotiator can use framing and offering multiple options to shape what others want. For example, a property development firm was acquiring land for a new hospital. The purchasing agent could not convince the owner of the last and most central parcel of land to sell or, in fact, even to name a price for the property. The agent was convinced that the property owner intended to hold the hospital hostage to an excessive demand. The CEO of the hospital was a skilled negotiator and decided to take personal charge of the acquisition of the property. The CEO made an appointment and met with the elderly woman owner of the very modest house at issue. The CEO noticed a rather large collection of children's school photos on a bulletin board in the woman's kitchen where they were sitting over coffee. When the CEO commented on it, he learned that the woman had been a teacher at the school one block away for more than 30 years. Many of her students had grown up and now had children in the same school. On occasion, her former students would drop by her house after leaving their children at the school, and she was able to keep up with their lives. The CEO was aware that many of the school's families were members of the "working poor" struggling to make ends meet. He asked the woman's opinion of an idea he had been working on—to have the hospital offer a free half-day clinic to serve the residents in the immediate area of the new hospital as a way to be a good neighbor. He sought her advice on how such a clinic could be presented to residents without their seeing it as "welfare." The idea appealed to this former teacher, who still cared greatly about her students. By the end of the meeting, the CEO had reached an amicable settlement with the owner at a very reasonable price and a commitment on her part to help launch the new clinic.

Of course charisma is not the only personal attribute that negotiators find valuable. They can also derive reference power through the ability to use knowledge, determination, and confidence to build consensus.[7] Individuals who possess an understanding of people and the confidence that they can control the processes and outcomes of interaction with others can build social capital as a way to achieve a desired goal.

Negotiators can also create reference power through reputation and performance. If someone has a reputation for getting things done, that person may have considerable power to influence the actions of others.

LEVERAGING POWER THROUGH PERSUASION

Peter Thompson, in his book *Persuading Aristotle*, credits the Greek philosopher with presenting the following principles of persuasion that can be used successfully in a negotiation to persuade a person to one's point of view, with or without an objectively persuasive argument:[8]

- Frame the question that you believe is at issue.
- Marshal persuasive arguments to answer that question.

- Choose the most persuasive language to support your position.
- Match nonverbal communications to the verbal communications you are using to persuade.

Framing the Question

As discussed in earlier chapters on negotiating strategies, after identifying the issues to be negotiated, you should frame each issue for presentation to the other side in a way that creates a positive definition of the problem and an equally positive set of solutions. Framing is useful because people perceive their interests differently depending on how their options are presented.[9] The goal, of course, is to present the issue in the light most favorable to your position.

Using Aristotle's principles of persuasion, a skilled negotiator can characterize the object of the negotiation in a way that lends itself to persuasive arguments. For example, in the Chapter Case, the widow was caught off guard by the officer's about-face at the beginning of the negotiation. And as long as the heart of the issue was to assign blame for the young man's death, there was little hope of reaching an agreement. However, if the widow could have reframed the issue as "How do we both move forward from this tragic incident?" then she might have been able to keep the officer at the bargaining table.

Creating Persuasive Arguments

There are three keys to formulating a persuasive argument, which Aristotle identified as *logos, pathos* and *ethos. Logos,* or *logic,* focuses on the rationality of the argument. Rational arguments are information-based—they include analysis, calculation, and an examination of the pros and cons of a certain action. Logic-based arguments are often the basis for integrative bargaining because in integrative bargaining the goal is to focus on interests, not positions. The parties try to identify their real desires, concerns, and interests and try to leave "personalities" out of the investigation. Interest-based bargaining (IBB) also lends itself to a rational approach to persuasion because the parties are engaging in joint problem solving, generating a variety of possible options before a decision is made, and basing some of the solutions upon an objective, external standard—calling, perhaps, upon an expert to evaluate the suggested settlement of the negotiation.[10]

Pathos, or *passion,* focuses on the emotion involved in one's argument. Most current negotiation literature appropriately discourages exhibiting unproductive emotion in bargaining, such as anger or frustration. But without some positive emotion, such as a sense of fairness or pride, arguments fail to persuade. Passion often addresses the intangibles that are a part of every negotiation—the needs and motivations of the parties at the bargaining table. Emotions are strongly related to ego and they establish a connection with another person that cannot be created by facts alone. Distributive bargaining, which focuses on one's rights rather than one's interests, often relies upon the underlying emotions within an argument, such as an appeal to fairness or equity.

Finally, *ethos,* or *character,* focuses on the person who is making the argument—that person's reputation for truthfulness and fair-dealing and/or the person's position of authority. One's reputation may stem from a traditional base of power, such as expertise, controlling resources, controlling information, charisma, or formal position. The strengths and weaknesses of negotiators are a part of every negotiation, whether the method used is integrative, interest-based, or distributive bargaining.

Now let's apply these three keys—logic, passion, and character—to the Chapter Case to understand just how different they are. A rational approach to persuading either party that the widow's claim against the officer was or was not valid would be to seek advice from a respected third party, perhaps a retired judge, who could analyze the evidence and list the pros and cons of both sides in proceeding to a jury trial. The party or parties could compare that list and try to arrive at a more realistic settlement point. An emotional approach might involve an opportunity for both parties to express their emotions without prejudicing their positions. Perhaps the parties could find a mediator who could facilitate a confidential discussion of the loss both women have experienced as a result of the shooting. Recognizing that each had suffered a loss might create a connection between them that could lead to a realistic settlement point. Finally, a character approach to persuading the parties in the Chapter Case might involve submitting the case to binding mediation-arbitration. In that type of third-party intervention, a mediator-arbitrator who is mutually accepted by the parties attempts to lead them to an equitable solution by mediation, but if that fails, the mediator-arbitrator is in a position to dictate what the parties will accept.

Using Persuasive Language

There are different types of *rhetoric* or persuasive arguments for different purposes. Judicial arguments are based on logic; the individual uses rhetoric for the purpose of persuading someone to look at past events the way that individual wants those events to be seen. A lawyer starts with a legal premise favorable to his or her client and then presents the facts and arguments that support the premise. In such an argument, the lawyer does indeed want the facts to "speak for themselves."

Demonstrative arguments are based on emotion; the rhetoric used is for the purpose of challenging the listeners' views or beliefs. Many religious speakers use a demonstrative rhetoric to extol the congregation to have faith and to commit themselves to a particular belief.

Deliberative arguments combine logic, emotion, and character; the rhetoric used is to persuade others, based on their existing values, to take some action or to agree to some proposal. Deliberative arguments are used in negotiations to persuade the listener to accept an agreement beneficial to the speaker. The speaker may use metaphor, humor, visual or auditory aids, or even storytelling to make that argument persuasive.

Metaphor Persuasive communication can appeal to all types of listeners by joining an idea or an image with an emotion or feeling. A metaphor is the most powerful way to carry meaning across from one thing into another. A *metaphor* is a figure of speech that contains an implied comparison between two seemingly disconnected concepts. That comparison creates a symbolic meaning that is loaded with emotion.[11] It is a shortcut to the meaning; it sets two unlike things side by side, to demonstrate the likeness between them. Examples of metaphors used by political or business leaders that have become part of everyone's reality include reference to the Soviet occupation of Eastern Europe as the "iron curtain," the justification for the Vietnam War under the "domino theory," the Internet as the "information super-highway," and the discrimination against women in top management as a "glass ceiling." In everyday discourse people describe something with intense heat as "white hot," or identify Ireland as the "Emerald Isle." These metaphors create an idea that makes others react to the underlying truth. The idea of an "iron curtain" conveys the totalitarian rule of the former Soviet Union, with its isolation from the West; the notion of a "glass ceiling" conveys both the availability of top management positions within an organization that could be seen to exist and the reality that women are not going to be allowed to reach them. Use the exercise in Figure 5.1 to practice creating metaphors.

Humor   Humor can be used to form a connection for the people in a negotiation. It can create a pleasant atmosphere and generate good feelings, as well as conveying the message that the parties, while perhaps on opposite sides, are still people.

Figure 5.1 Creating a Metaphor

Using the Chapter Case, role-play first as the police officer and then as the widow. In both cases, assume you have been given the opportunity to convey one message to the other person in order to persuade her that you are right.

1. *Decide what you believe is your best reason why the lawsuit should be settled in your favor.* For example, Officer Jones believes that she should prevail in the lawsuit because otherwise police officers will be afraid to react in a dangerous situation if they believe they will be exposed to criminal and civil liability.

2. *Brainstorm images that might be appropriate. Sources of images that might be useful in this case include nature (life cycle, vastness, chaos), transitions (journey, voyage, passage), human body (heart, hand, senses), and war (courage, heroism, pressure, drama).* An appropriate image might focus on the effect of police officers being afraid to act, such as tying their hands or leaving them exposed.

3. *Choose an image that you believe the other party can identify with and not one to shock or hurt the other party. The goal is not to blame or excuse, but to have one party see the situation through the other's eyes.* For example, "Don't shackle police officers" might be hurtful since it was alleged that James Mathis was engaged in an illegal activity.

4. *Write down the reasons why your image explains the message you want to convey.* For instance, using an image suggesting "aloneness" would convey Officer Jones's feeling of vulnerability when doing undercover work.

5. *Develop your image by focusing on a few details of the picture.* You might focus on Officer Jones's struggle with James Mathis over her gun, which was a frightening moment for her because she knew the officers who were there as her backup could not reach her in time if Mr. Mathis got the gun and intended to use it.

6. *Avoid clichés. Decide whether your image is new or unique enough to have an effect.* Avoid such overused phrases as "war on drugs" or "rite of passage."

7. *Try the metaphor on a classmate and record his or her reaction to it.* If your metaphor elicits agreement, then you have probably created a persuasive metaphor.

Sources: Adapted from Peter Thompson, *Persuading Aristotle: The Timeless Art of Persuasion in Business, Negotiation, and the Media* (Crows Nest, Australia: Allen & Unwin, 1998), 54; and Shaul Fox and Yair Amichai-Hamburger, "The Power of Emotional Appeals in Promoting Organizational Change Programs," *Academy of Management Executive* 15 (November 2001): 88.

Humor relaxes the listener and has the power to bridge differences.[12] In *The Intelligent Negotiator,* author Charles Craver shared this example during a labor negotiation that had become acrimonious:

> After an impasse had been reached, the parties stared intently at one another across the bargaining table. The chief negotiator from the union arose from his seat and began to walk slowly around the table toward the employer side. The room became completely silent by the time he arrived next to the chief negotiator for the employer. He squatted beside that individual and looked at his union colleagues on the other side of the table. When he said, "From here, you guys do look like sons of bitches," everyone laughed and much of the prevailing tension was broken.[13]

Using Props   Senses also influence how a spoken or written message is perceived. Highly visual people create and respond to images, auditory people create and respond to articulation, and kinesthetic people create and respond best to a demonstration or hands-on situation. Studies have shown that 40% of people respond primarily to visual stimuli, 40% through auditory stimuli, and 20% through kinesthetic stimuli.[14] Visual messages include facial expressions, a tilt of the head, posture, and appearance. Auditory messages are not only the words used but also the sound of the voice and how rapidly or slowly the words are spoken.[15] A negotiator might use visual strategies to focus the parties during a negotiation. A flip chart or PowerPoint presentation can be brought into the negotiations, with the issues separated one to a page. The negotiator can get agreement that they will discuss each item one at a time—and once they have thoroughly discussed an item, they will either agree or move on. That item will not be revisited until all other items have been discussed.[16]

Storytelling   Storytelling is an example of a right-brain activity that uses imagination to convey the parties' interests behind their arguments. Negotiation, after all, is not just a left-brain activity, a rational and analytical process by which parties calculate and use reasoning to achieve their goals. Negotiation requires the use of both reasoning *and* imagination; it is not left-brained or right brained, but utilizes the whole mind.[17] Storytelling is effective as persuasive speech because by telling stories, parties can define for themselves what the negotiation is about and what their real interests and concerns are. By telling stories, they can explore their inner feelings, their wishes and fears. They can also remember stories about alternative approaches to problem solving or solutions to various disagreements at the bargaining table. Thus storytelling can act similarly to brainstorming, letting people explore different options and predict various outcomes.[18]

Storytelling makes abstract ideas concrete. Storytelling is used as a way of opening people up, to talk and listen, and to pave the way for improved communication and understanding. It allows people to get to know each other better, and to understand why people on the other side in a negotiation feel the way that they do. By listening to the opponent's story, people will often say to themselves, "Oh, I understand—that has happened to me too," or "Yes, I can see how that would have made you feel the way it did." It makes people's beliefs more valid and their abstract ideas more real. In the Chapter Case, an observer might imagine that Wilma, a young widow mourning her young husband, has a story she could tell Officer Jones that might foster understanding. Her life was changed by violence; she and her deceased husband were subject to the public's scrutiny after the incident and had to endure newspaper and TV news reports that painted them in simplistic, and therefore inaccurate, ways.

Focusing on the Listener's Perspective

It is essential for negotiators to be able to connect to the other side, either by appealing to logic or emotion. Richard Petty and John Cacioppo,[19] leading researchers in the cognitive process of *attitude change,* or persuasion, describe both a central and a peripheral route to influencing a listener based upon the commitment of the listener.

The *central route* to persuasion emphasizes the *analytical* basis for the argument, the ideas, and the content of the message. The listener pays attention to the argument, attempts to understand it, and evaluates it. The effectiveness of this approach is dependent upon the ability and/or motivation of the listener to think about and evaluate the *content of the message.* Such motivation and ability is derived from many factors, including the relevance of the issue to the individual and the strength of the argument. Persuasive tactics typical in integrative and interest-based bargaining appeal to the listener's analytical side. These include controlling the agenda, presenting multiple alternative solutions or options, and framing and reframing the issues to address the listener's objections. In a negotiation, for example, integrative or interest-based bargaining focuses on the problem and not the people involved in the problem. The skilled negotiator engages the other side to participate in joint problem solving rather than in value exchange. Imagine a health services company that wants to increase the level of its employees' medical skills, but needs to protect itself from high turnover that may result when the employees enhance their skills. The employees want to receive more training for their job security, but do not believe the employer will give it to them because they know how volatile the health care market can be. There is a potential for the negotiations on "job training" to get caught up in the fears of both parties. By focusing on the positives of a joint goal for "more training" without mentioning the different reasons the parties have for more training, the negotiators can begin the process of persuading the parties to agree on a fair training program.

The *peripheral route* to persuasion emphasizes the *creative* nature of the listener in which the influence comes from the *source of the message or its presentation* rather than its content. The listener associates the message with such factors as perceived rewards or punishments or the attractiveness or expertise of the person delivering the message. According to Petty and Cacioppo, the peripheral route results from a listener's inability or lack of motivation to engage in thoughtful analysis of the issues.[20] Such lack of motivation or ability can stem from a lack of comprehension by the listener or the lack of a coherent argument. If the issue is important to the listener, then in the absence of a coherent argument the listener is guided by his or her preexisting attitude on the subject, rather than the argument being presented. Many times in a negotiation, the content of a position may not be particularly strong, in which case the peripheral route to persuasion becomes more important. Persuasive tactics typical in distributive bargaining—such as proposing throwaway items in order to make a real offer look better, appealing to an objective standard such as a contract or law as the basis for an argument, being friendly or flattering, or modeling the other's gestures or body language to create a similarity or "likeness"—often succeed in these cases. Thompson, in *Persuading Aristotle*, focuses on the extrovert–introvert and thinking–feeling pairs to demonstrate how to use *logos, pathos,* and *ethos* to persuade.[21] His pairs are set out in Figure 5.2. These pairs are comparable to two of the dimensions and their opposites in the Five Factor Model discussed in Chapter 1, which is a representation of personality traits in the workplace (see Table 1.2). As you recall, the five factors are neuroticism, extroversion, openness, agreeableness, and conscientiousness. The two dimensions Thompson refers to are *extroversion,* which is described as a trait characterized by a keen interest in other people and external events, and *openness,* which refers to how willing people are to make adjustments in notions and activities in accordance with new ideas or situations.

Referring to the figure and going clockwise from the top, if someone is a thinking-extrovert, then he or she is a *shaker* (as in a "mover and a shaker"). Shakers are outcome-oriented, quick-witted, and focused on facts. They are also self-confident, intense, often impatient with others. Shakers have a real advantage in negotiations because they can focus on the real point and not get off track with unnecessary concerns. To influence a shaker, use logic—focus on the bottom-line issues, be succinct and prepared. For shakers to persuade others, they need to know when to push ahead and when to hold back. In a negotiation, shakers have to use their intellect and leadership skills to bring others along to their side—but at the other party's pace, not the shaker's.

Figure 5.2 Personality Types

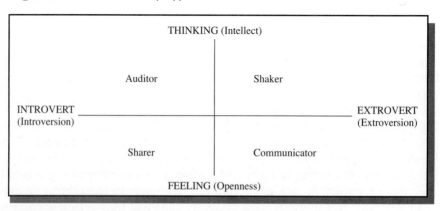

Source: Peter Thompson, *Persuading Aristotle: The Timeless Art of Persuasion in Business, Negotiation, and the Media* (Crows Nest, Australia: Allen & Unwin, 1998), 65. Used with permission.

A *communicator* is a feeling-extrovert—talkative, outgoing, enthusiastic, intuitive, and often charismatic. A communicator can also be glib, impulsive, and a poor listener. Communicators have an advantage in negotiations because they display excitement and a sense of mission for their position. To influence a communicator, use passion—focus on stories and metaphors that convey the emotion underlying an idea. Expect communicators to respond to your body language as well as your persuasive language. For communicators to persuade others, they need to create images and metaphors that will focus the listener on their message and that will relay their enthusiasm. In a negotiation, communicators have to use their intuition and empathy to really listen to the other side's position in order to connect and influence.

If you are a feeling-introvert, you are a *sharer*. Sharers are even-tempered, thoughtful, reliable, and idealistic. They can also be indecisive and ineffective. Sharers have an advantage in a negotiation because they have empathy for people and display sincere warmth and concern for the well-being of others. To influence a sharer, use character—relate to his or her sense of fairness and equity and build a relationship of trust. For sharers to persuade others, they must bring some substance, as well as the warmth of feeling, to the negotiations.

If you are a thinking-introvert, you are an *auditor*. Auditors are rational, cautious, reserved, reliable, and experts in their field. Auditors can also be inflexible, cynical, and so single-minded as to be boring. They have an advantage in negotiations because they enjoy complex argument and have the patience to listen long and thoughtfully. To influence an auditor use logic—include detailed analysis with extensive supporting documents. Expect detailed questions and a slow, prodding process of examination. For auditors to persuade others, they must be prepared to add some feeling to the expert or detailed argument being used in the negotiation.

Now let's see how these different personalities might approach the negotiation from the Chapter Case. Lee Ann, a lawyer and a "shaker" personality, has been asked by Officer Jones to negotiate with Wilma's attorney on her behalf. In preparation for the negotiation, Lee Ann not only researches the case law on the necessary facts that Wilma will have to prove to prevail in an "excessive force" case, but also the local jury verdicts in similar cases, the prior rulings of the judge assigned to the case, and the record of Wilma's attorney in wrongful death cases. She prepared an outline of the points she wanted to convey when she met with Wilma's attorney. She would emphasize the fact that Officer Jones would prevail if the jury believed she was in fear of her life and that local juries tended to believe police officers. Because the judge was inclined to allow plaintiffs great latitude in pleading their case to a jury, she did not intend to bring up this issue. Her research indicated that Wilma's attorney preferred cases with speedy resolution, so Lee Ann intended to emphasize the time this case will take to get through the court system.

Originally, Officer Jones had engaged Paul to be her attorney. Paul is a "sharer" personality. He gave Officer Jones a great deal of comfort in their initial meetings because he was sincerely interested in how she was handling this terrible event. But after three such meetings, Officer Jones worried that there was little substantive work being done. At an earlier meeting between the parties, Paul connected with Wilma because he also had empathy for her loss. Officer Jones thought that if there was going to be a settlement, Paul might be the right one to pursue it. However, after the young police officer was killed, Officer Jones decided not to discuss settlement.

Wilma's lawyer, Chris, is a "communicator" personality. His preparation for the negotiations was to revisit in his mind his first interview with Wilma, a 17-year-old widow whose husband, as far as she was concerned, had been executed by a police officer. He had a law clerk find examples of every shooting of an African American male by a white police officer and committed the most egregious examples to memory. His outline for the meeting contained phrases and images that he intended to use during the trial to focus the jurors on the tragic loss of life.

The law clerk assisting Chris in this case, Gail, is an "auditor" personality. She fills in the intellectual gaps that Chris leaves with rational arguments and reliable information. She anticipated Lee Ann's research and has prepared a counterargument to each of her points. Gail has never listened to Wilma's story and prefers not meeting clients. But she has meticulously gone over every detail of the night in question and has already formulated pages of questions for the trial.

Although a case like this would be hard to settle under any circumstances, the mix of personalities representing the parties would certainly complicate a negotiating effort.

TOOLS FOR PERSUASIVE COMMUNICATION

If you are to create a persuasive argument to gain leverage in a negotiation, the essential fact to remember is that the parties are *communicating.* In a face-to-face meeting, such communication is both verbal and nonverbal. A successful negotiator develops techniques to turn verbal and nonverbal communication into persuasive communication—thereby *creating leverage through persuasion.* In this section we will explain how communication is more than simply talking, and we will look at ways to use communication to persuade others. Moreover, we will examine the filters that may cause the parties' perception of what is going on to be different from what is actually going on—filters such as conflicting frame of reference, semantics, value judgments, and cultural diversity. Effective communication to override these filters includes several factors: active listening (discussed in Chapter 4), employing effective verbal communications, reading nonverbal communications, recognizing time and space issues, recognizing one's own stereotyping and prejudices, and understanding how emotions can influence the thought process.

Verbal Communication

In negotiations a speaker should remember that the goal is to persuade. Dialogue should be simple, expressing a position, followed by silence that allows the other party to digest what was said. A speaker should avoid confusing the other party by knowing what he or she is going to say before saying it. Talking consists of positive and negative elements. Positive elements are questions, doubts, uncertainties, and approvals because these indicate that the issues being discussed are still open. Negative elements include conclusion statements and flat assertions, which will indicate that the discussion is for all practical purposes over.

Voice   Persuasive communication does not come from the words of the message alone. It includes the ways people communicate with their voice and body. It is important for a negotiator to match nonverbal and verbal communication to avoid giving mixed signals. Voice qualities such as tone, pitch, emphasis, volume, or rate of speech can sometimes carry more meaning than the actual words being used. To be persuasive, the voice qualities should mirror the message. A logical and well-thought-out argument should be delivered in a calm and confident voice; an appeal to emotion, or *pathos* in Aristotle's principles of persuasion, should convey some emotion—happiness or disappointment.

Nonverbal Communication

From the moment two people come in contact with each other they are communicating. Before the first word is spoken, messages have been sent and received. Unfortunately, very few people think about those unspoken messages and, therefore, may not evaluate them properly.

The image you present at a negotiation will have an impact upon the reception you get from the other party. In Western culture, for example, it is a sign of honesty to look someone in the eye when talking to him or her. It may be a sign of being closed-minded to sit back with arms folded during a discussion. Such external manifestations of internal thinking can send more powerful messages than the spoken word. Nonverbal communication thus provides an informative background to the negotiation's verbal foreground.

Besides body language and facial expressions, we communicate nonverbally through such signals as personal appearance, the choice of a negotiation room, the look of printed materials, arriving on time (or not), and the absence or presence of distractions such as cell phones or pagers. Negotiators frequently resort to sending a message nonverbally through dramatic action—walking out of a negotiation, or pounding the table, or falling into stony silence. It is a well-known adage for lawyers that when the law is on your side you argue the law, when the facts are on your side you argue the facts, and when neither are on your side you pound the table.

It is important for a negotiator to read the nonverbal messages being sent by others because the failure to do so may cause the negotiations to get off track before they even begin. *Perception,* from the perspective of communication, is the meaning given to a message by both sender and receiver. An individual's perception is influenced by the objects that are seen, the way in which these objects are organized in the individual's memory, and the meaning attached to the objects. For example, a clenched fist raised in the air by a football player can be interpreted by members of the other team as a challenge or threat and by his own team members as a sign of solidarity.

Nonverbal communication can help you persuade in a negotiation by adding information (implications and subtext), emphasis (showing what is most important), subtlety (leaving open a suggestion), and rapport (relationship building). The basic types of nonverbal communication include the following:[22]

1. Kinesics—body motions, posture, degree of tension and relaxation
2. Eye movement—direct eye-to-eye contact, shifting eyes
3. Facial expressions—happiness, sadness, distress, fear, anger, surprise
4. Gestures—deliberate, symbolic (arbitrary), iconic (imitating)
5. Spatial relations—distance between individuals, personal space
6. Display—presentation of self, clothing, punctuality

Kinesics   Physical movements and postures during negotiations are very telling. How you carry yourself sends a message that you are (or are not) confident, at ease, and able to relate to people quite comfortably. You are seen as inclusive if your arms are unfolded, and if you are facing the opposing negotiator directly, not turning your body at an angle.

Eye Movement   Eye movement and eye contact is an often-discussed communication trait in negotiation. Researchers have shown a connection between eye contact and perceived power dynamics. Speakers feel more powerful and valued when listeners maintain eye contact, which shows the listener is paying attention and respects the speaker.[23] The reaction to a speaker is better if the speaker maintains eye contact as a signal of truthfulness and sincerity and focuses for a few seconds on each person at the negotiation as a way to include all of the parties.

Facial Expressions   Some nonverbal expressions of emotion are genetic rather than learned. These include expressions of happiness, sadness, anger, fear, surprise, and disgust.[24] But you cannot know for sure *why* the person is happy, sad, mad, or afraid from facial expression alone. Communicating nonverbally is limited because it is imprecise, it cannot explain complex ideas or send more than one message, and it doesn't transmit factual information and is easy to misread.

Gestures   Gestures can be understood only in the context of the entire interaction. For instance, negotiators are often cautioned that by crossing their arms and scooting back from the table, they will send a message that an issue is closed for discussion. Of course, if that is the message they want to send, it may be an effective way of communicating it. However, single, isolated gestures or expressions rarely have a defined or predictable meaning, especially if you don't know the other party well. For example, crossed arms can signal hostility or closed-mindedness, but the gesture can also mean that you are feeling cold, feeling defensive—or that you just have a habit of sitting that way.

Common nonverbal cues are identified in Table 5.2.

Time and Space   We communicate nonverbally by other symbols or signals. How we deal with time is one example. In Western cultures, being on time signals competency and respect. Management being late for an appointment or a negotiating session with a union, for instance, can communicate an unwillingness to reach agreement. In cultures with a cyclical vision of time, on the other hand, being punctual does not mean very much.

Table 5.2 Common Nonverbal Behaviors

MAY INDICATE CAN BE TRUSTED	MAY INDICATE DISHONESTY	MAY INDICATE CLOSED-MINDEDNESS	MAY INDICATE WILLINGNESS TO LISTEN
Direct speech	Fidgeting	Using briefcase or papers to "guard" body	Leaning forward in seat
Open gestures	Excessive smiling	Crossing arms	Keeping arms and palms open
Open behavior	Sheepish smiles	Turning body away	Maintaining great eye contact
Smiling	Overly serious tone		Nodding
Pointing	Lack of emotion		
	Averting eyes		
	Lack of eye contact		
	Being too quiet		

Use of space is another nonverbal communication symbol. The location and size of a person's office often communicates that person's importance to the organization. Also, having a private office as opposed to sharing space can be seen as a symbol of success. In companies that are changing the way they organize the workplace from a pyramid to an inverted pyramid, walls for private offices are coming down. Shared spaces by all employees—managers and line workers alike—are sending a powerful message of participatory management.

Stereotyping and Prejudice

Pre-judging a person on sight because of that person's age, sex, race, height, weight, physical disability, or sexual orientation can lead to poor communication. If you assume certain negative things about the other party only because of some perceived difference, then you may evaluate any future messages from that person in that light. Therefore it is important to recognize your own stereotyping and prejudices.

An equally inaccurate pitfall is giving someone a "halo." That is, because of having an initial *favorable* impression of someone for one reason or another, your continued perception of that person is positive no matter what. For example, some U.S. officials who participated in the initial formation of the Iraqi Governing Council may have formed favorable impressions of some of the participants in the early deliberations and then failed to adjust those perceptions as the process continued and those same members became obstacles to agreement.

Understanding Emotions

Purposeful use of emotions in a negotiation can help the bargaining process. Researchers Michael W. Morris and Dacher Keltner—studying how emotions shape, direct, or guide an internal thought process—have identified three mechanisms that account for a relationship between emotions and decisions.[25] First, they say that emotions trigger related associations that feed into the thought process. Thus, when a negotiator is angered in the context of a negotiation, he or she will likely recall other anger-producing events. Second, emotions can contribute directly to the way a negotiator is processing particular information. For example, an angry negotiator can use the feeling of anger to evaluate the fairness or unfairness of the opponent's proposals rather than rationally evaluating them. Finally, emotions can cloud judgment, perhaps prompting an angry negotiator to process relevant information in superficial ways.

Emotions affect not only a negotiator's behavior, but also that of the other party and the negotiating process itself. Displays of emotion can convey information about the beliefs and intentions of the parties to a negotiation or whether the negotiations are heading in the right or wrong direction. Displays of dominance by negotiators, for example, convey the nature and importance of their preferences and positions, while embarrassment and shame convey submissiveness. Anger at the bargaining table may signal the importance of the issue to both sides, whereas positive emotions can signal that the opponent is satisfied with a proposal and no additional concessions are necessary.

Emotions tend to evoke either *reciprocal* or *complementary* responses. A flash of anger at the negotiating table may cause an equally angry reaction resulting in an impasse, or it could cause the other party to offer some concession as a way to reduce the negative feelings caused by the outburst.[26] Or, emotions can operate as an incentive, reinforcing the behavior of the party. For example, if a display of anger is "rewarded" at the bargaining table by a concession, then that negotiator may use anger again to gain more concessions. Studies have shown that people express anger in negotiations specifically to induce a concession.[27] And even if there is no immediate reaction to the display of anger, an outburst may cause the opponent to change some of his or her demands in order to avoid another outburst in the future.

Emotions can be used to track or even influence the progress of a negotiation through its different phases. Initially, because the parties are making a decision to engage in a negotiation, sometimes in an uncertain environment certain fears arise: Is this person trustworthy? Is he sincerely interested in making a deal? Can she deliver on her promises? Thus, the first emotions that must be triggered in a negotiation may be *liking* and *interest*. Liking signifies a willingness to enter into a cooperative relationship, and the related expression of interest serves to convey an individual's need to appear as a person worthy of the relationship. Interest is flattering, so it begets a positive mood in response.

Next, the parties begin their positioning phase. This exercise is generally contentious because the parties are presenting their strongest claims to the subject of the negotiation. Either or both parties can express their claims in a dominating manner, which may elicit an angry response. *Anger* can convey information that a negotiator cares deeply about an issue and may be prone to rash action. Anger can elicit a like response or a complementary response of *fear* or *shame*. A display of dominance can also be met with a contempt emotion, such as *pride*. Reacting to demands in a negotiation with pride can be perceived as placing oneself on a higher status that the opponent. The counterresponse to *contempt* may be, again, more anger and an impasse—or perhaps a concession from the original dominating party because he or she wants to resolve the "relational" problem this position phase created.

The third phase of negotiating, the discussion and exchange of counterproposals, and perhaps problem-solving using collaborative techniques, is when the parties are engaged in relatively free discussion, exchanging information about priorities, brainstorming, and mutually evaluating options. If the negotiations are to accomplish their goal, this phase has to include a relationship of trust. The emotional transition from positioning to collaboration can involve embarrassment on the part of the party who has been overly demanding, or can involve the establishment of *rapport*—that is, a state of mutual positive response and interest that is evidenced by such nonverbal displays as nodding, leaning forward, and gesturing.

The endgame in a negotiation is the final phase when the parties shift from problem solving and value creation to actually getting an agreement. The emotions in play at this phase can be *exasperation, accusation,* and *ultimatums.* Another possible emotion that the parties might exhibit at this point in the negotiations is a *fear of commitment.* (Incidentally, some metaphors associated with this fear included a speeding train barreling into a train station, a turbulent sea overwhelming a small boat, and walking a tightrope.[28]) In order to reach agreement, the parties may have to find a way to reestablish the rapport relied upon earlier. There is a point when neither party is willing to make any more concessions; they must either agree, walk away, or engage in the conflict behaviors discussed next. A summary of the kinds of emotions in the different phases of negotiation is presented in Table 5.3.

Table 5.3 Possible Emotions in Negotiation Phases

Negotiation Phases	Goals	Possible Emotions	Characteristics of Emotions
Opening moves	Initiate positive process	Liking, interest	Greeting, eye contact, smile, personal questions, cocked head, forward lean
Positioning	Present one's strongest position	Anger, contempt	Hostile criticism, chopping gestures, dismissive tone, refusing to look at the person speaking
Problem-solving	Engender trust	Embarrassment, empathy	Apologies, blushing, submissive posture, simultaneous smiling, nodding and laughter
Endgame	Create commitment	Exasperation, anger, fear of commitment	Surprise at opponent's reluctance, walking away from negotiations

Source: Adapted from Michael W. Morris and Dacher Keltner, "How Emotions Work: The Social Functions of Emotional Expression in Negotiations," in *Research in Organizational Behavior,* eds. B. M. Staw and R. I. Sutton, (Amsterdam: JAI Press, 2000), vol. 22, 1–50.

PERSUASION THROUGH PROCESS

Michael Watkins, a leading scholar on developing leadership within organizations, identifies core techniques used by skilled leaders to shape the perception of interests and to foster buy-in by members of the organization.[29] His core tasks are as follows:

- Identify who needs to be persuaded and how that person can be influenced.
- Influence the person's belief about what he or she wants.
- Shape the person's belief about what options exist that satisfies his or her need.
- Use a decision-making process that fosters buy-in.

We can apply these tasks to the negotiation process as an effective way to persuade bargaining partners.

Who to Influence and How

In a negotiation, it is important to identify the ultimate decision maker, whether or not that person is the one you are actually negotiating with. In a labor negotiation, for example, the union negotiating team represents the employees and will ultimately present the negotiated agreement to them for approval. The team members are presumed to have influence with the bargaining unit by their presence on the committee. The goal in that negotiation, then, is to influence the negotiating team so that they will influence the members' vote on the agreement that is finally reached.

Many times, you can influence team members by addressing their individual needs or interests rather than the needs or interests of the overall group. For instance, in one recent negotiation of a new contract that had dragged on for almost a year, one of the two union members of the negotiating team wanted to make sure there was a *retroactivity clause* in the contract (a clause that allows any benefits of the contract to be retroactively applied). Numerous proposals from the employer were turned down because they did not contain such a clause. When the employer's negotiators found out that the member of the bargaining team who insisted on retroactivity was planning on retiring as soon as the contract was approved, the personal interest became clear. A subsequent proposal that did allow for a retroactive payment of wages was endorsed by the union negotiating team and accepted by the employees.

In everyday encounters where a bargaining opportunity presents itself, you may not be talking to the actual decision maker. A hotel clerk may be very sympathetic to your complaints about noisy neighbors but may lack the authority to discount your bill. You should quickly identify who has such authority and take your complaint to them.

Shape Perceptions of Interests and Goals

Framing, as discussed throughout this text, involves the use of argument, analogy, and metaphor to create a favorable definition of an issue to be addressed, as well as a set of potential solutions. In a negotiation, people's perception of their interests may be vague or diffused until they are faced with a choice. And they perceive their interests differently depending on how the choices are presented. Some framing techniques to use at the negotiating table are to invoke the *common good* as opposed to an individual benefit, to link the choice to the *core values* of the parties in the negotiation, and to point out *potential gains or losses* from certain choices.

In a neighborhood dispute over the location of a halfway house for teens with drug abuse arrests, an advocate for the home talked about some of the teenagers from the neighborhood who had lost friends or classmates to drugs and alcohol. He reminded their parents how devastating it was when their children had to face a friend's death at such a young age. And how that, but for the grace of God and the supportive families in the neighborhood, their children could be the ones needing a place to go that wasn't jail. By reminding his neighbors that they had a responsibility to try and prevent more such tragedies, and that caring for each other's children was a core value in the neighborhood, he persuaded them to support the halfway house's location.

Use a Negotiating Process That Fosters Buy-In

The key elements to a process that fosters buy-in can be found in *Getting to Yes*, by Roger Fisher and William Ury.[30] The elements of integrative bargaining—including separating the people from the problem, focusing on interests, not positions, offering options for mutual gain, and using objective criteria—support a negotiating style that gains acceptance from the participants. A shared diagnosis of the problem or issue makes it easier to negotiate because both sides acknowledge the existence of the issue or problem. Creating an atmosphere where the negotiating partners are listened to and their ideas are given weight is seen as a fair process. Active listening and a commitment to explore options encourage creative solutions and frame choices by the participants.

LEVERAGING POWER THROUGH PRESSURE TACTICS

In negotiation literature there has been significant support for the use of integrative and interest-based negotiation strategies to reach better agreements. Parties may choose to focus on *interests*—the underlying needs, desires, and goals of the parties—with an intention of constructing an agreement that addresses the needs of both parties. However, people find themselves most often engaging in the more traditional distributive bargaining as they conduct their day-to-day business. In distributive bargaining parties may focus on *rights*—determining by objective standards of fairness, contract, or law what the proper agreement should be. Too often, however, parties focus on *power*—trying to coerce each other to make concession they would not otherwise make.

Researchers Anne L. Lytle, Jeanne M. Brett, and Debra L. Shapiro found that many negotiators actually use both interest-based and power-based techniques at various times in the negotiations.[31] In a study using a simulated dispute between the president of a small printing company and a large computer company, 25 graduate students were paired with non-classmates to resolve a contract dispute in which the small printing company did not receive the software product it thought it should from the large computer company. Both companies stood to profit from a successful installation of computer equipment, so the *interests* of the parties were compatible. However, the printing company felt the parties' contract gave it the *right* to demand performance from the computer company, while the computer company felt the contract clearly relieved it of any obligation to provide software. And because the printing company faced bankruptcy if the computer equipment was not operational, it had *power* at the negotiating table because the computer company would not like the bad publicity. The study showed that parties move frequently among interests, rights, and power, most often in a reciprocal manner. That is, a communication on interests was answered 42% of the time with the other party's interests; rights were answered 22% of the time with the other party's rights; and power was answered 27% of the time with a power response.

This research indicates that it is not really a question of *whether* to use power in negotiations, but rather of *when* and *how* to use it. The strategic use of power in a negotiation can bring parties to the bargaining table, resolve an impasse to keep the parties negotiating, or cause the parties to make and abide by an agreement.[32] Figure 5.3 lists some key concepts when considering the use of power tactics in a negotiation.

For a negotiator to make a threat that has a positive outcome, it is essential that he or she is willing to follow through on the threat and that the demand or action required of the other party is doable. In the simulated contract dispute just described, the printing company was willing to go into bankruptcy if the computer company did not supply the software necessary to make the computer work—and both parties knew that the computer company could supply the software if it was willing to absorb the expense.

If you make a threat, it is important to make sure that it helps achieve your goals and satisfies your interests. Threats should not be made in anger, but should be planned in advance; recognizing the reciprocal nature of threats in negotiations, you should consider the potential impact of a retaliatory response; and you have to determine if the threat will cost you more than it costs the other side. The officer in the Chapter Case came to the litigation negotiations with a plan. She believed it unlikely that her lowball offer would be accepted and would leave the widow with no other option than to pursue the case in court. But she had already calculated the risk of a court decision and was satisfied that it was in her interest to fight the case in court rather than to settle it by making a seven-figure offer.

Most negotiations involve some level of threat or exercise of power in an attempt to change the other party's behavior or position. To be successful, the threat has to be credible. The negotiator must make the opponent believe the threat.[33] For example, after 15 years, Lee Ann wanted to renegotiate her share of her law partnership with Michael, Robert, and Tom. She was motivated by a growing dissatisfaction with the direction of the firm. She felt that she had been shouldering most of the firm's burden through her work for her city clients and not receiving the benefit. She had made statements in the past couple of years that she wanted the firm to change her partnership share or else she would leave—but as those statements generally followed a discussion of how much more work she brought into the partnership than others did, the other partners did not take it seriously. Finally, she had enough and announced her intention to leave the firm by the end of summer if they could not reach agreement on

1. Power is always relative in a negotiation—otherwise why bother to negotiate?
2. Power can be real or apparent.
3. Self-confidence gives you bargaining power.
4. If the other party believes that action can and will be taken against him or her, it may be unnecessary to actually exert power.
5. You don't need a strong position as long as the other side thinks you have one.
6. Power's range is limited by outside influences.
7. Power exists to the extent that it is used.
8. The ends of power can't be separated from the means used.
9. The exercise of power entails cost and risk.
10. Balance of power changes over time in a relationship.

Source: From Chester L. Karrass, Beverly Hills, CA, *The Negotiating Game,* rev. ed. (New York: HarperCollins, 1992), 57–58. Used with permission. www.karrass.com

a larger partnership share for her. Michael was tasked with handling the issue. Lee Ann sought to convince her partners she was serious by using the following tactics:

1. *Change the circumstances so that the cost of not following through on the threat is significant, and is recognized as significant by the other party.* Lee Ann made her announcement in front of the partnership's other employees that either she had a new compensation package or she was leaving. If she didn't follow through on her threat, her credibility with those employees would suffer and the partners knew that.
2. *Visibly and irreversibly restrict your options.* To further prove her point, Lee Ann let the city contract lapse at the end of June and did not ask for it to be renewed.
3. *Expend resources to create a fallback position and make sure the opponent knows it.* And while Lee Ann did not ask for a contract renewal, she did meet with the city's general counsel and discussed the possibility of becoming an in-house attorney for the city's police department. She made sure that Michael was aware of the meeting.
4. *Delegate the authority to carry out the threat so it is just a matter of execution at the appropriate time.* Lee Ann's vacation was scheduled for the last week in August, but she decided to take more time and leave in early August. She let Michael know that if the issue was not resolved by the time she left, she would give her secretary instructions to move her belongings out of the office while she was out of town. Lee Ann's deadline committed both parties to a course of action, as is noted in Box 5.1.
5. *Develop a reputation for following through on threats.* Michael knew Lee Ann well enough to know that she never threatened something in a negotiation that she wasn't willing to do.
6. *Give a convincing preview of the future.* Lee Ann hoped that her long vacation out of the office would convince the partners that they did not want her to leave the partnership and that they would make the changes to the partnership agreement as requested.

BOX 5.1 Traps to Avoid

Setting a Deadline

The owners and players of the National Basketball Association (NBA) reached an impasse in contract negotiations in the summer of 1998. The owners locked out the players and delayed the start of the 1998–1999 pro basketball season. Negotiations were still ongoing in December when the owners declared that if the contract was not resolved by January 8, the entire season would be canceled. Setting the deadline publicly committed the owners to either reach agreement or carry out the threat—which would cost owners and players alike hundreds of millions of dollars. In the early morning hours of January 6, an agreement favorable to the owners was reached. How, then, does this become a trap to avoid?

1. *Deadlines are a two-way street.* Setting a deadline can be a powerful negotiating tool because without a deadline, the other side can use stalling tactics hoping to pressure you for a better deal. But while setting a deadline can move stalled negotiations forward, it can also limit your ability to get the best deal by causing you to concede too quickly. Negotiators who recognize that deadlines affect both sides equally can use deadlines to defuse costly stalling tactics. One way to do this is to establish the deadline at the start of negotiations rather than after an impasse has been reached.

2. *Disclose your deadline.* If you are negotiating under a deadline that the other side doesn't know about, disclose it. If you don't then you will be accelerating your concessions in an effort to get done, but your opponent will not, resulting in a less favorable deal for you. If both sides know there is a deadline they are more likely to work toward an agreement to reach that deadline.

3. *Don't disclose time costs.* Don't confuse a time deadline with time costs. For example, a collective bargaining agreement between a city and its police officers was set to expire on June 30. Both parties were trying to complete negotiations by the deadline. The parties had already agreed on two provisions in the contract—one increased pay for one group of employees but the other reduced pay for a different group, to the city's advantage. Passing the deadline without agreement would cost the city money, which unfortunately the union knew. So on the last day of the expiring contract, the city conceded to a number of items that favored the union.

4. *Don't disclose BATNAs.* Unless your best alternative to a negotiated agreement is strong, do not reveal it even when revealing or setting a deadline. In the preceding example, even though there was a cost to the city for not meeting the deadline, the city's BATNA was stronger than the union's because until the contract was agreed upon, half of the employees would not receive any pay increase.

Source: Adapted from Don A. Moore, "Deadline Pressure: Use It to Your Advantage," *Negotiation* 7 (August 2004): 1–3.

Michael began to explore his options. He first had to decide if he believed not only that Lee Ann could follow through on her threat, but also that she actually would leave. If he thinks she will, then he has to decide if her leaving is more harmful to the partnership than changing her share of ownership in it. In other words, what is the partnership's BATNA? Michael had been in enough negotiations himself to recognize that much of Lee Ann's dissatisfaction stems from her belief that the partners do not truly value her services. Michael decided to offer to sit down with Lee Ann and engage in a joint problem-solving session. They would generate a variety of possible options that could possibly satisfy Lee Ann and the partnership's needs before a decision had to be made. Michael considered asking one of the retired partners from the firm, who had been a mentor to Lee Ann, to join in the discussion and evaluate the suggested solution. Michael had a good idea of the firm's BATNA and understood Lee Ann's needs and was confident he could resolve the issue before her deadline.

SUMMING UP

Drawing upon your experience in an actual negotiation or one of the negotiation exercises from earlier chapters, apply the principles and practices discussed in this chapter.

1. Describe the situation. You believe your BATNA (best alternative to a negotiated agreement) is significantly better than your bargaining partner's BATNA. Discuss the negotiating strategy you might use.

   _____

   _____

2. Your bargaining partner is negotiating as if your BATNA is weak. Describe three tactics you can use to change that perception and/or the reality.

   a. _____

   b. _____

   c. _____

3. Apply the traditional sources of power as appropriate in this negotiation for you and your bargaining partner.

   a. *Your power bases:*

      Control of resources _____

      Position _____

      Control of information _____

      Personal attributes _____

   b. *Your bargaining partner's power sources:*

      Control of resources _____

      Position _____

Control of information _____

Personal attributes _____

4. Formulate three "open-ended" questions to gather information from your bargaining partner.

   a. _____

   b. _____

   c. _____

5. Integrative and interest-based bargaining appeal to a listener's analytical side or one's evaluation of an argument. How would you leverage the *content of your argument* to persuade your bargaining partner?

   _____

   _____

6. Tactics used in distributive bargaining appeal to a listener's intuitive side or to a listener's reaction to the argument. How would you leverage the *presentation of your argument* to persuade your bargaining partner?

   _____

   _____

7. Decide whether you are an *auditor, shaker, sharer,* or *communicator* and decide how you would persuade your bargaining partner if he or she were an *auditor, shaker, sharer,* or *communicator.*

   Persuade an auditor by _____

   Persuade a shaker by _____

   Persuade a sharer by _____

   Persuade a communicator by _____

8. Describe the appropriate communication you should use for an analytical and intuitive presentation of your argument as indicated in the following table:

Communication	Analytical	Intuitive
Voice		
Kinesics		
Eye movement		
Facial expressions		
Gestures		

9. What step would you take to convince your bargaining partner to take seriously your threat to walk away from the negotiation without an agreement?

   _____

   _____

LEARNING EXERCISE: UNHAPPY CO-OWNERS

The purpose of this exercise is to apply the five negotiation skills presented in this chapter to an actual negotiation situation. You have inherited from your parents half of an undivided interest in a summer home with some prime acreage on a nearby lake. Your co-owner was your father's friend and partner in a number of enterprises. For years your two families have shared this summer house on alternating weekends and holidays without any problems. Your co-owner, however, is ready to sell the property and believes someone will buy it to redevelop it from a summer cottage to four upscale vacation homes. You are not interested in selling, but are willing to buy out your co-owner at the current fair market value. That value is considerably less than your co-owner believes the property is worth. When you can't reach agreement, your co-owner simply sells his interest to a third party, who may or may not be the potential developer.

This new co-owner tries to buy you out, and when you refuse he begins to make changes to the property without consulting you. When you complain, he threatens to petition a court to force the sale of the land—which would mean both of you would lose control, which he thinks you are not willing to allow. You decide to try to negotiate a deal so you can continue to use the property as you did when you were growing up. In order to do so, your co-owner will have to shelve any improvement plans he has for the property.

Apply the chapter negotiation skills as you answer the following questions.

Skill 5.1. Assuming your BATNA is letting a court sell the property, can it help you reach an agreement? Why or why not?

Skill 5.2. What are your power sources and your co-owner's power sources in this negotiation? How can you strengthen your power position?

Skill 5.3. Can you present a logical and an emotional argument to persuade your co-owner to agree to a deal?

Skill 5.4. What nonverbal communication technique might you use to persuade your co-owner that your proposal is a win-win proposition?

Skill 5.5. What threat can you make to force your co-owner to make concessions?

ENDNOTES

1. Steven Greenhouse, "UPS and Teamsters Reach Deal for a 25% Raise," *New York Times,* July 17, 2002, A10.

2. C. Marlene Fiol, Edward J. O'Connor, and Herman Aguinis, "All for One and One for All? The Development and Transfer of Power Across Organizational Levels," *Academy of Management Review* 26 (April 2001): 224–242.

3. Deepak Malhotra, "Make Your Weak Position Strong," *Negotiation* 8 (July 2005): 1–4.

4. David Lax and James Sebenius, "The Power of Alternatives or the Limits to Negotiation," in *Negotiation Theory and Practice,* eds. J. William Breslin and Jeffrey Z. Rubin (Cambridge, MA: Harvard Law School Program on Negotiation, 1991), 97–114.

5. Ibid., 107.

6. Joseph S. Nye Jr., "Soft Power and Leadership," *Compass: A Journal of Leadership* 1, (Spring 2004): 28–31.

7. Patricia S. E. Darlington and Becky Michele Mulvaney, *Women, Power, and Ethnicity:*

Working Toward Reciprocal Empowerment (Binghamton, NY: Haworth Press, 2003).

4. Russell B. Korobkin, "Bargaining Power as Threat of Impasse," February 2004, UCLA School of Law, Law and Economics Research Paper No. 04-6, available at the Web site of the Social Science Research Network, http://ssrn.com/abstract=516066 (accessed September 10, 2006).

8. Peter Thompson, *Persuading Aristotle: The Timeless Art of Persuasion in Business, Negotiation, and the Media* (Crows Nest, Australia: Allen & Unwin, 1998), 5–7.

9. Michael Watkins, "Principles of Persuasion," *Negotiation Journal* 17 (April 2001): 115–135.

10. William Ury, *Getting Past No* (New York: Bantam Books, 1993).

11. Shaul Fox and Yair Amichai-Hamburger, "The Power of Emotional Appeals in Promoting Organizational Change Programs," *Academy of Management Executive* 15 (November 2001): 84–93.

12. George Fuller, *The Negotiator's Handbook* (Upper Saddle River, NJ: Prentice Hall, 1991), 63.

13. Charles Craver, *The Intelligent Negotiator* (Roseville, CA: Prima, 2002), 128.

14. Thompson, *Persuading Aristotle*, 43.

15. Donald B. Sparks, *The Dynamics of Effective Negotiation*, 2nd ed. (Houston: Gulf Publishing, 1993), 57.

16. Michael R. Carrell and Christina Heavrin, *The Everyday Negotiator* (Amherst, MA: HRD Press, 2004), 138–140.

17. Virgil Peterson, "The Rabbi's Resolution and the Power of Stories," *Conflict Resolution Notes* 11 (September 1993): 29–30.

18. Deborah M. Kolb and Judith Williams, *Everyday Negotiation* (San Francisco: Jossey-Bass, 2003), 250–254.

19. Richard E. Petty and John T. Cacioppo, *Attitudes and Persuasion: Classic and Contemporary Approaches* (Boulder, CO: Westview Press, 1996), 255–269.

20. Michael T. Stephenson, William L. Benoit, and David Tschida, "Testing the Mediating Role of Cognitive Responses in the Elaboration Likelihood Model," *Communication Studies* 52 (Winter 2001): 324–337.

21. Thompson, *Persuading Aristotle*, 60–78.

22. Michael Wheeler and Dana Nelson, "Nonverbal Communication in Negotiation: An Introductory Exercise," Harvard Business School Note 903-081, January 13, 2004 (Boston: Harvard Business School Press), available from Harvard Business Online, http://doi.contentdirections.com/mr/hbsp.jsp?doi=10.1225/903081.

23. Nicholas Gueguen and Celine Jacob, "Direct Look Versus Evasive Glance and Compliance with a Request," *Journal of Social Psychology* 142 (June 2002): 393–396.

24. Wheeler and Nelson, "Nonverbal Communication in Negotiation," 4.

25. Michael W. Morris and Dacher Keltner, "How Emotions Work: The Social Functions of Emotional Expression in Negotiations," in *Research in Organizational Behavior*, eds. B. M. Staw and R. I. Sutton, (Amsterdam: JAI Press, 2000), vol. 22, 1–50.

26. Jeanne M. Brett, Debra L. Shapiro, and Anne L. Lytle, "Breaking the Bonds of Reciprocity in Negotiations," *Academy of Management Journal* 41 (August 1998): 410–424.

27. Morris and Keltner, "How Emotions Work," 37.

28. Michael Wheeler, "Overcoming Stage Fright: How to Prepare for a Negotiation," *Negotiation* 7 (August 2004): 7–8.

29. Watkins, "Principles of Persuasion," 115–135.

30. Roger Fisher and William Ury, *Getting to Yes* (Boston: Houghton-Mifflin, 1981).

31. Anne L. Lytle, Jeanne M. Brett, and Debra L. Shapiro, "The Strategic Use of Interests, Rights, and Power to Resolve Disputes," *Negotiation Journal* 15 (January 1999): 31–51.

32. Adam D. Galinsky and Katie A. Liljenquist, "Putting on the Pressure: How to Make Threats in Negotiations," *Negotiation* 7 (December 2004): 4–6.

33. Deepak Malhotra, "Making Threats Credible," *Negotiation* 8 (March 2005): 1–4.

Chapter 6

Strategy

*I*n this chapter we address the issue of **negotiation strategy**, which can be defined as the overall approach chosen when confronted with a bargaining situation. We have found that most novice negotiators either jump right into their first negotiating session without having given much thought to an overall strategy, or they look for assistance from someone because they are not sure how to start a negotiation process. Students in negotiation classes, for example—even after weeks of preparation and careful delineation of their priorities—are sometimes perplexed when they first enter a room to negotiate with another party and often ask teammates "So what is our strategy?" or "What's the big picture?" or even "How do we do this?"

The terms *strategy* and *tactics* are often confused and/or used interchangeably. What one experienced negotiator might think of as her primary *strategy* in approaching a negotiation, another might just as easily refer to as his primary negotiating *tactic*. In fact, former U.S. trade representative Charlene Barshefsky, who has negotiated with hundreds of companies and governments, noted that many people confuse tactics with strategy. Barshefsky explains that strategy comes first: A negotiator must know what the objectives are to develop a broad negotiation strategy. Negotiating tactics are the techniques used at the bargaining table. Tactics do not encompass the underlying substance of strategy determination and efforts that occur away from the table, to set up the most promising situation.[1]

Negotiation Skills

In this chapter we present five negotiation skills that can be learned and developed by the novice negotiator, and applied to the end-of-chapter Learning Exercise, "Buying a New Car."

Skill 6.1   *Before choosing a particular strategy, carefully identify and consider the three key elements—**time (deadlines)**,*

CHAPTER CASE: WEST COAST MUSIC INC.

Kevin Carter is president of West Coast Music, a family-owned and -managed chain of music stores in California, Oregon, and Washington. Kevin and his three sisters and two brothers are the third generation of Carters to own the business. In the last 20 years under Kevin's aggressive leadership, the company expanded from three stores in San Luis Obispo County, California, to 12 stores along the West Coast. All of the stores are located in shopping malls and they primarily sell and rent musical instruments, sheet music, organs, and pianos to individuals and school bands. Some of the stores provide private booths for lessons, or larger rooms for group lessons. Kevin over the years has realized that the negotiation of leased space within a mall is the most important management skill he had developed. Usually store owners and managers like Kevin find themselves at a disadvantage when negotiating with mall leasing agents who have much more experience and may feel they have leverage over owners—especially if they control the only mall in a county. As one agent once commented to Kevin, "I have three people that will take your space this week if you don't agree to my terms."

In most situations Kevin is negotiating with a mall's director of leasing for an empty or soon-to-be empty store. Generally five issues are central to the negotiated lease: (1) rent, which averages between $18 and $25 per square foot, or $180,000 to $250,000 per year, for a 10,000-square-foot store; (2) monthly common mall area maintenance charge for security and cleaning the mall open space; (3) store allowance for carpet, lighting, alarm system, computer system, and other fixtures; (4) length of the contract, which averages between 5 and 10 years; (5) mall location, which can include choice of space in a new mall or when two or more vacancies occur, and also variable rents, which apply in some cases and change if the mall experiences high vacancies. Mall location can be critical to some types of retail stores that depend on a high-traffic location to generate customers. Such high-traffic locations are termed "A" traffic locations and are generally close to an anchor tenant, while "B" traffic locations are still on the main floor of the mall but are not close to an anchor tenant store, and "C" traffic locations are generally on the second floor or isolated main floor locations.

KEY STRATEGY ELEMENTS

In deciding what overall strategy should be employed in a given negotiation, the negotiator should first identify and weigh the critical elements. Several experienced negotiators, including Herb Cohen[2] and consultants Peter B. Stark and Jane Flaherty, have identified the basic elements as *time, information,* and *power.*

Time (Deadlines)

The first strategy element—*time*—plays a critical role in many negotiation situations. **Pareto's law** or the "80/20 rule" often applies in negotiations. Pareto's law* simply states that 80% of what is accomplished occurs in 20% of the effort, while the remaining 20% of what is accomplished takes 80% of the effort. In negotiation this often results in 80% of the deal being agreed to in the last 20% of the time spent in bargaining.

Negotiators who effectively use deadlines can cause the last 20% of the time to produce results. As an example, Stark and Flaherty cite the historic 1999 NBA negotiations between the owners and the player's union. The NBA team owners had locked out the players in 1998 and several months of negotiations produced no progress. Then NBA commissioner David Stern set a deadline of January 7, 1999, after which he would cancel the season. On January 6, 1999, within only a few hours of the deadline, both sides reached agreement and season play resumed.[3] Herb Cohen, in his classic book *You Can Negotiate Anything,* also cites time as a critical element to be considered when determining strategy. He asks some telling questions, such as, "When do most people file their tax returns?" and "Given a two-month lead, when do most students start a term paper?" and perhaps most telling of Americans, "When state and city elected bodies must pass an annual budget by July 1st, the start of the new fiscal year, on what day and at what hour is it usually passed?" In most cases both sides have some sort of deadline or preference as to when they'd like a settlement—and given that fact, if negotiators on the other side know your deadline, but you don't know theirs, who has the advantage? Exactly. They do—because they know you will likely make more concessions and/or make poor decisions due to the pressure as your deadline nears.[4]

Therefore, if you in fact have a firm deadline, what should you do? Choose one of three strategies:

1. Without revealing your deadline, work to reach a settlement well in advance.
2. Declare an earlier "deadline" before your *real* deadline.

---

*Named for Vilfredo Pareto, a 19th century Italian economist.

3. Question negotiators on the other side about their deadline—and if you find out their deadline is before yours, agree to it and work to meet it. If it's a deadline for both sides, then neither has an advantage.

Time and deadlines can favor either party and significantly alter the outcome of a negotiation. Stark and Flaherty, however, offer several suggestions (see Box 6.1) that can enable a negotiator to use time effectively. It is very important to realize that you may not be able to identify the critical time or deadline factors at the start of negotiations, and thus during the bargaining process you must always be listening carefully to pick up any important piece of information. For example, a few years ago the elected city council of a major U.S. city held a special meeting on December 31 to decide whether or not the city should enter into a special partnership with a developer on a multimillion-dollar downtown project. The special federal tax incentive, which was a key to the financing of the project, expired at midnight. The council had met on the issue several times before and the vote always ended in a 6–6 tie, thus the

BOX 6.1   Tactics for Success

Use Time to Your Advantage

1. *Have patience.* Because most concessions and settlements occur in the last 20% of the available time, remain level-headed and wait for the right moment to act. As a general rule, patience pays.

2. *Be persistent.* Your counterpart is most likely not going to concede to your needs and desires in the beginning of the negotiation. If your first request does not work, try a different frame, or provide additional information that might persuade your counterpart to make a concession. Don't give up on your first try. Patience and persistence pay off in negotiations.

3. *Move quickly when possible.* There will be times when one or both parties will benefit if negotiations are resolved quickly. If this is the case, sell your counterpart on the benefits to him of a speedy resolution.

4. *Realize that deadlines can be moved, changed, or eliminated.* As your deadline comes near, do not panic. You can change it! Have you ever wondered why so many people run to the post office to file their tax returns at the last minute on April 15 when they could easily file an extension, gaining another four months or more to send in their forms?

5. *Know your counterpart's timeline.* In most negotiations, you are better off if you know your counterpart's deadline and she does not know yours. As you near her deadline, your counterpart's stress level will increase, and she will be more likely to make concessions.

6. *Make time work for you.* As a rule, you will not achieve the best outcome quickly. Although there are some exceptions, you will usually be better off moving slowly and with perseverance, even if it means changing your deadline.

Source: Peter B. Stark and Jane Flaherty, *The Only Negotiating Guide You'll Ever Need* (New York: Broadway Books, 2003), 20. Used by permission.

project had not been approved. Due to a tax law change, if the council did not pass the legislation, the project would die at midnight. At 3:00 P.M. another vote was taken and the result was, again, a 6–6 tie. During a break, the tired and weary pro-project group was ready to concede when someone told the council president, their leader, that one member of the anti-project group would be leaving at 5:30 to attend a church service he had never missed in 27 years. When the meeting resumed at 5:00 P.M., the president asked his members to filibuster on the next vote until he gave them a signal to call for the vote. At 5:45 he gave the signal and the project passed 6–5, and the meeting was adjourned. The president realized that timing—not an issue of substance and not a negotiated compromise—was what gave him the outcome they had sought for weeks.[5]

Information

The second critical element—*information*—has been called "the heart of negotiations." Why? Information shapes our appraisal of reality, our negotiation strategy, our BATNA, our expectations of what can be achieved and the outcome of a negotiation.

Consider, for example, how information shapes your appraisal of the price of a new Ford Escape Hybrid SUV. The sticker price is $36,000 for one with the options you desire. You call the dealer in your small town where you bought your last car and a saleswoman tells you the Escape Hybrids are brand new, hot-selling models. You read a newspaper article, which confirms that and says some people even pay above the sticker price to buy one of the first ones delivered. The price of gas is skyrocketing, notes the article, and thus all hybrid vehicles are selling like hotcakes.

At this point, what would you expect to pay for a new Escape Hybrid? Now suppose that a week later you read an ad in the newspaper—the dealer has a "special weekend price" on all Escape Hybrids, a $1,500 discount! You call the saleswoman and she says the one you drove and liked just sold, but more will be arriving each week. Then you see one in your neighbor's driveway, and he tells you he "got a great deal" through a friend—and paid only $2,000 below sticker. Your daughter then brings you a *Consumer Reports* article that tells you how to get the lowest price on a new car. You try it, and the *Consumer Reports* estimated price is exactly what your neighbor paid. At this point what would you expect to pay for one?

Finally you decide to use the Internet to find the lowest price within 100 miles. After a few days and several e-mails, you decide that the lowest price is at a dealer 80 miles away in a large city, and that price is $3,000 below sticker, or $33,000. You make the trip and purchase the Escape. A week later a co-worker tells you she bought the identical vehicle from the largest Ford dealer in Dallas, about 200 miles from your home. She paid $28,500. *Now* what would you expect to pay for a similar Escape Hybrid? If you are like most people, the price you would expect to pay changed as you received more information!

Often, but not always, more information discovered both before and during a negotiation process makes you a better negotiator. The party that has more and better information is more likely to negotiate a better outcome. Why, given this fact—which probably doesn't surprise anyone—do people fail to get adequate information? Experienced negotiators offer several possible answers based on their observations. For one, people regard a negotiation encounter as a limited or one-time event and simply fail to anticipate that they will need information until they are heavily involved in negotiations, when by then it's too late and they have become convinced by a shrewd negotiator that they "can't get a better deal anywhere else" or "this one won't last long" or they are under a deadline.[6] Another reason is that novice negotiators believe the process doesn't start until they meet the other party face-to-face, and thus they don't prepare at all, giving the other party the distinct advantage of framing its own information as "complete and objective" and anchoring the discussion with its opening offer. As discussed in Chapter 3, this lack of preparation can provide a great advantage to the other party. A third reason negotiators may fail to obtain the information they need can be summed up in a simple word: Homework! Some people view preparation as another form of homework, which it is, but it's also something they developed a dislike for in school. If you are one of those people, ask a friend, relative, or neighbor who likes "doing their homework" to help you prepare before the negotiations—or hire someone!

The most important piece of information, of course, is your BATNA. As discussed in Chapter 2, you should never enter into a negotiation situation without deciding your BATNA. In our Chapter Case, Kevin always starts a store lease negotiation by determining his BATNA or walk-away price—the lease cost per square foot. In one instance the leasing agent insisted on an amount that exceed Kevin's BATNA. The location had been empty for more than two years because it was near a "gentleman's club" and thus other businesses were not interested in it. Kevin, however, realized that the operating hours of the club were different from the hours of his store, and thus he believed it posed little problem. After a year of not being able to negotiate a lease price below his BATNA, Kevin stopped calling the agent. Then one day he read in the newspaper that the owner had failed in his legal bid to get the city to issue a zoning restraint against the club, which would have closed it down. Kevin again called the agent, and was able to get a lease price below his BATNA.

Unlike Kevin, however, novice negotiators may make one or more of several mistakes regarding their BATNAs. First, they may set a broad or vague BATNA, which cannot be easily used as an absolute minimum or maximum (for example, "I won't take less than what it was worth last year"), thus not exactly realizing when their BATNA has been crossed. Or, they may allow a savvy negotiator to talk them out of their BATNA with ploys such as "I don't want you to pay any more than you can afford" or "How much per month do you think you can afford?" Another mistake is that they simply don't stick to their BATNA because they become psychologically entrapped by the process itself. This tends to occur when people find themselves bidding against each other, and the desire to "win" or "beat" the other person causes them to continue negotiating beyond their BATNA or other rational stopping point. A classic example of such **psychological entrapment** (or auction fever) occurs when buyers are looking for a new house or attending an auction. Entrapped bidders, who win the auction but pay too much, often experience the "winner's curse" (see Chapter 3) because they later realize that they paid well above the item's value.[7] Box 6.2 offers suggestions from experienced negotiator Leigh Thompson on how to protect your BATNA by avoiding these traps.[8]

Protect Your BATNA

1. Set a *specific* BATNA—*before* you start negotiating—and stick to it! It must be an exact amount or value, not a vague reference such as "over costs" or "more than last year."
2. Write down your BATNA (or reservation point) on a piece of paper, put it in your pocket—and whenever you receive an offer, refer to it. If you are tempted to settle for less than your BATNA, stop negotiating, go home, and reassess your BATNA before you consider the offer.
3. Never reveal your BATNA! Many salespeople as well as other experienced negotiators will work hard to get you to reveal your BATNA. Consider how much *your* position would be improved if you knew *their* BATNA!

Source: Adapted from Leigh Thompson, *The Mind and Heart of the Negotiator* (Upper Saddle River, NJ: Prentice Hall, 1998), 18–20, 26–28.

Power

The third critical element—*power*—was discussed in detail in Chapter 5. As you review the critical elements of time, information, and power before determining a negotiation strategy, it may be useful to consider the words of Patrick J. Cleary, former chairman of the National Mediation Board: "More than anything else—yes, even more than money—the negotiation process is about power, ego, leverage, and saving face."[9]

In most negotiation situations either one party has substantial power, and thus leverage to influence a settlement—or else there exists a general balance of power, and to reach a settlement both sides must realize a gain that is greater than if no settlement is reached. How does one side gain substantial leverage, and what will they do with it? Cleary cites "the world's best example of leverage": his Uncle Bernie, who bought a parcel of land where he hoped to build his retirement home some day. Then, many years later when he visited the lot again, he discovered that someone had built a house on his lot! As Cleary notes, no one ever had greater leverage than his Uncle Bernie, who didn't even need to file a lawsuit to get the builder of that house to build him a beautiful home on a much better lot.[10] Keep in mind, however, that few of us find ourselves in a situation like Uncle Bernie's. Instead, we need to carefully review the three critical elements of our negotiation—time, information, and power—and decide how these factors frame the entire negotiation situation, and therefore what strategy we should pursue as we begin to negotiate with the other party.

Therefore, we present five broad strategies that can be employed in various negotiation situations. These five strategies, summarized in Table 6.1, include (1) increments of concession (focus on "the number"); (2) principled negotiation (integrative bargaining); (3) multiple equivalent simultaneous offers (MESOs); (4) the economic matrix; and (5) 3-D negotiation.

Table 6.1 Five Negotiation Strategies for Various Situations

Strategy	When to Consider	Description/Objective
1. Increments of concession (focus on "the number")	For distributive bargaining; single issue such as price; no long-term relationship	To create a pattern of concessions that will enable you to negotiate the best deal
2. Principled negotiation	Method of integrative bargaining; positive long-term relationship important; multiple issues	To move both parties beyond setting and defending their "positions" to discussing their true "interests," which may enable them to discover new settlement points that satisfy their true interests
3. Multiple equivalent simultaneous offers (MESOs)	For negotiations involving multiple issues, some objective and some subjective	To identify all the issues and prioritize them, identify different possible outcomes for each issue by assigning "points," and then develop multiple options of equal value to present to the other party
4. Economic matrix	For negotiations involving multiple issues, all of which can be assigned an objective value, usually dollars	Same as for MESO strategy, except all options are given dollar values instead of points, and then multiple equal-valued options are presented to the other party
5. 3-D negotiation	When negotiations stall or do not proceed well	To reframe the entire setup of the overall negotiation situation to influence the outcome

STRATEGY 1: INCREMENTS OF CONCESSION (FOCUS ON "THE NUMBER")

A common and often successful strategy in many distributive bargaining negotiations—especially one-time purchases of a house or car, dealings with vendors, or labor negotiations—is how to make concessions that will enable you to achieve a price (or cost) that is within your reservation point or BATNA. Often you expect both sides to make extreme opening offers, and then the majority of the negotiation is focused on "the number"—a final number or price, within the opening offers, that both sides will agree upon. Most homebuyers have gone through a similar process. The listed price is $390,000, and you want the house, but of course at the lowest price possible. You can defend your opening offer of $310,000 because another house in the neighborhood sold for that price (even though you also know it's not an identical home). You expect your offer to be rejected, and it is, and no counter is offered by the seller—so now what? What will determine the final price ("the number") between the opening offers of $390,000 and $310,000 that both sides will agree upon? The answer, to a great extent, depends on what strategy of concessions is utilized.

In this situation, consider a strategy of **increments of concession**, which means that you choose a pattern of concessions that will lead the other party to guess that

Figure 6.1 Increments of Concession

A seller's listed house price is $390,000, and the seller rejects the buyer's first offer in each of the following three patterns without making a counteroffer, and continues to reject additional offers until an agreement is reached. From the pattern of the buyer's additional offers, what would the seller likely estimate to be the buyer's BATNA? In each case the buyer's increments of concession lead the seller to estimate a different BATNA held by the buyer.

Pattern A: Split the Difference
Buyer's opening offer = $310,000
Buyer's second offer = $ 350,000
Buyer's third offer = $ 370,000
Buyer's fourth offer = $380,000

Pattern B: Equal Increments
Buyer's opening offer = $310,000
Buyer's second offer = $330,000
Buyer's third offer = $350,000
Buyer's fourth offer = $370,000

Pattern C: Decreasing Increments
Buyer's opening offer = $310,000
Buyer's second offer = $330,000
Buyer's third offer = $ 340,000
Buyer's fourth offer = $345,000

you have a certain BATNA (usually not the actual figure)—and thus they will offer concessions that enable you to achieve your *real* BATNA and get the best deal.[11] This strategy can also sometimes work if you allow the other party to guess your real BATNA.

Consider the three different patterns of concession in Figure 6.1 and picture yourself as the seller. For each of the three buyer patterns, what would you guess is the buyer's BATNA? The buyer in pattern A is simply *evenly splitting the difference* between your price and his last offer—a simple and common strategy likely to end up very close to your listed price. Thus you can estimate the buyer's BATNA to be very close to your asking price, or you might even assume that the buyer has not set a BATNA. With pattern B, the buyer is increasing his offer by *the same increment* each time—again a simple strategy likely to end up close to your listed price. In pattern C, however, the buyer makes offers of *decreasing increments* and appears to be closing in on a number, probably $350,000. Therefore, the pattern of increments would lead you to believe that $350,000 is the buyer's BATNA, and therefore once it is offered would be his last and highest offer. You would thus be more likely to respond to pattern C with a lower counteroffer than to patterns A or B, and therefore the buyer is more likely to achieve a lower settlement price. A negotiator, when faced with a similar negotiating situation, should very carefully consider what pattern of concessions to make because the pattern is likely to affect the settlement point.

While it may seem like an obvious tactic to retain a focus on "the number" when that number represents a party's BATNA or reservation point—and for most experienced negotiators this is indeed what happens—for novice negotiators, this is not always true. Our research with novice negotiators indicates that when they must negotiate several economic or other complex issues over several days or weeks, they will in fact exceed their reservation point in the "heat of battle" or simply to bring the negotiations to closure. On the other hand, when a team of 3 to 5 negotiators is used and one individual is given the almost exclusive duty of maintaining a running total of the cost of the issues that have been settled, the probability of exceeding the reservation point is lessened.

STRATEGY 2: PRINCIPLED NEGOTIATION

The strategy to practice integrative bargaining makes sense in many situations that include a valued relationship between the parties, many issues, and a desire to develop mutual-gains for parties. If integrative bargaining is preferred, then the "principled negotiation" strategy can be practiced. Roger Fisher and William Ury, in their landmark book *Getting to Yes*, introduced the strategy of "principled negotiation," which has gained tremendous support since then and today is commonly employed. Fisher and Ury explain how most traditional negotiators use the strategy of **positional bargaining**, which means that in a distributive bargaining situation, each side determines its BATNA, makes an opening offer, guesses the BATNA of the other side, and then begins to haggle over the perceived difference. Each side gives reasons why its position is the "best" and offers to make concessions in order to reach an agreement. The entire negotiation process is about each party presenting and defending its position. Often the negotiators get emotionally involved and locked into their arbitrary positions. The more negotiations focus on these positions, the less they discuss what the negotiators are really interested in—the issues.

The **principled negotiation** strategy differs from positional bargaining in several ways, according to Fisher and Ury:

1. Principled negotiators don't bargain over arbitrary positions, but instead openly discuss the issues and interests that are important.
2. Principled negotiators separate the people from the positions.
3. Principled negotiators develop mutual-gain options.
4. Principled negotiators focus discussion on objective criteria such as principles and facts, instead of on arbitrary positions.[12]

Positions Versus Interests

Many negotiators engage in positional bargaining because they mistakenly believe that they must keep their real interests to themselves. Therefore they reveal only their position—often a specific value—to the other party, and assume the other party will reveal only its position. Then they proceed with the "ritual dance" of trading concessions, trying to find a middle-ground number that both will accept. Principled negotiation, on the other hand, requires both parties to go beyond their stated positions and instead discuss the desires, needs, fears, and other factors—in other words, the *interests*—that led them to their stated position.

A **position** may be defined as the specific demand that a party has chosen, while its **interests** include the needs, desires, concerns, and fears that caused the party to choose that position. Principled negotiation involves revealing and reconciling interests rather than simply defending and exchanging positions on issues. It works because in most cases several positions exist that may satisfy an interest. Thus if the other side's stated position is unacceptable, then it is likely that other positions exist that are acceptable but can only be found by discussing each side's underlying interests. By openly discussing their true interests, both sides have a greater probability of reaching a settlement. It is naïve to think that the other side's stated position on an issue is the only position that will satisfy its interests.

For example, consider the true story of two next-door neighbors—let's call them Smith and Jones—who once fought constantly over the dogs owned by the Jones family. The Smiths had called the police to complain at least 20 times over the past few years, and finally forced Jones to court over the issue. The judge required the parties to negotiate a peaceful settlement. In their first meeting Smith took the position that Jones must get rid of the dogs, and Jones responded he had a right to keep the dogs. Smith, a wealthy home builder, then suggested that the Joneses sell him their house for $200,000. Jones was insulted and responded with "We lived on this street long before you did! Our children love their school, our best friends live just down the street, and we won't sell just to satisfy you!" Both sides then returned to their positions regarding the dogs, and nothing was achieved. The judge then ordered a mediator to sit down with both parties.

The mediator asked whether both agreed that they could not live next to each other in harmony. Both agreed they could not, that something had to give. The mediator then asked each what they wanted as far as their home and the dogs. Smith responded that he and his wife had built their custom home only five years ago, and had no idea they were moving next door to three large dogs, whose barking was a constant annoyance and kept them awake most nights. They wanted peace and quiet. Jones responded that they moved into their house 32 years ago, and although their home was a little small for their family of six, they loved the street and neighborhood. They noted that their best friends lived on the street. The mediator then asked Smith, as a builder, what might he be able to do to accommodate both interests. The next day Smith responded that he could build the Jones family a new, slightly larger home on the vacant lot on the next block, and pay all moving costs. However, he would expect the Jones house and property in exchange. With this proposal, the Jones family would be able to stay on the street near their friends but move into a better home, and the Smith family would acquire the house next door, which they could rent or tear down—either way controlling the noise. Smith and Jones both agreed to the proposal because both their interests were being met. If they had discussed only their original positions—the fate of the dogs—they would never have resolved the situation. A summary of their positions and interests is presented in Table 6.2.

Separate People from Positions

People (not computers) most often conduct negotiations—and people have feelings, egos, anger, and other human emotions that can interfere if not in fact prevent a settlement from being reached. Human responses to the positions taken by other parties can easily derail a bargaining situation that might otherwise be successful. This is particularly true if the parties have maintained a long-term relationship. The classic

Table 6.2 The Positions Versus Interests of Neighbors Smith and Jones

Party	Positions	Interests
Smith	1. The dogs must go!	1. We need peace and quiet.
	2. We will not move!	2. Our house is new, thus we prefer to stay in it.
Jones	1. The dogs must stay!	1. We must let the dogs out in our enclosed yard.
	2. We will not move!	2. We love the neighborhood and want to stay on the same street, near our friends.

case that comes to mind is between a wife and husband who are discussing where to spend Labor Day weekend. The husband wants to play golf with friends, but the wife wants to go to their cabin on a nearby lake.

To separate the *people* involved from their *positions*, the first thing to do is avoid any emotional outbursts or anger, which would likely be viewed as a personal attack on the other party. Second, don't discuss an issue on a personal basis, such as by saying, "You always want to go to the lake!" Instead, discuss the issue itself: "I understand you want to go to the lake—so what exactly do you want to do there?" Third, try to see the situation from their perspective, determine what their goals might be, and thus seek mutually agreeable options. In almost any negotiation, this skill can be critical. Most people have reasons for their positions—so if you can "step into their shoes" and view the situation from their perspective, you gain an appreciation for their position and often can find a mutually satisfying solution. Thus, if the wife in our example responds with "I need the peace and quiet of sitting on the porch and reading uninterrupted for hours—but I still want to be with you for dinner and for walks along the lake," then the husband might respond with "I understand—so how about if we go to the lake, but I invite my friends down for rounds of golf at the nearby course on Saturday and Monday?"

Focus on Objective Criteria

Positional bargaining is a contest of wills and emotions—a struggle to see which party can bluff the best, shout the loudest, talk the longest. Why? Because each makes arbitrary demands like "The price is $500, because I say it is." Then the other party counters with its own arbitrary demand of "I'll offer $350, and that's it." Too often either no settlement is reached or the person with the strongest will prevails. In positional bargaining, both sides constantly defend arbitrary positions, and their lack of objective criteria causes the other party to reject their position, and only defend their own.

In principled bargaining, on the other hand, the parties present offers based on **objective criteria** such as facts, principles, or a standard. Examples of objective criteria include such factors as cost, past precedent, documented market value, or similar results from recent transactions. The key is that when parties propose a solution, such as a price, they provide the criteria on which they based their number. They can answer a key question: "Why is that a fair number?"

Develop Mutual-Gain Options

In Chapter 1 we discussed the need to recognize the fact that parties will not agree to a proposed settlement unless they perceive it to be superior to no agreement at all. If you view a negotiation merely as the haggling over a single issue, such as price, then too often discussions will end unsuccessfully. Inexperienced negotiators often do not consider creating multiple options, for several reasons.[13] First, it is not natural to think in terms of what the *other* party might gain. What *is* natural is to think along the lines of "This is what I want—now how do I get it?" Also, people view bargaining as narrowing the gap between two initial offers, rather than as a means of finding a mutually agreeable solution to a problem. The fixed-pie constraint can further prevent negotiators from seeking **mutual-gain options**, as people assume there are a limited amount of resources to distribute. Finally, many people see the problems of the other party as the other party's problems, and don't easily recognize the need to find mutually satisfactory solutions.

How can negotiators develop mutual-gain options? Usually the first step is to agree to openly discuss the interests of both parties and then list them. Then consider different means by which each issue might be satisfied. Consider, for example, the Chapter Case. In one lease renewal situation that involved a location in a new upscale mall, Kevin Carter believed that a deal was not possible. West Coast Music simply could not risk $25 per square foot, or $250,000 per year, for the 10,000-square-foot store. The leasing director, however, was firm that he could not lower the price for Kevin when he had other new tenants paying that rate per square foot.

Kevin decided to find an option that was mutually beneficial to both, without jeopardizing his business. He strongly believed that West Coast Music would be an ideal store for the mix of retailers already signed in the new mall. Then one day he realized that the leasing agent for this particular new mall had never seen a West Coast Music store. Thus he arranged for the agent to visit him at one of his existing locations. During the visit Kevin focused their discussion on the quality of the store and how it would consistently bring new customers into the mall for music lessons (with parents often shopping in the mall while waiting for their child to finish a lesson). The leasing agent became convinced that the music store would be a good fit with the other stores, to the point that he was willing to hear a new rent proposal. Kevin then proposed a new lease formula that provided a fixed lease amount per year ($65,000) plus a variable amount that would rise as the store's sales volume increased (6% of sales up to $600,000; 8% of sales between $600,000 and $1.2 million, and 10% of sales above $1.2 million). In addition, the lease would be for a 10-year period instead of the usual 5-year period. The key to the leasing proposal was that it provided a mutual gain for both sides. The leasing agent avoided giving Kevin a lower rent deal than his other tenants but might realize a higher rent in the long run if the store was successful, and he also had a longer-term lease. Kevin could not afford the fixed annual rent in the original proposal, but he would be able to afford higher rent in future years if sales rose and the store had a greater "ability to pay."

Kevin's mutual-gains offer included the **ability to pay** concept, which has existed for many years in labor–management contracts. Union negotiators may insist that if an employer experiences higher profits or revenue, then the employer has the ability to pay higher wages and benefits. The movement to longer labor contracts in recent years (the average is more than three years) has created greater pressure on management to agree to methods by which increased ability to pay during the life of the contract will result in higher wages and benefits. Either a profit-sharing plan or a one-time bonus clause, for example, now appear in approximately 25% of all U.S. contracts as a means of providing higher wages if an employer experiences greater profits during the life of a contract.[14]

STRATEGY 3: MULTIPLE EQUIVALENT SIMULTANEOUS OFFERS (MESOs)

When setting the agenda for negotiation, you can narrow the focus on specific issues, identify alternatives, and establish the criteria for evaluating those alternatives. By making sure there are a number of alternatives, you increase the odds that the other side will be satisfied with one of them, and that an agreement will be reached. **Multiple equivalent simultaneous offers (MESOs)** provide a versatile strategy that allows you to create a scoring system to compare qualitatively different issues so that the best option can be identified.[15]

The MESO technique involves three basic steps: (1) Identify and then prioritize three or more issues in the negotiation, determining their *weights* or relative value to the parties. (2) Identify the different outcomes or options available for each issue, establishing one as the standard and thus worth 100 "points," and then consider the *relative value* of each other option by comparison to that standard. (3) Create three different but approximately equal offers by multiplying the weights by the values and generating the point total of the offer. Why three different offers? Research indicates that parties can effectively compare three offers without feeling overwhelmed by too many options.[16]

Now let's apply the MESO strategy to a situation in which an employee is preparing for a meeting with her employer about a possible career change. This situation is summarized in Table 6.3 and you may find it helpful to refer to the table as you read the following description.

The employee knows that there are various options to be discussed at the meeting. She wants to quantify the options and determine which are most important to her, and then determine how the different options will impact their relative importance. First she identifies what she believes to be the four most important issues: compensation, promotion opportunity, job responsibilities, and job location. She also assigns weights to each of the four issues: compensation at 40%, promotion opportunity at 30%, responsibilities at 20%, and location for the new position at 10%. Second, she identifies possible alternative outcomes for each issue and assigns a relative value to each. For example, the compensation could range from $155,000 to $200,000. Also, being located at an office within her hometown has more value to her than being assigned to a neighboring state. Third, she creates three packages of options, which are of approximate equal value in terms of points. The first, MESO #1, combines the highest compensation with lower values of the other three options. MESO #2 and MESO #3 include lower compensation with higher values of the other three options. Using this matrix, the employee will be able to emphasize the options that are most important to her and give the employer a number of opportunities to come to a satisfactory agreement.

Table 6.3 Calculating MESO Options

Issues and Options	Weight of Issue (W)	Value of Option (V)	MESO #1 • $200,000 • Another state promotion • Supervising other employees • Company's home office (W × V)	MESO #2 • $170,000 • Regional promotion • Manage a unit • Hometown (W × V)	MESO #3 • $185,000 • Regional promotion • Head of office • Another state (W × V)
Compensation	40%				
1. $200,000		100	40 pts.		
2. $185,000		75			30 pts.
3. $170,000		50		20 pts.	
4. $155,000		25			
Promotion opportunity	30%				
1. In home office		100			
2. In region		75		22.5 pts.	22.5 pts.
3. In another state		50	15 pts.		
Responsibilities	20%				
1. Manage a unit		100		20 pts.	
2. Manage an office		75			15 pts.
3. Supervising other employees		50	10 pts.		
Location	10%				
1. Hometown		100		10 pts.	
2. Home office (company)		75	7.5 pts.		
3. Another state		50			5 pts.
Package values			72.5 pts.	72.5 pts.	72.5 pts.

Source: Adapted from Victoria Husted Medvec and Adam D. Galinsky, "Putting More on the Table: How Making Multiple Offers Can Increase the Final Value of the Deal," *Negotiation* 8 (April 2005): 4–6.

This strategy enables the employee to frame three offers of approximately equal value to the employer, all of which represent approximately equal value to her (72.5 points). The strategy also enables her to anchor the negotiation in her favor! How? Because she set high and low anchor points on four issues. The employer can, of course, reject all three options, add additional issues, or change the values assigned to options. However, if that occurs, the employee has gained valuable information about the employer's interests, and it is very likely that some version of a MESO option will be accepted by both parties. Thus the MESO strategy has provided a valuable tool for shaping the negotiation process.

In general, a MESO strategy might be successful in the following instances:

1. When the other party has made a first offer and you need to reframe the negotiation in terms of the issues and options that are important to you

2. When the other party is a novice or unskilled negotiator who cannot easily package and compare all the issues
3. When you realize that you are in a lower power position and need a strategy that might level the playing field

In the example just discussed, the employee might easily believe she is in a lower power position than her employer, especially in terms of discussing salary, but the MESO strategy is likely one she would feel more comfortable presenting.

Why might the MESO strategy appeal to a negotiator? When one negotiator presents options of equal value instead of a single fixed position, the second party is likely to respond positively to the strategy because, for one thing, people like having choices—they generally prefer being able to choose among options rather than being asked to "accept or reject" one offer. Moreover, one of the MESO options is likely to have greater perceived value to the second party, and since they all are of equal value to the offering party, the preferred option may easily be acceptable to both, or at least provide a starting point to develop a settlement. Another reason MESO is successful is because most negotiators prefer to have input into a settlement. This strategy enables them to choose a preferred option or at least to provide additional issues and/or change the point values of options—all of which are significant inputs.[17]

The MESO strategy, however, does have disadvantages that you should consider before adopting it. First, it is a somewhat complex strategy that requires that several legitimate issues and options for each be developed. Second, astute opponents may try to "cherry-pick" the options they prefer for each issue and create their own MESO alternatives, which you may find unacceptable. In our example (refer to Table 6.3), the employer might respond with, "I prefer the $155,000 salary, promotion in another state, supervising other employees, and moving to another state"—which would have a combined point value of only 35 and thus not be nearly as attractive to the employee. The employee in that situation would need to respond with a new set of MESO combinations. A third potential disadvantage of the MESO strategy is the need to reveal much about one's own interests, perhaps more than is desired.[18]

STRATEGY 4: THE ECONOMIC MATRIX

The MESO strategy can be taken one step further when a negotiation situation involves several issues of economic value (usually approximate dollar values) and a fixed amount of resources available for the parties to negotiate. By estimating the dollar value of each option for each issue, the subjective assigning of points required in the MESO strategy is eliminated. The MESO strategy is likely to be more useful if some issues (such as location and responsibilities, in our previous example) are not easily reduced to dollar amounts. The *economic matrix* strategy, however, if appropriate, offers the potential advantages of the MESO strategy and the advantage of easier, direct comparisons of options measured by dollars instead of points.

In many cases, longtime negotiating partners develop bargaining patterns that can facilitate reaching an agreement quickly. However, such patterns developed after years of interactions can also work against the parties when one or the other wishes to change the bargaining relationship. In a recent negotiation between an employer and his employees, due to fiscal realities the employer had no choice but to demand that the employees make economic concessions in health care coverage. Over the years and through mostly good economic times, the employees had entered into each new contract negotiation with the understanding that all prior benefits would stay in place and that the negotiation was only about wage increases or new benefits. But a downturn in the economy and the rising cost of health care insurance had stretched the employer's resources to the limit. To avoid layoffs and actual wage decreases, the employer believed the union should be forced to accept only modest wage increases and a reduction of employee benefits.

The negotiating pattern established by this employer and the union was typical distributive bargaining. The parties would start with basic ground rules, including agreement to negotiate all noneconomic issues before tackling economic issues. The employer would propose modest changes in operational areas, which the union would object to just long enough to justify multiple negotiating sessions. This set the stage for the union to bring in its "economic package," which was always much higher than the union anticipated receiving. The employer would offer much less than he believed he would have to pay to reach agreement.

The employer believed that in order to get the union to accept lesser economic benefits, he would have to dramatically change the negotiating process the parties had followed for years. His strategy was to come to the initial meeting with a complete economic and noneconomic package, which included significant operational changes to the grievance and arbitration process in the contract as well as no increase in wages for the first year of the multiyear contract and very modest increases in the subsequent years. More importantly, the economic package proposed reducing and/or eliminating a number of employee benefits including eliminating or reducing annual bonuses based on years of service, eliminating free family health care coverage, reducing the benefits of the health care coverage, reducing the number of paid holidays, eliminating a clothing and equipment allowance, restricting the use of paid sick leave, and increasing employee contributions to the pension plan. The employer proposed in his ground rules that the parties agree on economic issues before starting on noneconomic issues. And the employer's negotiator let the union know that he had a complete proposal to give them when they were ready.

The initial reaction from the union's negotiating team was surprise, quickly followed by annoyance. The union's negotiator was not prepared to make an economic proposal and did not want to change the way the parties had negotiated in the past. He did not know why the employer wanted to start with the economic package, so he was unwilling to agree to the ground rules. However, the union members on his negotiating team wanted to know what was in the employer's proposal. Seeing it sitting on the table across from them was just too tempting. By the end of the day, the parties had agreed to discuss economic issues first before going on to noneconomic issues.

The initial proposal from the employer was certainly what the union could have expected—that is, far below what the employer could anticipate the union would accept. However, it became clear after more than two months of negotiating that *the union was not taking the employer's proposal seriously.* The employer hoped to have a contract in place when the existing contract expired at the end of the calendar year.

After several months with no progress, the employer's negotiator decided that something drastic had to be done to get the union's attention.

A totally new strategy was needed, and thus the negotiator created a new strategy called the **economic matrix**. In general, the strategy contains three core elements:

1. Bringing together several economic issues into one proposal
2. Limiting the total value of the economic issues, so that an increase in one requires a decrease in another
3. Providing options of equal value to the other party

Therefore the economic matrix strategy, like the MESO strategy, contains three potential advantages. First, instead of trying to negotiate the economic issues individually, the focus is shifted to the *total* value or cost of the economic issues. Second, the other party is likely to respond more positively because generally people prefer having choices, and one of the options might be of greater perceived value to the other party, whereas the first party (who created the matrix) doesn't have a preference among the choices and is only concerned with the total value or cost associated with each option. Third, a matrix of options gives the other party significant input into the negotiated decision—even if it is only choosing among options.[19] In this particular example, the total cost represented a decrease from the current value of the employee benefits, but the same strategy could also be utilized if the total represented an increase.

The employer's negotiator put together an economic matrix (see Figure 6.2), which in essence was a review of the economic variables on the table, and a forecast of future conditions to show the union why economic concessions were necessary. He also identified the amount of savings from the employees to balance the budget. Then the employer laid out a number of options on how to reach that goal in a matrix design with each option costed-out for the union negotiators to analyze. The employer's negotiator gave the matrix to the union's negotiating team and explained that the employer would let the union decide where to make the cuts to reach the necessary savings. The parties caucused and when they returned to the negotiations, the mood of the union's negotiating team was significantly different.

Seeing the anticipated cuts in benefits laid out as choices in a matrix had a sobering effect on the union. It became clear that the employer's intent to negotiate significant reductions in benefits was the reason he insisted on discussing the economic issues first, why he had a complete proposal at the initial negotiations, and why he had initially proposed such a lean total package.

The union ignored the employer's economic matrix at the next negotiating session, so at the subsequent session the employer proposed the matrix again, this time with some of the options removed. There was only one more negotiating session after that one. Then the union's chief negotiator and the union president began "back room" meetings with the employer's CFO and an agreement was reached.

The agreement froze wages for one year and then allowed a modest 2% increase in subsequent years. All employee benefits stayed in place, except that in the second year of the contract the employees began to contribute to the cost of health insurance premiums and their contributions would increase each year of the contract after that.

Figure 6.2 An Employer's Economic Matrix

November 15, 2004
EMPLOYER ECONOMIC PROPOSAL

Employee personnel average increase over four years was 5.2%. Employer average gross revenue increase over that same period was 2.5%. And, the CPI average increase was 2.15%.

If personnel costs had gone up to match revenue increases of 2.5%, it would have reduced recurring costs by about $10,400,000. To slow the growth of the employee personnel cost, personnel costs should be reduced by $5,200,000. Since the growth occurred over a four-year period, a four-year contract would be most appropriate with reductions of *recurring* costs of an average of approximately $1,300,000 a year. The Union was given the option to select reductions in three categories, recognizing that any increases would also have to be offset by reductions, that is, a cost of living raise (COLA) would increase the need for more concessions. An example of what the Union might have selected appears below.

Salary/Annual Bonus Options (SAB)	Health Care Options (HCO)	Fringe Benefits Options (FBO)	Year 1	Year 2	Year 3	Year 4
1. Reduce annual "step" increases by 50% *Savings: $450,000*	1. Reduce benefits of health care plan in one year *Savings: $500,000*	1. Eliminate equipment allowance (employer provide as needed) *Savings: $1,000,000*				
2. Eliminate annual "step" increases *Savings: $900,000*	2. Reduce benefits of health care plans over two years *Savings: $250,000 per year*	2. Equipment allowance reduced by 50% *Savings: $500,000*	FBO—2 $500,000			
3. Forgo COLA of 2% *Cost: ($2,400,000)*	3. Employees con-tribute 25% for family coverage *Savings: $750,000*	3. Vacation/holiday triple overtime eliminated *Savings: $1,500,000*	HCO—3 $750,000	FBO—3 $1,500,000		
4. Forgo half of COLA—1% *Savings: $1,200,000*	4. Employees con-tribute 50% for family coverage *Savings: $1,500,000*	4. Vacation/holiday double overtime eliminated *Savings: $750,000*			SAB—4 $1,200,000	HCO—4* $750,000
	5. Employees con-tribute 75% for family coverage *Savings: $2,250,000*	5. Eliminate clothing allowance (employer provide as needed) *Savings: $860,000*				
	6. Employees con-tribute 100% for family coverage *Savings: $3,000,000*	6. Clothing allowance reduced by 50% *Savings: $450,000*				FBO—6 $450,000
Total projected savings by year needed			$1.25 mil.	$1.5 mil.	$1.2 mil.	$1.2 mil.

*First year 25% savings on family health coverage offsets this reduction.

STRATEGY 5: 3-D NEGOTIATION

Up until now we've discussed generally straightforward types of bargaining strategies based on long-accepted principles. More recently, negotiators David A. Lax and James K. Sebenius developed a creative new strategy, which they labeled **3-D negotiation**. (For a word about *truly* unconventional tactics, see Box 6.3.)

The first dimension Lax and Sebenius suggest consists of the tactics used at the bargaining table once discussions begin. The second dimension is the deal design (specifics of a proposal). And the third dimension is the setup of the negotiation. According to Lax and Sebenius, too often negotiators focus solely on just the first two dimensions. For example, they select tactics to be employed at the table, and discuss designs that enable them to create value, as we discussed in Chapter 2. However, they overlook the third dimension, which is *the setup of the whole negotiation situation*—the parties involved, the issues, the sequence of issues to be decided, outside influences, and the timing of the negotiation. Furthermore, research by Lax and Sebenius suggests that negotiators will be most successful if they involve all three dimensions in their bargaining (see Table 6.4). Thus one strategy is to review these "setup" or third-dimension issues and possibly reshape them to influence the outcome.[20]

What strategies do 3-D negotiators practice? They might solicit outside offers from other parties, or they might bring a new party into the situation (as shown in the accompanying cartoon). They might decide to improve their BATNAs. Or they might shift the issues under consideration. All of these 3-D strategies can significantly alter the "setup" or third dimension of the negotiation situation.

An example of the effect of soliciting outside offers occurred in 1996 when America Online (AOL) was seeking to negotiate a deal for an Internet browser. Netscape and

---

BOX 6.3 Tactics for Success

Be Unpredictable

Mark Walker, professor of economics at the Eller College of Business at the University of Arizona, advises negotiators to be "unpredictable"—at least some of the time. Why? It's a lesson from game theory, which Walker teaches. If, for example, in a card game with only aces and kings and both players receiving only one card before betting, the dealer always folds when a king is drawn, and always bets when an ace is drawn, he will always win, right? No. The other player would catch on quickly to the dealer's strategy, and thus learns to fold whenever the dealer bets (because the dealer only bets when he has an ace). If however, the dealer bluffs unpredictably a specific fraction of the time, he wins.

This need for unpredictable behavior also shows up in other "games" such as tennis, contends Walker. Research by Walker and John Wooders found that that the world's top tennis players use randomized serving patterns. Major-league baseball pitchers of course try to remain unpredictable both in their type of pitch (fastball, slider, curve) and its location (inside–outside, high–low) and velocity, to keep batters guessing!

Source: Adapted from "Knowing How to Play the Game," *Eller Progress* (Winter 2005): 10–11.

Table 6.4 The Three Dimensions of Negotiation

DIMENSION	FOCUS	COMMON BARRIERS	APPROACH
1-D	Tactics (people and process)	"Hardball" tactics"; interpersonal issues; poor communications	Act at the table to improve interpersonal issues and tactics
2-D	Deal design (value and substance)	Lack of feasible or desirable agreements	Go "back to the drawing board" to design deals that unlock value
3-D	Setup	Number of parties; issues; BATNAs; outside offers	Make moves "away from the table" to create a more favorable situation

Source: David A. Lax and James K. Sebenius, "3-D Negotiation: Playing the Whole Game," *Harvard Business Review* (November 2003): 67. Used by permission.

For Better or For Worse

A man and woman confer with their real estate agent about making an offer on a house. By noting that another party is interested in the house and might also make an offer, the woman (who *really* wants the house) has created a 3-D negotiation!

Source: For Better or For Worse, syndicated by Universal Press Syndicate. Used by permission.

Microsoft were competing to sign with AOL, and Netscape was the heavy favorite to win because it dominated the market with a browser that was technically superior to Microsoft's. Microsoft's Bill Gates, however, shifted the issue from simply purchasing a browser for millions of dollars to something much broader, in which Microsoft had a decisive edge: access to the 50 million people who utilized the Microsoft Windows operating system. Microsoft agreed to place the AOL icon on the Windows desktop right next to Microsoft's own MSN, which was a competitor. AOL saved millions in promotion expenses to reach new customers and Microsoft won the Internet browser war, as Netscape began to fade in terms of number of customers.[21]

A good example of how bringing in a new party can affect the outcome occurred between the city of Louisville and the local Professional Firefighters Union. In 1981, when contract talks stalled, the union successfully began building citizen support for its cause, and then threatened a strike. Some firefighters warned the public of massive fires raging out of control in the older sections of the city where wooden houses stood only a few feet apart. The thought of not having firefighting protection caused many citizens to rally behind the union and to pressure the mayor and aldermen to give in to the demands of the firefighters. The city negotiators, on the brink of a called strike, sealed a deal to bring county volunteer firefighters into the city should the union firefighters not report to work as threatened. The union leaders quickly called off the strike, and a contract settlement was reached within days. The 3-D strategy of bringing in county volunteer firefighters as a third party to the picture (but not into the contract talks) reshaped the entire scope of the situation. Why? The union had strong dislike for its county volunteer counterparts, and feared that if the city successfully withstood a strike utilizing the county units, then the elected city leaders might question the value and expense of their full-time paid workforce. In addition, the union firefighters simply didn't want the county firefighters "on their turf."

Another excellent example of the 3-D strategy of bringing in other parties to change the scope of negotiations is found in the Chapter Case. Kevin met with a mall leasing agent to renegotiate the lease of his most profitable store. It was his best performing store in terms of gross profit per year and also in terms of lowest ratio of cost of rent to sales volume. During the first meeting, the mall leasing agent informed Kevin that his cost per square foot in the new lease would be considerably higher. After a few calculations Kevin realized that the rent would be the highest per square foot of any of his stores, and yet even with the current level of sales the store would still be his most profitable. In their second meeting Kevin was determined to minimize the increase and thus proposed a counteroffer. The leasing agent then responded, "I've got three people that are ready to take your space next month at my lease rate, and here are their names if you want to check them out." With a little work, the agent's claim did in fact check out, and Kevin knew why. There simply was no other mall in this city—and suddenly the entire scope of the negotiation had changed and entered the "third dimension," and thus Kevin quickly signed the new lease agreement.

SUMMING UP

Think about a situation in your life or work in which you need to choose a negotiation strategy. First answer the questions below regarding the key elements of the situation (time, information, power), and then answer the strategy questions that can help you select a preferred overall strategy to use as you start negotiating.

Key Elements:

1. Describe the situation. Is there a deadline that will affect the timing of the bargaining? If not, can you "create" one in the mind of the other party that would work to your advantage?

   _____

2. What is your exact BATNA? (Write it down and keep it with you during the bargaining.) What is your best estimate of the other party's BATNA?

   Your BATNA: _____

   Other party's BATNA:_____

3. What other information do you need to collect before you start the negotiation ?

_____

_____

4. Is the power between the two sides roughly balanced? If you have the power advantage (like Uncle Bernie) should you exploit it, or is your desire to maintain a long-term positive relationship more important?

_____

_____

5. Consider all the key elements together and summarize the general situation and the effects on your choice of strategy.

_____

_____

_____

Strategy Questions.

6. Can you and the other party agree on a principled negotiation strategy?

_____

If so, can you identify the likely interests (not positions) of both sides?

_____

_____

_____

What are the key objective criteria to be considered?

_____

_____

_____

Can you identify possible mutual-gain options that can be put on the table at the start of the bargaining?

_____

_____

_____

7. Would a strategy of creating value potentially provide the best outcomes for both sides? If so, how would you approach the other party in the discussion?

_____

_____

_____

8. If several economic issues are involved, could you develop a MESO or an economic matrix of outcome alternatives to offer to the other side? If so, choose either the MESO or the economic matrix strategy and list the issues and options for each issue in a matrix, with options of approximate equal value to you.

_____

_____

_____

_____

_____

_____

_____

9. Can you utilize a 3-D strategy by bringing an outside party into the setup, or by soliciting a third-party offer? By shifting the focus to a new issue that provides you with greater leverage? By improving your BATNA?

_____

_____

10. Will negotiations primarily focus on one number, such as price (which means you should consider a strategy of "increments of concession")?

_____

If so, what are the likely initials offers, and what will be your pattern of concessions?

_____

_____

_____

_____

LEARNING EXERCISE: BUYING A NEW CAR

The classic negotiation situation involves a man or woman who is somewhat of a "car buff" and trades in his or her current automobile every 3 to 5 years for a new one. In this exercise the buyer, Ward Jackson, currently has a seven-year-old Ford Windstar but now, with his children out of school, is ready for a sedan. Ward has two golfing buddies that recently bought the new model of the Toyota Avalon. Ward has ridden in their cars and really likes them. To prepare himself, he decided to utilize the Consumer Reports New Car Price Service to learn more about the different models, availability, and true dealer cost of an Avalon.

Thus one sunny Friday afternoon he pulls into the local Toyota dealer just "to browse." A Toyota sales representative, Shelley Kowalski, approaches Ward and after a few minutes has him taking a new red Avalon XL for a test drive. Ward likes the car, but is not in a hurry to buy—unless he believes he is getting the best deal. Shelley asks him the classic sales representative question, "Would you like to take this car home today?"

Ward responds with, "Who at the dealership can authorize the lowest price?"

Shelley responds, "The sales manager."

Ward says, "Then you ask him for the lowest cash price on this car, if I write the check today, and keeping in mind that I have the *Consumer Reports* information, and thus I know what the dealer paid for the car."

Review the information and answer the following skills questions:

Skill 6.1: Before choosing a particular strategy, carefully identify and consider the three key elements for this particular situation—*time (deadlines), information,* and *power*—and decide how they may impact the negotiations.

Skill 6.2: Develop a strategy of *increments of concession* for Ward that will lead the sales manager to guess that he has a certain BATNA or walk-away price—in this case a minimum above the *Consumer Reports* invoice amount—and thus enable you to get the best deal. The manufacturer's suggested retail price (MSRP) for the Avalon XLS is $31,225, and the invoice plus $200 profit for the dealer (*Consumer Reports'* recommended minimum) is $26,400.

Skill 6.3: Consider whether or not Ward could successfully utilize the *principled negotiation strategy* in this car-buying negotiation. Why or why not?

Skill 6.4: The Consumer Reports Car Buying Service identified three other cars (Buick Lucerne, Volkswagen Passat, Mercury Montego) that it recommended as generally equal to the Avalon. If the two parties fail to agree on a price, how could Ward utilize this comparison information (or other information) to take the negotiation to a new third dimension (*3-D negotiation*), and thus change the setup of the whole negotiation situation?

Skill 6.5: Assuming that Ward, like most buyers, would prefer some options that cost extra, utilize the information from the Consumer Reports New Car Price Service as presented in the following table, as well as Ward's option preferences (color: metallic blue; sound system: JBL 6-CD in-dash; DVD navigation system; seats: power, heated front; safety: traction control/stability control, front and side curtain airbags; moonroof: power, tilt/slide), to develop three *MESO* or *economic matrix* packages to present to the sales manager.

Factor/Option	Avalon	Lucerne	Passat	Montego
1. MSRP	$31,225	$27,265	$29,950	$26,885
2. MPG	22city/31hwy	19city/28hwy	19city/28hwy	21city/29hwy
3. Destination charge	$580	$725	$630	$700
4. DVD navigation system	$1,950	$ 1,450	$1,600	$1,375
5. Colors available	pearl white; metallic blue or green; black; red	pewter; red; metallic green or blue; black	pearl white; metallic blue or green; black; red	pewter; red; metallic green or blue; black
6. JBL sound system (6-CD, in-dash)	$1,095	$795	$995	$795
7. Traction control/ stability control	$3,450	$2,750	$3,225	$2950
8. Heated, power front seats	$975	$750	$1,050	$875
9. Moonroof (power, tilt/slide)	$1,250	$795	$1,025	$1,375
10. Airbags	Std: front & side curtain	Std: front only (no side curtain)	Std: front & side curtain	Std: front & side curtain

ENDNOTES

1. David A. Lax and James K. Sebenius, "3-D Negotiation: Playing the Whole Game," *Harvard Business Review* (November 2003): 66.
2. Herb Cohen, *You Can Negotiate Anything* (New York: Bantam Books, 1980), 91–98.
3. Peter B. Stark and Jane Flaherty, *The Only Negotiating Guide You'll Ever Need* (New York: Broadway Books, 2003), 17–20.
4. Cohen, *You Can Negotiate Anything*, 91–98.
5. Michael R. Carrell and Christina Heavrin, *The Everyday Negotiator* (Amherst, MA: HRD Press, 2004), 30–31.
6. Cohen, *You Can Negotiate Anything*, 101.
7. Charles Craver, *The Intelligent Negotiator* (Roseville, CA: Prima, 2002), 117–121.
8. Leigh Thompson, *The Mind and Heart of the Experienced Negotiator* (Upper Saddle River, NJ: Prentice Hall, 1998), 18–20, 26–28.
9. Patrick J. Cleary, *The Negotiation Handbook* (Armonk, NY: Sharpe, 2001), 15.
10. Ibid.
11. Cohen, *You Can Negotiate Anything*, 110–112.
12. Roger Fisher and William Ury, *Getting to Yes* (New York: Penguin Books, 1981), 1–14.
13. Ibid., 56–62.
14. Bureau of National Affairs, *2002 Sourcebook on Collective Bargaining* (Washington, DC: BNA Press, 2002), 37.
15. Victoria Husted Medvec and Adam D. Galinsky, "Putting More on the Table: How Making Multiple Offers Can Increase the Final Value of the Deal," *Negotiation* 8 (April 2005): 4–6.
16. Ibid.
17. Carrell and Heavrin, *The Everyday Negotiator*, 115–117.
18. Medvec and Galinsky, "Putting More on the Table," 6.
19. Carrell and Heavrin, *The Everyday Negotiator*, 115–117.
20. Lax and Sebenius, "3-D Negotiation," 66–74. Also see the Harvard Business School Web site, www.people.hbs.edu/jsebenius/hbr/3-Dnegotiation.
21. Ibid.

Chapter 7

Impasse and Alternative Dispute Resolution (ADR)

A negotiation or dispute between parties will likely result in one of four possible outcomes: (1) an agreement being reached with both parties gaining something of greater value than if no agreement is reached; (2) the negotiation ending with no agreement reached and neither party gaining anything—often caused by one party walking away from the discussions, possibly exercising its BATNA; (3) negotiations reaching an impasse or stalemate, with both parties desiring to move forward but not seeing how current bargaining can achieve any progress; or (4) both parties realizing they are at an impasse but willing to find a method of moving discussions forward either by using a third party or by some method of alternative dispute resolution. Some negotiators might consider litigation as a fifth possible outcome, but for our purposes the use of the court system is another (and less desirable) third-party method not examined in this text.

In previous chapters we have discussed how parties can prepare for and conduct negotiations with the general goal of reaching a settlement that benefits both parties. In addition, we have explained why no agreement is, in some cases, the only possible ending, probably because one party realizes it has a better alternative to a negotiated agreement—another buyer/seller, a possible advantage that timing may give them in the future, or another method by which the goal can be reached. Although some may view this outcome as a "failed" negotiation, that is not always true. For example, consider a new car buyer who cannot reach a settlement with a dealer and walks away from the negotiations. The buyer then negotiates an almost identical deal with another dealer on a similar car—a deal the first dealer might have offered. The first dealer sells the car that the buyer walked away from to another customer who is very happy with the deal—and thus two agreements were reached. Was the first negotiation really a failure, or did the buyer, by walking away, enable two dealers and two buyers to successfully reach settlements on two cars?[1]

165

Without a doubt, most people might call a negotiation that ends up with no agreement "a failure." For example, the 1979 International Harvester plant strike in Louisville, Kentucky, which resulted in a closed plant, and thousands of management and union workers either without jobs or with significantly lower-paying jobs, was certainly viewed by most people involved and the general public as a failed negotiation. But also consider the 2003 negotiation between the owners of two Major League Baseball teams, the Boston Red Sox and the Texas Rangers. The deal was designed to send Alex Rodriguez, a player who many considered to be the best in baseball, from the Texas Rangers to the Boston Red Sox, in exchange for Boston's Manny Ramirez. A tentative deal was reached between the clubs, and Boston fans were thrilled—thinking they had the key player needed to finally beat their rivals, the New York Yankees. Then, when it looked like the deal was final, it suddenly fell apart when the Major League Baseball Players Association (MLBPA) rejected it. Yankee owner George Steinbrenner then quickly stepped in and negotiated his own deal to bring "A-Rod" to the Yankees from Texas. Boston fans were enraged, and Steinbrenner embarrassed Red Sox owner John Henry in the press for weeks with statements like, "We understand John Henry must be embarrassed, frustrated, and disappointed by his failure in this transaction."[2]

Certainly Red Sox fans, if not the majority of all baseball fans as well as many negotiators, would have called the Red Sox–Rangers negotiation a complete failure. To Red Sox fans it was a worst-case scenario—they lost the chance to bring baseball's best player to Boston *and* he landed with the rival, hated Yankees instead. Thus the 2004 season started with Boston fans in despair. But then, at the end of the season, the Red Sox met the Yankees in the American League Championship Series. Within one game of elimination at the hands of the hated Yankees, the Red Sox came back from an 0–3 deficit to beat the Yankees and win the pennant, and then went on to win the World Series—their first title in 86 years! In the playoffs, one of Boston's best players was Manny Ramirez, while the Yankees' new star, A-Rod, struggled. The failed negotiation at the start of the season suddenly appeared to be just what the Red Sox needed to end the 86-year "curse of the Bambino" (a reference to the Sox trading Babe Ruth to the Yankees after their 1918 World Series victory). Thus, in rare circumstances, even a failed negotiation may in the long run result in a happy ending.

However, most failed negotiations do not result in "happy endings," and thus negotiators often seek alternatives to a negotiation failure. In this chapter, then, we discuss the third and fourth possible negotiation outcomes: impasse, and methods of resolving an impasse through third-party intervention or alternative dispute resolution (ADR). There are many common reasons why a negotiation results in a deadlock—including the lack of a zone of possible agreement (ZOPA) on one or more issues, as discussed in Chapter 3; parties who become entrenched in "the heat of the battle" and are unwilling to consider alternative proposals;

or simply negotiators who lack effective skills. Whatever the reason, it may be helpful to think of the impasse or deadlock not as the endpoint, but rather as one point that exists along a "negotiation process continuum," which can be visualized as follows:

Preparation → Opening offers → Bargaining → Impasse → Third-party intervention → Settlement

Negotiation Skills

In this chapter we present five negotiation skills that can be learned and developed by the novice negotiator, and applied to the end-of-chapter Learning Exercise, "The Common Driveway."

Skill 7.1 *Recognize that a negotiation process may encounter an* **impasse,** *which can become merely a temporary situation if an appropriate resolution strategy is implemented to reach a settlement.*

Skill 7.2 *As a negotiation approaches a potential settlement, recognize that you may encounter* **settlement pressure** *and will need to firmly remain aware of your resistance point or BATNA to avoid potentially agreeing to an unfavorable settlement.*

Skill 7.3 *If a negotiation reaches an impasse or deadlock, do not consider it terminated, but instead consider established* **mediation** *programs. This step can be viewed as "mediated negotiation," in which a third party facilitates the parties' development of their own settlement.*

Skill 7.4 *When negotiation and mediation have failed to produce an agreement, and both parties desire a final resolution, carefully consider the pros and cons of* **arbitration.** *The only remaining alternatives in most disputes are arbitration or court litigation, and arbitration does offer certain advantages in comparison to the courts. However, the risks of a public process in which a third party will render a final and binding decision should be carefully considered.*

Skill 7.5 *Recognize that newer, less common methods of alternative dispute resolution, called* **hybrid forms of ADR,** *are available and should be considered if negotiation fails to produce a settlement.*

CHAPTER CASE: HUNT MANUFACTURING COMPANY

Douglas Hunt is an Austrian immigrant who came to the United States after World War II and started a machine products company, Hunt Manufacturing Company, in St. Louis. The company makes machines that mass-produce consumer plastic products including bottles, resealable bowls, and containers. In 2000 Hunt decided at age 70 that it was time to retire and sell the business. Rick Thomas, a member of the Hunt Board of Directors, knew the business well and decided that his own company was interested in acquiring Hunt Manufacturing. Once both parties agreed to a tentative price, Thomas initiated a *due diligence process* (research done in preparation for a business transaction) and found something that quickly emerged as a possible deal breaker—a pending lawsuit.

The week after Hunt announced to his employees his intention to sell the business, Lynn Stephan, the former sales director, filed a sexual harassment suit against both Douglas Hunt and Hunt Manufacturing Company. Stephan had worked at Hunt Manufacturing from 1990 to 1999 as the director of sales and was generally regarded by other employees as very professional and quite successful. She left suddenly without notice to accept a position with another firm. The suit alleged that Hunt had created a "hostile work environment," which is unlawful according to the 1964 Civil Rights Act, through a pattern of actions including displaying pictures of naked women in internal presentations, constantly telling off-color jokes in Stephan's presence during staff meetings, and the "final straw"—rubbing up against her at the annual company picnic while making crude remarks. The lawsuit asked for $500,000 in damages.

After an initial investigation from the human resource director, the Hunt Board of Directors took control of the company because the investigation uncovered several eyewitnesses whose testimony left little doubt that the incidents cited by Stephan had in fact occurred. Thomas made it clear to the Hunt Board of Directors that they must settle the lawsuit before any acquisition could take place. The directors realized that any potential buyer would have the same concerns.

The directors contacted the Hunt Manufacturing insurance company about the lawsuit. The insurance company investigated the case as well and indicated that it might be willing to pay the claim up to $250,000 (the coverage maximum), if and only if Stephan and Hunt Manufacturing would attempt to settle the case through mediation. Both had agreed to mediation when Douglas Hunt suddenly suffered a massive heart attack, and his health quickly deteriorated until he was confined to a wheelchair and required 24-hour medical care. Now the Hunt directors became even more anxious to sell the company because no internal person was a logical successor to Hunt. The directors again contacted Rick Thomas about a possible acquisition. He responded that any deal was dead unless the lawsuit was settled. The directors approached Hunt about a settlement but he refused to talk with them. Both the directors and Rick Thomas agreed that they had reached an impasse and the talks ended.

IMPASSE

Regardless of what method of negotiation is employed, how well intentioned the parties involved are, or how long and involved the discussions have been, some negotiations will result in a stalemate or **impasse**. Why? There are several common causes of an impasse. The most obvious is that the interests of the two parties were not resolved. Simply stated, they could not discover a proposal that contained terms better than no agreement at all. Recall the point we emphasized in Chapter 2: It is absolutely critical for both parties to realize that any settlement must include gains by both parties, or one party will likely walk out. A second possible reason is that one or both parties had no real intention of reaching a settlement in the first place. Sometimes people are just gathering information, possibly to be used in another negotiation. Have you ever just browsed a car dealership, with no real intention to buy a car?

A third possible reason for an impasse involves **settlement pressure**, which may occur when the parties are involved in a genuine negotiation and are close to reaching an agreement. As they approach their resistance points, they realize a potential end point is near and that every proposal might be the final one—and thus they feel greater pressure to settle than is warranted. To illustrate settlement pressure, in Figure 7.1 we return to the Chapter 3 figure that illustrated the typical two-party, single-issue negotiation. If you were the buyer in this situation, keeping in mind that the absolute maximum you can pay (your resistance point) is $11,000, would you feel greater settlement pressure if the seller lowered the listed price of $12,500 to $12,000 or $11,750 or $11,100? When the price is $12,000 or $11,750, you probably would not feel much pressure because it is still well above your resistance point, but at $11,100 it becomes very close to your resistance point, and the next counteroffer is likely to be within your range, and therefore you would feel the pressure of a deal coming close to reality.

Under settlement pressure, some negotiators exude weaknesses and agree to terms that fall short of their BATNA or bottom line. However, in such a situation skilled negotiators recognize that it would be irrational to accept terms that do not meet their bottom line or BATNA. Thus, negotiations can become stalled.[3]

Finally, a fourth possible cause of an impasse is "the heat of the battle." The parties may become so engaged in defending their position and attacking that of the other side that they become entrenched, unwilling to compromise and move the negotiations forward. But whatever the exact cause of a deadlock or impasse in the negotiation process, if the parties desire a settlement then the impasse can be viewed as just a *temporary* pause in the negotiation process, until a method of resolution is initiated.

Figure 7.1 Two-Party, Single-Issue Negotiation, Revisited

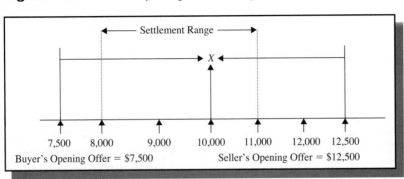

ADR: An Overview

When both parties have declared an impasse and negotiations have ceased, but at the same time *both have a true desire to reach a settlement,* then they may turn to a third-party intervention or alternative dispute resolution as a means of assistance, and ultimately reach a settlement. **Alternative dispute resolution**, or **ADR** as it is commonly known, can be defined as the use of various methods by which neutral third parties assist individuals engaged in a conflict or negotiation stalemate to reach an agreement without resorting to the courts. Increasingly, ADR is viewed as almost a panacea for a society that has become overly litigious. In general, ADR involves methods of mediation, arbitration, or, occasionally, a "hybrid" form of the two.

Mediation and arbitration both have a long and successful history in the field of collective bargaining or union–management relations. However, in recent years ADR has expanded into a variety of other fields including commercial disputes, employment issues, consumer products, landlords and tenants, international disputes, physicians and hospitals, divorce cases, and neighbor-to-neighbor disputes.[4] In fact, the use of ADR outside the field of labor relations more than doubled between the years 1995 and 2000, according to the American Arbitration Association (AAA), which handled more than 62,000 cases in 1995 and 140,000 cases in 2000. The majority of cases heard by the AAA were business-to-business, with consumer-to-business cases representing another large group, and labor–management cases representing only 11% of the AAA's caseload.[5]

Why has the use of ADR increased so rapidly in recent years? The rise has usually been directly attributed to the desires of parties on both sides of disputes to avoid litigation, which is the only other third-party method available. ADR in comparison to litigation has several advantages, in terms of the following factors:[6]

- *Cost:* The litigation process often involves several rounds of pretrial discovery, investigations, hearings, direct court costs, and of course attorney fees. Some of these costs are avoided with ADR.
- *Complexity of issues:* The court system does not guarantee that judges, jury members, or other involved individuals will have the technical expertise to understand and fairly decide complex or technological issues. This situation increases the risk of decisions based on a lack of knowledge or understanding of the issues involved. If ADR is utilized, however, the parties can choose a mediator or arbitrator who has extensive knowledge about the issues. The parties can even access the past decisions of individuals being considered to provide them a relevant framework.
- *Time concerns:* The legal process is almost always more lengthy than an alternative dispute resolution, especially if appeals are involved. A lengthy process can be emotionally draining on those directly involved and can be the source of bad publicity for a business, not-for-profit agency, or governmental entity. In addition, uncertainty about the outcome may cause other costly delays to an organization, which cannot make strategic plans until the case is settled.
- *Confidentiality:* The ADR process can provide a private and confidential means of settling negotiations, which the public court system cannot provide.
- *Avoiding disastrous decisions:* Because the parties are not forced to accept any particular decision, mediation can avoid a disastrous decision—one that could

Any dispute, controversy, or claim arising out of or in connection with this contract, or the breach, termination, or invalidity thereof, shall first be referred to mediation in accordance with the Rules of the Mediation Institute of the Stockholm Chamber of Commerce, unless one of the parties objects. If one of the parties objects to mediation, or if the mediation is terminated, the dispute shall be finally resolved by arbitration in accordance with the Rules for Expedited Arbitration of the Arbitration Institute of the Stockholm Chamber of Commerce. The place of arbitration will be Indianapolis, Indiana, the language to be used in the arbitral proceedings shall be English, and the arbitral tribunal shall be composed of a single arbitrator.

Source: Robert C. Beasley, "Dispute Resolution—Pros and Cons of the Three Basic Options," *Licensing Journal* 25 (February 2005): 30. Used by permission of Aspen Publishers, Inc.

Figure 7.2 Contract Clause Specifying the Use of Mediation and Arbitration to Settle International Disputes

possibly be even worse than if one party had walked away from the negotiations or accepted the last offer made by the other party.

Thus, when the parties are involved in a "good faith dispute," mediation and arbitration provide many potential advantages compared to the litigation process. It is important to point out, however, that in some cases the courts may provide the most desirable route to resolve a dispute. Robert Beasley, general counsel and director of business affairs for Paws Inc., which directs and manages the worldwide legal affairs for the comic character "Garfield," has discussed the advantage of not specifying mediation or arbitration in business contracts, but instead maintaining immediate access to U.S. courts, if the majority of disputes that might arise simply involve someone not paying money owed to another party. In such cases, Beasley argues, the courts are faster and cheaper than mediation or arbitration, and judges are more likely to provide a simple order to pay.

On the other hand, Beasley also advises that *international* contracts—even those involving someone owing money—should specify the use of arbitration to resolve disputes. Why? Decisions by arbitrators are more easily recognized as legally binding in foreign jurisdictions due to various international conventions adopted by most commercial countries in the world. In addition, the contract can specify the place, currency, and language to be utilized in the arbitration proceedings, substantially lowering the costs.[7] A sample of such a contract clause specifying the use of mediation and arbitration appears in Figure 7.2. One issue that is missing from this example, but included in others, is payment of costs. For example, the clause might specify that the costs associated with any mediation or arbitration will be paid by the loser, will be split 50-50 between the parties, or will be determined by the parties at the start of the case.

MEDIATION

As explained earlier in this chapter, *mediation* is one form of ADR. It has emerged over the last 30 years as a preferred method of resolving negotiation impasses as well as disputes involving employers and employees, businesses, families, or communities. The most important advantage of mediation over arbitration or other methods of ADR is that the parties themselves develop the settlement. In fact, most state courts have established mediation programs to assist litigants in settling disputes that they have been unable to settle for themselves, before the cases are brought to the state courts for action. In addition, at the federal level, the Alternative Dispute Resolution Act of 1998[8] requires all federal district courts to adopt local rules for the use of mediation. Mediation has even expanded to the arena of "cyber" commerce, with many e-business sites adopting mediation programs as a means of resolving conflicts largely through e-mail communications.[9]

In fact, mediation today is the most commonly utilized method of ADR. **Mediation** can be defined as a private dispute resolution process in which the parties involved in a disagreement receive the assistance of a third party who facilitates the resolution of the issues. This definition contains three critical characteristics of mediation:

1. It is **private** process, not conducted in a public setting such as a court of law.
2. The mediator is a **third party,** and thus both parties involved must trust the mediator to be an objective individual with whom they will share their true interests.
3. The mediator strives to **facilitate** a mutually acceptable resolution of the dispute, and generally does not offer proposals or have any authority or power to force either party to accept any proposal on any issue.

Mediation works best when the third party is a skilled, impartial facilitator who is viewed by the parties as neutral.

How Mediation Works

Mediation begins when the parties involved in a dispute recognize they are at an impasse and yet desire to reach a settlement. Therefore they jointly request the services of a mediator. This joint request may be triggered by a contractual agreement such as the one in Figure 7.2, or simply occurs when two parties sincerely desire to resolve their differences and recognize that mediation might provide a means to achieve that goal.

The next step is for the parties to request the services of a mediator through one of many formal mediation services such as the American Arbitration Association (AAA), which provides mediation services as well as arbitration services. The AAA is a public service not-for-profit organization that since 1926 has offered a broad range of ADR services to businesses, individuals, unions, consumers, and governmental units. The AAA also provides excellent publications on mediation and arbitration, available at its Web site, www.adr.org. Another excellent source of mediators is the Federal Mediation and Conciliation Service (FMCS), which has provided facilitation and mediation services for over fifty years—more than any other agency of government—and can be found online at www.fmcs.gov. The FMCS was originally formed to provide services in labor–management relations, but today a majority of its cases are non-labor-related. In addition to the AAA and FMCS, many community associations, private enterprises, university-based providers, and governmental mediation services are available.

The agency contacted will then assign a mediator from a master list of available mediators in the region. The mediator generally has no past or present relationship with either party and is free to refuse or accept the appointment. At the same time, the parties are given information about the mediator and are free to ask for a different mediator for any reason. They are also free to stop the mediation process at any time once it has begun and may request another mediator at any time.

Once a mediator is agreed upon, the parties are informed about any fees involved (some federal and state mediators do not charge fees) and may be required to sign a payment agreement that splits the fees evenly. The steps commonly followed in the mediation process are listed in Figure 7.3 and are also discussed on the following pages.

It is critical for the parties to recognize that mediators are not judges and have no authority to impose a settlement or choose a proposal as the "best" or "right" one.[10] The success of mediation depends on several factors, including the skills of the mediator; the willingness of the parties to divulge their true underlying interests to the mediator and cooperate in finding a solution; whether one or both parties wants to "even the score" or "win at any cost" rather than reach a settlement (both parties should ask themselves if this is their motivation—and if so they may be better off to skip mediation in favor of arbitration or litigation, and save themselves the time and expense!); and the nature of the issues involved—that is, is there a potential common ground or ZOPA that both parties will accept as a settlement?

Approaches to Mediation   How, exactly, does a mediator succeed in finding a mutually agreeable solution to disputes that the parties by themselves could not discover? Norman Brand, the respected editor of *How ADR Works*, suggests that there is

Figure 7.3
Steps in the Mediation Process

1. *Request:* The parties involved in a dispute voluntarily and jointly request the services of a mediator from an agency, and after an initial interview they agree to a mediator.
2. *Initial conference:* The mediator and parties meet, and the mediator's role and responsibilities as well as the rights of the parties are explained.
3. *Schedule of sessions:* The mediator designs a schedule of private sessions with the parties, some jointly with both parties, but often many are held separately, particularly if the parties have engaged in heated dialogue.
4. *Formal retainer:* The parties sign an agreement to share the fees. The parties may or may not be represented by an attorney during the process. Parties in employment and business disputes usually retain attorneys.
5. *Information gathering:* The parties submit information about the issues involved and their positions.
6. *Facilitation:* The mediator identifies areas of agreement, defines the unresolved issues, and assists the parties in negotiating a possible resolution.
7. *Settlement proposed:* At some point the mediator usually summarizes a proposed settlement that the parties have themselves developed and find agreeable. The mediator then drafts a report confirming the agreement.
8. *Agreement:* A formal document such as a settlement agreement is submitted to the attorneys or court and signed by the parties.

Source: Steven Mitchell Sack, *The Employee Rights Handbook* (New York: Warner Books, 2000), 348–352. Used by permission.

no concrete answer to this question. Although mediators are usually trained and experienced in their trade, they vary greatly in the methods they employ to achieve a settlement. Instead, contends Brand, mediation is an art, and sometimes seems more like magic than an exact science.[11] Others contend that mediation is both an art *and* a science because a mediator needs to be knowledgeable about the substance and details of the disputed issues—the science—and at the same time work as a combination of facilitator, high priest, and sorcerer to keep discussions moving forward and not allow them to deteriorate into finger-pointing and name-calling—the art.[12] The key factor in mediation is the trust and confidence that the parties involved have with the mediator. Brand has developed a classification of the most common successful approaches used by mediators. These approaches, in ascending order of intervention by the mediator, are as follows:[13]

- *Collaborative mediation:* The mediator, in joint sessions, strives to get each party to understand the other's point of view and position on the issues. This provides a starting point for both sides to identify the zone of possible agreement (ZOPA) for each issue and therefore discover potential solutions. This process is more likely to be successful when the parties share a long-term, positive relationship.
- *Evaluative mediation:* The mediator meets with the parties separately in an effort to fully understand their points of view on issues, and then shows them the relative strengths and weaknesses of their positions on each issue. Finally, the mediator seeks some movement in their positions, which will provide a possible settlement.
- *Directive mediation:* When the mediator at some point in the process believes that a particular goal or settlement proposal is appropriate and achievable, a directive approach may be successful. The mediator meets with both parties together, but allows each party to speak directly only to the mediator, not to the other party. The more agitated party often goes first. A goal of the process is to force both parties to listen intently to the other party and not only hear the other party's concerns, but also feel their passion. The other party is instructed to listen without interruption, but is reminded that it, too, will be given a chance to talk. The parties are forbidden to make personal attacks. Caucuses are often required to cool tempers and allow the parties to have confidential communications with the mediator.

Functions of a Mediator   Regardless of which general approach a mediator chooses, there are five functions that the mediator performs as he or she assists the parties involved in a dispute. Nationally recognized mediator Theodore W. Kheel describes these roles as (1) the one who sets the ground rules, (2) the ringmaster, (3) the educator, (4) the communicator, and (5) an innovator.[14]

First, the mediator specifies the *ground rules* of the mediation process. For example, a ground rule might state that the mediator will keep all the records of the sessions, or that the mediator will set the time and place for joint and separate sessions. Another ground rule might be that disputed issues will be resolved one at a time, but no agreement is binding until all issues have been resolved, or that the parties will not cite anything said by the other side. Other ground rules might require that the process be private, but if public statements are necessary, they can be made only by the mediator.

Second, the mediator serves as a *ringmaster* for the sessions, and thus chairs the meetings, determines if a recess is needed, and decides whether sessions should be held jointly or separately. In this ringmaster capacity, a mediator allows the parties to tell their stories and then requires them to define the issues in dispute. This function may appear to be obvious, but in fact is a critical part of the mediation process and is often very helpful in moving the negotiations forward. The parties involved usually have a strong need to tell their story to an impartial person. The mediator will ask both sides to define each unresolved issue and state their positions in the presence of the other party; having the opponent present has a leveling effect on exactly how the position is stated. Then the mediator confirms that if all the issues presented are resolved, the parties will have an agreement. If a party disagrees, then the mediator presses them as to what other issues must be resolved, and thus should be put on the table. As ringmaster, the mediator will also confirm exactly who speaks for each party and is authorized to make decisions on issues, and exactly how the parties will indicate their agreement on issues. For example, parties might indicate acceptance by having the spokesperson for each side initial a briefly worded position statement.

The third function of a mediator is to serve as an *educator* to both parties on the issues. While a mediator never tells the parties how they should resolve an issue, he or she will direct them as they develop proposals that achieve their own primary objectives as well as those of the other party.

A fourth function is to be a *communicator,* because it is usually easier for the parties involved to communicate through a third party than directly to each other, particularly if negotiations have become heated. Mediators must be careful to communicate messages and offers exactly as intended, and thus often take careful notes and review them with the sender before delivering the communication.

As the fifth and last function, a mediator must be an *innovator,* to find new ways of resolving issues while at the same time being careful not to make specific proposals. This is often achieved through suggestions such as, "This idea may not have merit, but could you find a way of including the issue of health care in the pension package proposal?"

Now let's return to the Chapter Case to see how a mediator performs these five functions. After Hunt Manufacturing and Lynn Stephan reached an impasse, Hunt's insurance company contacted a local not-for-profit mediation agency that handled employment and family disputes. A mediator was assigned to the case and was found acceptable by both Stephan and Hunt Manufacturing. In the first session all parties sat around a table and the mediator asked each to present their opening statements, witness testimony, other evidence and the results of the investigation. Then, after a recess, the mediator asked Lynn Stephan to openly discuss the incidents and express how they and the case had affected her emotionally, in an effort to ensure that she had the opportunity to directly tell all of the directors her full story. Finally, the mediator asked the directors to express the position of Hunt Manufacturing. The directors were obviously affected by her story, and apologized to Stephan for the actions, but also presented their case. The entire session lasted about four hours.

The second session was held a week later. The mediator kept the two parties in separate rooms, far away from each other. He began by presenting, separately to each side, what he believed were the critical facts, as well as the weaknesses in their cases and why he thought each might have difficulty winning a jury trial. He stated that if the case proceeded to a state or federal court, Hunt Manufacturing would effectively be admitting that the incidents cited by Stephan had occurred. He told Stephan that her case had three major weaknesses: First, under federal law she was required to notify someone in the company of her complaint and give the company the opportunity to correct the situation—which the Hunt Board of Directors had effectively done when it took control shortly after hearing the results of the investigation. Second, the case was not a "quid pro quo" case—that is, according to her own testimony, Hunt had never requested sex in exchange for a job, a promotion, or some other favor. Instead it was a "hostile environment" case—which is still unlawful, but not considered as serious by many jurors. Finally, if the case went to a jury trial the company's defense would likely focus on Hunt, now a 70-year-old man in poor health, confined to a wheelchair, who simply was guilty of practices that were commonplace in his generation. In addition, the witness accounts varied in their view of whether the acts were of a serious nature or just harmless pranks.

After a recess the mediator started asking both sides what amount would settle the case that day, while keeping them in separate rooms. This separation tactic enabled the company's directors to reject any offer that would exceed the insurance company's maximum coverage and thus kill the acquisition deal. The starting offers were $5,000 (Hunt Manufacturing) and $500,000 (Stephan). After about two hours the two sides agreed to a mediated settlement of $63,000, to be paid within 24 hours. They evenly split the $5,000 mediation fee. If the case had gone to court, the estimate of combined legal fees and court costs would have totaled $35,000 to $50,000. Both sides believed they had received a fair settlement, and in a faster and less expensive manner than if they went to court.

Benefits of Mediation

As just described, mediation may or may not produce a settlement but it definitely offers several distinct potential advantages over litigation or arbitration, including the following:[15]

1. *Psychological benefits:* Agreements reached through mediation enable the people involved to avoid the anxiety, trauma, and uncertainty of arbitration or litigation. They directly participate in the formulation of the terms of agreement, and this involvement means they are more likely to freely abide by and support the agreement than one imposed on them by a third party. In addition, because the parties involved had direct input into the selection of the impartial, third-party mediator, they believe their positions have been heard and considered by a reasonable, fair, and neutral person.

2. *Savings in time and money:* Effective mediation programs generally save the parties involved significant time and money in comparison to arbitration or litigation.

Of course, if the case is not successfully resolved in mediation and must proceed to the courts or an arbitrator and thus still incur those expenses, mediation will have added to the total cost. However, a recent study of court-mandated mediation in two states found that most attorneys believe effective mediation programs do save their clients both time and money.[16]

3. *Focus on issues:* The mediation process must focus on the underlying issues involved if a jointly agreeable solution is to be achieved. By comparison, judicial and arbitral proceedings focus primarily on which side is "right" or which should "win" in efforts to gain the favor of the decision maker. This advantage holds even when the only issue involved is the payment of money. Generally, mediation is a more conciliatory process in which both parties recognize that the interests of both must be met if an agreement is to be reached, and therefore it is more of an extension of the negotiation process. In fact, mediation has been called *facilitated negotiation.* Experienced mediators are able to induce the parties involved to reevaluate their underlying needs and interests and more realistically evaluate the other party's interests, and therefore achieve a settlement.

4. *Successful outcomes:* Mediation works! For example, it is estimated that 85% of labor–management grievance disputes are settled through mediation even though these cases had already been involved in several resolution attempts before mediation.[17] Why? Perhaps because the process occurs in a more comfortable, relaxed atmosphere, with a communications flow taking place directly between the parties, and not through a third party. This encourages mutually developed solutions that in the long run may help maintain positive relations between the parties.

5. *Control:* The most important benefit to the parties involved is that mediation allows them to control the outcome. They recognize that should mediation fail and the case go to arbitration or litigation, the arbitrator, judge, or jury can make a decision that is beyond their bottom line or resistance point—and that they will have no control over that decision, which often is final and binding. Therefore, they usually prefer to have some input into a less-than-perfect decision than have no input into what may be a disastrous decision. Also, when a mediated settlement is reached, because they have participated in forming the outcome, the parties are more likely to abide by the terms of the agreement than if the terms were imposed on them by a third party.[18]

6. *Confidentiality:* Mediation is a process that occurs between the parties and the mediator only—and therefore all discussions, proposals, name-calling, and other interactions remain confidential. The parties are not required to present their positions in a public court, testify under oath, or even put their thoughts in writing. There is not a written trail of what occurred during mediation. It is entirely a private process. By comparison, court and arbitration hearings take place in a public forum. The parties must provide evidence that is made public and sometimes must testify under oath. Details of the case are recorded. Outcomes, such as decisions by judges or juries and arbiters, are made public.

Mediators can be most successful when they follow the rules provided in Box 7.1.

BOX 7.1 Tactics for Success

Rules for Mediators

Patrick J. Cleary, former chairman of the National Mediation Board, suggests that mediators and even negotiators can utilize common "mediator rules" to move a stalled negotiation forward. Successful mediators often utilize the following rules or practices.

CREATE A POSITIVE ATMOSPHERE

Some simple but effective methods for changing a negative atmosphere to a positive one include these: (1) Mediators that find parties sitting across the table from each other in a hostile atmosphere often begin their work by *seating the parties on the same side of the table, across from the mediator.* This simple physical change can give the parties a sense of shared purpose or problem and helps them focus less on what divides them than on what unites them. People may act differently toward others sitting beside them than if they sit away from them across a table. (2) If the tension in the room is too great to the point of distracting the parties, a mediator may *move them to separate rooms.* This change can easily lower the tension because then they are only dealing directly with members of their own side. A mediator may take this move a step further and meet with only one or two calmer members of each side until the tension has been lowered. (3) Creating a sense of shared success or momentum often helps move things forward. Sometimes negotiations stall because the parties feel no sense of urgency, and thus a mediator will *create a deadline.* Setting a deadline to discuss one issue, for example, before moving on to the next may cause the parties to stop pursuing perfection on the wording of the issue but instead agree in principle and move on to the next issue. "Don't let perfect stand in the way of good" and thus bog down progress.

MAINTAIN NEUTRALITY

Mediators must, above all else, project neutrality in everything they do during negotiations. While easy to say, staying neutral is not easily achieved. Sometimes on one side the people involved are polite and well mannered, while those on the other side resort to name-calling, swearing, and yelling. Yet a mediator must treat them the same and not take sides, or ask leading questions, or cut one side off while letting the other side ramble. Why? If either side senses the mediator is not neutral they will likely stop cooperating, or ask for a new mediator.

ABSORB CONFLICT

It is common for the parties involved in a heated negotiation to solicit support or even evoke a reaction from a mediator. But the mediator must remain as expressionless as possible, letting the parties know that he or she is listening with a nod of the head or a response such as, "I sense you are angry about this issue" (which is very different from "I certainly see your point, but the other side thinks …"). Negotiators will not argue for very long with a mediator who won't argue with them.

PROVIDE REALITY CHECKS

Mediators are not consultants. They should not give advice or suggest solutions. But they can provide a reality check to help a party maintain realistic expectations. They do not characterize a proposal as "good" or "reasonable" but instead ask if the party is ready to offer the proposal to the other side. However, if a proposal, idea, or fact is extreme, to avoid wasting time or an angry response by the other side, a mediator may offer a reality check. For example, if one party is about to ask for an extreme concession by the other side, a mediator might suggest, "Do you really want to jeopardize the progress you've made on many other issues by suggesting a price on this issue that is at least triple that of any other competitor?"

NO CONSCIENCE

A mediator's job is to help the parties reach an agreement. A mediator's job is not to decide if the parties are making a "fair" or "good" deal. If the parties agree to it, then it is right. If the parties agree on an issue, no matter how bizarre it might appear to the mediator, the mediator "puts it on the agreed stack of issues" and moves the discussions on to the next item. Mediators should not try to stop parties from making what they perceive to be a bad deal. Their job is only to keep the parties moving forward. Why? For the same reason mediators don't make proposals: No matter how fair a proposal appears to the mediator, it can easily be viewed by one party as slightly favoring the other party, and thus the mediator no longer appears as a neutral to that party and has lost their trust. However, sometimes, such as in divorce cases involving young children, a mediator may make an exception to this "no conscience" rule if he or she believes the best interests of the children are at stake.

Cleary calls the temptation for inexperienced mediators to make what they believe to be a completely neutral proposal that can bring closure to the negotiations the *"novice's curse"*—a mistake most mediators make only once. He recalls his own novice's curse when, during a labor–management mediation, he drafted a proposal that combined the union's top issue with that of management—a "pay freeze." The proposal broke the impasse, but then in the final session to sign the agreement, the union's chief negotiator asked, "Just to be clear, by *pay freeze* you mean no increase in hourly wage rates, but we can continue to move up the pay scale, right?"

"No!" responded management's chief negotiator. "We mean no increase in wage rate *or* movement up the scale—everyone's pay will be frozen during the term of the contract."

In such a situation, which is not all that uncommon—people defining a key term differently—having one of the parties deliver the proposal, and not the mediator, would cause the blame for the lack of clarity to reside with that party, and not the mediator.

Source: Adapted from Patrick J. Cleary, *The Negotiation Handbook* (Armonk, NY: Sharpe, 2001), 137–162.

ARBITRATION

Arbitration is a distinctly different process from mediation. The informality, the parties' voices in deciding the outcome, and the private characteristics of mediation are largely absent. Instead arbitration is a formal, quasi-judicial win-lose process in which one person (or a tripartite panel) controls the process and decides the outcome. The aspect of a third party alone deciding the outcome, which is final and binding on the parties involved, is why many parties choose a mediated settlement rather than risk going to arbitration and receiving an unacceptable decision. Why, then, would parties agree to arbitrate a dispute rather than seek mediation? When negotiation and/or mediation fail to produce a resolution, and one or both parties believe that a settlement must be determined, the only remaining alternatives in most disputes are arbitration or court litigation, and arbitration does offer certain advantages in comparison to the courts. In most cases arbitration is less costly, less

Zits
Today even teenagers may consider using arbitration to resolve a dispute.

Source: Zits is syndicated by King Features Syndicate, Inc. Used by permission.

time-consuming, less rule-driven, and friendlier than the courts. And like litigation, arbitration will produce a decision and end the dispute in the vast majority of cases. Today arbitration as a possible method of resolving a variety of disputes has become common—as illustrated in the accompanying cartoon.

In fact, arbitration today is the most common form of settling disputes when negotiation and mediation have failed to produce an agreement. **Arbitration** can be defined as a process in which one or both of the parties involved have agreed by contract to submit unresolved issues to a neutral third party whose decision shall be final and binding on all parties involved. This definition contains three critical elements of arbitration:

1. It is initiated when the parties sign a **contract** in which they agree to settle any unresolved disputes through arbitration.
2. The arbitrator is a **neutral third party,** and thus both parties involved trust the arbitrator to be an objective individual who has no conflict of interest with the parties involved, their attorneys, or organizations.
3. The arbitrator shall render a **decision that is final and binding** on the parties involved, who through the language of the contract have agreed to accept and implement the decision.

Contracts that contain arbitration agreements are generally of two types—collective bargaining agreements that specify arbitration for settling any grievances that arise under the contract, and business contracts such as those between an employer and an employee, a buyer and a seller, or between two businesses.

Arbitration as it is practiced today in the United States largely developed in the field of labor–management relations. It was first written into a clause as a means of resolving disputes in the 1829 constitution of the Journeymen Cabinet-Makers in Philadelphia. The first recorded arbitration hearing occurred in 1865, when Pittsburgh ironworkers arbitrated a wage dispute.[19] George Washington was a "staunch believer" in arbitration and specified in his Last Will and Testament that should a dispute arise, it was not to be settled by litigation, but by "three impartial and intelligent men ... two chosen by the disputants and the third chosen by those two … such decision to be binding on the parties." This was one of the first uses of a tripartite arbitration board.[20]

In the United States, three statutes govern the private sector arbitration of disputes: the 1947 Labor–Management Relations Act (LMRA), also known as the Taft-Hartley Labor Act, which provides for the arbitration of disputes involving collective bargaining agreements as discussed in this chapter; the 1926 Railway Labor Act (RLA), which has jurisdiction over disputes between employees and a carrier in the railroad and airline industries; and the 1925 Federal Arbitration Act (FAA), also called the United States Arbitration Act. The Federation Arbitration Act governs commercial arbitration situations such as business–business, employer–employee, and buyer–seller. It provides the parties with guidelines and enforcement mechanisms for arbitrated disputes. For instance, when an arbitration agreement exists between the two parties, the act enables one party to force the other party to arbitrate a dispute. The U.S. Supreme Court has stated that with the Federation Arbitration Act, Congress "declared a national policy favoring arbitration" over the more expensive, slower court litigation process. The FAA also provides that an arbitration award can be confirmed by a court judgment.[21]

The foundation of the arbitration process in labor relations as we know it today, however, was set by the U.S. Supreme Court in a series of four cases known as the *Lincoln Mills* case (1957) and the *Steelworkers Trilogy* (1960).[22] The decisions supported the premise that arbitration was preferred to the courts as a route for ending disputes and providing industrial peace. Arbitration was determined to be a matter of contract. Parties are not required to submit disputes to arbitration, but if they have entered into a contractual obligation to do so, then they are required to arbitrate. If a question of *arbitrability* (whether a dispute falls under the terms of a contract's arbitration clause) exists, courts should decide in favor of arbitration. In addition, the courts in reviewing arbitration decisions should enforce them without examining their merits. These historic decisions led to a rapid rise of arbitration clauses in labor contracts, until today approximately 98% of all private sector agreements provide for binding arbitration as the final step in resolving employee grievances.[23]

How Arbitration Works

The arbitration process begins when one or both parties involved file a *submission* (or stipulation) requesting arbitration to settle certain disputed issues such as payment of funds, the termination of an employee, or the provision of services. The complaint is filed with the source of arbitrators specified in the contract or ordered by a court, such as the American Arbitration Association (AAA), the Office of Arbitration Services (OAS) of the Federal Mediation and Conciliation Service, or a state or local agency.

The agency involved either assigns an arbitrator to the case or provides a list of available arbitrators for the parties to review and crosses off any names for whom they have objections. Arbitrators are not required to have any specific education or technical training unless so specified in the contract. Most, however, are attorneys, retired judges, labor negotiators, or college professors. The qualifications of arbitrators are generally believed to include the following:

- *Impartiality:* Past decisions that indicate they have not favored either side in similar cases
- *Integrity:* Fairness and good judgment in past decisions

- *Expertise:* Knowledge of the law, industry, or past practices relevant to a specific case
- *Training or education:* Legal training, experience in a specific field, or higher education[24]

The chosen arbitrator first reviews the contract or other document that gives him or her the authority to decide the case, and then makes a full disclosure of any potential conflicts of interest with any of the parties involved. In general, arbitrators have often complete control over the formal proceedings, including a series of steps similar to those outlined in Figure 7.4.

Figure 7.4   Steps in an Arbitration Proceeding

The arbitration proceeding is largely under the control of the arbitrator, who must, under accepted procedural rules of arbitration, give the parties a full and fair hearing. In addition, the arbitrator must be satisfied that all the information necessary to decide the case has been presented. Thus, arbitrators may actively participate in the hearing by asking questions or seeking further information. The rules of the procedure in some cases may be specified by the contract signed by the parties involved in the dispute.

1. *Preliminary hearing:* A primary purpose of the first meeting is to resolve procedural matters so the case may proceed smoothly. The parties involved, or their attorneys, are asked to provide brief written statements of their claims as to the nature of the dispute—such as wrongful termination, failure to make payments, breach of contract, and so forth. The parties also provide exhibits, lists of witnesses, and other supporting information.
2. *Opening statements:* Made orally and/or in writing, the opening statements are brief and general outlines of the issues to be resolved, the positions of the parties, remedies sought, and the relevance of witnesses and other evidence.
3. *Rules of evidence:* Arbitrators have the authority to decide rules of evidence unless they have been specified in a contract provision. The rules of admissibility that would apply in a court of law are not observed by arbitrators. In general, any information the arbitrator believes will help in understanding the case and making a decision is accepted. Arbitrators often give the parties a free hand in determining what evidence they would like to present. A hearing will continue until both parties have nothing more to add. An arbitrator's understanding of a case may be improved by visiting the physical site involved in a dispute. Circumstantial evidence may be allowed by the arbitrator because in some cases, such as theft or drug use, it may be the only evidence available.
4. *Witnesses:* Witnesses are generally allowed to tell their story in their own way without interruptions. Each party has the right to use leading questions as is common in legal cases. Arbitrators generally allow cross-examination of witnesses, and unlike legal hearings may allow *hearsay* evidence (statements made by someone other than the person testifying). However, in many cases very little weight is given to hearsay evidence. The use of witness testimony by telephone is generally discouraged by arbitrators, who view it with skepticism and believe it impairs the other party's right to cross-examine.
5. *Summation:* Before the arbitrator closes the hearing, both sides are allowed to provide post-hearing briefs and make closing statements. These briefs and summations emphasize the evidence and witness testimony that supports their side, and try to discredit the evidence presented by the other side.
6. *Arbitrator's award and opinion:* The *award* refers to the arbitrator's decision in the case and specifies remedies such as compensation, reinstatement of terminated employees, interest, or back wages. The contract may provide that the prevailing party, as determined by the arbitrator, receive fees and costs from the other party—otherwise each party bears its own costs and they split the arbitrator's fee. The *opinion* refers to the arbitrator's reasons for deciding the case. A written, reasoned opinion can contribute to the parties' acceptance of the award.

Source: Adapted from Frank Elkouri and Edna Asper Elkouri, *How Arbitration Works,* 6th ed. (Washington, DC: BNA Books, 2003), 293–387.

Potential Drawbacks of Arbitration

As stated earlier, mediation has increasingly become the preferred method of settling disputes because it offers many advantages compared to litigation as well as arbitration. In addition, the process of arbitration has itself produced some unique negative consequences that the parties should at least be aware of before they enter into an arbitration process. Some of the major drawbacks associated with arbitration include the following:

- *"Playing God."* While some professionals can successfully perform roles of both mediator and arbitrator, there is a difference in the personal characteristics required. Mediators must possess empathetic, accommodating, and even therapeutic personalities, but arbitrators tend to have impersonal, fact-oriented, and decision-oriented personalities. Negotiators should not expect to encounter arbitrators with personalities similar to those of mediators. One highly successful mediator who became an arbitrator quit after only a few months because he believed that as an arbitrator he was "playing God."[25]
- *The Chilling Effect.* When negotiators are aware that a failure to reach a settlement will likely lead to arbitration, they may "cool" their efforts to reach a negotiated agreement. Why? This *chilling effect* occurs because they expect the arbitrator to review the offers on the table that were made during negotiations, and—at least to some extent—to split the difference between the last offers. Thus the negotiator is not as willing to make substantial offers during this phase, anticipating that those offers may be used by an arbitrator as anchor points for a settlement range.[26]
- *Surface Bargaining.* If negotiators anticipate that arbitration is the likely outcome of their deliberations, they may lose interest in the negotiations. In anticipation of an imposed settlement—and especially if they are tired from a long process—they may lose their initiative and engage in "surface bargaining" or halfhearted efforts, or may even prematurely declare an impasse as a means of initiating arbitration.

Final-Offer Arbitration

In the conventional type of arbitration just discussed, the arbitrator has unlimited authority to decide unresolved issues—but the arbitrator generally chooses a settlement point that lies between the final offers made by the parties on the issue. To choose a point outside of that range would simply not be logical because it would exceed one side's best offer. An exception is in cases involving interest arbitration, when an alternative method called **final-offer arbitration** can be selected. Final-offer arbitration follows the procedure outlined in Figure 7.4—except at the end, both sides submit their last offers on the issue and the arbitrator *must choose one of the two offers* and in fact cannot choose any other settlement point.

What is the potential advantage of final-offer versus conventional arbitration? In the conventional procedure, because the two parties realize their offers effectively create the zone of possible agreement, they may not make many concessions during the entire mediation and arbitration processes. This is what we described earlier as the *chilling effect*, which can "chill" the bargaining process (stop the parties from making concessions), since the arbitrator is likely to select a compromise position between the two final positions. If final-offer arbitration is utilized, however, the motivation of the parties involved, as they determine their final positions, is quite different. Both want their position to be the one selected by the arbitrator, and thus they have a strong incentive to make themselves appear as "reasonable" as possible. In theory the final positions in a final-offer process will move toward a center point in comparison to the last positions offered during mediation/arbitration, for example, and thus reduce the chilling effect of conventional arbitration.

Research on decisions involving the arbitration of Major League Baseball salaries supports this belief concerning final offers. When arbitrators are given a pair of final offers, if one appears to be "extreme" based on relevant facts (such as a player's hitting or pitching statistics), then the other is far more likely to be chosen by the arbitrator, whereas if both offers appear to be reasonable, then they have an equal chance of being selected.[27]

Combined Method   Recent research has also suggested that an even more useful method of reducing the chilling effect is to use an arbitration method that combines some aspects of conventional arbitration and final-offer arbitration. In the **combined method**, arbitrators choose the point that they believe is the best or fairest settlement point. The parties submit final offers under the rules of that process and then, if their fair settlement point lies between those final offers, the arbitrator chooses the settlement point—but if it lies outside their final offers, the arbitrator must choose one of the two final offers. The potential advantage of the combined method in comparison to the other two methods is that it combines the advantages of each: The parties will still make final offers that will tend to converge toward the middle, but arbitrators are able to select the settlement point that they believe is the fairest. Because the parties prefer voluntary, negotiated settlements and their last offers are converging, but because they know that one or the other is not necessarily going to be selected, they are more likely to reach a settlement voluntarily.

In practice, the conventional arbitration method is by far the most commonly utilized, while final-offer has been increasing in use, and the combination method is largely untried.[28] Figure 7.5 illustrates the conventional, final-offer, and combined arbitration methods.

HYBRID FORMS OF ADR

Two other forms of alternative dispute resolution are mediation-arbitration and arbitration-mediation, sometimes referred to as *hybrid forms*. Hybrid forms of ADR are methods that combine elements of the mediation process with elements of the arbitration process.

Mediation-arbitration, also called **med-arb**, although not as commonly utilized as either mediation or arbitration, is probably the best known and most utilized hybrid form of ADR. In the med-arb procedure, the contractual agreement prescribes that the same third party will serve as both a mediator and an arbitrator in an effort to resolve the dispute. The procedure typically consists of two steps: (1) a mediation process with an imposed deadline, followed by (2) an arbitration process in which

Two parties are disputing the value of a half-acre housing lot in a new subdivision. Other half-acre lots have sold in the past year in the range of $45,000 to $65,000 depending on exact size, location, flatness, existing mature trees, proximity to a proposed park or power lines, and other factors that affect desirability. The lot in question has no decided advantage or disadvantage in comparison to other lots. To achieve a quick resolution, the parties submitted the issue to arbitration. The last positions of the parties as revealed to the arbitrator were as follows: party A, $25,000; party B, $80,000.

The arbitrator then suggested a *final-offer* process, which the parties accepted, and their final offers were: party A, $45,000; party B, $68,000. The arbitrator, still not satisfied that he could render a fair decision, suggested the *combined* process, which the parties accepted. The arbitrator then carefully reviewed the distinct attributes of the other lots that had recently sold in comparison to the lot in question, and decided that $55,000 was the fair value.

If *conventional* arbitration had been utilized, the arbitrator would have had a more difficult time deciding a fair value because the last positions—$25,000 and $80,000—were so far apart. Even if the decision was the same $55,000, it would have represented a $30,000 "loss" to party A, and a $25,000 "gain" to party B. If final-offer had been utilized, the arbitrator would have been required to choose either $45,000 or $68,000 as the value—a substantial variation from what he believed to be the fair value of $55,000. By utilizing the combined method, the arbitrator is able to select a value that he, as an impartial third party, believes is fair and is within a reasonable range of the two final offers made by the parties.

A: Last Position	A: Final Offer	Arbitrator's Settlement	B: Final Offer	B: Last Position
		X		
$0 $25,000	$45,000	$55,000	$68,000	$80,000

Figure 7.5

Illustration of Three Arbitration Decision Methods: Conventional, Final-Offer, and Combined

the arbitrator will impose a final and binding decision, as in traditional arbitration. The arbitration decision may include any of the types described in Figure 7.5—conventional, final-offer, or a combined method.

Med-arb is typically chosen when the parties involved desire to employ the advantages of both methods to resolve their dispute. Thus, in general, the parties want a third party who can assist them in developing a voluntary settlement if possible, but in case that is not possible, they also desire a process that can guarantee a final settlement.[29] In addition, because the same third party serves as both mediator and arbitrator, the total time and cost should be less than if two separate procedures were employed with two individuals serving as impartial third parties, thus requiring less time and effort to become familiar with the issues, positions, and facts of the case. In fact, if the med-arb third party is adept at arbitration and has pushed the parties in a failed effort to achieve a voluntary settlement, he or she may not conduct an arbitration hearing, since little new evidence is likely, but instead will only ask for summary positions before making a binding decision. Recognizing that the third party has the power to implement a final decision as the arbitrator, the parties involved in the dispute are likely to give that individual greater authority and leverage during the mediation procedure.[30]

Arbitration-mediation, or **arb-med**, is a newer ADR procedure. Like the med-arb hybrid, the same third party individual serves in two capacities, as arbitrator and as mediator. Arb-med typically consists of three phases. First, an arbitrator holds an arbitration hearing on the disputed issues. At the conclusion of the hearing the arbitrator's decision is placed in a sealed envelope and not revealed to the parties. Next, the third party serves as a mediator, but the parties are well aware that if the mediation process should fail to produce a settlement, the decision in the envelope will be implemented, and thus they have a strong incentive to settle the dispute voluntarily to avoid an imposed decision. Finally, should the mediation fail, the third party removes the ruling from the envelope and reveals the final and binding solution to the parties. Thus the arb-med procedure differs from the med-arb hybrid process in one critical aspect: The parties have only one brief chance to influence the decision of the third party—in the first phase. After that, the parties recognize during mediation that they cannot affect the binding ruling of the third party, and therefore if they want to have any control over the outcome they must voluntarily agree to a settlement in the mediation phase. Therefore the advantage of the arb-med procedure is that it motivates the parties to reach an agreement during mediation and avoid an arbitrated decision.[31]

THE FUTURE OF ADR

The various methods of ADR discussed in this chapter experienced a boom period starting in the early 1990s. The primary advantages of ADR in comparison to a court suit not only remain, but have increased: faster, less costly, and less traumatic settlements. In addition, ADR maintains a distinct advantage in comparison to a court trial: maximum involvement of the parties in the dispute, including the opportunity to reach a voluntary settlement. Theodore J. St. Antoine of the University of Michigan Law School predicts that the future of ADR is likely to include an increase in the number of cases, and will include many new forms (such as hybrids) and new subject matter through several avenues including the following:[32]

1. *Employment arbitration:* It is estimated that as of 2000, more U.S. employees were covered by employer-imposed arbitration agreements as a means of resolving termination and other employee-disputed issues than were covered by union collective bargaining agreements. Research indicates that employees with discrimination claims actually succeed more often in employer arbitration systems than in the courts.
2. *Business contracts:* More employers such as retailers, utilities, medical providers, and insurers prefer contracts that specify arbitration as a means of settling disputes with customers, debtors, patients, insureds, and vendors.
3. *Court-ordered ADR:* Because the courts are faced with a rising number of other cases, courts and state agencies are increasingly referring more cases to mediation or arbitration.

A research study by the American Arbitration Association (AAA) reported in 2004 supports St. Antoine's predictions about the future of ADR. The study surveyed *Fortune* 1000 companies and found that the use of ADR is indeed increasing, and that those companies that best utilized ADR as a means to resolve disputes had lower in-house legal department expenses and used a wider range of ADR options (methods and content areas) than those companies that did not efficiently utilize ADR. The most common reported uses of ADR were employment and commercial disputes. The study also determined the following key characteristics of the "most dispute-wise" companies:[33]

- Top management support for ADR that results in greater acceptance and utilization of mediation and arbitration
- A legal department that is integrated into the strategic planning process and therefore has a greater understanding of the types of disputes encountered by the company
- Management that is more focused on preserving important long-term relationships with clients, customers, employees, and suppliers, rather than just winning cases through litigation

SUMMING UP

Think about a negotiation situation in your personal life or at work. Can it be categorized as a bargaining situation that has resulted in or might likely result in a deadlock or impasse?

1. Describe the situation. Is it likely that the parties involved would prefer a settlement of the disputed issues through mediation or as the result of a final and binding decision by an arbitrator, instead of no settlement? Why or why not?

   _____

   _____

2. What are the primary issues to be disputed?

   _____

   _____

3. What do you expect will be the final positions of the parties on each of the unresolved issues?

   _____

   _____

4. If the parties currently do not have a contractual obligation to settle disputes through ADR, should they agree to such an obligation to resolve future issues? Why or why not?

   _____

   _____

5. Draft a contract provision similar to the one in Figure 7.2, which would provide the use of a method of ADR to resolve future issues.

   _____

   _____

_____

_____

6. Which of the primary methods of ADR discussed in this chapter do you believe should be included in the contract provision? Why?

_____

_____

7. Which of the following situations should be considered for inclusion in the contract provision?

Employment _____ Supplier _____ Commercial _____

Consumer _____ Patient _____ Vendor _____

Competitor _____ Acquisition _____ Other _____

8. What advantages and disadvantages would you expect from utilizing mediation and/or arbitration instead of the courts to resolve the dispute?

_____

_____

_____

_____

LEARNING EXERCISE: THE COMMON DRIVEWAY

For more than 30 years David and Shari Wilson lived and raised a family in their dream house that they purchased shortly after their marriage. Now in their retirement years, the Wilsons have encountered an unexpected problem—their new neighbors. Until six months ago the Wilsons' best friends, Edna and Hazen Vrooman, lived next door in a house they built shortly after the Wilsons moved into their home. Because the two lots were small, the Vroomans and Wilsons agreed to have a shared concrete driveway poured the year they both built detached garages in their backyards. The two families never had a problem sharing the driveway even during the years when their children became teenage drivers and both houses had more than two cars. Everyone parked in the back, inside or near the garage, or else on the street, thus leaving the driveway open for entering or leaving either garage.

Last year both of the Vroomans died and their house was sold to a younger couple, George and Amber Green. The Greens have three teenage children, all of whom have cars. On several occasions since the Greens moved in, one or another member of the Green family has left a car parked in the shared driveway, thus blocking it from use by the Wilsons. On Memorial Day the driveway was again blocked, causing Mr. Wilson to call Mr. Green, and the following conversation took place:

MR. WILSON: Mr. Green, one of your cars is blocking the driveway again, and we need to leave.

MR. GREEN: Sorry, I'll find out which one it is and move it.

MR. WILSON:	Thanks, but this problem seems to occur every day, can we meet to discuss how to resolve it?
MR. GREEN:	Sure, I'll be right over ... (The Wilsons meet Mr. Green on their front porch.)
MR. WILSON:	We want to be good neighbors, but we should be able to get in and out of our garage without waiting for you to move a car.
MR. GREEN:	I understand. I tell the kids to park on the street or in the back, but you know how kids are these days.
MRS. WILSON:	Well, when our kids and the Vrooman kids were young and drove cars, we never had this problem—they knew not to park in the driveway.
MR. GREEN:	I'll talk to our kids—they are not bad kids, just forgetful.
MRS. WILSON:	You've said that before, but the problem has only gotten worse.
MR. GREEN:	Well, as long as we're here together ... Your oak tree is well past its prime. Last week I had a tree surgeon look at it because several large limbs have fallen on our property. He said it needs a considerable trimming of the deadwood, which could cost $3,000. He also said it needs to be done soon!
MRS. WILSON:	Edna Vrooman and I planted that tree together as a sign of our friendship the week they moved in. Whenever I look at it, I think of her—she was my best friend.
MR. GREEN:	Sorry, I didn't realize that—I'm sure you miss her—but some of the dead limbs reach out over our house and if they fell they could injure someone or do some real damage.
MR. WILSON:	Since you are bringing up other issues, can you ask your children not to hold their band practice in the garage so late in the evenings? They are good, but it keeps me awake.
MR. GREEN:	We could set a curfew for them, if you can have your tree trimmed.
MRS. WILSON:	But what about the driveway? We must be able to get in and out without calling you every day.
MR. GREEN:	Well, the driveway is right on the dividing line of our two properties, I had it checked out at the courthouse by my lawyer. She said we can do whatever we want on our half of the drive.
MR. WILSON:	But half a driveway is no good, you'd be driving on the grass and mud.
MR. GREEN:	Maybe we could look into widening it?
MR. WILSON:	That would be expensive! It's so long, and we live on Social Security and just don't have the money for something like that, or for trimming the tree.
MR. GREEN:	Well, we are not getting anywhere today. I need to talk with my wife and our lawyer ...

After reading this case of the common driveway, answer these skills questions:

Skill 7.1: Is this dispute at an *impasse*? Why or why not?
Skill 7.2: Is either party experiencing any *settlement pressure*?

Skill 7.3: If the dispute between the Wilsons and the Greens reaches an impasse, should they consider *mediation* to resolve their differences? Why or why not?

Skill 7.4: If further negotiation and mediation should fail to resolve the dispute, why might either the Greens or the Wilsons consider *arbitration* or litigation as a means of reaching a settlement?

Skill 7.5: What *hybrid forms of ADR* are available and should be considered if negotiation fails to produce a settlement?

ENDNOTES

1. Peter B. Stark and Jane Flaherty, *The Only Negotiation Guide You'll Ever Need* (New York: Broadway Books, 2003), 9–11.

2. Hal Bodley, "Red Sox, Yanks Fire Verbal Volleys," *USA Today*, February 18, 2004, available at www.usatoday.com/sports/baseball/al/redsox/2004-02-18-henry-cap_x.htm (accessed September 15, 2006).

3. Charles B. Craver, *Effective Legal Negotiation and Settlement*, 5th ed. (Danvers, MA: Matthew Bender, 2005), 180–181.

4. Norman Brand, ed., *How ADR Works* (Washington, DC: BNA Books, 2002), 1–3.

5. Casey J. Dickinson, "Arbitrator's Post Highlights Alternative Dispute Resolution," *Central New York Business Journal*, October 13, 2000, 5.

6. Raneta L. Mack, "ADR & Y2K: A Simpler Way to Resolve Complex Technology Disputes," *Journal of Alternative Dispute Resolution in Employment* (Summer 2000): 11–15.

7. Robert C. Beasley, "Dispute Resolution—Pros and Cons of the Three Basic Options," *Licensing Journal* 25 (February 2005): 30.

8. The Alternative Dispute Resolution Act of 1998 (28 U.S.C. 651), available at several locations online, including the Web site of the Departmental Office of Civil Rights, U.S. Department of Transportation, www.dotcr.ost.dot.gov/documents/ycr/adr1998.htm.

9. Craver, *Effective Legal Negotiation and Settlement*, 484–487.

10. Steven Mitchell Sack, *The Employee Rights Handbook* (New York: Warner Books, 2000), 348–352.

11. Brand, *How ADR Works*, 4–5.

12. Patrick J. Cleary, *The Negotiation Handbook* (Armonk, NY: Sharpe, 2001), 162–164.

13. Brand, *How ADR Works*, 4–5.

14. Theodore W. Kheel, *The Keys to Conflict Resolution* (New York: Four Walls Eight Windows, 1999), 59–81.

15. Craver, *Effective Legal Negotiation and Settlement*, 490–493.

16. B. McAdoo and A. Hinshaw, "The Challenge of Institutionalizing Alternative Dispute Resolution: Attorney Perspectives on Rule 17 on Civil Litigation in Missouri," *Missouri Law Review* 67 (2002): 473; and B. McAdoo, "A Report to the Minnesota Supreme Court: The Impact of Rule 114 on Civil Litigation Practice in Minnesota," *Hamline Law Review* 25 (2002): 401.

17. Craver, *Effective Legal Negotiation and Settlement*, 492.

18. Ibid.

19. Edwin Witte, *Historical Survey of Labor Arbitration* (Ithaca, NY: Cornell University Press, 1952), 29–33.

20. Frank Elkouri and Edna Asper Elkouri, *How Arbitration Works*, 6th ed. (Washington, DC: BNA Books, 2003), 4.

21. Elkouri and Elkouri, *How Arbitration Works*, 49–51.

22. *Textile Workers v. Lincoln Mills*, 353 U.S. 448 (1957); *United Steelworkers v. American Manufacturing Company*, 363 U.S. 564 (1960); *United Steelworkers v. Warrior & Gulf Navigation Company*, 363 U.S. 574 (1960); and *United Steelworkers v. Enterprise Wheel & Car Corporation*, 363 U.S. 593 (1960).

23. Bureau of National Affairs, *Basic Patterns in Union Contracts*, 14th ed. (Washington, DC: BNA Books, 1995), 35.

24. Elkouri and Elkouri, *How Arbitration Works*, 138–143.

25. Brand, *How ADR Works*, 3.

26. R. Lewicki, D. Saunders, and J. Minton, *Essentials of Negotiation* (Chicago, IL: Irwin, 1997), 203.

27. Daniel R. Marburger and Paul L. Burgess, "Can Prior Offers and Arbitration Outcomes Be Used to Predict the Winners of Subsequent Final-Offer Arbitration Cases?" *Southern Economic Journal* 71 (2004): 93–102.

28. David L. Dickinson, "A Comparison of Conventional, Final-Offer, and 'Combined' Arbitration for Dispute Resolution," *Industrial and Labor Relations Review* 57 (January 2004): 288–301.

29. William H. Ross and Donald E. Conlon, "Hybrid Forms of Third-Party Dispute Resolution: Theoretical Implications of Combining Mediation and Arbitration," *Academy of Management Review* 25 (2000): 416–427.

30. Val Buxton, "Pitfalls and Pratfalls of Impasse Resolution Procedures in the Federal Government: A Negotiator's Experience," *Labor Law Journal* 37 (March 1986): 167–180.

31. Ross and Conlon, "Hybrid Forms of Third-Party Dispute Resolution," 416–427.

32. Cited in Brand, *How ADR Works,* 9–13.

33. Richard Naimark, "Getting Dispute-Wise," *Dispute Resolution Journal* 59 (February–April 2004): 56–57.

Chapter 8

Ethics, Fairness, and Trust in Negotiation

*Y*ou negotiate every day. You may be negotiating for yourself or for other parties. It may be a formal negotiation carried out in your company's boardroom or at a car dealership. Or it may be an informal deal struck on the golf course or at a restaurant. Regardless of the circumstances, when you negotiate you bring your knowledge and information, strategies, skills, and goals to the table. You also bring your ethics and your value system. These factors are important because your own ethics and values, and the ethics and values of those with whom you negotiate, can determine behaviors during negotiations and influence the outcome.

As we note throughout this text, negotiating is a voluntary process that interdependent parties engage in to influence an exchange, balance interests, or resolve conflicts. Two necessary elements of a negotiation are *communication* and *motivation*. Negotiating is certainly a necessary feature of the business world and an indispensable activity for society in general. A negotiation that results in an agreement represents the bargain that the parties want, or at least the bargain they can live with. But, is the bargain *only as good* as the process used to get it? And is there an objectively good or bad bargain?

Whether the parties engage in distributive, integrative, or interest-based bargaining, the bargaining process commonly includes less than frank and open communication. Negotiators use such tactics as anchoring, framing, and trading, as well as concealment, bluffing, exaggeration, posturing, misrepresentation, and withholding or distorting facts. Why? These are all common techniques used to gain an advantage. The Gallup Poll asked a representative cross section of adults to pick the most important values in their daily lives from a list of moral values. The values most often selected were truth, responsibility, freedom, self-respect, fairness, and compassion.[1] How do we reconcile the seemingly deceptive practices used in negotiations—concealment, bluffing, misrepresentation, withholding or distorting facts—with two values people hold dear—truthfulness and fairness? We need to understand how ethics, values, and ethical behavior apply to the negotiation process. And we will discuss how truthfulness and fairness can be a part of the negotiation process even though some negotiating tactics challenge those values—and what it means to be "fair" and "unfair" in both the negotiation process and in negotiation outcomes.

Trust is another essential element in negotiations because each negotiation involves a risk. In this chapter we will explore why trust is essential, how to establish trust, and the tactics that impact trust.

Negotiation Skills

In this chapter we present five negotiation skills that can be learned and developed by the novice negotiator, and applied to the end-of-chapter Learning Exercise, "Settling a Lawsuit."

Skill 8.1   Identify **ethical systems** that may guide parties to a negotiation.

Skill 8.2   Determine the **substantive fairness** of a negotiation.

Skill 8.3   Ensure the **procedural fairness** of a negotiation.

Skill 8.4   Distinguish between **concealment behaviors** in negotiations that are ethical and those that are unethical.

Skill 8.5   Learn to **create trust** in a one-shot negotiation and in a long-term negotiating relationship.

CHAPTER CASE: WITHHOLDING INFORMATION

During recent labor negotiations, both parties knew that the rising cost of health insurance was going to be a major issue. Two years earlier in an attempt to curtail costs, the employer's management, without publicizing or concealing the fact, decided to become self-insured. The previous insurance provider had agreed to become a third-party administrator, so it was likely that the change would not have been apparent to the employees. During the current negotiations, the employer asked that the employees agree to change benefits in order to lessen the premiums the employer paid for the health insurance. The employer told the employees no other measures could be used to reduce those growing costs. In response, the employees asked the negotiator if the employer would consider becoming self-insured so their benefits could stay the same while the employer would be able to control the costs because there wouldn't be an insurance company realizing a profit from their contributions.

It became apparent to the employer's negotiator that the employees had not noticed the change to self-insurance two years earlier. Unfortunately, any savings by becoming self-insured had already been realized in the health care program and would not change the employer's need to have benefits reduced now in order to cut costs in the future. The negotiator worried that if the employees knew their employer had already become self-insured, they would not be willing to give up some of the plan's benefits, expecting rather that the employer absorb the cost. On the other hand, the negotiator wasn't sure it was right to withhold the information from the employees, regardless of the outcome of the negotiations.

ETHICS

Ethics is the study of morality—the worth of moral judgments and principles of conduct. Your ethical belief system is a basis for the **values** you develop. Your values can be influenced by the cultural setting in which you live and by those with whom you associate. Parents, friends, teachers, employers, and co-workers all influence your values. Values reflect your belief about "ends" to be achieved and about the "means" for achieving those desired ends.[2] That is, they determine what you want to accomplish and what you will be willing to do to reach that end.[3]

In addition, adherence to particular values establishes behavioral rules. **Behavioral rules** are the accepted customs, standards, or models you expect of yourself in the conduct of your life and what you expect of others with whom you interact. Thus, in a negotiation, ethics, values, and behavior rules are important because they influence how the parties view each other, how they evaluate the negotiation, and how they act during the negotiation. In the Chapter Case, the *end* that the employer's negotiator valued was an agreement that reduced the employer's cost for health care coverage. The *means* used to reach that end included withholding information that may or may not have influenced the outcome. Did the negotiator act ethically?

In Western civilization, three ethical theories have been used to describe alternate views of human nature. One ethical theory was developed by the Greek philosopher Aristotle (384–322 B.C.), who believed that the inherent nature of human beings was "good."[4] And he believed that no matter what the action, a human being's ultimate nature was to try to realize a truly good end. And, as it is inconsistent with "goodness" to use a "bad" means, both the means used and the ends achieved must be "good." Aristotle promoted a fairness or justice approach to ethics, or **ethics of purpose**.

Certainly in the employer–employee negotiations in the Chapter Case, the mutual *end* the parties wanted to reach was a contract—the employer wanted a contract that he could afford, and the employees wanted a contract that maximized wages and benefits. Of course, the employees realized that if their contract is not affordable, then the employer may go out of business and they will be unemployed. And the employer realized that an unfair agreement will not foster the type of workplace environment that is good for business. The *means* that the parties used to reach a fair and affordable contract was collective bargaining. Following an ethics of purpose, if the parties conduct their bargaining under acceptable behavioral rules then it could be argued that the means are good—even if the employer's negotiator withholds information. A "fair and affordable" contract covers economic issues (wages, overtime, bonuses), as well as noneconomic issues (grievance procedure, job security, promotions). The design of a health care program is just one issue. In this case the employer's need for a reduction of benefits would not be changed simply because the employees learned that the employer was already self-insured. One could argue that withholding information on this one issue in this context was necessary to reach agreement and therefore a good means.

A second ethical theory was developed by the German philosopher Immanuel Kant (1724–1804), who believed that, through reason, people would recognize that they should treat others as they wished to be treated, and therefore would devise rational rules of conduct by which to live. Any other approach would be inconsistent and irrational. Kant supported the classic rule of "do unto others as you would have them do unto you," or **ethics of principle**. However, as discussed in Chapter 1, the rational thought process is complex. People may evaluate the same information and reach totally different conclusions because they receive and judge information using their own unique knowledge and experience. Kant's theory relies upon a collective *rationalization* that establishes moral rules. In the Chapter Case, under Kant's theory, before making his own decision the employer's negotiator has to ask himself whether he would think the employees were unethical if they withheld information from him at the bargaining table.

A third theory was developed by the English philosopher and political economist John Stuart Mill (1806–1873), who believed that one can only judge the moral value of an action by its result. If an action benefits more people than it harms, then it is moral. Mill's *utilitarianism* suggests that ethical actions are those that provide the greatest balance of good over evil. To analyze an issue using the utilitarian approach, you first identify the various courses of action available; then you ask who will be affected by each action and what benefits or harms will be derived from each; and then you choose the action that will produce the greatest benefit and the least harm. Mill recognized that few moral decisions are without some negative effect. A pharmaceutical company rushes to market a new, inexpensive AIDS drug in Africa because it has great potential to stop the AIDS virus from spreading, although the side effects for some patients could be fatal. The drug is distributed because more people are helped than are harmed. Mill supported the theory that "the end justifies the means," or **ethics of consequence**. In the Chapter Case, the employer's negotiator can certainly argue that the end of reaching an affordable agreement justified the means used in the negotiation.

The three ethical theories can be summarized as follows:

Aristotle	Ethics of purpose	People are inherently **good**.
		They will strive to reach a **good end**.
		They will use **good means** to do so.
Kant	Ethics of principle	People are inherently **rational**.
		They will see the **right way** to do things.
		They will pursue **rational means**.

Mill	Ethics of consequence	People will determine the **outcome of an action.**
		They will do that which does the **most good.**
		They will use the **means necessary** to reach a good end.

In Box 8.1 you can test your understanding of these ethical theories by applying the philosophers' principles to the facts in the Chapter Case.

Values and Behaviors in Negotiations

As stated earlier, *values* are the patterns by which you orient yourself to the environment—basic beliefs about life that come from your ethics and that underlie your behavior. Values are both *self-centered* and *social-centered* because they involve both

---

BOX 8.1   Tactics for Success

Moral Decision Making

Using what you have learned about the philosophies of Aristotle, Kant, and Mill, test your ability to recognize whether a particular behavior is ethical by applying those principles to the Chapter Case. Consider the following question:

Should the negotiator tell the employees that the employer is already self-insured?

1. *Ethics of consequence: The end justifies the means.*

   What benefits will result if he does?

   _____

   What harm will result if he does not?

   _____

   Which outcome has the best overall consequence?

   _____

2. *Ethics of principle: Do unto others as you would have them do unto you.*

   Are the employees entitled to the information?

   _____

   Should the employer expect similar treatment from the other side?

   _____

3. *Ethics of purpose: A good end cannot be reached with bad means.*

   Does withholding the information subvert the negotiation process?

   _____

   If the employees do not have all the information, can they fairly evaluate the employer's offer?

   _____

---

the individual and society. The internal, self-centered aspects of values are standards that you have internalized and accepted for *your own behavior.* External, social-centered aspects of values are guiding principles established by the social environment in which you live. These values are what you would expect from *someone else's behavior.*

Milton Rokeach, who did extensive studies on values, explains that values are beliefs about what is good or desirable. These beliefs are enduring, and are stable enough for the behavior stemming from them to be reasonably consistent and predictable.[5] He distinguishes between values concerned with *ends* (what we want to achieve, or our **terminal values**) and values concerned with *means* (the way we go about our lives, or our **instrumental values**). Terminal values include such ends as a comfortable life, a sense of accomplishment, equality, freedom, happiness, self-respect, and social recognition. To achieve these ends, instrumental values include independence, honesty, ambition, courage, logic, responsibility, self-control, and broad-mindedness.

In a typical negotiation, the terminal value can usually be found in the object of the negotiation. For example, employees and employers negotiate an employment contract so that the parties can afford a comfortable life and provide their families with security. The parties resolving a conflict over a breached agreement may be seeking equality and/or self-respect as a part of their negotiation. Many of the instrumental values (the means) come into play in a negotiation. Skilled negotiators can use imagination and logic to create opportunities for the parties to achieve their mutual goals. Such bargaining techniques and strategies as being honest, cheerful and polite, and maintaining self-control play a part in a successful bargaining outcome.

Behavioral rules, as stated earlier, are implicit or explicit standards, customs, or models that spring from our values and guide our actions. There are two types of behavioral rules—descriptive and injunctive. *Descriptive behavioral rules* describe or show the common behavior in people in certain situations—that is, they describe what people do. *Injunctive behavior rules* judge or show what behavior is approved and disapproved within the culture—that is, they describe what people *should* do.

Injunctive rules prescribe the socially appropriate way to act or to respond in a given situation—that is, the "normal" course of action and actions to avoid if at all possible. Behavioral rules, if written down, become formal rules of proper conduct—laws, codes of ethics, and so forth. In most instances behavioral rules are adopted implicitly as people align their actions and reactions until a consensus of proper behavior emerges. This method of creating behavioral rules accounts for continuity in beliefs across generations and organizations: Children learn the rules of appropriate behavior in their culture; new employees learn the boss's list of dos and don'ts; newcomers to a club discover the group's standards and expectations.

FAIRNESS

According to Eleanor Holmes Norton, a professor of law at Georgetown University Law Center and Washington D.C.'s delegate to Congress, because bargaining is an indispensable activity that must continue and is not inherently unethical, some tactics used in negotiations appropriately deviate from ethical behavior under certain conditions.[6] **Fairness** underlies negotiations because negotiating is a voluntary endeavor, and unless the parties anticipate a "fair shot" they are not likely to engage in the negotiations. Fairness has both substantive and procedural qualities.

As you read earlier in the chapter, ethical negotiations involve upholding values and adhering to behavioral rules. According to educators David A. Lax and James K. Sebenius, areas to examine on the question of fairness in negotiations are the distribution of value created by the negotiations and the appropriateness of certain tactics. The *substantive fairness* of a negotiation may be seen in the distribution of value from that negotiation and the *procedural fairness* is seen in the appropriateness of certain negotiation tactics.[7]

Substantive Fairness in Negotiations

Substantive fairness is concerned with dividing the value claimed or created in a negotiation equitably. But is determining whether a division of value is *equitable* a subjective or objective test? If both parties to a negotiation are satisfied, does that mean that the negotiation has met the substantive fairness test? Whether a negotiated agreement is fair—that is, reasonable, evenhanded, and broadly acceptable—may be determined by applying four principles: proportionality, reciprocity, impartiality, and the requirement that all parties be heard.

First, fairness does not always mean identical or equal treatment or distribution of assets; it requires *proportionality*. A fair agreement takes the parties' circumstances into account. When negotiators talk about "dividing the pie," they seldom require that the pie be split 50-50. Circumstances surrounding the investment of the parties in making the pie can dictate a totally different but nonetheless fair split.

Second, fairness is associated with *reciprocity,* or mutual responsiveness to each other's concessions, which seems both intrinsically fair and is instrumental in achieving cooperation. As we will discuss later in this chapter in the section on trust, concessions from one party can generate comparable concessions from the other party, and that cycle triggers cooperation. Concessions do not need to be identical; again, commitments are sought from the parties in light of their different circumstances.

Third, fairness requires some *impartiality.* A fair agreement cannot be measured simply by the fact that the parties agreed to it. There must be some balancing of the different interests in the final bargain for it to be considered fair.[8]

And fourth, fairness requires that the parties *be heard.* People tend to judge a negotiation as fair when they have had an opportunity to voice their point of view and have it considered by the other party.[9]

Procedural Fairness in Negotiations

As stated earlier, fairness also involves procedural issues. People choose to negotiate when they are confident the process will result in a fair agreement that can be performed to mutual advantage. How critical is truth-telling in negotiations? A negotiation is about communication. Information is given, sought, analyzed, and used to reach agreement. But information can also be withheld or distorted. How do you reconcile the lack of truth-telling in negotiations and how do you ensure the fairness of the result?

One way to judge the fairness of the outcome of a negotiation is to judge the fairness of the process. This *functionalist model* for negotiations provides a way to test the ethics of the bargaining process through the bargaining tactics of negotiators. Bargaining is a self-regulated process—that is, there are no external rules or guidelines that regulate how the parties bargain and no external arbitrator to hold the parties accountable for unethical behavior. Unlike a court proceeding where the witness is put under oath to tell the truth and the judge ensures truth-telling, a negotiator can give evasive answers, fail to offer clarifying information, and engage in any manner of puffing. It is up to the parties to police the process by recognizing the tactics being used. Bargaining is an adversarial process, but its voluntary nature demands that the adversaries cooperate to reach agreement. So although you may use any number of tactics to advance your position, you must be willing to compromise to avoid a breakdown of the negotiations. The fairness of strategies used in a negotiation may only be determined by their success. A basic "take it or leave it" approach to negotiations may not be inherently unfair, but it may certainly be unsuccessful.

The assumptions of the functionalist model are that bargaining is an indispensable process; the purpose of bargaining is to reach a valid agreement; practices that threaten a valid agreement violate the purpose of the negotiation; and bargaining is a voluntary, adversarial process in which the parties knowingly use bargaining techniques to gain information and obtain fair treatment. Within this context, you can see how achieving truthfulness and fairness in negotiations is both essential and difficult. Fairness and truthfulness are important because they engender trust and enable the parties to reach agreement. However, parties using bargaining tactics that provide less than full "truthfulness" are not necessarily being unfair and are not necessarily threatening a valid agreement. True, giving totally false information in a negotiation violates the assumption that bargaining techniques will elicit accurate information and will result in a fair agreement and is, therefore, unethical. However, deceptive offers and counteroffers and settlement point deceptions do not always prevent accurate information, because the truthfulness of the parties' positions will come out as the negotiation progresses.

Avoiding a direct answer to a question, failing to volunteer information, puffing, and bluffing are such well-known bargaining techniques that, while they might limit the opponent's access to information, they do not necessarily violate the process. The parties are able to counter such techniques with other techniques to arrive at truthful information. The fairness of tactics has to be determined within the context of the particular negotiation. For example, it might be unfair for a lawyer negotiating with a layperson to use certain tactics that would be fair against another lawyer. In a long-standing relationship in which both parties have ample opportunity to know details about each other, concealment of one's agenda may not be unfair. In the Chapter Case, an argument can be made that the employer was not unfair when he did not tell the employees that he had already become self-insured, because that information was never kept from the employees—they just hadn't bothered to find it out.

Michael Wheeler contends there is no question that **procedural fairness** serves the interest of the negotiation process. It brings all needed parties to the negotiating table and keeps them there; it enables the parties to evaluate alternative proposals with an open mind; it facilitates resolving conflicting interests and claims so the parties can reach agreement; it legitimizes the outcome to important constituencies on both sides of the table; it helps to secure the implementation of and compliance with agreements; and it establishes and maintains successful cooperation in the long run. Citing a pragmatist's reasoning of enlightened self-interest—"what goes around comes around"—Wheeler suggests that negotiators should test their values when going into a negotiation because the issues at stake are not only the object of the negotiation, but also the relationship between the parties. His test for meeting the procedural fairness standard in negotiations is simple:

1. Does it meet the *reciprocity standard*—how would you feel about being treated in this way?
2. Does it meet the *universality standard*—would you advise others to behave in this way?
3. Does it meet the *publicity standard*—would you like to see your actions described on the front page of the newspaper?
4. Does it meet the *trusted friend standard*—would you be comfortable telling your best friend or spouse about your actions?
5. Does it meet the *legacy standard*—do you want to be known or remembered for acting in this way?[10]

Let's now return to the Chapter Case. The employer's negotiator in this case did not tell the employees that the employer was already self-insured. He stated again, however, that the employer's research indicted that the only savings that could be projected into the next year would have to come from a change in the benefits being offered to the employees. Eventually the employees agreed to those changes. How did the negotiator measure up on Wheeler's procedural fairness test? Would the negotiator want to have information withheld from him, even if the outcome of the negotiation would be the same (reciprocity)? Probably not. Negotiation is about information—sharing it, analyzing it, and acting upon it. Less than full disclosure of relevant information by one party puts the other at a disadvantage. Would the negotiator advise others to withhold information in this manner (universality)? Probably not. Even if in this circumstance an argument can be made that the non-disclosure was irrelevant to the eventual outcome, it would be difficult to justify such actions in most negotiations. Would the negotiator like to see his actions described on the front page of the newspaper (publicity)? Definitely not. The negotiator would prefer that this tactic be below the radar screen because it could very well damage the employer's future relationship with the employees. Would the negotiator be comfortable telling his best friend about it (trusted friend)? Probably so. Again, the information that was not disclosed by the negotiator was available to the employees elsewhere, and the information would not change the core issue regarding the need to address health care costs. Finally, would the negotiator want to be remembered for this action (legacy)? Probably not. Regardless of the fact that the nondisclosed information was probably irrelevant to the actual negotiations, it raises ethical concerns. The negotiator would know, as discussed throughout this chapter, that one of the characteristics of a negotiator is his or her reputation for trustworthiness.

Ethical dilemmas, such as the one faced by the negotiator in the Chapter Case, are something to be avoided. Box 8.2 suggests some ways to avoid being trapped into lying in a negotiation.

BOX 8.2 Traps to Avoid

Alternatives to Lying

If you find yourself trapped in an ethical dilemma, find alternatives to lying and thus maintain trust in the negotiations by using these techniques:

1. When asked what your bottom line is, instead of lying about it, ask your opponents for their bottom line or simply say you are not ready to reveal yours. One negotiator deftly deflects such demands by explaining his goal in the negotiation and assuring his opponent that he will reveal his bottom line in due time.

2. If you intend to claim "lack of authority" to give up a particular item at the negotiating table, don't seek such authority to do so before the negotiations begin. So when asked, you can truthfully say you do not have the authority or you can even indicate that you do not have the authority but that you will seek it if it means an item can be agreed upon.

3. If you don't want to volunteer available alternatives to a demand by your opponent because many of those alternatives may provide more than your opponent is actually hoping for, don't say there aren't any when you know there are. Rather, try to elicit your opponent's options, to which you can respond.

4. Don't lie about your intentions; only make promises you can keep. In a recent labor negotiation, the union was adamant about retaining a provision in the contract that would require the employees to join or stay in the union or the employer would fire them. The employer's negotiator explained that the law would not allow the employer to fire employees for refusing to join the union. The employer and the union could, however, require the non-member employees to pay a "fair share" amount to support the union's efforts in collective bargaining. The union wasn't satisfied because its officers believed that just seeing the requirement in the contract would be enough to discourage any employee from not joining the union. The employer refused to include the provision because it was not a promise he could keep.

5. Never lie about facts, focus on the uncertainty of certain facts, or limit your discussion to an expression of your opinion about facts. In the Chapter Case, for example, the negotiator truthfully told the employees that the changes in the health care benefits he was pursuing with them were the only changes that would reduce the employer's costs. He did not tell them that being self-insured did not save money, since it had but had already been taken into account.

Source: Adapted from G. Richard Shell, "Bargaining with the Devil Without Losing Your Soul: Ethics in Negotiation," in *What's Fair: Ethics for Negotiators,* eds. Carrie Menkel-Meadow and Michael Wheeler (San Francisco: Jossey-Bass, 2004), 57–78.

Appropriate or Inappropriate Negotiating Tactics

The essence of much bargaining involves convincing the other side of what you will or will not agree to in order to reach an agreement. Because concealing your bottom line while still moving the negotiations forward may result in a better outcome for you, you have an incentive, or at least may be tempted, to use various misleading tactics. There is nothing unfair about such tactics if both parties understand that such tactics are a part of the process. Certainly, for instance, you expect certain misleading tactics when buying a car. Representations by the car salesperson that he or she has no authority to cut the sticker price but will try to get approval from the manager *if* you will commit to buying the car is a familiar tactic that does not take advantage of most buyers. Why? Because such tactics have been displayed in movies and on TV for years. Parents have warned their children about encountering such tactics when they buy their first car. In fact, such techniques are so well known that the sellers of Saturn automobiles have pursued an aggressive ad campaign centered on the fact that their sales staff do not negotiate price. The sticker price is the sale price. Savvy buyers respond to misleading sales tactics with tactics of their own. They warn the salesperson that if he or she comes back from the manager without a substantial reduction in the price of the car, there will be no sale. Neither party is ready to stop the negotiation; they are simply trying to find each other's bottom line.

What tactics are commonly considered to be "fair" in negotiations may depend on how you view the negotiation process. If you view *negotiations as a game,* for instance, then like poker, bluffing is an acceptable tactic. In that situation, you have a realistic distrust of your opponent and expect the same from her. This view of bargaining as a game where lying or bluffing is okay may cause difficulties if your opponent does not share your view or if she's simply not playing the same game. Furthermore, if one of the parties cannot freely exit the negotiations, then the use of misleading tactics in that negotiation might be unfair. If you expect that both you and your opponent will do the right thing simply because it *is* the right thing, then you have an *idealistic view* of negotiations. Bluffing, posturing, or misrepresentations are tactics that take advantage of the other party and, therefore, are not "right." And finally, if you believe that "what goes around comes around," you have a *pragmatic view* of negotiations. You believe deception during negotiations may be necessary, but you know you cannot cross the line between what may be acceptable deception and what is unacceptable lying, or you will ruin your credibility.[11]

With business ethics much in the news today, the topic of ethical tactics in negotiations has become an even more complex topic. As noted earlier in the chapter, even philosophers disagree about the correct compass to use to measure our actions: Can we reach good ends if the means are questionable? Do unto others as we would have them do unto us? Or do the ends justify the means? Each of those measures requires subjective analysis and people often disagree about what is good, right, or harmful. But even if parties know what's right, they may be motivated by self-interest to do otherwise. Self-interest—defined as pursuing an opportunity for private gain or avoiding personal loss or hardship—is a powerful motivator.[12]

Roy J. Lewicki and Robert J. Robinson propose that the ethical problems in negotiations commonly involve one or more of the following lapses in truth-telling: (1) deception, (2) misrepresentation of one's position, (3) bluffing, and (4) falsification.[13]

Deception   In negotiations there are plenty of opportunities to deceive one another about the matters under negotiation. In the Chapter Case, the employer had to decide whether to withhold the information on the self-insurance health care plan or disclose the fact and risk losing a tactical advantage at the bargaining table. There are, however, disincentives to deceiving the other party that also spring from self-interest. In the Chapter Case the employer was aware that the employees could discover the information about self-insurance; it had not been concealed. If they discovered that the employer had deceived them about such an important issue, it might negatively impact not only the current negotiations but also all future negotiations between the parties.

Opportunities for deception about the matters under negotiation are greater when the *information disparity* between the parties is great. There is always some difference in the amount or type of information each party has when negotiations begin. If that difference is great, then unless the more knowledgeable party volunteers information, the other party might not know enough to ask the right questions. So through passive concealment, the more knowledgeable party can be deceptive.

There is also more opportunity for deception when the truth of the facts presented in the negotiations is *difficult to verify* by any objective standard. The employees in the Chapter Case would find it difficult to dispute the health insurance premium information provided to them by the employer because such costs are a result of a complex formula applied to the unique profile of the group being insured. Other instances when deception is likely are when a party has *insufficient resources* to make the kind of inquiry necessary to verify information, when interaction is a *one-shot deal* so the time available to confirm information is limited, and when the *intent to deceive* is hard to establish. In the Chapter Case, the employer could respond to the request to "consider" self-insuring by assuring the employees that all avenues available to cut costs have been explored and that reducing benefits is the only choice available at the time. Then if the employees discover that the employer had already become self-insured, the employer can claim that there was no intent to deceive because self-insuring would not have resulted in any additional savings.

Misrepresenting Your Position   Another opportunity for unethical tactics in negotiations concerns concealing your *settlement preferences*—that is, exactly what you will settle for in a given negotiation. As described by J. Gregory Dees and Peter C. Cramton, there is a fundamental clash between moral theory and negotiations practice embodied in the settlement-issue deception.[14] Although lying about your bottom line is arguably unethical in many situations, it is a widely condoned negotiation strategy and considered "shrewd" when successful. The authors do distinguish between misrepresenting your bottom line and lying about other issues at the bargaining table. For example, a homeowner might claim that she is in no hurry to sell her house, even though she needs to sell immediately—which is acceptable lying, as opposed to her false claim that the roof of the house is in great condition.

Dees and Cramton's **Mutual Trust Principle** rests on the fact that there are three types of negotiators: (1) *opportunists,* who will seek their own self-interest in a negotiation regardless of the other party's actions; (2) *moral idealists,* who act according to their own moral concepts, also regardless of the other party's actions; and (3) *pragmatists,* who are willing and able to constrain their self-seeking behavior on moral grounds, provided the other party does the same. A pragmatist believes it would be unfair to require you to take an action out of respect for your opponent, if you have no reason to believe that the other party will treat you with the same respect. Thus the Mutual Trust Principle requires you to reveal your bottom line only if you have reason to believe your opponent will reveal his bottom line. A unilateral decision to refrain from deceiving your opponent exposes you to exploitation, is not likely to solicit your opponent's real bottom line, and is not likely to have a positive outcome for you. This self-defense strategy of deception has come under some criticism, however, because it would seem to allow you to engage in any unscrupulous behavior if you have reason to believe that your opponent will also engage in any unscrupulous behavior, or at least you if don't know that your opponent won't.[15]

Bluffing There is a significant opportunity for unethical behavior in negotiations when *bluffing* about future actions—that is, when making false representations embodied in threats and promises. Threats are often a part of traditional pressure bargaining, ranging from a threat to leave the bargaining table to threats of closing a business and laying off workers. Likewise, promises are often made during a negotiation to reach agreement. In the Chapter Case, the employer could "promise" to look into self-insuring the health care plans as a ploy to reach agreement. *Deceptive* threats and promises, on the other hand, differ from simply not offering information to the other party or concealing one's bottom line, because they are acts of commission. That is, a party affirmatively makes threats or promises that it does not intend to act upon in order to get the other party to concede something in the negotiations.

When a party makes a threat to leave the negotiations unless you make a significant concession, here are some practical ways to assess your opponent's credibility:

1. Did he take any action that will make it *costly* for him *not* to follow through on the threat?
2. Did he take any action that would actually make it *impossible* for him *not* to follow through on the threat?
3. Did he turn over the control to follow through on the threat to someone else you have less influence over?
4. Is he known for following through on his threats?
5. Has he demonstrated that even though following through on the threat may cost him today, in the long run he will benefit?

For example, in an apparent push to speed up contract talks with UPS, Captain Tom Nicholson, president of the Independent Pilots Association (the pilots' collective bargaining unit), *publicly* called for a "last, best, and final" offer from UPS within seven days or he would take a strike vote to his membership. UPS initially refused to commit to the deadline. However, because the threat was made publicly, UPS had to weigh the union president's increased personal cost to his reputation for not following through if UPS did not satisfy his demands. In fact, Nicholson did leave himself some "wiggle room." He announced that he would pull together UPS's offers from recent talks and let members vote on those. If the contract didn't settle as a result of those actions, he would seek approval from his membership for a strike. Arguably, Nicholson in this example ceded control to his membership to vote for or against a strike, although the membership will typically follow the advice of its leaders on a vote such as this. UPS needed to assess whether the Pilots Association and its president were given to idle threats or if in the past they have done exactly as promised. The last strike of UPS workers, in 1997, cost UPS about $750 million in revenue and disrupted the supply chains of thousands of businesses across the country. Even though that strike was by a different union, the Pilots Association had to be aware of the Teamsters' success in forcing concessions from UPS as a result of their actions.[16]

Falsification   Steven P. Cohen, author of *Negotiating Skills for Managers*,[17] believes that ethical negotiations are a paradigm for good business. Business is about exchanging things of value with others in order to meet the interests of the companies involved. Negotiation involves the exchange of information. False information leads to bad deals and is bad for business. As an example, Cohen cites the corporate scandals of Arthur Andersen, Enron, WorldCom, and Tyco, in which company officers gave false accounting information (1) to investors, to induce them to purchase or hold stock while insiders were selling; (2) to employees, to accept corporate decisions that caused them to lose their jobs and their retirement funds; and (3) to lending institutions, to extend credit to non-creditworthy businesses. Their unethical dealings led not just to record bankruptcies, but also to jail terms for some company officials. Unethical negotiating tactics may induce parties to reach an agreement to which they cannot be truly committed. Reluctant parties make undependable partners. Ethical negotiation, like good business, furthers and strengthens the relationships of the parties, giving value to all the participants.[18]

Researchers have attempted to discern what tactics are acceptable in a typical negotiation. In two surveys, M.B.A. students were asked to rate 18 tactics, used in a variety of negotiation settings and with differing levels of dishonesty, on perceived ethical appropriateness and the likelihood that they might use the tactic (see Table 8.1). In both studies, the students generally agreed on four tactics they perceived to be appropriate, two they believed were marginal, and 12 they judged to be inappropriate. They also indicated they would likely use only those tactics they considered appropriate or marginal.[19]

Of course, Table 8.1 does not include an exhaustive list of potentially unethical tactics. Table 8.2 presents some typical gambits in negotiations that are potentially unethical, and some practical responses.

Table 8.1 Appropriate and Inappropriate Negotiation Tactics

In two surveys, M.B.A. students were asked to rate 18 negotiation tactics according to perceived ethical appropriateness. Here are the results:

APPROPRIATE TACTICS	INAPPROPRIATE TACTICS
• Gain information about your opponent by asking friends, associates, and contacts.	• Misrepresent factual information to support your own position.
• Make an unrealistically high opening demand.	• Misrepresent the nature of negotiations to third parties to protect confidentiality.
• Hide your real bottom line.	• Misrepresent nature of negotiations to third parties to improve your position.
• Give the false impression that you aren't in a hurry to pressure your opponent.	• Misrepresent factual information to your opponent because he has done so.
	• Falsely threaten your opponent.
	• Promise good things with no ability to deliver.
MARGINAL TACTICS	• Bypass your opponent's negotiator to undermine opponent's confidence in him.
• Make an unrealistically high or low first offer.	• Threaten to undermine your opponent with his boss.
• Lead your opponent to believe you are the only game in town, when you are not.	• Bypass your opponent's negotiator to get opponent to join your side.
	• Gain confidential information by paying associates and contacts.
	• Gain confidential information by hiring your opponent's employee.
	• Gain confidential information by cultivating your opponent's friendship with gifts or personal favors.

Source: Adapted from Roy J. Lewicki and Robert J. Robinson, "Ethical and Unethical Bargaining Tactics: An Empirical Study," in *What's Fair: Ethics for Negotiators,* eds. Carrie Menkel-Meadow and Michael Wheeler (San Francisco: Jossey-Bass, 2004), 221–245.

TRUST

A negotiation requires an interaction between at least two parties who have a *relationship;* there are various degrees of relationships, from casual to intimate. The parties must be *motivated* to negotiate. That is, each party must need or at least perceive that he or she wants or needs something that the other party has or can control. A negotiation requires the parties to *communicate.* Negotiation is about information—asking

Table 8.2 Unethical Negotiating Gambits

Negotiating Gambit	How It Works	How to Respond
The Decoy	Highlight an issue of no real importance to you in order to get a concession on another issue.	Stay focused on the "highlighted" issue and address it, not something else.
The Red Herring	Similar to the Decoy; make a demand you intend to drop in exchange for something you want.	Stay focused on the real issue being negotiated and watch for the issue your opponent seems willing to trade.
The Deliberate Mistake	One side leaves something out of or in the bargain advantageous to their opponent, only to "discover" it after the deal is made and insist it be taken out or added in.	Although you might be tempted to leave this advantageous mistake in the deal, the right thing to do is to point it out before the deal is finalized.
Escalation	After both sides are fully invested in the deal, make another demand because you have the leverage to do so.	Tie up all details before the deal is "done." Build personal relationships with your bargaining partner.
Planted Information	Surreptitiously plant false information so your opponent finds it.	Verify any information you get. Be wary if it comes from an unknown or unreliable source.
Never-Ending Negotiation	Make, break, or change verbal agreements when the other side believes the negotiations are concluded. Can include actually changing terms in the written agreement.	Don't be tempted to agree to the changes just to get done! The best defense is to keep a record of each part of the agreement as it is concluded and have both parties sign off on it.

Sources: Adapted from Roger Dawson, *Secrets of Power Negotiating*, 2nd ed. (Franklin Lakes, NJ: Career Press, 2001), 105–123; and Chester L. Karrass, *The Negotiating Game* (New York: HarperCollins, 1992), 183.

for it, giving it, analyzing it, and using it to reach agreement. And both parties must be able to *deliver on their agreement.* **Trust** plays a significant role in successful negotiations because all negotiations involve some level of risk. In order to be motivated to take a risk and enter into a bargain, there must be some level of trust between the parties based upon their degree of relationship and the strength of their belief that the party will perform.

Denise M. Rousseau, professor of organization behavior at the University of California–Berkeley and the 2004–2005 president of the Academy of Management, and her colleagues Sim B. Sitkin, Ronald S. Burt, and Colin Camerer are on the forefront of research on understanding "trust" within business organizations.[20] According to their research, trust is a complex phenomenon that requires analysis because of its essential need within the negotiation process. Trust enables cooperative behavior, reduces harmful conflict and transaction costs, and facilitates the work of the parties. Trust is not simply cooperation; cooperation may be coerced. The two essential elements of trust are *risk* and a *relationship.* **Risk** refers to the perceived probability of loss and some uncertainty regarding whether or not the other party intends to act appropriately. Trust also requires an *interdependent relationship* where the interests of one party rely to some degree upon the other party. Degrees of that dependency will alter the nature of the trust in a relationship as described in more detail in the following discussion.

Five Bases for Trust

According to Rousseau, there are five different bases of trust with varying degrees of intensity: deterrence-based trust, calculus-based trust (or self-interest trust), relational trust, identity-based trust, and institutional-based trust.

Deterrence-based trust is formed when you believe that someone else is trustworthy because there is a severe penalty imposed if that person does not perform. A construction contract often has automatic and specific dollar damages when the contractor fails to perform certain tasks. In such cases the damages, perhaps a daily amount for each day the project remains undone after a certain and agreed-upon finish date, are significant enough to be a deterrent to a breach of the contractor's obligation. Deterrence-based trust is at the narrowest end of a continuum of trust. The penalties involved in deterrence-based trust foster a certain amount of cooperation, but there is less risk or reliance when the exchange is highly structured and easily monitored.

Calculus-based trust or *self-interest trust* is a rational choice made on the belief that the other party intends to perform an action that is beneficial to both parties. The trust is formed not just because there is a penalty for nonperformance, but also because there is credible information on the reputation and/or qualifications of the other party upon which someone can rely. The foundation of this trust, however, is the self-interest of the party. So there must be some certainty that the value of the exchange will be realized. In other words, you trust—but verify! For example, a company's purchasing director would check out the references or qualifications of a potential supplier and make a decision based upon such research. The transaction would be limited in time and scope, so that failure to perform would show up immediately and the relationship could be easily terminated. Calculus-based trust involves more risk than deterrence-based trust, but does not significantly threaten one's real interests.

Relational trust is developed through repeated and positive interactions between parties over time. The trust is based upon the reliability and dependability of past performance that gives rise to a certainty that the other party will perform in the future. The repeated cycle of exchange, risk-taking, and successful performance strengthens the depth of trust between the parties and the formation of attachments. In this type of trust one anticipates not only a positive performance from the other party, but more importantly that the other party will not do anything negative in its performance. Both parties benefit from the exchanges and build strong bonds that support the relationship. A study of the business relationships established between bank managers and small firms found that relational trust, created by providing a customer orientation and a personnel stability, produces more customer loyalty than might be expected by the economic self-interest of the customer alone.[21]

Relational trust can survive a lapse of performance if the parties evidence a willingness to restore good faith and fair dealing. Major League Baseball owners and players tried to reestablish trust with their fans by evidencing an aggressive approach to eliminating steroid use by the players. In January 2005 they agreed to a tougher steroid-testing program that included penalties for first-time offenders and random, year-round steroid checks for all players, an expanded list of banned substances, and specific penalties for offenders.[22] The agreement was hailed as a significant accomplishment because it was done quickly and professionally. This agreement on steroid testing, a recently concluded agreement with the umpires' union, and a 10-year agreement with the minor leagues signaled a change in the way Major League Baseball owners and players negotiate. Between 1972 and the start of the 2002 negotiations, every round of negotiations between baseball's owners and players produced either a strike or a lockout. Baseball survived the 232-day strike in the 1994–1995 season, but the years of distrust between owners and players threatened the future of Major League Baseball. And although an agreement was reached without a work stoppage, the 2002 negotiations went down to the wire with a threat of a players' strike looming.[23] The quick resolution of the steroid-testing program was successful only because the parties had reestablished an atmosphere of trust that had been significantly eroded over three decades of labor disputes. They did this, some say, out of necessity because of congressional pressure to set national standards banning steroid use in all professional sports. But most players and owners cited a desire to reestablish baseball's popularity with the fans as the motivating factor.[24]

Identity-based trust is similar to relational trust in that it develops when the parties engage in a cycle of cooperation, shared resources, and information exchanges, but in this case the intensity of such exchanges creates an "us" culture rather than an "us and them" culture. A partnership, such as a law firm or an accounting firm, would be an example of an identity-based trust relationship established in business.

Institutional-based trust can be found in both organizational and societal systems that require reliance on the performance of others. Within organizations, "teamwork" cultures institutionalize cooperation and reliance by basing rewards upon the performance of the group. Collective bargaining laws that require employers to bargain with representatives of their employees can be the springboard to an actual trust relationship between management and labor. From a broader societal perspective, the creation of trust stemming from compliance with traffic laws can be seen in the basic ability to drive with some confidence that *most* other drivers will stop at a red light.

A person imposes penalties and conducts an arm's-length transaction when deterrence-based trust is involved because he or she is uncertain whether the other party can be trusted. And although research lessens the uncertainty about performance, calculation-based trust seldom establishes a relationship that transcends the transaction itself. Relational and identity-based trusts are firmly grounded in the interdependencies of the parties and the certainty that the other party intends to act appropriately. Institutional-based trust is created by the interdependencies of parties as a result of external forces, and there is a high certainty that other parties will act appropriately.

In Table 8.3 we compare the basis, qualities, and characteristics of these five different forms of trust, and the nature of the risk and interdependency found in each one.

Table 8.3 Forms of Trust

	DETERRENCE-BASED TRUST	CALCULUS-BASED TRUST	RELATIONAL TRUST	IDENTITY-BASED TRUST	INSTITUTIONAL-BASED TRUST
Basis	Penalty	Self-interest	Belief that other party has concern for welfare	Belief that both parties share concern for welfare	Organizational and societal systems that institutionalize cooperation
Qualities	Fosters cooperation, but not necessarily trust	Rational choice based upon research on competence and trustworthiness; trust but verify	Repeated cycle of exchange, risk-taking, and performance	Cooperation, sharing resources and information, creating an "us" culture	Cooperation or adherence to standards due to external controls
Nature of Risk and Relationship	High risk and no interdependency	Low risk and interdependency to extent of investment	Low risk and high interdependency	Low risk and high shared identity	Low risk and situational interdependency
Characteristics	Exchange highly structured, monitored; some question of whether this is a type of trust	Transaction limited; failure to perform noted immediately; relationship easily terminated	Anticipate positive and no negative performance; creates loyalty over and above what self-interest would dictate; more resilient to unmet expectations	Belief in positive performance, negative performance not considered; involves more than loyalty; can survive unmet expectations, although stronger sense of betrayal	"Teamwork" cultures where parties are functionally dependent upon trust; legal systems; codes of conduct

Sources: Adapted from Denise M. Rousseau, Sim B. Sitkin, Ronald S. Burt, and Colin Camerer, "Not So Different After All: A Cross-Discipline View of Trust," *Academy of Management Review* 23 (July 1998): 393–404; and Patrick A. Saparito, Chao C. Chen, and Harry J. Sapienza, "The Role of Relational Trust in Bank–Small Firm Relationships," *Academy of Management Journal* 47 (June 2004): 400–410.

Trust in Negotiating Relationships

One-shot negotiations (buying a car or house), repeat but arm's-length negotiations (supplier–customer), and long-term relationships (employer–employee; partnerships) all present different levels of interaction that can be described as dependent and *inter*dependent, shallow and deep. In a negotiation relationship the level of trust can differ based upon the nature and depth of the dependency and interdependency of the parties.

In a one-shot negotiation, such as buying a new car or a new home, the transaction is generally between casual acquaintances or strangers and is characterized by one party supplying the other party with services, goods, or other materials in exchange for some type of compensation, generally money. The risk is that the supplier is unreliable. The trust involved is one-sided—that is, the purchaser must trust that the supplier's product is worth the money being paid. Thus, the level of trust is shallow and can be easily lost.

Repeat negotiations, on the other hand, create a relationship in which the parties have more interdependency because the parties have the possibility of more shared interests in the future. This type of relationship would be characterized by both parties investing in the transaction in order to achieve their goals—such as a manufacturer and its suppliers, who must effectively coordinate their purchases and deliveries for both to profit. The risk is that the supplier is both unreliable and untimely. The trust involved is still essentially one-sided in that the manufacturer must trust that the supplier will perform in a timely manner. But the parties, while *inter*dependent in this one transaction, are still free agents—that is, nonperformance by a supplier would lead the manufacturer to drop him and seek other suppliers. Therefore the trust involved is still shallow.

A negotiation between parties in a long-term relationship in which power is asymmetrical, such as between an employer and her employees, involves significant dependency. The employer's behavior and knowledge is generally outside the employees' ability to control or even to monitor, and the employees' fate is in the employer's hands. Therefore there is a risk that the employer will use her position to the employees' disadvantage by cheating the employees or by abusing the relationship. This is a dependent relationship requiring significant risk and therefore trust is equally significant.

A negotiation between parties in a long-term relationship of equal power, such as in a business partnership, typifies a significant *inter*dependency. The parties enjoy independence but also a common identity, goals, risks, and rewards. The risk is that the parties' actions independent of one another will damage the partnership. Trust is inherent in the relationship, but communication is essential so one will not fail to anticipate the other's needs or actions of the other to both of their detriments.[25]

Thus, levels of trust are based upon the frequency and types of encounters, display different risks, and rely upon different levels of trust, as outlined in Table 8.4.

Table 8.4 Levels of Trust

FREQUENCY OF ENCOUNTERS	CHARACTERISTICS	POSSIBLE RISKS	LEVEL OF TRUST
One time	Parties are casual acquaintances or strangers; exchange of money for product.	Unreliable	Shallow dependency
Frequent but arm's length	Both parties invest in the transaction for equal benefit.	Unreliable, untimely	Shallow interdependency
Long-term, asymmetrical	One party has control of resources needed by the other party.	Cheating, abuse	Deep dependency
Long-term, equal	Parties have equal status and can act independently.	Fail to anticipate needs of each other	Deep interdependency

Source: Adapted from Blair Sheppard and Dana M. Sherman, "The Grammars of Trust: A Model and General Implications," *Academy of Management Review* 23 (July 1998): 422–437.

Trust and Distrust

Because it is essentially a voluntary process, parties must be motivated to negotiate, as we have stressed throughout this text. The motivation stems from a need or desire—or at least a perceived need or desire—to gain something another party has or controls, and also from the belief that a bargain can be made with that party. The risk involved in the negotiation means you might have to use mechanisms to create trust or to overcome distrust, because it is not always possible to pick the party with whom you are to negotiate. A manufacturer who is dependent upon the product of a supplier whose ownership has just changed hands will need to establish a trusting relationship with the new owner or risk harming his business. An employee may have to negotiate for a promotion with a supervisor whom she doesn't trust, or else lose the opportunity to advance.

Roy J. Lewicki, Daniel J. McAllister, and Robert J. Bies,[26] leading scholars in the study of trust development, negotiation, and conflict management, recognize that the uncertainty, complexity, and speed of change that typifies the global business environment makes collaboration critical for success. Collaboration requires trust. In this competitive and complex environment they warn that viewing *trust* and *distrust* as polar opposites may be too simplistic because to some degree both trust and distrust exist within most business relationships. Trust, as previously discussed, exists when you have a confident, positive expectation that the other party's conduct is motivated by good intentions toward you. Likewise, distrust can exist when you have a confident, but negative expectation that the other party's conduct has sinister intentions toward you. Normally one views *trust as good* and *distrust as bad* and the trust relationship as one-dimensional. That is, trust is a type of commodity, so that if one betrays your trust, you take it back and withhold it from that person in the future.

But business relationships are multifaceted, so parties can hold different views of one another that are both accurate and inconsistent. According to Lewicki and his colleagues, both trust and distrust reduce complexity by allowing desirable and undesirable conduct, respectively, to be viewed as *certain.* For example, traffic rules work because we believe other drivers will obey them (trust); but we still drive defensively and watch for drivers who violate traffic rules (distrust). Negotiators representing management and labor, who have established a rapport by meeting frequently across the bargaining table, accept each other's word or handshake when a deal is made (trust); but still verify facts and figures knowing that each represents opposing interests (distrust). In addition, multifaceted relationships in the business arena are not static, but rather are constantly changing with interaction frequency, duration, and joint challenges that are met or not met. Co-workers who have had little or negative contact with one another (distrust) may form a strong trust relationship after participation in a "teamwork" project (trust).

But trust and distrust are not just two sides of the same belief—that is, *low trust* is not the same thing as *high distrust,* nor are *high trust* and *low distrust* the same. You can have a trust relationship that runs the gamut from low to high trust, or you can have a distrust relationship that spans from low to high distrust—or any combination of the four. The difference is your belief in the "virtuous" or "sinister" intentions underlying the conduct and the intensity of the dependency. In relationships characterized by limited interactions and little or no need for consideration from each other, low trust would mean you have no reason to place much confidence in the actions of the other party, but at the same time you would have no reason to be wary, or to have low distrust. When buying a house you take the seller's representations about the house at face value. You would not anticipate that the seller has your interests at heart, but have no reason to believe the seller has it in for you, either. So you can engage in a negotiation with both low trust and low distrust. In a relationship characterized by pooled interdependence—that is where both parties are pursuing joint goals—high trust would mean you had reason to be confident that the other party will fulfill its obligations, and little reason to suspect the other party will not perform, or low distrust. Consider the example of two colleagues in a partnership acquiring rental property, for example. Each would feel confident that the partner's negotiation with the seller would be conducted for their joint benefit. And each would have little reason to think that the partner would not get the best deal possible.

As a contrast, in relationships characterized by monitoring or compelling each other's behavior, you have no reason to have confidence in the other party, so you have low trust—and you would have ample reason to be wary and watchful of the other party, so you also have high distrust. If the property partnership in our example broke up because of alleged wrongdoing by one or both of the partners and the parties were in litigation over the assets, a court could allow one of the parties to continue to manage the property under the court's direction until the case could be resolved. The non-managing partner would have both low trust and high mistrust of the former partner.

Finally, in a relationship characterized by a multifaceted and reciprocal interdependency where the parties have both separate and shared goals, high trust would mean you have many areas in which you have confidence in the other party and some areas in which you have reason to be extremely wary of the other's conduct, or high distrust. Relying again on our example of the property partnership, assume that the two partners operate one or more apartment complexes quite successfully because one of the partners does all of the day-to-day work. He has good relationships with the tenants and he's a reasonably competent plumber and electrician when the need arises. He has difficulty with money, however, because he likes to gamble—and while the amount of his gambling is not significant, it can cause cash flow problems. The other partner, therefore, insists on keeping control of the checkbook to ensure that the partnership assets are not at risk. The matrix in Figure 8.1 shows how low and high trust can be integrated with low and high distrust, depending upon the circumstances.

It is the ability to accept the possibilities of high and low trust, and high and low distrust, within one transaction or relationship that facilitates the negotiation process. The question is no longer "Do I trust?" but now becomes "In what areas do I trust, and in what ways?"

Establishing Trust

As detailed throughout this chapter, trust exists in an uncertain and risky environment; if you know something is *certainly* going to happen, then you would not need to *trust* that it will happen. Trust provides you with an expectation of predictability—that is,

Figure 8.1
High/Low Trust and
High/Low Distrust

Source: Adapted from
Roy J. Lewicki, Daniel J.
McAllister, and Robert J.
Bies, "Trust and Distrust:
New Relationships and
Realities," *Academy of
Management Review* 23
(July 1998): 438–458.

High Trust	• Interdependency • Joint goals • Reason to be confident • Little reason to be wary	• Multifaceted and reciprocal relationship • Separate and shared goals • Many areas for confidence • Many reasons to be wary
Low Trust	• Limited interactions • No reason for confidence • No reason to be wary	• Monitoring or compelling each other's behavior • No reason for confidence • Ample reason to be wary
	Low Distrust	**High Distrust**

you anticipate that another party's actions will result in certain outcomes. Trust in negotiations makes it easier to share information and jointly address contentious issues, understand interests, look for options, and eventually reach agreement. Trust, however, is a fluid concept. It can be created or lost in an instant. In the Chapter Case, the employer's negotiator had to make a decision about how much information to reveal to the other side. The decision could mean expanding the trust relationship, but negatively affecting the negotiation outcome. Or, it could mean a positive outcome for the employer, but damage to the trust relationship between the parties.

Trust between two negotiating parties can be developed naturally over time, but you do not always have the luxury of time to develop trust. Two techniques that negotiators can use to develop trust quickly include assessing the situation and building mutual trust.

Assessing the Situation   It is important for negotiators to do their homework and learn as much as possible about the other party's situation prior to starting a negotiation, for a number of reasons. First, *are there incentives for the other side to deceive you?* For example, you need to know what proprietary information the other party has that may be relevant to the negotiation, as well as the likelihood that the other party will share or withhold that information. In the Chapter Case, the employees could have discovered that the employer was self-insured before the negotiations took place. The issue of withholding information may never have come up.

Second, *are there time constraints on the opposing party?* You need to determine whether such a time constraint will cause the other party's negotiators to agree to something they really don't want to agree to or push you to reach agreement just to meet a deadline. Letting them know that you want to work around the time problem rather than take advantage of it can establish an atmosphere of trust.

Third, *how well do you know the other party?* If you have personal experience with the people you are negotiating with, you may already know whether they are trustworthy. If you know them only through reputation, you could try and find someone with firsthand knowledge.

Fourth, *how does the other side see you?* You have to be realistic as to how you are perceived in a negotiation. You may think of yourself as totally trustworthy—but will the other party have sufficient experience with you to believe that, or will they rely on your reputation, which may or may not be what you think?

Fifth, *are there common interests you can build trust around?* If the relationship is new, but there is a possibility that a successful negotiation will give you a chance to do business again in the future, then you might be willing to settle this initial negotiation in such a way as to ensure that future. Letting the other party know that you have taken the time to find out about their interests and concerns sends a message that the long-term relationship is important to you.

Building Mutual Trust   The level of trust within any negotiation depends upon the history of the parties, their reputations, their vulnerabilities, and the behavioral rules appropriate for the setting. In some negotiations, for instance, a handshake is the accepted form of agreement and suggesting a signed document would be insulting. Individuals tend to respond to the actions of others with similar actions. This norm of *reciprocity,* as discussed in Chapter 3, supports the general principle behind trust-building—that is, a negotiator needs to demonstrate both trustworthiness and the ability to trust.[27] Ways of engendering trust in a negotiation can be found both in the *process,* where trust is tied to the exchange itself, and in the *parties,* where trust is tied to the individuals involved.

Trust in the negotiating process can be built early on, perhaps by making a carefully crafted concession at the start of deliberations to let negotiators for the other party know that you trust them. Also, you can demonstrate your trustworthiness by following through on a promise or being candid with information. You should attempt to view or structure the negotiation as part of a long-term relationship rather than a one-shot deal. This view of the relationship fosters honesty and trustworthiness because parties who hope to meet again are less likely to take advantage of each other. Parties can build trust in the negotiation by emphasizing their interdependency and by recognizing that they have a vested interest in trusting each other.

Managing your own reputation is another important aspect of developing trust. It would be to your advantage to make sure the party you are negotiating with recognizes when you have made a concession to his advantage. This may cause a reciprocal concession and the creation of mutual trust. If the parties do not know one another, it might be beneficial to bring in a mutually trusted third party to vouch for both sides. Box 8.3 presents these and other ways to build trust in negotiations.

BOX 8.3   Tactics for Success

How to Build Trust in a Negotiation

1. *Speak their language:* Tell the other party you understand their perspective and needs. You can do this by active listening and paraphrasing your opponent's offers or demands.

2. *Manage your reputation:* It's a tool that can be used to successfully negotiate. Build your reputation by dealing with parties honestly, by keeping your word,

(continued)

by trying to *create* more value and not just *claim* more value in a negotiation.

3. *Recognize your interdependency:* Negotiating is a voluntary exercise. The parties must have mutual needs or else they wouldn't be at the bargaining table. Talk about those needs and the issues that brought both parties to the table, and what both parties hope to accomplish.

4. *Make a unilateral concession:* A concession can convey that you value the relationship enough to offer something in return for the goodwill it creates. Negotiators often agree to small or inconsequential items at the beginning of a negotiation to set the stage for future agreement. A concession of more import without a request for reciprocity can be quite effective in gaining your opponent's trust.

5. *Label your concessions:* Make sure the other party knows when you make a concession. This might trigger a concession on their part, which will increase the cycle of trust. To point out such a concession, you could simply say, "I know this issue is as important to you as it is to me, but I'm willing to resolve it in *your* favor to move the negotiations along."

6. *Explain your demands:* Reasons for a demand can create an atmosphere of trust, rather than the belief the demands are motivated by greed. In a recent labor negotiation, none of the members of the employees' negotiating team had ever negotiated before and simply demanded a substantial wage increase, which was met with understandable resistance by the employer. After four months of nonproductive meetings, the employees brought in an outside expert to help them. The first thing the new negotiator did was to go through the employees' demands and explain in detail the basis for each economic request, thereby establishing his own credibility and moving the negotiations along on a more positive path.

Source: Adapted from Deepak Malhotra, "Risky Business: Trust in Negotiations," *Negotiation* 7 (February 2004): 1–4.

SUMMING UP

Most adults consider the ethical values of *truthfulness* and *fairness* as important values in their daily lives. Truthfulness and fairness engender trust. But negotiation processes and tactics can challenge the parties' trust in each other and can threaten the success of the negotiation. Negotiators have to navigate through the process in an ethically acceptable manner. As you anticipate your next negotiation, prepare to negotiate ethically by answering the following questions.

1. Describe the situation. Describe the type of negotiation you are undertaking.

_____

_____

2. Which philosophy—ethics of purpose, ethics of principle, or ethics of consequence—best describes how you view the standards for this negotiation, and why?

_____

_____

3. If you viewed negotiations as a game, what ethical tactics could you use in your negotiation?

_____

_____

4. If you took a pragmatic view of negotiations, what ethical tactics could you use in your negotiations?

_____

_____

5. Why do deceptive offers and counteroffers, and settlement point or bottom line deceptions, not frustrate the purpose of negotiations?

_____

_____

6. How will you judge the *procedural* fairness of your negotiated deal? How will you judge the *substantive* fairness of your negotiated deal?

_____

_____

_____

_____

7. Why is trust an essential value for negotiations?

_____

_____

8. Which type of trust—deterrence-based, calculus-based, relational, identity-based, or institutional-based—would you expect to find in this negotiation, and why?

_____

_____

_____

9. Based upon the type of trust involved, what level of risk—high, medium, or low—are you undertaking? How did you arrive at this conclusion?

_____

_____

10. How can you quickly establish trust in this negotiation?

_____

_____

LEARNING EXERCISE: SETTLING A LAWSUIT

The purpose of this exercise is to apply the five negotiation skills presented in this chapter to an actual negotiation situation. As a result of a claim, 30 people, none of whom knew each other prior to the filing of the claim, are negotiating a settlement with a pesticide company. The company sold lawn products that it said were not harmful to pets. After hundreds of dogs and cats died from exposure to the pesticide, the company withdrew the product from the market. The 30 people are seeking compensation for their lost pets. The company has gone out of business and left $250,000 to settle all of these claims. You are a representative of the former company, given the task of negotiating a settlement with the 30 people. You will receive a bonus if you can settle for less than the full amount. You know the amount of money to be distributed but the claimants do not.

You are thinking of doing the following things: (1) demanding that the claimants appoint a representative for you to negotiate with, and then you can make sure the representative receives a premium for getting the parties to agree to settle; (2) telling the claimants that the company left only $100,000 for paying claims; (3) telling the claimants that the company also has other expenses to pay, so if they don't reach agreement by the end of the day, the money will be gone.

Now answer the following questions.

Skill 8.1: What *ethical values* should you use in this negotiation? How did you decide?

Skill 8.2: How would you determine whether the negotiation is conducted with *substantive fairness?*

Skill 8.3: What *concealment behaviors* would be ethical and unethical in this negotiation?

Skill 8.4: Are you employing *fair procedures* in this case?

Skill 8.5: How would you *create trust* in this negotiation?

ENDNOTES

1. Cited in "The Value Minute," Values Count LLC, 2004, available from the Values Institute of America, www.valuesinstitute. org/ (accessed September 23, 2006). Also see Peter Hyde and Bill Williamson, "The Importance of Organizational Values," *Focus on Change Management* 67 (September 2000): 9–13.

2. Milton Rokeach, *The Nature of Human Values* (New York: Free Press, 1973). Also see John Stevenson, "Exploring Workplace Values," *Journal of Vocational Education and Training* 51 (1999): 335–354.

3. Ibid.

4. Roger Scruton, *A Dictionary of Political Thought* (New York: Farrar, Straus & Giroux, 1982), 156.

5. Milton Rokeach, *Understanding Human Values* (New York, NY: The Free Press, 1979), 47–65.

6. Eleanor Holmes Norton, "Bargaining and the Ethics of Process," *NYU Law Review* 64 (1989): 494–539.

7. David A. Lax and James K. Sebenius, "Three Ethical Issues in Negotiations," *Negotiation Journal* 2 (1986): 363–370.

8. Cecilia Albin, "Negotiating International Cooperation: Global Public Goods and Fairness," *Review of International Studies* 29 (2003): 365–385.

9. Keith G. Allred, "The High Cost of Low Trust," *Negotiation* 7 (June 2004): 1–4.

10. Michael Wheeler, "Fair Enough? An Ethical Fitness Quiz for Negotiators," *Negotiation* 7 (March 2004): 1–4.

11. G. Richard Shell, "Bargaining with the Devil Without Losing Your Soul: Ethics in Negotiation," in *What's Fair: Ethics for Negotiators,* eds. Carrie Menkel-Meadow and Michael Wheeler (San Francisco: Jossey-Bass, 2004), 57–78.

12. Peter C. Cramton and J. Gregory Dees, "Promoting Honesty in Negotiation: An Exercise in Practical Ethics," *Business Ethics Quarterly* 3 (1993): 1–23.

13. Roy J. Lewicki and Robert J. Robinson, "Ethical and Unethical Bargaining Tactics: An Empirical Study," in *What's Fair: Ethics for Negotiators,* eds. Carrie Menkel-Meadow and Michael Wheeler (San Francisco: Jossey-Bass, 2004), 221–245.

14. J. Gregory Dees and Peter C. Cramton, "Shrewd Bargaining on the Moral Frontier: Toward a Theory of Morality in Practice," *Business Ethics Quarterly* 1 (1991): 135–167.

15. Alan Strudler, "On the Ethics of Deception in Negotiation," *Business Ethics Quarterly* 5 (1995): 805–822.

16. Deepak Malhotra, "Making Threats Credible," *Negotiation* 8 (March 2005): 1–4; and Bill Wolfe, "Pilots Set Deadline for UPS to Offer Contract," *The Courier-Journal,* June 24, 2005, E1.

17. Steven Cohen, *Negotiating Skills for Managers* (New York: McGraw-Hill, 2002).

18. Steven P. Cohen, "Negotiation as a Paradigm for Business: Ethical Negotiations Lead to Ethical Businesses," *The Negotiator Magazine,* October 2002, www.negotiatormagazine.com/ article22.htm (accessed September 16, 2006).

19. Lewicki and Robinson, "Ethical and Unethical Bargaining Tactics," 226–227, 232.

20. Denise M. Rousseau, Sim B. Sitkin, Ronald S. Burt, and Colin Camerer, "Not So Different After All: A Cross-Discipline View of Trust," *Academy of Management Review* 23, (July 1998): 393–404.

21. Patrick A. Saparito, Chao C. Chen, and Harry J. Sapienza, "The Role of Relational Trust in Bank–Small Firm Relationships," *Academy of Management Journal* 47 (June 2004): 400–410.

22. "New Steroid Rules for Baseball," CBS Broadcasting, New York, January 13, 2005, available at the CBS News Web site, www.cbsnews.com/stories/2005/01/13/ entertainment/main666580.shtml (accessed September 16, 2006).

23. Paul D. Staudohar, "Baseball Negotiations: A New Agreement," *Monthly Labor Review* 125 (December 2002): 15–22.

24. Hal Bodley, "Baseball Officials Announce Tougher Steroids Policy," *USA TODAY,* January 12, 2005, available at http://www. usatoday.com/sports/baseball/ 2005-01-12 steroid-policy_x.htm (accessed on September 23, 2006).

25. Discussion based on Blair Sheppard and Dana M. Sherman, "The Grammars of Trust: A Model and General Implications," *Academy of Management Review* 23 (July 1998): 422–437.

26. Roy J. Lewicki, Daniel J. McAllister, and Robert J. Bies, "Trust and Distrust: New Relationships and Realities," *Academy of Management Review* 23 (July 1998): 438–458.

27. Cramton and Dees, "Promoting Honesty in Negotiation,"15.

Chapter 9

The Influence of Culture and Gender on Negotiations

*A*s discussed throughout this text, negotiating is a key part of every-day business transactions and conflict resolution. It is an inherently *personal* activity, in that every negotiation requires an interaction between at least two parties who have a relationship. Individuals make judgments during the course of a negotiation and those judgments influence the decisions made and ultimately the outcome of the negotiation. In this chapter we will explore how the *culture* or *gender* of a negotiator impacts the negotiations. We will focus on aspects of negotiations that are particularly sensitive to cultural influences—specifically heuristics and biases, emotions, negotiation patterns, and trust and fairness. *The Handbook of Negotiation and Culture,* edited by Michele J. Gelfand and Jeanne M. Brett,[1] was an invaluable resource for this chapter. It is an in-depth review by noted researchers of negotiation theory as applied to cross-cultural bargaining, including the psychological process of negotiating and the social context of cross-cultural negotiation.

New York Times columnist Thomas L. Friedman, in his book *The World Is Flat: A Brief History of the Twenty-first Century,*[2] argues that the world has gone through three eras of globalization. The first lasted from 1492 until about 1820 and was built around *countries* globalizing—Spain exploring the New World, Britain colonizing India, and the Portuguese setting up trade posts in the Indian Ocean. The second great era of globalization, from the early 1800s up to the year 2000, was spearheaded by *companies* globalizing for markets and labor. The final era is now, the 21st century, in which the world economy is flattening through the activities of *individuals* and small groups. Many of the influences that Friedman details in the 10 events he contends launched this current era of globalization involve one-on-one opportunities for individuals from diverse cultures to interact. For example, the massive investment in fiber-optic cables signaled the rise of computer applications that enabled faster, closer coordination among far-flung sites and allowed everyone, everywhere, to use the Internet as a personal supply chain of knowledge. The migration of business functions and the movement of manufacturing plants to Third World economies caused midlevel managers to relocate. Revolutions in transportation allowed logistics giants like UPS and FedEx to take control of customer supply chains and enabled even mom-and-pop shops to go global.[3]

In this "flat world," no one can afford to ignore the influence of cultural differences on doing business. And because negotiation is a critical business activity, you need to know the impact that cultural differences can have on the negotiation process.

Negotiation Skills

In this chapter we present five negotiation skills that can be learned and developed by the novice negotiator and applied to the end-of-chapter Learning Exercise, "Negotiating a Franchise Agreement."

Skill 9.1   *Recognize the* **cultural-based and gender-based traits** *that may influence the negotiation process.*

Skill 9.2   *Avoid* **negotiation biases** *that may arise in a cross-cultural negotiation.*

Skill 9.3   *Determine negotiation strategies that* **respond to diverse negotiation patterns and practices** *in a cross-cultural negotiation.*

Skill 9.4   *Identify practical steps to use* **gender-specific traits** *in both integrative and distributive negotiating situations.*

Skill 9.5   *Develop a negotiating strategy* **combining the cultural and gender differences** *explored in this chapter.*

CHAPTER CASE: BRIDGING THE CULTURAL GAP

Toyota Motor Corporation announced in May 2005 that its subsidiary, Toyota Motor Manufacturing, Kentucky Inc. (TMMK), which is one of Toyota's production plants in North America, would be in charge of producing the hybrid version of its highly successful Camry model starting in the second half of 2006. According to the announcement, Toyota would invest $10 million to start hybrid production and to reach the expected monthly production target of 4,000 Camry hybrids. This decision was possible because in 1986, then-Governor Martha Layne Collins succeeded in convincing Toyota to locate a production plant in Georgetown, Kentucky. Larry Hayes, the governor's chief of staff at the time, made numerous trips to Japan to negotiate the investment by Toyota of more than $5 billion in a plant that now employs 7,000 people in the central Kentucky area.

In a recent interview, Hayes discussed the negotiation. He recounted two examples of how culture impacted the negotiations. First, he observed how Governor

Collins "courted" the chairman of Toyota Motor Corporation, Shoichiro Toyoda. Toyota boasts of its efforts to be responsible corporate citizens in every community where the company operates, describing that effort as establishing close relationships with people and organizations in the local community and participating in community activities from the sponsorship of educational and cultural programs to international exchange and research.[4] Recognizing that the culture of Toyota favored developing personal relationships and committing to the community it serves, Governor Collins made numerous trips to Japan to meet with Shoichiro Toyoda personally. She emphasized how establishing the plant in Georgetown would be beneficial to Toyota, its shareholders, and employees, as well as to the residents of Kentucky, whom she represented. Governor Collins never referred to the location of the plant in Kentucky as an *economic* development project, but rather as a *community* development project. Hayes is convinced that the governor's appeal to the Japanese sense of collectivism was crucial in Toyota's decision to locate in Kentucky.

In the second example, cultural differences almost caused the deal to fall through. All the terms and conditions of the transaction had been negotiated and Hayes traveled to Japan with his negotiating team for a final meeting with Toyota's negotiating team, led by the current chairman of Toyota International, Hiroshi Okuda. Hayes's team included the bond counsel who would be handling the Commonwealth of Kentucky's issuance of economic development bonds to provide money for the incentives that the state was giving Toyota to locate in Kentucky. Toyota was presented with a contract for Okuda's signature. Okuda was surprised and uncomfortable because, as he explained, even though the company intended to do everything that had been agreed upon, he could not sign a contract because the company might be *prevented* from doing all that was agreed upon. Hayes discovered later that in Japan a verbal agreement was as binding as a written document because not to comply with a commitment would cause the loss of face and would harm long-term relationships, which are highly regarded. And yet, signing a document that specified those commitments was not possible. Hayes explained that he could not return to Kentucky and present the multibillion-dollar deal and ask the Kentucky Legislature to take the necessary actions without an enforceable contract, which meant a signed agreement. The negotiation session for the day ended without a resolution of the problem. Hayes contacted Governor Collins, and she called Chairman Toyoda to explain the situation. The next day when the teams resumed, Okuda signed the contract without further explanation. Despite its rather precarious beginning, locating Toyota in Kentucky was a huge economic boom for both the immediate area and the entire state.

Understanding Cultural Differences

Culture encompasses the values and norms shared by members of a group and the economic, social, political, and religious institutions that shape and mold their activities. At a fundamental level, these cultural values frame and guide the interpretation of experience, the processing of information, and the ways people communicate. It is possible to describe culture as a shared set of basic assumptions and values, with resultant behavioral norms, attitudes, and beliefs that manifest themselves in systems and institutions as well as behavioral and nonbehavioral patterns. There are various levels to culture, ranging from the easily observable outer layers, such as behavioral convention, to the increasingly more difficult to grasp inner layers, such as assumptions and values. Culture is shared among members of a group or society and has an interpretative function for the members of that group. Culture is situated between human nature on the one hand and individual personality on the other. Culture is not inheritable or genetic, but rather is *learned.* Although all members of a group or society share their culture, expressions of culture-resultant behavior are modified by an individual's personality.

People create their culture as a way to adapt to their physical environment. Customs, practices, beliefs, and traditions for development and survival are passed along from generation to generation. Your culture facilitates day-to-day living by making sense out of your surroundings. The following characteristics of cultures can influence the way an individual might negotiate:

- *Self-identity:* Cultures provide an individual with a sense of self, which can be manifested anywhere from extreme independence to extreme interdependence. In a negotiation, this cultural sense of self may dictate whether the parties see negotiations as a competition or an opportunity to collaborate.
- *Relationships:* Cultures also organize the relationships between individuals according to age, sex, status, or degree of kinship. Such relationships may influence a negotiation by dictating who the culture recognizes as its leaders, who makes the decisions, and who will be governed by those decisions.
- *Communication:* Verbal and nonverbal communication distinguishes one culture from another. A multitude of languages, dialects, and colloquialisms combine with body language and gestures to make communication unique within cultures and subcultures. Another aspect of communication relevant to negotiations is whether the culture exchanges information in a direct or indirect manner.
- *Time and time consciousness:* In some cultures time may be viewed as a cycle, constantly reoccurring so that it involves many simultaneous experiences and people. Or time can be viewed as a lineal, sequential event. In that case, time once lost is never regained. A culture that views time as lineal and finite will expect negotiations to begin on time and to finish as soon as possible.
- *Values and norms:* The needs of a culture will dictate its values and norms. These values include both those accepted by the individual for his or her own behavior and those established by the social environment to guide someone else's behavior. As the parties to a negotiation interact, both sides are making judgments based upon their own culture's value system, and they may not realize they are sending the wrong message until it is too late.
- *Mental process and learning:* Each culture has a reasoning process and an accepted system for learning. One culture might emphasize abstract thinking and another might emphasize rote memory.[5] Such traits will dictate how information given in a negotiation is received.

Hofstede's Cultural Dimensions

Cultures can be dissected to identify critical dimensions that impact negotiating styles. Geert Hofstede and Michael Harris Bond formulated five such dimensions from research studies: (1) power distance, (2) uncertainty avoidance,

(3) individualism–collectivism, (4) masculinity–femininity, and (5) long-term orientation.[6] Hofstede's value dimensions, however, are not meant to create stereotypes by suggesting that all individuals within a certain culture possess all of the exact same characteristics. As Hofstede explained in a recent interview:

> Countries aren't king-size individuals; they are social systems. It is like the forest and the trees. Forests are not king-sized trees; they are eco-systems of different trees, shrubs, animals, and other organisms. National cultures are eco-systems of different individuals, institutions, and resources.[7]

Individuals may certainly fail to display the "cultural dimension" that has been listed as the predominant dimension within that individual's country.[8] These cultural paradoxes contradict attempts to fit individual negotiators neatly into one or another category. Nevertheless, they are useful as a tool to anticipate *possible* negotiating differences that may arise in a cross-cultural negotiation.

Power Distance   The first dimension, *power distance,* focuses on the degree of equality or inequality between people in the country's society. A high power distance ranking indicates that inequalities of power and wealth have been allowed to grow within the society and that the ordering of people into a high or low place is "correct" and should be protected; some individuals in the culture are considered superior to others because of their social status or family background. A low power distance ranking indicates that the society de-emphasizes the differences between its citizens' power and wealth. In these cultures, equality and opportunity for everyone is stressed and people accept the hierarchy only as a necessary convenience. Individuals gain a position in such cultures by earning it through work and achievement.

Negotiators from cultures with a high power distance tend to be more comfortable with hierarchical structures, clear authority figures, and the use of power in a negotiation. Negotiators from cultures with low power distance tend to be more comfortable with democratic structures, flat organizational hierarchies, shared authority, and limited use of power. The United States has a moderately low power distance orientation and Japan has a moderately high power distance orientation. (See Figure 9.1 for a comparison of the two countries in terms of Hofstede's five dimensions.) Martha Layne Collins was able to use her position as governor of the Commonwealth of Kentucky to meet *as an equal* with Toyota's chairman, Shoichiro Toyoda, in order to negotiate the deal outlined in the Chapter Case. The power distance characteristic also came into play in the Toyota negotiation when it became evident that Toyota's negotiator, Hiroshi Okuda, was not the decision maker and could not sign the contract without authority from the corporation's chairman.

Uncertainty Avoidance   *Uncertainty avoidance* focuses on the level of tolerance for uncertainty and ambiguity within the society in its unstructured situations. A high uncertainty avoidance ranking indicates that the society has a low tolerance for uncertainty and ambiguity. This creates a rule-oriented culture that institutes laws, rules, regulations, and controls in order to reduce the amount of uncertainty. A low uncertainty avoidance ranking indicates the society has less concern about ambiguity and uncertainty and has more tolerance for a variety of opinions. This is reflected in a culture that is less rule-oriented, more readily accepts change, and takes more and greater risks.

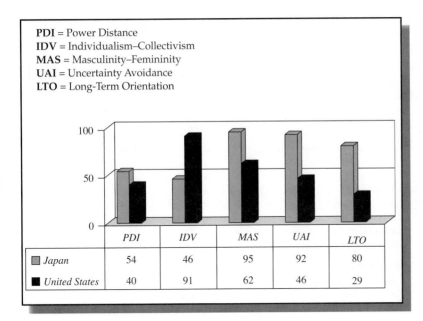

Figure 9.1
Hofstede's Cross-Cultural Comparisons, U.S. and Japan

PDI = Power Distance
IDV = Individualism–Collectivism
MAS = Masculinity–Femininity
UAI = Uncertainty Avoidance
LTO = Long-Term Orientation

	PDI	IDV	MAS	UAI	LTO
Japan	54	46	95	92	80
United States	40	91	62	46	29

As discussed in Chapter 8, every negotiation involves some level of risk. Part of a negotiator's challenge is to establish the level of trust appropriate to or necessary for a negotiation to succeed. In risk-averse cultures, the ability of an outsider to engender such trust is often compromised.

Individualism–Collectivism   The dimension of *individualism–collectivism* focuses on the degree that the society reinforces individual or collective achievement and interpersonal relationships. A high individualism ranking indicates that individuality and individual rights are paramount within the culture. Individuals in these societies may tend to form a larger number of looser relationships. The "I" is predominant; identity is based on the individual. Involvement with organizations is calculative—that is, done only for a purpose. Leadership, individual performance, and initiative are valued in individualistic cultures.

A low individualism ranking typifies societies of a more collectivist nature with close ties among individuals. There is a tight social framework in which in-groups look after each other and expect absolute loyalty. In a collectivist culture, the "we" consciousness is paramount. Involvement with organizations is moral, membership is an ideal, and public service is a duty. Order, duty, and security are valued, and are provided by reliance on individuals in the group itself and not outsiders. In a collectivist culture there is an emphasis on the *context* of a communication (*how* it is said), rather than the *content* of the communication (*what* was said).[9] As you saw in the Chapter Case, negotiators from a collectivist culture are more likely to respond to an argument based on how a project will benefit the many people involved, rather than trying to sell it on a purely economic basis.

Now refer to Figure 9.2, which compares various countries on the five dimensions of cultures.[10] The United States is listed first for *individualistic* orientation; Japan tends

Figure 9.2
Nations Exhibiting Extremes in Hofstede's Cultural Dimensions

Low Power Distance
- Austria
- Denmark
- New Zealand
- Israel
- Ireland

(U.S. tends to have low power distance.)

High Power Distance
- Malaysia
- Philippines
- Panama
- Mexico
- Venezuela

Low Uncertainty Avoidance
- Singapore
- Denmark
- Sweden
- Hong Kong
- Jamaica

(U.S. tends to have low uncertainty avoidance.)

High Uncertainty Avoidance
- Greece
- Belgium
- Portugal
- Poland
- Uruguay

Individualistic
- U.S.
- Australia
- Great Britain
- Netherlands
- Canada
- New Zealand

Collectivist
- Pakistan
- Taiwan
- Indonesia
- Costa Rica
- Columbia

(Japan tends to have a collectivist orientation.)

Masculinity
- Japan
- Austria
- Hungary
- Venezuela
- Italy

(U.S. tends to be masculine.)

Feminist
- Sweden
- Norway
- Netherlands
- Denmark
- Costa Rica

Low Long-Term Orientation
- Canada
- United Kingdom
- U.S.
- Pakistan
- Philippines

High Long-Term Orientation
- China
- Hong Kong
- Singapore
- Japan
- South Korea

Sources: Adapted from Geert Hofstede, *Culture's Consequences: International Differences in Work-Related Values* (Thousand Oaks, CA: Sage, 1984); Geert Hofstede and Michael H. Bond, "The Confucius Connection: From Cultural Roots to Economic Growth," *Organizational Dynamics* 16 (1988): 4–21; and Geert Hofstede, "Motivation, Leadership, and Organizations: Do American Theories Apply Abroad?" *Organizational Dynamics* 9 (Summer 1980): 42–63.

to have a more *collectivist* orientation. As you might expect, U.S. negotiators tend to be more competitive in their approach, will argue fine points of their position with enthusiasm, and focus on areas of disagreement as problems that need to be solved one at a time. And, as seen in the Chapter Case, U.S. negotiators like closure—such as having a signed agreement in hand when the negotiations conclude. Japanese negotiators, on the other hand, tend to put less emphasis on the words used in a negotiation and more emphasis on the relationship established *before* the negotiation began. They tend to listen more than talk, and to focus on areas of commonality and agreement rather than disagreement.

Masculinity–Femininity   The *masculinity–femininity* dimension focuses on the degree that a culture reinforces, or does not reinforce, the traditional masculine trait of assertiveness. A high masculinity ranking indicates that the society values achievement, control, and power and has a high degree of gender differentiation. In these cultures, males dominate a significant portion of the society and power structure; men are assertive and women are nurturing; and sex roles are clearly delineated. Japan, for example, is a highly "masculine" culture. Martha Layne Collins, as indicated in the Chapter Case, was able to overcome the fact that she was a woman when negotiating with the chairman of Toyota because of her position as governor of Kentucky.

A high feminine ranking indicates that a society has a more nurturing orientation and a lower level of differentiation and discrimination between genders. In these cultures, females are treated as more equal to males; sex roles are more fluid; and its people, the quality of life, and the environment are valued. Service and cooperation count; sympathy for the unfortunate is appreciated. The so-called "male" and "female" traits of assertiveness and nurturing are certainly evident in the use of distributive and integrative bargaining styles and will be discussed later in the chapter, when we explore gender differences.

Long-Term Orientation   The final dimension, *long-term orientation*, refers to the selective promotion of a particular set of ethics found in Confucian teachings. It focuses on the degree to which a culture is devoted to traditional, forward-thinking values. A high long-term orientation ranking indicates that a society values long-term commitments and respect for tradition. Therefore, it looks toward future rewards rather than immediate recognition and values—in particular, perseverance and thrift. It supports a strong work ethic where long-term rewards are expected as a result of today's hard work. A low long-term orientation ranking indicates that a society is inclined more toward immediate results and "saving face" by keeping up appearances. In this culture, change can occur more rapidly as long-term commitments do not become impediments to change. Governor Collins found that the long-term orientation of her Japanese counterparts helped her land the Toyota plant for Kentucky. The phased expansion over a number of years, longer perhaps than a U.S. competitor might have been willing to do, gave Kentucky time to relocate and train the necessary workforce.

The GLOBE Study on Cultural Dimensions

The GLOBE (Global Leadership and Organizational Behavior Effectiveness) study[11] was a research project designed to develop empirically based theories to describe, understand, and predict the impact of cultural variables on business practices. The study included 62 societies around the world and was based on surveys of more than 17,000 middle managers in the telecommunications, food processing, and banking industries. Those managers were asked to report their perceptions of the common behaviors and institutional practices in their societies—that is, the *way things are*—and what they perceived to be the values, desires, and aspirations of their societies—that is, the *way things should be*. The study differed from Hofstede's study in that the survey sought to identify not only where the society was at the time, but where the society saw itself going.

The GLOBE study identified nine cultural dimensions that could be used for comparing different societal cultures: (1) performance orientation, (2) in-group collectivism, (3) institutional collectivism, (4) power distance, (5) uncertainty avoidance, (6) future orientation, (7) gender egalitarianism, (8) assertiveness, and (9) humane orientation. Six of the nine dimensions have their origins in Hofstede's cultural dimensions: Power distance and uncertainty avoidance reflect the same constructs; in-group collectivism and institutional collectivism are refinements of Hofstede's individualist–collectivist dimension; and in lieu of Hofstede's masculinity–femininity dimension, the GLOBE study developed its gender egalitarianism and assertiveness dimensions. Future orientation, humane orientation, and performance orientation have their origins in other organizational behavioral studies.[12]

The GLOBE project reduced the complexity of its findings by grouping the 62 societies it targeted into 10 regional clusters, shown in Figure 9.3. The GLOBE project was able to characterize the way the societies within a cluster shared cultural dimensions as well as each society's aspirations. The nine GLOBE dimensions along with rankings of representative clusters are as follows:

1. *Performance Orientation:* The degree to which a culture's people (should) encourage and reward people for performance. (*High:* Germanic Europe, Confucian Asia, and Anglo; *Low:* Eastern Europe and Latin America)
2. *In-Group Collectivism:* The degree to which a culture's people (should) take pride in and (should) feel loyalty toward their families, organizations, and employers. (*High:* Southeast Asia, Confucian Asia, Eastern Europe, and Middle East; *Low:* Anglo, Nordic Europe, and Germanic Europe)
3. *Institutional Collectivism:* The degree to which individuals are (should be) encouraged by institutions to be integrated into broader entities, with harmony and cooperation as paramount principles at the expense of autonomy and individual freedom. (*High:* Nordic Europe and Confucian Asia; *Mid:* Anglo; *Low:* Latin America, Germanic Europe, and Latin Europe)
4. *Power Distance:* The degree to which a culture's people are (should be) separated by power, authority, and prestige. (*High:* Southeast Asia, Eastern Europe, and Latin America; *Mid:* Anglo and Confucian Asia; *Low:* Nordic Germany and Germanic Europe)
5. *Uncertainty Avoidance:* The degree to which a culture's people (should) seek orderliness, consistency, and structure. (*High:* Nordic Europe and Germanic Europe; *Mid:* Anglo and Confucian Asia; *Low:* Middle East, Eastern Europe, and Latin America)
6. *Future Orientation:* The degree to which a culture's people are (should be) willing to defer immediate gratification for future benefits. (*High:* Germanic Europe and Nordic Europe; *Mid:* Anglo and Confucian Asia; *Low:* Middle East, Latin America, and Eastern Europe)

Figure 9.3 The 10 Clusters of GLOBE Countries

Latin Europe	Germanic Europe	Nordic Europe	Anglo	Eastern Europe
• France	• Austria	• Denmark	• Australia	• Albania
• Switzerland (Fr.)	• Germany	• Finland	• Canada (Eng.)	• Georgia
• Israel	• Netherlands	• Sweden	• United States	• Greece
• Italy	• Switzerland (Ger.)		• New Zealand	• Hungary
• Portugal			• Ireland	• Kazakhstan
• Spain			• United Kingdom	• Poland
			• South Africa (Cau.)	• Russia
				• Slovenia

Confucian Asia	Latin America	Southern Asia	Sub-Sahara Africa	Middle East
• China	• Argentina	• India	• Namibia	• Egypt
• Hong Kong	• Bolivia	• Indonesia	• Nigeria	• Arab Rep.
• Japan	• Brazil	• Iran	• South Africa (Afr.)	• Kuwait
• Korea, Rep.	• Colombia	• Malaysia	• Zambia	• Morocco
• Singapore	• Costa Rica	• Philippines	• Zimbabwe	• Qatar
• Taiwan	• Ecuador	• Thailand		• Turkey
	• El Salvador			
	• Guatemala			
	• Mexico			
	• Venezuela			

Source: Mansour Javidan, Gunter K. Stahl, Felix Brodbeck, and Celeste P. M. Wilderom, "Cross-Border Transfer of Knowledge: Cultural Lessons from Project GLOBE," *Academy of Management Executive* 19 (May 2005): 59–76. Used with permission.

7. *Gender Egalitarianism:* The degree to which a culture's people (should) support gender equality. (*High:* Eastern Europe and Nordic Europe; *Mid:* Anglo and Confucian Asia; *Low:* Middle East and Germanic Europe)

8. *Assertiveness:* The degree to which a culture's people are (should be) assertive, confrontational, and aggressive. (*High:* Germanic Europe and Eastern Europe; *Mid:* Anglo and Confucian Asia; *Low:* Nordic Europe and Southeast Asia)

9. *Humane Orientation:* The degree to which a culture's people are (should be) fair, altruistic, generous, caring, and kind toward others. (*High:* Southern Asia and Sub-Sahara Africa; *Mid:* Anglo and Confucian Asia; *Low:* Latin Europe and Germanic Europe)

Characteristics of the various GLOBE dimensions that have a direct impact on how an individual from such a society might negotiate are suggested in Figure 9.4. Figure 9.5 shows the relative scores on the nine GLOBE dimensions for the U.S. and Japan.

In summarizing its findings from the 10 society clusters, the GLOBE study noted the following:[13]

1. The **Anglo cluster,** consisting of the predominantly English-speaking developed nations that were formerly British colonies, is characterized by an individualist performance orientation. Although their societies value gender equality,

Figure 9.4 Representative Characteristics of GLOBE Dimensions

High PERFORMANCE ORIENTATION *societies have characteristics such as …*	*Low PERFORMANCE ORIENTATION* *societies have characteristics such as …*
Value competitiveness and materialism. Value what one does more than who one is. Expect direct, explicit communication.	Value societal and family relationships. Value harmony with the environment. Value who one is more than what one does. Expect indirect, subtle communication.
High INSTITUTIONAL COLLECTIVISM *societies have characteristics such as …*	*Low INSTITUTIONAL COLLECTIVISM* *societies have characteristics such as …*

Group loyalty is encouraged, even if this
  undermines the pursuit of individual goals.
Rewards are driven by seniority, personal needs,
  and/or within-group equity.
Critical decisions are made by groups.
	Pursuit of individual goals is encouraged,
	  even at the expense of group loyalty.
	Rewards are driven very largely by an
	  individual's contribution to task success.
	Critical decisions are made by individuals.

High IN-GROUP COLLECTIVISM *societies have characteristics such as …*	*Low IN-GROUP COLLECTIVISM* *societies have characteristics such as …*

Duties and obligations are important
  determinants of social behavior.
A strong distinction is made between in-
  groups and out-groups.
People emphasize relatedness with groups.
The pace of life is slower.
	Personal needs and attitudes are important
	  determinants of social behavior.
	Little distinction is made between in-groups
	  and out-groups.
	People emphasize rationality in behavior.
	The pace of life is faster.

High POWER DISTANCE societies have *characteristics such as …*	*Low POWER DISTANCE societies have* *characteristics such as …*
Society is differentiated into classes. Power is seen as providing social order. Information is localized and hoarded.	Power is linked to corruption and coercion. Information is widely shared.
High UNCERTAINTY AVOIDANCE societies *have characteristics such as …*	*Low UNCERTAINTY AVOIDANCE* *societies have characteristics such as …*
Use formality in interactions with others. Rely on formalized policies and procedures. Take moderate, carefully calculated risks. Show strong resistance to change.	Use informality in interactions with others. Rely on informal norms for most matters. Are less calculating when taking risks. Show only moderate resistance to change.
High HUMANE ORIENTATION *societies have characteristics such as …*	*Low HUMANE ORIENTATION* *societies have characteristics such as …*

The interests of others are important.
People are motivated primarily by a need for
  belonging and affiliation.
Members of society are responsible for
  promoting the well-being of others.
	One's own self-interest is important.
	People are motivated primarily by a need
	  for power and material possessions.
	The state provides social and economic
	  support for individuals' well-being.

High FUTURE ORIENTATION societies have characteristics such as …	Low FUTURE ORIENTATION societies have characteristics such as …
Emphasize working for long-term success. Organizations tend to be inflexible and maladaptive.	Prefer gratification as soon as possible. Organizations tend to be flexible and adaptive.

High ASSERTIVENESS societies have characteristics such as …	Low ASSERTIVENESS societies have characteristics such as …
Value competition, success, and progress. Communicate directly and unambiguously. Try to have control over the environment. Build trust on basis of calculation.	Value cooperation and warm relationships. Communicate indirectly; try to "save face." Try to be in harmony with the environment. Build trust on basis of predictability.

Sources: Robert J. House, Paul J. Hanges, Mansour Javidan, Peter W. Dorfman, and Vipin Gupta, eds., *Culture, Leadership, and Organizations: The GLOBE Study of 62 Societies* (Thousand Oaks, CA: Sage, 2004). Used with permission. Also see Cornelius N. Grove, "Worldwide Differences in Business Values and Practices: Overview of GLOBE Research Findings," 2005, Dare to Be WorldWise Professional Knowledge Center, Grovewell LLC, www.grovewell.com/pub-GLOBE-dimensions.html (accessed September 19, 2006).

they tend to be male-dominated in practice. They aspire to improve performance, future, and humane orientation as well as in-group collectivism.[14] Negotiators from these cultures can be expected to use a competitive negotiation style, to communicate directly, to value personal needs and attitudes, and to attempt to persuade with rational arguments.

2. Societies in the **Middle East cluster** share many commonalities in norms and practices reflecting their common historic and religious heritage. They are highly group-oriented, hierarchical, and masculine. They aspire to increase their uncertainty avoidance and their future orientation.[15] As negotiators, they might be highly suspicious of outsiders, reluctant to share information, but inclined to communicate directly. They might attempt to control the environment, would not be reluctant to use power tactics, and would be invested in winning.

3. The **Southern Asia cluster** has a total population of almost 1.5 billion. The cluster has a high power distance rating and strong group and family collectivism practices. These societies aspire for stronger future and performance orientations and lower levels of power distance.[16] Negotiators from this cluster would not be inclined to share information, would not be reluctant to use power tactics, would feel a high sense of duty and obligation to the parties they represent, and could be persuaded by emotional arguments.

4. The countries grouped as the **Latin Europe cluster**—Spain, Portugal, Italy, French Switzerland, France, and Israel—land in the mid-range on all of the studied dimensions, except they have a high power distance and low humane orientation. The cluster's values are particularly high on performance

Figure 9.5 GLOBE Cultural Dimensions, United States, and Japan

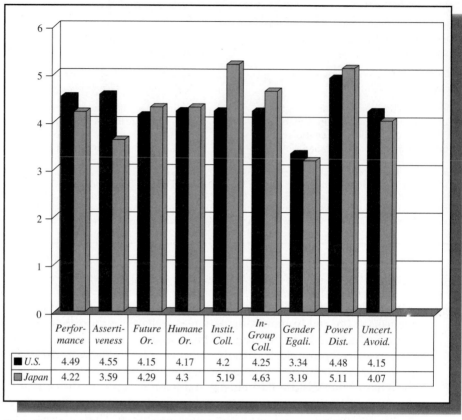

	Perfor-mance	Asserti-veness	Future Or.	Humane Or.	Instit. Coll.	In-Group Coll.	Gender Egali.	Power Dist.	Uncert. Avoid.
■ U.S.	4.49	4.55	4.15	4.17	4.2	4.25	3.34	4.48	4.15
▨ Japan	4.22	3.59	4.29	4.3	5.19	4.63	3.19	5.11	4.07

Source: Based on information from Mansour Javidan, Peter W. Dorfman, Mary Sully de Luque, and Robert J. House, "In the Eye of the Beholder: Cross Cultural Lessons in Leadership from Project GLOBE," *Academy of Management Perspectives* 20 (February 2006): 86–87.

orientation, perhaps reflecting the participants' understanding of the impact of global competition.[17] Negotiators from this cluster would tend to hoard information, not be reluctant to use power tactics, and be motivated by self-interest.

5. The **Germanic Europe cluster** is distinguished from other clusters by its industrial relations, which emphasize cooperation between "labor" and "capital" through co-determination and work councils. They are characterized by a strong tendency for standardization and rules, hierarchy, assertiveness, and gender inequality, although they aspire to increase gender egalitarianism, and to reduce uncertainty avoidance and assertiveness.[18] Negotiators from these cultures are likely to use a competitive negotiation style, to communicate directly, and to value personal needs and attitudes over any group needs. They may try to control the

environment, attempt to persuade with rational arguments, and use power tactics—and will be very invested in winning.

6. The **Eastern Europe cluster** exhibits distinctive cultural practices including assertiveness, high power distances, gender egalitarianism, and in-group collectivism. This cluster, in converting from a communist philosophy to a market-based economy, aspires to increase its future and performance orientation.[19] Negotiators from this cluster are likely to use a competitive negotiation style and would communicate directly, but also would tend to hoard information. They generally feel a high sense of duty and obligation to the parties they represent and would not be reluctant to use power tactics.

7. Results from the GLOBE study on the **Latin America cluster** include a concern by the participants that these countries are excessively elitist and highly collectivist, in the sense of marked family and group loyalty values and having a high tolerance for ambiguity. On the other hand, the societies aspire to reduce their power distance rankings and increase both future and performance orientations.[20] Negotiators in this cluster would tend to be driven by a group interest rather than individual interests, and would allow all of the group to take part in the decision making. They might hoard information and would not be reluctant to use power tactics.

8. The **Nordic Europe cluster** shared a strong tendency for standardization and rules with Germanic Europe but had a low score on assertiveness and has embraced gender equality. The cluster aspires to reduce the power distance within its societies and to increase in-group collectivism. Negotiators from this culture would enter the negotiations with formalized policies and procedures and would be reluctant to change positions. They would be driven by a group interest rather than individual interests, would allow all of the group to take part in the decision making, and would be more interested in the long-term benefits of the negotiation than in the immediate results.

9. The **Confucian Asia cluster** emphasizes its in-group and institutional collectivism and performance orientation as its current practice and seeks to reduce its power distance and improve its future orientation. Negotiators would be driven by a group interest rather than individual interests and by their duty and obligations to the group. They are likely to use a competitive negotiation style and be reluctant to share information.

10. Finally, the **Sub-Sahara Africa cluster** also emphasizes its in-group collectivism and has a high power distance, which it hopes to reduce, and low future and performance orientations, which it hopes to improve. Negotiators in this cluster would not readily share information and would not be reluctant to use power tactics, but would pursue the group's interest and rely on the group to make the decisions.[21]

In Box 9.1, reviewing one company's experience in failing to recognize cultural differences can help you avoid the same mistakes.

BOX 9.1 Traps to Avoid

Ignoring Cross-Cultural Differences

A company's "knowledge base" is an important resource. It is a product of human experience and thought, which is embedded within a company's rules, processes, or routines. Creating partnerships requires the sharing of such knowledge. Five principles for successful transfer of knowledge are: (1) recognizing the value of the knowledge; (2) ensuring the motivation of the organization that is sharing the knowledge; (3) developing clear communication channels to transfer knowledge; (4) ensuring the motivation of the organization that is receiving the knowledge; and (5) ensuring that the receiving organization has the capacity to absorb and assimilate the knowledge.

Culture and cultural differences can impact how well knowledge can be shared. Researchers studied a failed attempt by a Nordic Europe business school (NORDED) to market its training program for "Leadership and Management of Change" to a Southern Asia bank (Tai Bank), to determine if there were core problems to avoid. The GLOBE study determined that the Nordic Europe and Southern Asia clusters showed the greatest variance in the dimensions of power distance, in-group collectivism, and uncertainty avoidance. Nordic Europe had a low power distance, low in-group collectivism, and high uncertainty avoidance. Southern Asia had the opposite. Because NORDED was marketing a knowledge product, it needed to satisfy the five principles for the transfer of knowledge just described, which it had difficulty doing because of the cultural differences. Here is a summary of the problem areas:

- *Recognizing different cultural values:* NORDED's program was designed around its belief that organizations are better off if their managers are involved in decision making because that leads to better quality decisions. This value is understandable for a low power distance culture (Nordic Europe), but it doesn't necessarily translate to a culture with a high power distance that values hierarchical management (Southern Asia).
- *Understanding different motivations:* Sharing knowledge takes time and resources. NORDED's personnel may have been motivated to share what they considered a valuable product, but Tai Bank's managers may not have shared that motivation because a culture with an orientation toward in-group collectivism would be reluctant to spend time and energy working with out-group members.
- *Communication:* How the knowledge is communicated is an important aspect of knowledge exchange. In a culture with high uncertainty avoidance, such as NORDED's, there would be a preference for advanced planning, high attention to detail, and organization *before* the delivery of the program. Tai Bank's low uncertainty avoidance, on the other hand, would tend to support a more fluid program that could be monitored and adjusted *during* its presentation.

- *Assimilation:* The degree of similarity between two cultures contributes to the ability of one to assimilate knowledge from the other. In this case, NORDED and Tai Bank's cultures were so dissimilar that the ability of Tai Bank to actually incorporate the knowledge base that NORDED was attempting to share was limited.

Source: Adapted from Mansour Javidan, Gunter K. Stahl, Felix Brodbeck, and Celeste P. M. Wilderom, "Cross-Border Transfer of Knowledge: Cultural Lessons from Project GLOBE," *Academy of Management Executive* 19 (May 2005): 59–76.

NEGOTIATION ISSUES SENSITIVE TO CULTURE

Heuristics and Biases in Cross-Cultural Negotiations

As previously discussed in Chapter 1, a behavioral decision theory has been applied to the study of judgment and choice in the negotiation process.[22] Under the *rational choice theory,* negotiators would gather sufficient information, evaluate the information appropriately, compare the pros and cons of reaching agreement, and then make a rational decision—resulting in good agreements. In practice, however, negotiators are just people who may or may not have the time, inclination, or ability to act so rationally. When negotiators react to uncertainty in a cross-cultural setting by relying upon *heuristics,* or rules of thumb, to simplify decision making, they can create **biases,** preconceived notions that cause them to make faulty or irrational decisions. Examining the role of culture in negotiator cognition is useful in determining which of these negotiation biases are most culturally variable and which are not.

Cognitive Biases Noted researchers Michael W. Morris and Michele J. Gelfand[23] distinguish between biases that are learned and biases that arise from the human perceptual system, theorizing that the former would be culturally variable but the latter would not. Biases based on numerical judgments—anchoring, insufficient adjustment, and framing—are examples of biases based on a natural human sensitivity to change. Research supports the theory that the party making the higher first offer fares better in a negotiation. Research also shows that negotiators, when presented with a choice between a certain gain by settling versus the possibility of a greater gain by not settling, will settle—but when presented with a choice between a certain loss by settling versus the probability of a larger loss by not settling, will not settle.[24]

Learned Biases *Overconfidence* or *self-serving evaluations* are examples of biases based on learned behavior. In highly individualist societies, negotiators tend to view their own behaviors as more fair than others. The origin of this **egocentric bias** is the privileged status of one's self-concept in individualistic cultures, such as the United States, when society reinforces individual achievement over relationships. The self is served by focusing on one's positive attributes to "stand out" and be better than others. In contrast, in collectivistic societies, such as Japan, negotiators conceive of themselves more in terms of their relationship to others and are therefore more likely to see the other's viewpoint as being just as valid as their own. The self is served by focusing on shared characteristics to blend in.[25]

Morris and Gelfand discuss **availability bias** as an example of a culturally significant bias. Using a software metaphor, they note that a knowledge structure first must be *available* (like a program existing on your computer), it must be *accessible* (like a frequently used program), and it must be *activated* (like selecting a particular program to prepare a spreadsheet). Just because an individual possesses a knowledge structure doesn't mean that he or she will be able to easily access that knowledge or that he or she will activate the knowledge to make a judgment. A knowledge structure that views negotiations as a win-lose proposition may be available in a "masculine" society, but unavailable in a "feminine" society. Or such a view of negotiations may be known, but not easily accessible—that is, negotiators from a feminine society may have engaged in distributive bargaining at one time in their careers, but because it is not a common occurrence, it is not readily accessible. Finally, there might be cultural reasons influencing the availability of a knowledge structure, even if the person were familiar with it. A female negotiator from a society with gender egalitarianism may refuse to be drawn into a distributive bargaining pattern, preferring instead an integrative bargaining process.

Finally, *representativeness* is certainly a culturally significant bias. Representativeness is one of the heuristics that people use to judge the likelihood that some event or item is part of a broader category, based solely on the degree of similarity between the event or item and the category, rather than on statistical likelihood or actual information. It is, in effect, **stereotyping.** In a cross-cultural negotiation, making assumptions about negotiators based upon stereotyping is certainly easy to do, but will not further the goals of the negotiations.

Negotiation Patterns in Cross-Cultural Negotiations

The negotiation process involves the general strategy or approach taken, the tactics used by the parties, and the flow of the process itself during negotiation phases. As you recall, the negotiation strategies discussed throughout this text are, in brief, *competitive-distributive bargaining,* a win-lose process in which each side views the object of the negotiation as a "fixed pie" and the goal is to maximize the amount of the pie your side gets, and *cooperative-integrative bargaining* and *interest-based bargaining,* which are win-win strategies emphasizing shared interests, maximizing the return for both parties, and creating or maintaining a long-term relationship. Tactics include such things as various forms of verbal and nonverbal communication, persuasion techniques, use of experts, and the manner in which information is shared. Phases include the pre-negotiation preparation, exchange of information, relationship building, problem solving, exchange of concessions, and resolution.

The way in which tactics are combined to form a strategy and the way strategies are employed to reach a goal creates a *pattern of negotiation.* This pattern is displayed in (1) the general *strategic approach* of the parties toward the particular negotiation, as evidenced for instance by the frequency of certain tactics; (2) the influence of one party over another, as evidenced by the *sequence of tactics;* and (3) the *flow of the process* toward an outcome during the phases of negotiation.

Strategic Approach   The first indication of the pattern of a negotiation is seen in the strategic approach taken—whether the negotiator begins with a goal of maximizing individual gain and therefore uses more distributive tactics, or with a goal of maximizing joint gains and therefore uses integrative tactics more frequently. As negotiations progress, it is likely that the players will use both distributive and integrative elements in order to keep the process going.[26]

From what you have learned thus far in the chapter, and including the topics to be covered in the remainder of the chapter, it is obvious that cultural issues will come into play in this aspect of the negotiation pattern.

Sequence of Tactics   There is evidence that the frequency with which integrative or distributive tactics are used, particularly as to information exchange, has an impact on the outcome of the negotiation. *Integrative* information exchanges that give or seek to establish the priorities of the parties tend to result in larger joint gains than *distributive* information exchanges that focus on preferences or positions.[27] Cultural aspects obviously play a role here.

The sequence of tactics can follow a pattern that is either reciprocal or nonreciprocal. A reciprocal response is one in which negotiators match each other's moves exactly—for example, a minor concession by one side elicits a minor concession by the other, or an angry outburst is matched in kind. A reciprocal sequence can signal that the parties are on the same page in the negotiation, but whether that page is positive or negative depends upon the nature of the reciprocity. Nonreciprocal responses include countering a tactic with its exact opposite, or countering with a similar but not the same tactic. An example of the former is when a negotiator counters a defensive stonewalling tactic with an offensive tactic of establishing a deadline for completion of the negotiations. An example of the latter is countering a defensive stonewalling tactic with a different defensive tactic such as picking holes in the opponent's position.

Again, the cultural differences discussed in this chapter emphasize how important it is to understand that the party you are negotiating with may not react to your tactics in a way that you would expect.

Flow of the Process   Finally, in looking at the flow of the negotiation process itself, the timing and intensity of tactics used will differ between distributive and integrative strategies, and thus will differ across cultures. In a distributive negotiation there is an escalating exchange of messages over time and an increased number of proposals and offers immediately before a deadline is met; in an integrative negotiation there is a peak exchange of messages or proposals during the problem-solving stage; and in a mixed integrative-distributive negotiation there is a linear exchange of information and proposals over time, but significant increase during the problem-solving and resolution stages.

Wendi Lyn Adair and Jeanne M. Brett,[28] preeminent scholars on cross-cultural negotiation, contend that competition (distributive) and cooperation (integrative) strategies are both central elements of a negotiation regardless of the location. However, the behaviors that negotiators from different cultures use to gain cooperation or to engage in competition are different. For purposes of illustration, we can compare a Western individualist culture to an Eastern collectivist culture. In the Western culture where people believe that negotiation is primarily about distribution of resources, the interplay between cooperation and competition is to create joint gains and to claim the largest portion possible. In the Eastern culture where people believe that negotiation is primarily about relationships, the interplay between cooperation and competition is to create a long-term relationship on favorable terms that will result in claimed value.

The frequency of information exchange and persuasion tactics is examined by comparing cultures with low- and high-context communication. In low-context cultures, such as the United States, information sharing is explicit and direct with a goal of making one's priorities clear, whereas in high-context cultures, such as China, information sharing is implicit and indirect so that the other party must infer priorities. In low-context cultures persuasion tactics are primarily appeals to rationality, relying upon logic and reasoning to argue a point and making more commitments to influence the other side. In high-context cultures, on the other hand, persuasion tactics are primarily appeals to emotions, relying on social roles and relationships to press a point and using strategic questioning and patience to influence the other side.[29] In Box 9.2 you can see the difference in the use of information in high-context cultures.

BOX 9.2   Tactics for Success

Consensus Building

A consortium of U.S. companies submitted a proposal to build a dam in China's Yangtze River and prepared to negotiate with the Yangtze Valley Planning Office. The Yangtze Valley Planning Office, as is the tradition in China, was of equal rank with other organizations that had a say in the governance of the region. When disagreements occurred between such organizations, the decision could be sent up to the highest authority possible or the bureaucracy could attempt to reach consensus. In this instance, the affected groups engaged in complex bargaining to establish compatible goals and protect interests. In consensus cultures, relationship building is critical not only to reaching agreement but in making sure that the agreement is carried out. If the project was to move forward, the U.S. negotiating team had to adapt its negotiating strategy to the Chinese consensus-building culture.

Here are some consensus-building tactics that would be helpful in negotiations with the Yangtze Valley Planning Office:

1. Be patient. Consensus building takes time.
2. Be prepared to provide demands for significant amounts of information. All of the parties to the process require enough information to augment their arguments.
3. Identify the most significant doubters among the group and focus information that can dispel some of their doubts.
4. Shift the focus of your efforts from "formal" negotiations to informal negotiations where you can interact with the individuals trying to reach consensus.
5. Adjust your timetable to account for the time needed to satisfy all of the interests involved.
6. Recognize that the relationship building involved in the consensus process can result in better deals that are implemented more quickly because of the "buy in" by the affected parties.

Source: Adapted from James K. Sebenius, "The Hidden Challenge of Cross-Border Negotiations," *Harvard Business Review* (March 2002): 4–11.

Emotions in Cross-Cultural Negotiations

Negotiators make many decisions, and more or less use logic to make those decisions. But decision making is a cognitive process where the outcome is a choice between alternatives—and deciding between alternatives often involves not only logic but also emotion. Many decisions have pros and cons on both sides: "Shall I have the fish or the beef?" With no rational way to decide, a negotiator relies on emotion to make the decision: "Which do I like better, fish or beef?"

Emotions play a predictor role in negotiations, in that researchers have found that positive moods going into a negotiation resulted in higher joint gains and fewer contentious tactics, whereas expressing negative emotions caused the parties to have less regard for each other's interests and ultimately lowered joint gains. Negative emotions also resulted in a reduced desire by the negotiators to have future interactions.[30] Emotional reactions are also a consequence of negotiations. Researchers have found that negotiators who regard the negotiation process as fair were more likely to experience positive emotions. Emotion can be a negotiating tactic when a strategic display of an emotion such as anger is used when not actually felt.

Emotions have an effect not only on a negotiator's own negotiating behavior, but also on the other party. Emotions can evoke reciprocal or complementary emotions, convey information about how the individual feels about the situation, and indicate whether the negotiations are heading in the right or wrong direction. Positive emotions can signal that your opponent is satisfied with your proposal and that no additional concessions are necessary—while negative emotions, such as anger, may elicit more cooperation by signaling dissatisfaction with what is currently on the table and causing you to offer more favorable terms.[31]

Emotions are a part of every negotiation. In cross-cultural negotiations, reading those emotions may be more difficult.[32] To begin with, the mere anticipation of cross-cultural negotiations can produce negative emotions for a number of reasons. The perceived dissimilarity between the cultures produces a lack of attraction to the other culture and makes it difficult for negotiators to find a common frame of reference. Cultural distance lessens the negotiators' sense of control, making the situation more ambiguous and unpredictable than would otherwise be the case. Because there is a concern that the negotiation will be more difficult and less likely to result in an agreement, the trust level at the beginning of the negotiation may be reduced.

Theorists have categorized emotions in negotiation as associated with either a promotion focus or a prevention focus. A **promotion focus** is when a negotiator is more concerned with the presence or absence of positive outcomes; a **prevention focus** is when a negotiator is more concerned with the presence or absence of negative outcomes. A negotiator from an individualist culture would likely have a promotion focus because a positive outcome would reflect well on him or her personally, whereas negotiators from a collectivist culture would likely have a prevention focus because a negative outcome would indicate that they had failed in their obligations.

Cheerfulness-related emotions (happy, joyful) when meeting the desired goal and dejection-related emotions (sad, disappointed) when not meeting it are typical for someone with a promotion focus. Typical for someone with a prevention focus would be acquiescent-related emotions (calm, relaxed) when negative outcomes are believed to be unlikely and agitation-related emotions (tense, restless) when negative outcomes arise.

Cross-cultural negotiations may also invoke ego-focused and other-focused emotions. Ego-focused emotions—anger, frustration, guilt, or pride—are associated with achieving or not achieving an individual's goals or desires. Other-focused emotions—shame, anxiety, fear, or satisfaction—are associated with an ability or inability to nurture interdependency with in-group members.

How emotions influence cross-cultural negotiations may be different from how they influence intracultural negotiations. As already noted, in Western cultures positive emotions can signal that your opponent is satisfied with your proposal and that no additional concessions are necessary, while negative emotions such as anger may elicit more cooperation by signaling dissatisfaction with what is currently on the table and cause you to offer more favorable terms.[33] However, in a cross-cultural negotiation with a party who has a prevention focus, if a person with a promotion focus exhibits anger, this emotional display will not cause the prevention-focused negotiator to make concessions. Rather, it is likely to evoke an acquiescent response—achieving the goal of preventing a bad outcome. Thus, Pierre Casse of the Economic Development Institute of the World Bank lists the following five negotiating behaviors that are helpful to international negotiators:

1. *See the world as other people see it and understand others' behavior from their perspective.* Larry Hayes, in the Chapter Case, was surprised by the Toyota negotiating team's reaction to *signing* a contract. He knew that the deal had been concluded to everyone's satisfaction and that Toyota had every intention to carry out its part of the bargain. Hayes did not initially understand that signing a contract document did not mean the same to Hiroshi Okuda as it did to him.
2. *Demonstrate the advantages of your proposals in a way that can persuade your bargaining partner.* Governor Collins was able to appeal directly to Chairman Toyoda and convince him that in her culture *not signing* the agreement indicated that there was some doubt as to whether the party had actually accepted the deal.
3. *Manage stress, ambiguous situations, and unpredictable demands.* Larry Hayes reported that although almost 20 years had elapsed since his final negotiation with Hiroshi Okuda, he can still remember how stressful it was to think that this critical project was not going to happen because of a single signature.
4. *Express your ideas clearly, so you are accurately understood.* Hiroshi Okuda was probably equally surprised by the insistence of the Kentucky negotiators that he sign an agreement *that had already been made.* He was not able to communicate exactly why his reluctance was not a reflection of any intention of not carrying out the project as agreed.
5. *Adjust your suggestions so that you are sensitive to cultural constraints and limitations.* Larry Hayes was correct in asking Governor Collins to speak to Chairman Toyoda directly to get a signed agreement, because in the Japanese hierarchical culture it would not have occurred to Hiroshi Okuda to sign the agreement without the chairman's approval.[34]

Communication in Cross-Cultural Negotiations

As previously discussed, parties to a negotiation are communicating. In a face-to-face meeting such communication is both verbal and nonverbal. Verbal communication in a negotiation actually begins with listening. There are, of course, different ways of listening. *Defensive and offensive listening* is hearing with an agenda. *Information gathering* is listening for facts; it involves no evaluation of what is heard. *Polite listening* is really just waiting for the other person to finish so you can start talking. *Active listening* requires understanding, empathy, and active involvement to understand the content of the message (the idea) as well as the feeling or attitude of the message (the emotion).

Individuals, in their roles as senders or receivers of communication, are influenced by their own culture. Communication does not always mean comprehension. Understanding is dependent upon the sender and the receiver interpreting the symbols used—verbal and nonverbal—in the same way. Communication in the global context can be anything but simple. Often there is a basic barrier because of language differences. The negotiator needs to communicate in cross-cultural settings and may use interpreters, rely on bilingual team members, or may learn the language.[35] Language is more than words, however, and a language barrier in the relationship between negotiators can include the following features:

- The "second language" users will have some language proficiency but not enough for effective or comfortable communication.
- Communication can be stilted or impersonal.
- Team members with more language proficiency may intervene in the communication process between chief negotiators, undermining one or the other's role.
- Poor communication exaggerates the tension at the negotiating table.[36]

Nonverbal communication may be an even more difficult area for a negotiator. Nonverbal communication includes *sign language*—such as a gesture for a waiter's attention—and *action language*—movements that accompany normal activities, such as making or not making eye contact when conversing. In some cultures, people stand very close to each other when talking. In the United States, on the other hand, people like a "comfort zone" around them and are uncomfortable when someone comes in too close. Americans, insensitive to this difference, have been known to back up continually during social events in a foreign country, just to be followed by the person who could not understand the distancing.[37]

High- to Low-Context Communication

One cultural anthropologist has studied cultures around the world and has developed a concept that may be useful in communicating with people from diverse backgrounds. Edward T. Hall identified two classic dimensions of culture: high-context and low-context. These concepts primarily refer to the way in which information is communicated. *High-context* cultures place value on the context in which the communication takes place—on body language, setting, and other cues in the environment in addition to the spoken word. High-context cultures use communication for interaction and use information exchange as a way to establish and maintain a relationship, with only minimal information in the transmitted message itself. *Low-context* cultures are the reverse. Low-context communications rely heavily upon the spoken word. External surrounding factors are screened out and objective facts are relied upon for the information gathered. Most of the information has to be in the transmitted message in order to make up for what is missing in the context.[38]

Individuals from high-context cultures place great value on being a member of a group, starting with the family. Achieving harmony within the group often requires considering the good of the whole, as opposed to one's own advancement. The low-context culture values and rewards individual achievement, initiative, and independence. Hall warns that of course not everyone within a cultural group will display the extremes of the high-context or low-context culture, but there are definite patterns. Table 9.1 shows his findings.[39]

For communication in a negotiation to be persuasive, it must appeal at some level to both the analytical and the emotional side of the listener. As described in Chapter 5, Richard E. Petty and John T. Cacioppo's *central route* to persuasion emphasizes the analytical basis for the argument—that is, the ideas and content of the message. The *peripheral route* to persuasion emphasizes the emotional nature of the listener, with the influence coming from the source of the message or its presentation rather than its content.[40] Petty and Cacioppo's central and peripheral routes to persuasive communication can easily be compared to low- and high-context communications. Low-context cultures rely upon direct information sharing and analytical arguments, while high-context cultures use indirect, inference information sharing and emotional arguments.

Time Management Differences in Cross-Cultural Negotiations

Hall also studied the different cultural concepts of time and time management in low- and high-context cultures. *Monochronic time,* which is typical of low-context cultures, is a linear concept of time, measured in days and years that once used are never replaced. People in these cultures tend to focus on one thing at a time and schedules and deadlines are important. Their comfort level with a negotiation is higher when there's a definitive list of issues in which each one is dealt with and decided before moving on to the next. *Polychronic time,* which is typical of high-context cultures, is circular in nature, constantly reappearing like the rotation of the seasons. People can do many things simultaneously in a polychronic culture and to the extent these activities interfere with completing a task or a communication, schedules and deadlines are

Table 9.1 High to Low Context, by Culture

HIGH	MIDDLE	LOW
Japanese	Spanish	German-Swiss
Chinese	Italian	German
Arabic	French	American
Greek	French Canadian	Scandinavian
Mexican		English
Russian		English Canadian
Vietnamese		

Sources: Mary O'Hara-Devereaux and Robert Johansen, *Globalwork: Bridging Distance, Culture, and Time* (San Francisco: Jossey-Bass, 1994), 54; and Philip R. Harris and Robert T. Moran, *Managing Cultural Differences* (Houston: Gulf Publishing, 1991), 36.

unimportant. Their comfort level with a negotiation is higher when the parties spend time establishing a relationship before bringing up issues. Issues are discussed all at once and then discussed again without ever reaching a decision on any of the issues. People with a polychronic sense of time prefer to think about the whole package before committing to any part of it.[41]

Behavior Responses in Cross-Cultural Negotiations

The concept of low-context versus high-context extends to negotiator behavior, which is another area that is sensitive to culture. Studies have shown a difference in negotiators' behavior responses—reciprocal or nonreciprocal—between low-context and high-context cultures. Negotiators from a low-context culture like the United States will reciprocate direct and indirect information exchange equally, while negotiators from a high-context culture like Japan, consistent with its culture, are more likely to reciprocate indirect information exchange and less likely to reciprocate direct information exchange. However, inconsistent with cultural leanings, studies showed that negotiators from high-context cultures reciprocated rational forms of influence behaviors more than negotiators from low-context cultures, and there was no difference in how negotiators from both cultures reciprocated emotional influence behaviors.[42]

During the phases of negotiation, the behavior of negotiators from low- and high-context cultures seems to follow the same pattern as in intracultural negotiations—that is, influence attempts focused on relationship goals, followed by information exchange, then interplay of competitive and cooperative behaviors, and a final phase dominated by offers.

Trust and Fairness in Cross-Cultural Negotiations

Trust is essential to the negotiation process. As discussed at length in Chapter 8, the essential elements of trust are *risk* and *a relationship.* Risk refers to the perceived probability of loss and some uncertainty regarding whether or not the other party intends to act appropriately. Recall that the five bases of trust are *deterrence-based, calculus-based, relational, identity-based,* and *institutional-based.* These in turn are somewhat dependent upon cognitive processes used in U.S. culture: calculating the costs and rewards of the other party acting in an untrustworthy manner; predicting the other party's behavior; evaluating the other party's motives; assessing the other party's ability to deliver on a promise; and transferring trust from one known trustworthy party to an unknown party. Consider how each of these processes relies on underlying behavior assumptions. For example, when calculating the cost of another's untrustworthy behavior, you assume that the party is motivated by self-interest and will, therefore, weigh such factors just as you do. But you cannot predict another's behavior unless such behavior is consistent and predictable, nor can you evaluate another's motives unless those motives are based on values similar to your own. Looking at these same processes in different cultures demonstrates why trust is difficult to establish in cross-cultural negotiations.

In cultures with high collectivism and femininity rankings, basing trust on the ability to calculate the other party's costs and rewards for acting in an untrustworthy manner may be difficult because individuals are either not motivated by self-interest (group-orientation) or tend toward more cooperative behavior (nurturing). Conformity—and therefore predictability—is high in these cultures but is low in cultures that tend to be more individualistic and masculine. Evaluating motives might be difficult in highly individualistic and masculine cultures because there would be no reason to believe the other party would be acting in your interest. But the norms in collectivist and feminine cultures would provide a strong indication of such motives. Basing your trust on the capability of a party to deliver on a promise in an individualistic or masculine culture would make sense. After all, those cultures rely upon individual achievement, whereas, the group-oriented collectivist and feminine cultures discourage such rugged individualism. But basing your trust within a collectivist and feminine culture on one member of a group by transference from another trustworthy member of the group makes sense because it is a norm of these kind of cultures for members of the group to take responsibility for the other members of the group.[43]

Trust is linked to one's belief in the fairness of the negotiation, and in U.S. culture fairness is associated with *reciprocity*—mutual responsiveness to each other's concessions, which seems both intrinsically fair and is instrumental in achieving cooperation. Applying the concept of justice, or fairness in the negotiation context, in cross-cultural negotiation requires an analysis of whether there is a universal concern for fairness, whether individuals from different cultures conceptualize fairness the same way, and whether fairness is manifested the same way across cultures. The consensus of psychologists and anthropologists is that all cultures share a concern for fairness, recognizing that such power-limiting rules are essential to a stable social system.

There is, however, culture-specific application of those rules. For example, although people from different cultures may agree that resources should be allocated "fairly," they may disagree on what that means. Those from individualist or collectivist cultures will likely differ on whether the allocation of resources should be based on equity (according to one's contribution), equality (equally divided among all members of the in-group), or need (obligation to others). In an individualist culture, for example, when determining a fair salary, one's contribution may be measured by the number of hours worked or tasks completed. But in a collectivist culture, a fair salary might be measured by one's contribution to the team effort or to its harmony. In a culture with high power distance, paying more to someone of a higher rank just because of that rank does not offend the equality concept, whereas in a low power distance culture, equality demands an equal allocation of resources. And allocating resources according to one's need in a collectivist culture is consistent with its sense of loyalty and obligation toward families and in-group members.[44]

GENDER ISSUES IN NEGOTIATIONS

An often-cited study by Judy B. Rosener on women's management style offers some evidence that a negotiator's gender may affect his or her negotiating style.[45] The study was based on a survey of 456 men and women in a variety of organizations nationwide. It concluded that women tend to encourage participatory management while men tend toward a "command and control" style. Table 9.2 summarizes the gender differences as discussed by Rosener and others.

Table 9.2   Management Styles That May Affect Negotiating Styles

	MALE MODEL	FEMALE MODEL
NEGOTIATING STYLE	Competitive/command and control	Cooperative/interactive
ORGANIZATIONAL STRUCTURE	Vertical and hierarchical	Horizontal and egalitarian
OBJECT	Winning	Quality output
PROBLEM-SOLVING STYLE	Rational and objective	Intuitive and subjective
KEY CHARACTERISTICS	Direct	Facilitate
	Strategic	Empathetic
	Unemotional	Collaborative
	Analytical	High performance

Source: Adapted from Judy B. Rosener, "Ways Women Lead," *Harvard Business Review 68,* (November–December, 1990) 119–125; Nanette Fondas, "Feminization Unveiled: Management Qualities in Contemporary Writings," *Academy of Management Review 22* (1997), 257–282; Marilyn Loden, *Feminine Leadership on How to Succeed in Business Without Being One of the Boys* (New York: Times Book 1985).

A more recent survey of managers to elicit the eight characteristics that the respondents believed managers had to have for effective leadership found that the males' lists included *aggressiveness, confidence,* and *objectivity* in their top five—all hallmarks of a competitive style of negotiating. But the females' responses listed *appreciation, recognizing strengths, fairness,* and *accessibility* as the most important characteristics of a leader[46]—all qualities that encourage a more collaborative negotiation style.[47]

Much has been written since Rosener's study, notably by authors Deborah M. Kolb and Judith Williams,[48] who outlined the hidden context within every negotiation. That hidden context, dubbed the *shadow negotiation* (see Chapter 2), acknowledges that although people negotiate over issues, they also negotiate on how they are going to relate to each other. As bargainers try to turn the discussion of the problem to their advantage or persuade the other party to cooperate in resolving it, they make assumptions about each other—what the other person wants, his or her weaknesses, how he or she is likely to behave. In effect, the shadow negotiation is where bargainers decide just how cooperative they are going to be in reaching a mutual solution.[49]

If gender differences in negotiation styles stem from the fact that relationships play a more central role in the lives of women than in men, it naturally flows that women's attitudes toward negotiation reflect their need to value the relationship among parties as well as the object of the negotiations. This suggests that the recognition of the advantages of integrative (win-win) over distributive (win-lose) negotiations should cause a reevaluation of the so-called feminine and masculine negotiation styles. Some studies have shown that a focus on cooperation and relationship building not only wins acceptable short-term results, but actually produces solutions that are objectively superior to those produced by competitive tactics.[50] So if integrative negotiations result in better agreements than distributive negotiations, then it follows that women would actually make better negotiators by using integrative techniques at the bargaining table. In the Chapter Case, Martha Layne Collins took the time and expended the effort necessary to form a personal relationship with Shoichiro Toyoda in pursuit of the negotiations for the Toyota plant. While any skilled politician—male or female—would recognize the necessity of doing this, Governor Collins may very well have had an advantage in that it reflected her natural style.

Women Negotiating on Their Own Behalf

The exception to women's negotiating style being equal to or actually superior to a more masculine negotiating style is when women are negotiating for themselves rather than for someone else. A key element in negotiations is to recognize that you have an opportunity to negotiate. In a study of people's ability to see the possibility of change to their circumstances, women were 45% more likely to score lower than men.[51] In another study that measured the extent to which individuals believe that their behavior influences their circumstances, women scored low on "locus of control," meaning that men believe more than women that their fate is within their own control. Therefore, men are more likely to recognize an opportunity to negotiate.[52]

Individuals have an internal sense of who they are and what they are like—an "interior self-portrait" made up of how they see themselves and how they believe others see them. This interior self-portrait is a filter through which a person processes information, understands events, and is motivated. Studies have shown that men have more "independent" self-portraits and women more "interdependent" ones. A person with a more independent self-portrait, like many men, sees himself as distinct from others with less attention to how he affects others. He is focused on promoting his personal preferences and goals and seeking out relationships that tend to be more useful than intimate. A person with a more interdependent self-portrait, like many women, defines herself in terms of her connections to others and how she influences the people around her. Her focus is on developing strong relationships and protecting them. Because negotiation is necessitated by a conflict of some type and because conflict can have a negative effect on the relationship of the parties, women with these more interdependent self-portraits often avoid negotiations or perform poorly in a traditional negotiation situation.[53] When negotiating on her own behalf, then, a woman's concern over relationships tends to suppress her negotiating outcomes.[54]

Women Negotiating for Others

Women who negotiate for others are not influenced in the same way. Linda Babcock and Hannah Riley conducted a study in which 194 students were given a negotiation simulation involving a single-issue distributive price negotiation over the hourly compensation of a worker. Some women participants were asked to negotiate for themselves and some were given a representative role negotiating for another. The shift in representation role resulted in women setting higher pre-negotiation targets and higher initial offers. On average, the women entered the negotiation intending to ask for 22% more per hour for someone other than themselves.[55]

Additional research has been conducted on the theory that gender differences in negotiations are not based on individual traits so much as on the negotiating situation. In one study, the goal was to test whether gender differences in negotiation goals and outcomes would be influenced by the ambiguity of the negotiating situation. An **unambiguous negotiation** is one in which the zone for potential agreement is fairly well known or established. An **ambiguous negotiation** is one in which there is no information on what the scope of the agreement should be. Part 1 of the study, using ambiguous settlement information, was conducted over three years with 1,634 MBA students; part 2, using unambiguous settlement information, was conducted with 238 adults recruited from college campuses to participate. The results supported the theory that the role of gender in negotiation is situational: In high ambiguity situations, men entered into the negotiation with more optimistic goals and higher initial offers than the women and ultimately negotiated significantly higher payoffs, whereas, in the unambiguous negotiations there were no perceptible differences in the men's and women's goals, first offers, or outcomes.[56] In an ambiguous negotiation situation, a woman's reaction differs from a man's because the parties are called upon to improvise a response rather than to follow a clearly prescribed script. Such improvisation requires the negotiator to draw on internal attitudes, traits, and values. Under these circumstances where one's past experience and individual attitudes, traits, and values are called upon, gender-based social roles and stereotypes are likely to have more influence.[57]

SUMMING UP

Suppose that you are in a cross-cultural negotiating situation for a computer manufacturer. Apply the principles and practices discussed in this chapter as you answer the following questions.

1. Select two of the dimensions of culture, identified either by Hofstede or the GLOBE project, and discuss how best to negotiate a deal favorable to market your company's product in an East European country and an Asian country in terms of those dimensions.

   Dimensions: _____

   East European negotiation: _____

   _____

   _____

   Asian negotiation: _____

   _____

   _____

2. The dimensions of culture attributed to the United States reflect its origins and history as valuing the "rugged individualist" who carved out a democratic nation from a vast and rich environment. The United States joins other Anglo cultures as a highly individualistic society; as tolerant, but tending to be masculine; as egalitarian and accepting of ambiguities and differences of opinion. Select two clusters from the GLOBE project groups and describe how the history and tradition of the countries in those clusters are reflected in their cultural dimensions. How can this information help you in your negotiations?

   Cluster 1: _____

   _____

_____

_____

Cluster 2:_____

_____

_____

_____

3. Explain why the heuristic of *availability* is a culturally significant bias in your negotiation to sell the computer product in a highly feminine society.

_____

_____

4. Explain why the pattern of negotiating you probably used successfully in Australia to settle a dispute about your company's computer product would probably not work in Pakistan.

_____

_____

5. One's emotions can have either a *promotion focus* (concern for the presence of positive outcomes) or a *prevention focus* (concern for the absence of negative outcomes). Which type of focus is a negotiator from a collectivist society likely to have, and why?

_____

_____

6. a. If you believe the allocation of resources should be based on *equity* (according to one's contribution), you probably live in what kind of culture?

    _____

   b. If you believe the allocation of resources should be based on *equality* (equally divided among all members), you probably live in what kind of culture?

    _____

   c. If you believe the allocation of resources should be based on *need* (obligation to others), you probably live in what kind of culture?

    _____

7. The *shadow negotiation* is the hidden context of a negotiation that values the _____ as much as the _____.

8. Do you view yourself as an *independent* or *interdependent* person, and how will that impact the way you negotiate for your company?

_____

_____

9. The parameters of your negotiation on this new computer product are somewhat ambiguous. Would you predict you would be *very successful* or *somewhat successful* in selling it to both of your target markets? Why? _____

_____

_____

LEARNING EXERCISE: NEGOTIATING A FRANCHISE AGREEMENT

The purpose of this exercise is to apply the five negotiation skills presented in this chapter to an actual negotiation situation. You are negotiating the expansion of a Kentucky Fried Chicken (KFC) franchise with a Japanese company. You have worked with the company's representatives before and you believe you have a good relationship. In fact, it is your intent to encourage the representatives to branch out on their own in order to double the number of franchise locations in a short period of time. Recently KFC has instituted a number of programs to encourage global expansions of its franchises, including the following:

1. Waiving part of the franchise fee for a first-time franchisee if the individual has a history with KFC
2. Bonuses paid directly by KFC to participating franchisees based on sales volumes
3. Allowing multiple companies to apply as co-owners of franchises
4. Waiving the franchise fee altogether if the franchisee commits to having the restaurant open within three months

Answer the following skills questions:

Skill 9.1: What *cultural-based traits* will and will not influence this negotiation process? Why?

Skill 9.2: What *negotiation bias* will you need to be aware of and how would you avoid it?

Skill 9.3: How can you *respond to the negotiation patterns* used by the Japanese negotiator?

Skill 9.4: What *masculine or feminine characteristics* could be helpful in reaching agreement?

Skill 9.5: How would you advise KFC's negotiator to *reach a "good" agreement* for both parties?

ENDNOTES

1. Michele J. Gelfand and Jeanne M. Brett, eds., *The Handbook of Negotiation and Culture* (Stanford, CA: Stanford Business Books, 2004).

2. Thomas L. Friedman, *The World Is Flat: A Brief History of the Twenty-first Century* (New York: Farrar, Straus & Giroux, 2005).

3. Ibid., 48–172.

4. See "History of Toyota," Toyota Motor Corporation, www.toyota.co.jp/en/about_toyota/history (accessed September 19, 2006).

5. Jim Kennedy and Anna Everest, "Put Diversity in Context," *Personnel Journal* (September 1991): 50–54; and Sondra Threderman, "Managing the Foreign-Born Work Force," *Manage* (October 1988): 26–29.

6. Geert Hofstede, *Culture's Consequences: Comparing Values, Behaviors, Institutions, and Organizations Across Nations,* 2nd ed. (Thousand Oaks, CA: Sage, 2001); Geert Hofstede, *Culture's Consequences: International Differences in Work-Related Values* (Beverly Hills, CA: Sage, 1984); and Geert Hofstede and Michael H. Bond, "The Confucius Connection: From Cultural Roots to Economic Growth," *Organizational Dynamics* 16 (1988): 4–21.

7. Michael H. Hoppe, "An Interview with Geert Hofstede," *Academy of Management Executive* 18 (February 2004): 76–77.

8. Joyce S. Osland and Allan Bird, "Beyond Sophisticated Stereotyping: Cultural Sense-Making in Context," *Academy of Management Executive* 14 (2000): 65–77.

9. Harry C. Triandis, "The Many Dimensions of Culture," *Academy of Management Executive* 18 (February 2004): 88–93.

10. Geert Hofstede, "Motivation, Leadership, and Organizations: Do American Theories Apply Abroad?" *Organizational Dynamics* 9 (Summer 1980): 42–63.

11. Mansour Javidan, Gunter K. Stahl, Felix Brodbeck, and Celeste P. M. Wilderom, "Cross-Border Transfer of Knowledge: Cultural Lessons from Project GLOBE," *Academy of Management Executive* 19 (May 2005): 59–76. Also see Robert J. House, Paul J. Hanges, Mansour Javidan, Peter W. Dorfman, and Vipin Gupta, eds., *Culture, Leadership, and Organizations: The GLOBE Study Of 62 Societies* (Thousand Oaks, CA: Sage, 2004).

12. Robert House, Mansour Javidan, Paul Hanges and Peter Dorfman, "Understanding Cultures and Implicit Leadership Theories Across the Globe: An Introduction to Project GLOBE," *Journal of World Business* 37 (Spring 2002): 3–10.

13. Javidan et al., "Cross-Border Transfer of Knowledge," 62.

14. Neal M. Ashkanasy, Edwin Trevor-Roberts, and Louise Earnshaw, "The Anglo Cluster: Legacy of the British Empire," *Journal of World Business* 37 (Spring 2002): 28–39.

15. Hayat Kabasakal and Muzaffer Bodur, "Arabic Cluster: A Bridge Between East and West," *Journal of World Business* 37 (Spring 2002): 40–54.

16. Vipin Gupta, Gita Surie, Mansour Javidan, and Jagdeep Chhokar, "Southern Asia Cluster: Where the Old Meets the New?" *Journal of World Business* 37 (Spring 2002): 16–27.

17. Jorge Correia Jesuino, "Latin Europe Cluster: From South to North," *Journal of World Business* 37 (Spring 2002): 81–89.

18. Erna Szabo, Felix C. Brodbeck, Deanne N. Den Hartog, Gerhard Reber, Jurgen Weibler, and Rolf Wunderer, "The Germanic Europe Cluster: Where Employees Have a Voice," *Journal of World Business* 37 (Spring 2002): 55–68.

19. Gyula Bakacsi, Takacs Sandor, Karacsonyi Andras, and Imrek Viktor, "Eastern European Cluster: Tradition and Transition," *Journal of World Business* 37 (Spring 2002): 69–80.

20. Enrique Ogliastri, "Culture and Organizational Leadership in Colombia," July 1998, available from Thunderbird, the Garvin School of International Management, www.thunderbird.edu/wwwfiles/ms/globe/publications_2001.html (accessed May 31, 2005).

21. Cornelius N . Grove, "Worldwide Differences in Business Values and Practices: Overview of GLOBE Research Findings," 2005, Dare to Be WorldWise Professional Knowledge Center, Grovewell LLC, www.grovewell.com/pub-GLOBE-dimensions.html (accessed September 19, 2006); and Robert J. House, Paul J. Hanges, Mansour Javidan, Peter W. Dorfman, and Vipin Gupta, eds., *Culture, Leadership, and Organization: The GLOBE Study of 62 Societies* (Thousand Oaks, CA: Sage, 2004).

22. Max H. Bazerman and Margaret A. Neale, "Heuristics in Negotiation: Limitations to Effective Dispute Resolution," in

Negotiating in Organizations, eds. M. H. Bazerman and R. J. Lewicki (Beverly Hills, CA: Sage, 1983), 51–67; and Howard Raiffa, *The Art and Science of Negotiation* (Cambridge, MA: Harvard University Press, 1982), 20–32.

23. Michael W. Morris and Michele J. Gelfand, "Cultural Differences and Cognitive Dynamics," in *The Handbook of Negotiation and Culture,* eds. Michele J. Gelfand and Jeanne M. Brett (Stanford, CA: Stanford Business Books, 2004), 45–70.

24. Charles Craver, *The Intelligent Negotiator* (Roseville, CA: Prima, 2002), 44–45.

25. Michele J. Gelfand, Marianne Higgins, Lisa H. Nishii, Jana L. Raver, Alexandria Dominguez, Fumio Murakami, Susumu Yamaguchi, and Midori Toyama, "Culture and Egocentric Biases of Fairness in Conflict and Negotiation," *Journal of Applied Psychology* 87 (October 2002): 833–845.

26. Joan F. Brett, Gegory B. Northcraft, and Robin L. Pinkley, "Stairways to Heaven: An Interlocking Self-Regulation Model of Negotiation," *Academy of Management Review* 24 (July 1999): 435–451.

27. Laurie R. Weingart and Mara Olekalns, "Communication Process in Negotiation: Frequencies, Sequences, and Phases," in *The Handbook of Negotiation and Culture,* eds. Michele J. Gelfand and Jeanne M. Brett (Stanford, CA: Stanford Business Books, 2004), 143–157.

28. Wendi Lyn Adair and Jeanne M. Brett, "Culture and Negotiation Process," in *The Handbook of Negotiation and Culture,* eds. Michele J. Gelfand and Jeanne M. Brett (Stanford, CA: Stanford Business Books, 2004), 158–176.

29. John L. Graham and N. Mark Lam, "The Chinese Negotiation," *Harvard Business Review OnPoint* (October 2003): 1–11.

30. Bruce Barry, Ingrid Smithey Fulmer, and Gerben A. Van Kleef, "I Laughed, I Cried, I Settled: The Role of Emotion in Negotiation," in *The Handbook of Negotiation and Culture,* eds. Michele J. Gelfand and Jeanne M. Brett (Stanford, CA: Stanford Business Books, 2004), 71–94.

31. Jeanne M. Brett, Debra L. Shapiro, and Anne L. Lytle, "Breaking the Bonds of Reciprocity in Negotiations," *Academy of Management Journal* 41 (August 1998): 410–424.

32. Rajesh Kumar, "Culture and Emotions in Intercultural Negotiations," in *The Handbook of Negotiation and Culture,* eds. Michele J. Gelfand and Jeanne M. Brett (Stanford, CA: Stanford Business Books, 2004), 95–113.

33. Brett et al., "Breaking the Bonds of Reciprocity in Negotiations."

34. Philip R. Harris and Robert T. Moran, *Managing Cultural Differences,* 3rd ed. (Houston: Gulf Publishing, 1991), 58.

35. Michael Kublin and Robert Brady, "International Business Negotiating," *NBDC Report,* no. 145 (December 1992), 1–4.

36. Alan J. Feely and Anne-Wil Harzing, "The Language Barrier and Its Implications for HQ–Subsidiary Relationship," paper presented at the 64th Annual Meeting of the Academy of Management, New Orleans, LA, August 2004.

37. C. Barnum and N. Wolniansky, "Taking Cues from Body Language," *Management Review* (June 1989): 59–60.

38. Edward T. Hall, *Beyond Culture* (Garden City, NY: Anchor Press, 1976), 101.

39. Jim Kennedy and Anna Everest, "Put Diversity in Context," *Personnel Journal* (September 1991): 50–54.

40. Richard E. Petty and John T. Cacioppo, *Attitudes and Persuasion: Classic and Contemporary Approaches* (Boulder, CO: Westview Press, 1996), 255–269.

41. Graham and Lam, "The Chinese Negotiation," 7.

42. Adair and Brett, "Culture and Negotiation Process," 167–168.

43. Patricia M. Doney, Joseph P. Cannon, and Michael R. Mullen, "Understanding the Influence of National Culture on the Development of Trust," *Academy of Management Review* 23 (July 1999): 601–620.

44. Kwok Leung and Kwok-Kit Tong, "Justice Across Cultures," in *The Handbook of Negotiation and Culture,* eds. Michele J. Gelfand and Jeanne M. Brett (Stanford, CA: Stanford Business Books, 2004), 313–333.

45. Judy B. Rosener, "Ways Women Lead," *Harvard Business Review* 68 (November–December 1990): 119–125.

46. Jonathan Segal, "Women on the Verge of Equality," *HR Magazine* 30 (June 1991): 117–123.

47. Deborah M. Kolb, "More Than Just a Footnote: Constructing a Theoretical Framework for Teaching About Gender in Negotiation," *Negotiation Journal* 16 (October 2000): 347–357.

48. Deborah M. Kolb and Judith Williams, *The Shadow Negotiation: How Women Can Master the Hidden Agendas That Determine Bargaining Success* (New York: Simon & Schuster, 2000).

49. Deborah M. Kolb and Judith Williams, *Everyday Negotiation: Navigating the Hidden Agendas in Bargaining* (San Francisco: Jossey-Bass, 2003), 12–13.

50. Linda Babcock and Sara Laschever, *Women Don't Ask: Negotiation and the Gender Divide* (Princeton, NJ: Princeton University Press, 2003), 165.

51. Babcock and Laschever, *Women Don't Ask*, 20.

52. Ibid., 20–23.

53. Ibid., 118.

54. Lee E. Miller and Jessica Miller, *A Woman's Guide to Successful Negotiating* (New York: McGraw-Hill, 2002), xix.

55. Hannah Riley and Linda Babcock, "Gender as a Situational Phenomenon in Negotiation," paper presented at the IACM 15th Annual Conference, Salt Lake City, June 2002, and KSG Working Paper No. RWP02-037, available from the Social Science Research Network, http://ssrn.com/abstract=305159 (accessed September 19, 2006), 1–28.

56. Ibid., 17.

57. Hannah C. Riley and Kathleen L. McGinn, "When Does Gender Matter in Negotiation?" September 2002, paper presented at the AOM Conflict Management Division Meeting, and KSG Working Paper No. RWP02-036, available from the Social Science Research Network, http://ssrn.com/abstract=320363 (accessed September 19, 2006).

Chapter **10**

Closing the Deal

"What we have here is a failure to communicate" is an often-quoted line from the movie *Cool Hand Luke*. This film, made during the turbulent '60s, was the character study of a nonconformist, antihero loner who bullheadedly resists authority and "the establishment," represented in the movie by a southern prison warden. The statement is ironic, of course, because the conflict in the movie involved much more than just "a failure to communicate." Luke and the prison warden had major disagreements over Luke's defiant attitude; Luke undermined the authority of the sun-glassed prison guard during prison-work detail; and Luke challenged the state's control over him by his repeated attempts to escape. In other words, the movie portrayed the classic elements of a conflict: at least two parties who are *interdependent* and who have *incompatible* goals or needs.

Negotiating is one way to resolve such conflicts. And at some point the parties complete the bargaining stage, possibly utilizing third-party intervention, and thus reach the closing stage. The feeling of relief and sense of closure tells them that an agreement has been made. All issues have been addressed and settled—and now all that remains is to finalize the deal.

But what do you do when negotiating is simply not working? We have emphasized throughout this text that negotiating is a *voluntary* process and that the parties may decide that the option *not* to reach agreement is better than accepting the agreement on the table. However, there are times when walking away is not that easy. The voluntary aspect of negotiating in these cases may simply be the right to agree or not to agree to *certain issues* rather than a clear-cut right not to negotiate. For example, employers are required by law to negotiate with employees who have unionized. The rights and responsibilities of both sides during labor negotiations or a labor dispute are contained in federal and state laws, in rulings by arbitrators, and in court decisions. An employer cannot refuse to meet with a union representing his employees and cannot refuse to negotiate in good faith—but he can refuse to give his employees a pay raise. The parties generally have to demonstrate that they are bargaining "in good faith" before they can avail themselves of the right to "walk away." Many commercial transactions, such as construction contracts or consumer purchases, contain grievance procedures that compel the parties to try resolving a dispute that might arise under the contract by negotiation before proceeding to formal arbitration or court action. A consumer may have to use the procedure called for in a contract—one that presents the possibility of a negotiated agreement, but if not satisfied the consumer may still be able to sue. In these instances, the desire to reach agreement may not be strong enough to overcome the obstacles to agreement.

In this chapter we will look at closing the deal without giving in, and getting buy-in by the parties so that the agreement reached is appropriately *memorialized* and *implemented*. We will look at some of the reasons why it is difficult for parties to reach agreement at the end of a negotiation and how to overcome those difficulties without giving up. And finally, we will present some ways to incorporate strategies into the negotiations that will help you manage the bargaining relationship going forward.

Negotiation Skills

In this chapter we present five negotiation skills that can be learned and developed by the novice negotiator, and applied to the end-of-chapter Learning Exercise, "Keeping a Client."

Skill 10.1 Be able to create an **agreement template** *to ensure that important aspects of a negotiated deal are properly memorialized.*

Skill 10.2 *Learn how to* **claim value *or* retain value** *at the closing stage of a negotiation.*

Skill 10.3 *Learn to identify the* **causes for stalemate** *and techniques to move past them.*

Skill 10.4 *Recognize* **bargaining traps** *and learn how to avoid or eliminate them.*

Skill 10.5 *Employ techniques during negotiation that* **builds a relationship** *between the parties.*

CHAPTER CASE: TO AGREE OR NOT TO AGREE—THAT IS THE QUESTION

In 1983, after months of intense four-party negotiations, the Commonwealth of Kentucky, the City of Louisville, Jefferson County, and Humana (a private for-profit hospital company), had agreed that Humana would operate the new state-built teaching hospital that was a part of the University of Louisville School of Medicine. Humana agreed to assume responsibility for financial support of the hospital, including uncompensated care for the community's poor, in exchange for a commitment of $20 million a year from the state and approximately $6 million a year from the local governments. The medical school was to supply doctors and interns and would be allowed to use the facility as its teaching hospital. The signing of this unique and historic agreement was to be held at the newly completed hospital at a festive press event. But after all of the parties had arrived, local dignitaries and staffs, hospital employees, and members of the press were kept waiting while Governor John Y. Brown Jr. had an impromptu private meeting with Mayor Harvey Sloane and Jefferson County Judge/Executive Mitch McConnell. In the meeting, the governor refused to sign the agreement unless the mayor and the county judge/executive agreed to issue $12 million in previously authorized bonds to defray part of the cost of the hospital.

Fifteen years earlier, the city and county had proposed renovating the local public hospital, which the city and county governments owned and the University of Louisville managed—and at that time, local voters had approved issuing $12 million in bonds for the renovation. The bonds were never issued. However, in the ensuing years the state agreed to build a new University of Louisville teaching hospital. And although the issue of the city and county contributing to the cost of the hospital through that prior bond issue had come up during negotiations, the state had not previously made it a condition of the agreement because there was some doubt as to whether the bonds could still legally be issued.

So now, after about an hour of discussion and delay, Mayor Sloane and County Judge/Executive McConnell, with help from their legal advisers, convinced Governor Brown that they could not change the agreement they were about to sign at the very public event without going back to their respective legislative bodies for approval—which would take at least a month, if their legislative bodies would even agree. Nor could they assure the governor that the bonds could be sold legally. The best offer they could make was to sign a *side letter* that said they would use their "best efforts" to have the bonds issued and the money turned over to the state.

Reluctantly, the governor accepted their offer and the agreement was signed.

Reaching an agreement can be a quick and easy process, a long and difficult process, or somewhere in between. At some point in most situations, all issues are resolved and the parties conclude the negotiations. In some cases a nod of the head or a handshake is all that is needed to settle, as when two friends agree where they want to go to dinner and what movie they want to see. However, in most business negotiations, as well as many personal negotiations, *reaching* an agreement is just the first step. *Writing* the agreement is next, and then *abiding by* the agreement follows and lasts as long as the agreement itself. This chapter presents some techniques to enhance all three steps.

AGREEMENT TEMPLATE

Experienced negotiators have developed **agreement templates**, which are standard documents that include all of the critical elements of an effective agreement. An effective agreement is one that includes the important aspects of the issues negotiated. It answers potential what-ifs of the deal—*what if* a payment is late, *what if* the product is the wrong color, *what if* maintenance is unsatisfactory, and so forth. An agreement template could have helped the parties in the Chapter Case avoid the last-minute negotiations that almost derailed their unique and historic public–private partnership.

What are the key elements of an effective agreement? Unfortunately no list is exhaustive and can foresee all the what-ifs—but for a starting point, consider including the following template elements:[1]

1. *Parties:* Name the parties involved, even those who may not have participated in the negotiations but will be involved at some point.
2. *Intent:* Describe the big picture of what the agreement is intended to accomplish.
3. *Roles:* Describe exactly what duties the parties involved have each agreed to perform.
4. *Time:* State deadlines for actions and penalties for failure to meet the deadlines.
5. *Measurement of satisfaction:* Use language to specify objectives, such as: "final plans approved in writing by the buyer" or "to the expressed satisfaction of ..."
6. *Consequences:* Specify the consequences that would occur if the actions specified in the agreement do not materialize. For example: "Failure of party A to deliver specified services to the destinations listed will cause party A to pay a fee equal to 10% of the goods delivered that month to all destinations under the agreement."
7. *Point persons:* Each party should specify one person as the contact person who is responsible for meeting the terms of the agreement during the life of the agreement. The larger the organization, the more important it is to specify a point person.
8. *Exit strategy:* Specify a process for terminating the agreement for any reason, in case one of the parties wishes to do so in the future. For example: "Either party may terminate the contract at any time without reason, by giving a 30-day written notice to the other party."

Before the parties say they have reached agreement, it is important to restate with as much specificity as possible the main points of the deal that has been reached. Negotiations can conclude with an understanding of the deal and agreement on the relevant points. But often a written document memorializing the agreement is also necessary.

Put It in Writing!

Many times oral agreements or handshake deals in business only include the price and quantity of goods or services to be provided. All other aspects of the deal are left unaddressed—and too often must be decided by a judge or jury when "friends" part ways or when business associates discover significant differences.[2]

To make sure both parties abide by the agreement, they should put it in writing! The degree of formality and detail required depends on the value, length of time, and past relationship of the parties involved. Reducing the agreement to writing serves three purposes:

1. *Communication.* People often hear what they want to hear, they don't listen carefully to details, or their memories of verbal agreements fade quickly. A written agreement can eliminate all of these problems.
2. *Commitment.* Reducing an agreement to writing often causes the parties to commit themselves to that agreement. Seeing the terms in writing can help one to understand issues better than just hearing them spoken. For instance, if a spouse, friends, or children, have trouble recalling exactly which chores or actions they agreed to, showing them a piece of paper that they signed can quickly increase their commitment.
3. *Contract.* Reducing an oral agreement to writing and signing and dating it, usually creates an enforceable contract. Simply providing a copy of the written agreement at a later date may cause a party to realize it is a binding contract, or if court action is necessary the signed agreement is critical evidence.

With a written, signed, and dated document in hand, the parties involved can feel confident their negotiating produced an agreement that achieves gains for both sides. In addition, they have a document that can be referred to at a later date if needed. Such a written document should be clear on the distribution of responsibilities under the agreement and the expectations of the parties; each side should identify the risks they are willing to assume and those they are not; the parties might want to include a "dispute resolution" procedure in the agreement, so that any problems arising under the agreement can be quickly resolved; and there should be a clear "exit" or "extension" strategy so the parties know, to the extent possible, what the future holds for this relationship.

The party who drafts the document should reflect the actual agreements made—all of them. The non-drafting party should read the document carefully to verify that the language being used is clear and represents the understanding of the parties. This might entail reviewing notes from the negotiations and making sure the notes and the written document are consistent. Finally, if "boilerplate" or standard contract terms have been included—even if those items were not actually discussed or agreed to—review them to make sure these standard terms do not adversely affect the deal that was made. Often, the inclusion of such terms in the final agreement will cause the parties to discuss those details, which could help avoid problems in the future. For example, in a price contract the parties might realize, when adding boilerplate language on how payments will be made, that one party will not be able to use wire transfers for the first year of the agreement. Knowing this, the parties can rewrite the provision to state how payment will be made the first year and when wire transfers will commence.

THE CLOSING STAGE

Negotiations come to a close when all alternative options are ruled out, or when integrative and distributive solutions converge. Knowing that an agreement has been reached, the people involved become psychologically committed to the agreement and are often eager to move quickly to sign the papers, shake hands, exchange money for goods, or otherwise finalize the deal. However, it is very likely that additional concessions will be made. Why? Consider the quote often attributed to Yankee great Yogi Berra:

"It ain't over till it's over!"

If the other party senses that you are *overly anxious* to close the deal, then it may try to extract last minute concessions. Patience at this point is critical. Take your time to finalize the deal—remember that *both sides* want the agreement. In the Chapter Case, Governor Brown may have waited until the press conference to raise the issue of the $12 million commitment in order to pressure the mayor and the Jefferson County Judge/Executive to agree. Their solution, a "best efforts" commitment letter, fell far short of the governor's demand. So in the end, the pressure that Mayor Sloane and Judge/Executive McConnell put on the governor to conclude the deal won out.

Don't make last-minute concessions just to close a deal. Remember, last-minute concessions are just as valuable as any of the initial concessions—maybe even more so. If any such concessions are made, they should be reciprocated. If the other side makes a last-minute demand, such as "I forgot one item, which we can handle easily …" consider one of these three responses:[3]

1. *Silence:* At this stage of the negotiations, judicial use of silence is advisable. Say nothing, because any response may be perceived as a sign of weakness. Continue to close the deal at hand with no changes.
2. *The Walk-Away:* You may be able to project a *personal indifference* to settling that will concern the opposing side, which has certainly become invested in reaching an agreement. This may be the best time to suggest that you can—and will—walk away from the deal if the other side tries to extract a final concession.
3. *The Promise Technique:* Using the promise technique when the other party makes a last-minute demand, you respond by indicating your willingness to agree—*if* they make a similar concession, and then conclude the negotiations. Thus: "To take care of this last item of yours, I promise to pay the delivery charge, if you decrease the final cost by $200." Or, as in the Chapter Case, the promise technique resulted in the mayor and county judge/executive getting the governor to sign the previously agreed-upon deal without reference to the $12 million, if they would use "best efforts" to have the bonds issued.

Of course, as a negotiator, when you are about to conclude negotiations not only should you be prepared to respond to last-minute demands by the other party, but you should also consider making one yourself—perhaps using the classic **nickel-and-diming** tactic. If you believe the other side is anxious to settle, before signing any papers consider insisting on the addition of one, small overlooked, item—a nickel-or-dime item—which might be one that the other side can easily agree to and increase the value of your negotiated settlement. The tactic works particularly well when purchasing large items, with the price set by the company or an owner who is not present, and thus the salesperson has limited authority. However the salesperson usually can provide something—free furniture delivery, a 64 MB memory card for a digital camera, and so forth.

To give a personal example, this author fondly recalls negotiating a great price on a new Corvette and then telling the salesperson, "OK, we have a deal—if you throw in the dealer extended warranty for free." "I can't do that!" responded the salesperson, who saw me walk away. The salesperson then checked with his manager and later called me at home: "We have a deal." The purchase was large enough that the dealership was willing to absorb the cost of the extended warranty—and I had wisely waited until all the papers were drawn up before asking for one more "dime" item that could be easily added to the deal.

If however, you misjudge the situation, the nickel-and-dime item could become a deal breaker when the other party walks away—unless your nickel-and-dime request is quickly withdrawn.[4]

Ultimately, however, when the parties have all but reached agreement and only a small gap between the sides still exists, it may be to your long-term benefit to voluntarily cover the gap. This cooperative approach generates goodwill and gives your opponents the sense that they made a good deal.[5]

MOVING PAST STALEMATE

When negotiations reach a stalemate, it is important to recognize that deadlocks at the end of a negotiation are a common part of the bargaining process. A stalemate may be thought of as a conflict within a conflict. Stalemates can be addressed by many of the same basic approaches used to resolve conflicts. When confronted with a stalemate, parties should ask what or who is causing it, what the stalemate is accomplishing (if anything), what alternatives the parties have to meet each other's negotiating goals, and whether there is a way past the stalemate.

Cognitive, Emotional, and Process Issues

Cognitive Issues Stalemates can occur on the cognitive, emotional, or process levels. On the cognitive level in a typical negotiation, negotiators have kept, or have tried to keep, certain information private—such as their BATNA, their cost of not agreeing, or their cost of a delay in reaching agreement. This makes the parties mutually uncertain about the other side's reservation price, so they make assumptions. People have a tendency to arrive at assumptions that reflect a *self-serving bias* to conclude what is fair is what benefits oneself.

Self-serving assessments can impede negotiations and promote stalemate in a number of ways. First, if negotiators estimate the *value* of their BATNA in self-serving ways, this could rule out any chance of settlement by eliminating the zone of agreement. Second, if the negotiators believe that their own notion of *fairness* is impartial and shared by both sides, then they will interpret the other party's unwillingness to agree to their demands as an exploitative attempt to gain an unfair advantage. Third, if negotiators are willing to *make economic sacrifices* to avoid a settlement perceived as unfair, and their ideas of fairness are biased in directions that favor themselves, then negotiators who are "only trying to get what is fair" may not be able to settle.[6]

Skilled negotiators are aware of the possibility of a self-serving bias at this stage of the negotiations and attempt to reframe the final offers in ways to moderate the bias. For example, the negotiator may review the concessions that have been made by both parties during the negotiations in a positive light to remind the parties that they have been dealing fairly with one another.

There are times when the parties genuinely cannot move forward with the resolution process. There may be an inability to close the deal because of a reluctance to actually share their best offer. This reluctance may stem from a fear that they will be giving away too much if the offer is accepted, or to the contrary, that their best offer—their real bottom line—will not be enough to close the deal and they are not prepared to end the negotiations. A possible solution to this barrier would be for both parties to share their bottom line with a trusted third party. If the parties are actually in the zone of agreement with their bottom lines, then the third party can facilitate making the final offers.

Emotional Issues   On the emotional level, when a negotiation become difficult it can become stressful, resulting in participants displaying strong emotions such as anger, disgust, or disapproval, and triggering equally strong reactions from the other party. And although it is *possible* to prevent a negotiation from escalating by suppressing emotions, it is often difficult to do so. Furthermore, there is no guarantee that suppressing emotions will prevent difficulties from developing on other fronts. Those suppressed emotions can find expression in negative nonverbal behaviors, reduced flexibility in offers, and reluctance to give any concessions.[7]

Negotiators must recognize that humans have normal reactions to certain provocations. Learning what those reactions are and how to handle them can help you avoid the trap of pushing your opponent's hot button or allowing your opponent to push yours—and instead you can push negotiations past stalemate, as outlined in Box 10.1 and discussed here.

First, *label the opponent's behavior to yourself,* calling it "immature," "counterproductive," or even "hurtful" if that describes it. Next, *label your own feelings,* taking the time to acknowledge those feelings, and if necessary take a break to allow yourself time to move past the emotion. Third, recognize that in most negotiating situations, experiencing emotions may mean *stepping out of your comfort zone.* Expressing

---

BOX 10.1   Traps to Avoid

Handling Emotions

Don't fall into an emotional trap during the final stages of a negotiation! Learn to handle stress, disapproval, anger, and other emotions—both your own and those of your opponent.

1. Label your opponent's behavior to yourself.
2. Acknowledge your own emotions.
3. Recognize that emotions may move you out of your comfort zone.
4. Identify your own assumptions that may be causing the emotion.
5. Express your emotions appropriately.

strong negative emotions is not acceptable in most settings, so working through emotions in a negotiating situation may cause anxiety over violating social norms. Fourth, *identify the assumptions* that may have lead to the emotional response—for example, did the opponent violate your sense of fairness by offering a hollow concession? Once the assumption is unearthed, determine if your assumption is correct, or if perhaps your opponent's concession is not so hollow from his perspective. Finally, *express your feelings appropriately.* Deborah M. Kolb, co-author of *The Shadow Negotiation,*[8] advises negotiators to counter the move that provoked the negative emotions by *reframing the situation* or by shifting the conversation back to the *key issue,* rather than the provocation, by asking a question or correcting a misstatement.[9]

When your opponent's hot button is pushed and he or she reacts in anger, you also need to understand what caused that reaction. Looking past the emotion, is your opponent indicating an important underlying interest that would not otherwise be expressed? Can you put yourself in your opponent's shoes and identify the reasons for the angry reaction? Would acknowledging the emotion satisfy the interest that motivated the reaction? Can you uncover the underlying concern by asking questions and seeking more information, such as those in Box 10.2?

BOX 10.2 Tactics for Success

Asking the Right Questions

When bargaining becomes a debate between opposing positions, the conversation can block discovery of common goals and joint gains. One way to break through such a stalemate, according to communications educator Linda L. Putnam, is to ask the right kind of questions. The following scenario provides some examples of the right kinds of questions.

The city and its police officers' union were in labor negotiations. The union was concerned because the economy was not good and they had been following the news of other cities where proposals had been floated to lay off police. The city did not believe it would actually have to lay off any employees, but even if it did, it did not anticipate laying off police. However, unions representing the city's other employees felt if layoffs became necessary, the "no-layoff" clause protecting police was unfair because it meant

almost a fourth of the city's employees would be excluded from layoffs. The city was attempting to negotiate the deletion of the no-layoff clause as a sign of "good faith" with the other unions rather than as an indication that layoffs were imminent. In addition to the deletion of the no-layoff clause, the cost of health care coverage for the city's employees had become so expensive that the city had stopped providing any contribution for non-union employees' family coverage and was attempting to delete that item from the police union contract as well. The union was adamant that it would not agree to either change. The negotiation sessions had become quite heated, with the union accusing the city administration of not caring about its employees who put themselves in harm's way to protect and serve the community. The union also accused the city of not caring about its citizens because it was willing to

(continued)

(Continued)

reduce the number of police serving the community. For all practical purposes, a stalemate now existed in the contract negotiations.

1. Use *open-ended questions* with an explanation that invites the other side to think through the inquiry; such questions aid in gathering information and the search for alternatives. The city negotiator trying to get agreement on the removal of the no-layoff clause might ask this question: *I appreciate that you are concerned about layoffs of police in other cities, but that has never been done here and I wouldn't think it would be done here. But the no-layoff clause is a lightning rod for all of our other unions. Do you think there's some way we can assure your members that their jobs are not in jeopardy and still take the clause out?*

2. Use questions to interrupt and redirect a negotiation that has become a debate. For example, use a *window question,* one that calls for the opponent to explain his understanding of the situation. The city negotiator, in trying to stop an argument about the city's concern or lack thereof for its employees by proposing changes to the health care coverage, might ask this question: *I am not sure we are really that far apart. What were you saying was the most important part of a health insurance plan for your members?*

3. Use *circular questioning,* or a series of questions that promotes dialogue by expanding the scope of the discussion beyond the immediate negotiation. The union negotiator who wants to keep the dialogue on the health care coverage going, but recognizes that the discussion isn't getting anywhere, might ask this question: *Exactly how does the city decide who the health care insurance provider will be? What flexibility is there in how those policies are written? Is the city a fairly significant client or is it just a small fish in a large pond?*

4. Use questions to *uncover underlying concerns.* The union negotiator, believing that the possibility that police would be laid off was very slim, might ask the city negotiator this question: *There doesn't seem to be a financial crisis here as there has been in other cities. Is there something looming in the future that we're not aware of that would make the concessions you've asked for necessary?*

5. Use questions to *enhance creativity* of settlements. Learning more about the opponent's interests can give new insights to win-win solutions. The city negotiator could ask this question: *I know we're in this thing together. I wonder if you've given any thought to some alternative approaches to the need to find some savings within the police department budget?*

Source: Linda L. Putnam, "Are You Asking the Right Questions?" *Negotiation* 8 (March 2005): 7–9. Used with permission.

Process Issues   On the process level, a stalemate might be the result of the actions of some members of the negotiating team—or perhaps resulting from the instructions that those members feel they must carry out or the authority they have or do not have. Therefore, the negotiators may need to move the negotiations *from formal negotiations to informal negotiations,* especially if the negotiations involve two teams. This will allow the chief negotiators to hammer out the last details more candidly than they might be able to do otherwise. Or, they may need to *turn over the final nego-tiations to someone else* who has the authority to expand the zone of agreement to more than what authority the negotiating teams had. In the Chapter Case, the governor's decision to speak one-on-one with the mayor and county judge/executive over an issue that was not in the agreement that had been hammered out over a number of months with their representatives was obviously designed to expand the zone of agreement to include the $12 million issue.

The manner in which negotiating parties communicate can also be considered a process issue. Improved communication can help move negotiations forward. True dialogue occurs when both parties *speak* and both parties *hear.* Exploring, by appropriate inquiry, what each is saying and what each is feeling about the negotiation can change the course of the negotiation and move it out of a stalemate. Other tactics to enhance communication include the following: (1) focusing attention on the issue at hand, and not letting the discussion revert to a recitation of past acts; (2) avoiding distractions; (3) delaying the discussion if emotions are becoming difficult to control; (4) trying to see issues from the other side's perspective; (5) not interrupting, but rather letting the speaker complete the argument or presentation; (6) not agreeing or disagreeing, but encouraging the train of thought; and (7) actively responding to questions.

Bargaining Traps

Participants in a negotiation, especially a complex and/or lengthy negotiation, can begin to lose perspective as the negotiation nears a conclusion. They can fall into a number of bargaining traps that are difficult to avoid. Following are some common bargaining traps and techniques to address them.

Conflict Spirals   One of the most common bargaining traps that can lead to a stale-mate in negotiations is the **conflict spiral** created by incompatible negotiating styles. A conflict spiral, once begun, has its own momentum and is very difficult to reverse. A *spiral* is defined in Merriam-Webster's Collegiate Dictionary as "the path of a point in a plane moving around a central point while continuously receding from or approaching it." Visually, it is circular and continuous as it rotates in repeating circles like a corkscrew. A conflict spiral occurs when one party initiates a contentious communication, and the other party responds with a contentious communication, and then the first party responds in a consistent manner, and so on, and so on.

Research into the nature of conflict has found that five transformations occur during conflict escalation using a competing strategy:

1. Tactics can go from light to heavy—that is gamesmanship, persuasion, and promises can turn into threats and irrevocable commitments.
2. What starts as a small conflict over one specific issue grows into a larger conflict over a number of issues.
3. The conflict shifts from the specific to the general.
4. The goals of the parties change from doing well to harming the other side.
5. More people get involved.[10]

Conflicts with an imbalance of power or a lack of mutually beneficial options are more likely to escalate. The negative attitudes of the parties toward each other keep the conflict alive, whether the conflict is spiraling through a vicious cycle of action and reaction, or whether the parties have become invested in the conflict and cannot end it without prevailing. The parties have *selective perception* of their counterparts—that is, they select the perceptions about the other that confirm their existing attitudes and discount the perceptions that do not. They assume that the other party will react in a negative way, and when their adversary reacts to aggressive behavior with aggressive behavior, it confirms that belief. Finally, the parties to a conflict stop talking to each other and the lack of communication escalates the conflict.

As noted throughout this text, parties in negotiations tend to model or reciprocate their bargaining partners' behavior: integrative (win-win) communications, distributive (win-lose) communication, procedural statements, and emotional statements. It is not unlikely, then, that the parties to a negotiation will reciprocate threats and initiate a conflict spiral. Authors Jeanne M. Brett, Debra L. Shapiro, and Anne L. Lytle conducted a simulation of a conflict and recorded the contentious communications in order to gauge how often such a communication was reciprocated.[11] The study had four hypotheses about conflict spirals:

1. Conflict spirals that eventually result in an agreement result in a one-sided agreement.
2. A negotiator can refocus his or her bargaining partner off of the contentious communication by not reciprocating.
3. A negotiator can refocus his or her bargaining partner off of the contentious communication by reciprocating with both a contentious and a noncontentious communication.
4. A negotiator can refocus his or her bargaining partner off of the contentious communication by labeling the behavior as unproductive.

The experiment confirmed the first hypothesis—that agreements made in highly contentious negotiations are one-sided. The end result of a conflict spiral in a contentious negotiation is like losing a game of tug-of-war. When one party finally gives in, he or she is pulled far into the opponent's side. The study also confirmed all three of the other hypotheses: Rights and power statements, both considered contentious communications, were "significantly likely to be reciprocated,"[12] whereas by not reciprocating rights or power statements or by including a communication that moved the focus away from contentious communications, the conflict spiral can be avoided.

Psychological Entrapment   Another bargaining trap is known as **psychological entrapment**. Psychological entrapment is a decision-making process whereby a party escalates his or her commitment to a previously chosen, though failing, course of action in order to justify or make good on the prior investments. In negotiations, psychological entrapment occurs when the parties become so caught up in the negotiation "game," and in the time and effort they have put into the negotiation, that they become determined to get an agreement, even if the agreement turns out to be worse than the no-agreement alternative.

Negotiators hope to obtain a good bargain when they negotiate. To protect themselves during the heat of negotiations, they need to have established their BATNA. When the negotiations go in a direction that is worse than their BATNA, they need to be able to walk away and accept that they will not reach agreement. However, the more time and effort that people put into a negotiation, they more they want to get an agreement. The greater the costs that a party incurs, the more they become invested in achieving the goals they were pursuing. And the more contentious the process, the more invested the parties can become.[13]

A way to de-escalate such conflicts and move the parties along past the stalemate and to agreement is to engage in joint problem solving. A four-step problem-solving process includes (1) diagnosing the problem, (2) reexamining one's own interests at stake in the conflict and setting reasonable goals, (3) jointly engaging in creating win-win options, and, if necessary, (4) reducing one's reasonable goals and trying again.[14] Using the scenario outlined in Box 10.2, here is an explanation of the joint problem-solving technique:

1. *Diagnose the problem.* Start by focusing on the critical issues of the negotiation and the factors that led up to the stalemate. In doing this, identify all of the parties to the negotiation—not only the obvious parties, but also any others who are likely to care or be affected by it and, therefore, may be part of the reason the parties cannot reach agreement. In the labor negotiation example in Box 10.2, the interest of other labor unions was definitely a factor in the stalemate. Determine if the source of the stalemate is a failure to communicate (that is, some type of misunderstanding), a substantive disagreement over limited resources or incompatible goals, or a struggle over the relationship.[15]

2. *Reexamine goals to set a realistic target.* Decide what interests are really at stake—both the surface interests and those that lie below the surface. Such deeper interests may actually be shared by the parties and can be used to reestablish the relationship necessary for agreement. For example, in the labor negotiation, it is possible that the city's goal of changing some of the provisions of this contract in order to send a message to other bargaining groups is an unrealistic target. If the city could get the union to suggest other, less emotional changes to the contract, those changes might be enough to send that same message. If the original goals set were overly optimistic, those goals can be readjusted.

3. *Engage in joint problem-solving techniques.* Joining together with an opponent to address the problem is a learned technique. The parties can look at options to "expand the pie" by increasing the available resources at issue in the conflict. They can identify and trade *nonspecific resources*—that is, something of value that has not been in the conflict. For example, the city and union might agree that while there will be no layoffs, the number of public safety employees would be reduced by attrition, early retirements would be encouraged, and they would agree to abolish "light duty" (allowing the employees who have been injured to perform clerical tasks until they improved or retired on a disability). The parties can trade high-priority items for low-priority items, which not only narrows the conflict scope but also establishes a pattern of cooperation.[16] The parties can try to satisfy the needs of one with minimal loss to the other; or the parties can try to establish a "bridge" between each other's goals—by reframing the change in direction of the negotiation

not as a "retreat" from a previous position, but as a movement "forward" to a better solution.[17]

4. **Reexamine goals again, and set a lower target.** If the parties are unable to use the above techniques to reach the goals each have set, then one or both have to reduce their expectations so that the joint problem solving can begin again. In order to do this, there must be a way to allow the parties to back away without backing down and without losing face. One method is to show how circumstances have changed since the original goals or expectations were set. With health care costs escalating, the city's goal of eliminating its subsidy of the police officers' coverage overnight and the union's goal not to change it at all may have become unrealistic. A technique to save face could be to agree to bring in a third party to make a recommendation as to what would be fair and reasonable.

Other Barriers to Agreement

Ideologically Based Conflict Individuals come to a negotiation with different attitudes and beliefs. In a conflict situation when the object of the negotiation is ideological rather than financial, reaching agreement may be much more difficult. When the parties differ on core beliefs, their individual values and often the influence of outside constituent groups are barriers to a negotiated agreement.

The reason why values in ideologically based negotiations can become barriers to agreement is that the collaboration necessary for any mutually beneficial outcome is perceived to involve *trade-offs* and *compromises.* In a dispute over money, such trade-offs and compromises might be fairly easy to do. However, if the issue involves basic beliefs or values, such trade-offs and compromises may offend the negotiator's moral identity. In Figure 10.1, an ideologically based negotiation for war reparations sought by Jewish victims of Nazi Germany is an example of such difficult negotiations involving moral values.

Figure 10.1 Negotiating for the Victims of Nazi Germany

Stuart Eizenstat negotiated for six years with private companies, banks, Jewish organizations, class-action lawyers, and the governments of Germany, Austria, France, and Switzerland to seek justice and reparations for the victims of Nazi Germany. The survivors of slave labor camps, and families of the victims of the Holocaust who did not survive, were looking for restitution for slave labor, compensation for confiscated property, and benefits from unpaid insurance policies. Eizenstat represented the U.S. government, which became involved in these essentially private causes of action because of sympathy for the Jewish, Polish, and Ukrainian Americans who had suffered. But Eizenstat described his role, not as an impartial mediator, but as a representative of a party with "conflicting interests that balanced each other. We wanted justice for the victims and ... to preserve our relations with foreign governments."

The claims being made against Swiss banks, German companies that employed the slave laborers, French banks, and Austrian insurers were not the strongest legal cases to negotiate, but this was a moral negotiation as well. The ultimate money settlement was $8 billion. But the most valuable outcome was the change in how these countries revisited their histories and their involvement in Nazi Germany. Eizenstat noted that while the allocation of the money between the 1.5 million camp survivors was small, enclosed with each check was an apology from the presidents of Germany and Austria, asking for forgiveness.

Source: Adapted from Susan Hackley, "Negotiating for the Victims of Nazi Germany," *Negotiation* 7 (May 2004): 4–6.

Values, as central elements of the "self," can further your own interests (self-enhancement), explain yourself to others (self-identity), and teach yourself about your own beliefs (self-perception). However, these same values can create biases, such as cognitive biases, which color a party's ability to agree. Some biases become more pronounced when ideological differences are involved. For example, the **fairness bias** arises in ideological disputes because the parties' notion of fairness generally stems from their core values. Therefore, in a specific conflict, they evaluate their position as being fairer, because it is consistent with *their own value system*.[18] If you place a higher value on rewarding individual achievement than on concern for morale in the workplace, for example, you will perceive your proposal for merit raises as "fairer" than a proposal for cost-of-living raises for those barely making minimum wage.

A **self-identity bias** that develops during an ideologically based conflict can be a significant barrier to agreement. Although it is common for people to identify with a particular group without prejudicing their ability to negotiate, when the group itself is a reflection of an individual's beliefs and values, it is less likely that the individual will separate from the group and its core beliefs in order to reach agreement. As described in Figure 10.1, Eizenstat, who was negotiating on behalf of the United States involving reparations for primarily Jewish victims of Nazi Germany, had to make sure that the fact that he was Jewish did not prevent him from being an effective negotiator. He had to make it clear that he represented the United States government and *its* interests in seeking justice for individuals who had been victims of Nazi Germany.

Finally, some psychologists believe that values pay a role in one's *self-perception*. Individuals may have limited knowledge about their own value systems but can discover their values by observing their own behavior.[19] In general, people perceive themselves as causing good and not harm by their actions. If an action does harm, it challenges their self-perception. Therefore, if necessary they create an omission bias. An **omission bias** attempts to justify *inaction* by believing that inaction is less harmful than *action*—if action may result in some harm. Inaction, in the context of negotiations, is a stalemate.

Decision-Making Conflict Remember, the parties to a negotiation are making decisions. Those decisions address needs and values, knowledge, and generalization. At the *needs and values level,* decision making is the process that orients action to address unfilled needs or attain a high decree of fulfillment. The *knowledge level* links a decision to the ability to understand the problem. And the *generalization level* corresponds to the use of tools to simplify the mass of information or the complexity of the problem in order to make a decision. All of the parties' decision-making processes are situation-specific—that is, each negotiation presents the players with a unique opportunity. So an analysis of the situation includes the party making the decision, the other participants in the process, and the environment in which they are negotiating. The environment is often unstable. It may change either spontaneously or because of the decisions the players make in the negotiation; it is influenced by the relationship of the parties and the strategies they use to negotiate. The parties may make decisions intuitively, based on common sense and knowledge acquired through experience. Or they may make decisions based on analogy, comparing the problem in hand to problems previous solved, or on generalization, based on composite cases or schemata.

The difficulty that arises in a negotiation stems from the interaction of parties who feel they must (1) communicate their needs without revealing too much information, (2) assimilate the information provided, and (3) discern the needs of the other party.

Decisions during negotiations become messages and are an indication of the real objectives, goals, and preferences of the parties. Concessions can be assessed as indicating either that the party making the concession has decreased his or her needs to some degree or that a need has been fulfilled in a way the opponent did not anticipate. The sequential nature of negotiation, the time it takes to reach agreement, and the actions and reactions of the parties are significant to the process because they offer opportunities to change the direction of the negotiation.

The sequential decision-making process allows the parties to make a single decision that makes subsequent decisions possible. As discussed in Chapters 2 and 3, initial agreements to fairly simple issues establish the rapport necessary to find solutions to more complex issues. To feel comfortable in doing so, and to come to the correct conclusion based upon the opponent's concession, the parties assume that their opponents are rational. But because purely rational behaviors are sometimes hard to identify in a negotiation, one way to break through a stalemate is to focus on *understanding* the opponent's position no matter how irrational it might seem; maintaining *flexibility* as the negotiation unfolds so that the negotiators can react to an altered situation; and allowing for *revisions* to one's goals as the negotiating landscape changes.[20] Resist the temptation to label another negotiator as "irrational" simply because his or her behavior fails to fit your own style or expectations. What should you do when confronted with an opponent who cannot be convinced by the merits of your evidence or arguments and seems to be making arbitrary or irrational decisions in a negotiation? How can you determine if the negotiator is truly irrational or is merely employing a negotiating strategy? Noted mediator Lawrence Susskind has suggested the following possibilities for consideration:[21]

1. Your opponent is perfectly rational, or at least should be assumed so, and you need to see the negotiation from your opponent's perspective. You need to find out more from your opponent by asking questions and being cooperative to the extent you can without prejudicing your position.

2. Your opponent is rational, but has adopted a seemingly irrational position as a competitive bargaining strategy. You can counter by adopting a cooperating bargaining strategy, focusing on interests not positions, pursuing joint problem-solving techniques, and by proposing objective criteria. If necessary, try to bring in other parties to change the dynamics of the negotiation and reduce all exchanges to written notes so that there is a paper trail evidencing your collaborative efforts and your opponent's irrationality.

3. Your opponent is truly irrational, and the likelihood of reaching a mutually beneficial agreement is compromised. Your only option is to commit your offers to paper and offer it to your opponent, with a definite deadline for the negotiations to end. If the opponent refuses to respond in kind and you are unable to involve other players from your opponent's side who might be more willing to negotiate, it is probably time to walk away.

Then, Susskind suggests seven steps for coping with an irrational bargaining opponent, as follows:[22]

1. Don't respond to irrational behavior in kind. You'll only make things worst.
2. Don't make unilateral concessions to win over the other side. You'll just encourage more bad behavior.
3. Don't lose your cool out of frustration. Walk away before you lose your temper.
4. Focus on meeting your own interests—even if you don't like the way the other side is behaving.
5. Prepare for each exchange carefully. Talk with others in your organization and rehearse as often as possible.
6. Summarize each negotiation exchange in writing. Try to keep others on both sides in the loop.
7. Know when it's time to walk away—then do it.

BUILDING A RELATIONSHIP

Usually the *end of a negotiation* signals the *beginning of a relationship*. Some forethought on how to conduct negotiations, and what steps to take after the deal is signed, can determine whether that relationship is a success or failure. For example, if you start negotiations with the idea of creating relationships and not just of making a deal, you will select the right people to do the negotiating, those who have interpersonal skills, knowledge, and sensitivity—in other words, skilled negotiators who considered a wider range of outcomes or options, who give more attention to areas in which the parties might agree rather those in which they might disagree, who have developed a range of possible settlement points rather than a goal, and who understand the parties' long-term considerations.

Both negotiators should make sure their respective sides have been briefed on the contents of the agreement, so there will be, ideally, no surprises as the deal is implemented. If this is a new relationship, keep the negotiators involved during the initial phase of implementation. No matter how thorough a drafter might be, a written contract never covers everything that can happen, so having the negotiators available to make sure the understandings of the parties are followed, even if the agreement is silent on the issue, is important.

Establish effective two-way communications, preferably on a set schedule, so that face-to-face meetings to discuss the positive aspects of the deal are more frequent than meetings to resolve problems. When possible, structure the deal with an increasing level of effort and cooperation as the parties perform under the agreement. For example, your contract could include a provision stating that if the supplier meets your delivery deadlines for the first 100 computers, then you would pay a 1% premium on the purchase price on each subsequent order, thereby strengthening the commitment of your supplier to meet your deadlines.[23]

Renegotiating an Agreement

Creating a relationship could be invaluable if something happens and the deal has to be renegotiated. A need to renegotiate may be triggered by a change in circumstances significant enough for one side to decide it is cheaper to abandon the agreement than to fulfill it. For example, a long-term contract to supply oil may have to be renegotiated because of the damage Hurricane Katrina did to offshore drilling operations. Or, an agreement may need to be renegotiated because of an imperfect contract. This may be a negotiator's worst nightmare. A long and complex negotiation finally concludes with a mutually satisfying result, and after numerous draft exchanges an agreement is signed. After the parties begin to implement the negotiated agreement, one side notifies its negotiator that she has to go back and renegotiate the deal because they have discovered a mistake. No contract can cover every contingency, nor can the parties be certain that everyone who has a hand in implementing such an agreement will understand it the same way. So when a mistake is made and it is significant enough, the only option may be to try to renegotiate.

A renegotiation is different from the original negotiation because (1) the parties know much more about each other, having been through one negotiation; (2) walking away from the deal is likely to be more difficult because of the investment of time and probably money; and (3) the renegotiation is probably taking place against a backdrop of bad feelings and/or disappointed expectations. Some things you can do if you are called upon to renegotiate is to try to avoid hostility, look for an opportunity to create value, have a realistic assessment of what it will cost if the agreement can't be renegotiated, make sure all the players are at the table, and consider hiring a mediator.

SUMMING UP

For the first four questions below, assume the role of one of the five parties from the Chapter Case as you form your answers. Note here which party: _____

1. What reasons do you have for sticking with the negotiations at this point?

   _____

   _____

2. Describe three tactics you can use after agreement is reached and your bargaining partner asks for one more thing.

   a. _____

   b. _____

   c. _____

3. Detail the parts of an agreement template and explain why it helped you in this negotiation.

   _____

   _____

   _____

4. Can you identify an ideological issue in this negotiation? If so, explain why it is more difficult than financial negotiations to resolve.

_____

_____

_____

Answer questions 5–10 based on a negotiation situation in your own life. Describe the situation:

_____

5. What three purposes does a written agreement serve? Explain each.

a. _____

_____

b. _____

_____

c. _____

_____

6. You are in a conflict spiral with your bargaining partner, what can you do to get out of it?

_____

_____

_____

_____

7. Your bargaining partner is being irrational. List seven techniques to deal with him or her.

a. _____

b. _____

c. _____

d. _____

e. _____

f. _____

g. _____

8. You have agreed to try joint problem solving with your bargaining partner. What does this entail?

_____

_____

_____

9. List five types of questions you can ask to break a stalemate, and give an example of each:

a. _____

b. _____

c. _____

d. _____

e. _____

10. List the steps can you take during negotiations to help establish a long-term relationship with your bargaining partner.

_____

_____

_____

_____

LEARNING EXERCISE: KEEPING A CLIENT

The purpose of this exercise is to apply the five negotiation skills presented in this chapter to an actual negotiation. Your business is helping retailers find good locations for their stores and helping them work with neighbors and local governments so that the development of the shopping area goes smoothly. You have been cultivating as a client a national company that develops designer clothes-outlet shops, and have finally reached an agreement whereby you can represent it on its next project. You have drawn up your normal engagement letter and expect to finalize the deal with Mr. Black at your next meeting. However, Ms. White attended the next meeting and began to ask detailed questions about the work you intend to do and the expected outcomes. She was particularly interested in your strategy for answering questions about traffic issues, because the developer had recently learned that there might be organized opposition to the particular location the developer hoped to purchase. Although many of the details of the job that Ms. White raised were not mentioned in the engagement letter, you and Mr. Black had discussed them and they had been resolved, you believe, to his satisfaction. Ms. White seemed unaware of those discussions, and you are afraid you are starting all over again to negotiate this deal. A major concern to you is that she has asked you to limit your travel expenses by agreeing not to go to the out-of-state location more than one overnight a month for the anticipated year-long project. You know that one visit a month will not get the job done. Answer the following questions:

Skill 10.1: How would an *agreement template* facilitate closing this deal?

Skill 10.2: How can you *react to the particular demand* for limiting your time at the site, which is totally unacceptable, but not risk losing the deal?

Skill 10.3: What technique can you use to *move Ms. White past* her apparent problems with your engagement?

Skill 10.4: How can you avoid the *psychological trap* of agreeing to an arrangement guaranteed to fail, just to keep this client?

Skill 10.5: What techniques can you use during this impromptu negotiation to *build a relationship* with Ms. White?

ENDNOTES

1. Henry S. Alford, "Small Business Contracts" *The Lane Report* 19 (February 2004): 36.
2. Michael R. Carrell and Christina Heavrin, *The Everyday Negotiator* (Amherst, MA: HRD Press, 2004), 191–194.
3. Carrell and Heavrin, *The Everyday Negotiator,* 118–121, 181–183.
4. Stewart Levine, *Getting to Resolution* (San Francisco: Berrett-Koehler, 1998), 143–147.
5. Charles Craver, *The Intelligent Negotiator* (Roseville, CA: Prima, 2002), 197–201.
6. Linda Babcock and George Loewenstein, "Explaining Bargaining Impasse: The Role of Self-Serving Biases," *Journal of Economic Perspectives* 11 (1997): 109–126.
7. Barbara Gray, "Negotiating with Your Nemesis," *Negotiation Journal* 19 (October 2003): 299–310.
8. Deborah M. Kolb and Judith Williams, *The Shadow Negotiation: How Women Can Master the Hidden Agendas That Determine Bargaining Success* (New York: Simon & Schuster, 2000).
9. Deborah M. Kolb, "Staying in the Game," *Negotiation* 6 (December 2003): 1–4.
10. Dean G. Pruitt and Sung Hee Kim, *Social Conflict: Escalation, Stalemate, and Settlement* 3rd ed. (New York: McGraw-Hill, 2004), 89–91.
11. Jeanne M. Brett, Debra L. Shapiro, and Anne L. Lytle, "Breaking the Bonds of Reciprocity in Negotiation," *Academy of Management Journal* 41 (August 1998): 410–424.
12. Ibid., 418.
13. Charles B. Craver, *Effective Legal Negotiation and Settlement,* 5th ed. (Danvers, MA: Matthew Bender, 2005), 377–384.
14. Ibid., 144.
15. Nancy G. Neslund, "Why Teach Conflict Resolution in Business Schools?" *American Business Law Journal* 26 (1988): 557–573.
16. Joyce L. Hocker and William W. Wilmot, *Interpersonal Conflict,* 3rd ed. (Dubuque, IA: Brown, 1991), 216–217.
17. William Ury, *Getting Past No: Negotiating Your Way from Confrontation to Cooperation* (New York: Bantam Books, 1993), 108–110.
18. Kimberly A. Wade-Benzoni, Andrew J. Hoffman, Leigh L. Thompson, Dona A. Moore, James J. Gillespie, and Max H. Bazerman, "Barriers to Resolution in Ideologically Based Negotiations: The Role of Values and Institutions," *Academy of Management Review* 27 (January 2002): 41–57.
19. Richard E. Petty and John T. Cacioppo, *Attitudes and Persuasion: Classic and Contemporary Approaches* (Boulder, CO: Westview Press, 1996), 170–173.
20. Gregory E. Kersten and David Cray, "Perspectives on Representation and Analysis of Negotiation," 1997, InterNeg Research Papers, http://interneg.concordia.ca/interneg/research/papers/ (accessed June 11, 2005).
21. Lawrence Susskind, "Stubborn or Irrational? How to Cope with a Difficult Negotiation Partner," *Negotiation* 7 (December 2004): 9–11.
22. Ibid.
23. Jeswald W. Salacuse, "The Deal Is Done—Now What?" *Negotiation* 8 (November 2005): 1–4.

INDEX